Illinois
Local
Government

A HANDBOOK

Edited by James F. Keane
and Gary Koch

With a Foreword by James D. Nowlan

SOUTHERN ILLINOIS UNIVERSITY PRESS

CARBONDALE AND EDWARDSVILLE

Copyright © 1990 by the Board of Trustees,
Southern Illinois University
All rights reserved
Printed in the United States of America
Edited by Yvonne Mattson
Designed by Joanna Hill
Production supervised by Natalia Nadraga

93 92 91 90   4 3 2 1

Library of Congress Cataloging-in-Publication Data

Illinois local government.

   Bibliography: p.
   Includes index.
   1. Local government—Illinois—Handbooks, manuals,
etc. I. Keane, James F., 1934–   . II. Koch, Gary,
1950–
JS451.I35I39 1989   352.0773   89-5997
ISBN 0-8093-1445-2
ISBN 0-8093-1446-0 pbk.

The paper used in this publication meets the minimum requirements of
American National Standard for Information Sciences—Permanence
of Paper for Printed Library Materials, ANSI Z39.48-1984. ∞

Contents

v

Figures
and
Tables

Figures

Tables

Foreword

We practice democracy with gusto in Illinois. There are more governments in the Prairie State than in any other state in the Union, 6,621 in all. One is our state government; the other 6,620 are so-called local governments. These range from school districts and municipalities with hundreds of employees and budgets of millions of dollars, to tiny rural townships where annual meetings take place in white clapboard town halls right out of a Norman Rockwell painting, to important, yet obscure, mosquito abatement districts. Gary Koch estimates that there are sixty-five thousand elected and appointed government officials in Illinois—one official for every 177 citizens. If we add the thousands who are former officials as well as the additional thousands who have sought office without success, it is clear that a high percentage of our citizenry—at some time or other—offers to take on the responsibilities of governing in Illinois.

We do so in good faith, but with little idea of what governing is all about. I know this to be true in Illinois state government, where I have served as a member of the Illinois House and as a director of state agencies. Once Governor James Thompson asked me to become—the next day—the acting director of an agency about which I knew next to nothing!

As a result of my experiences, I put together *Illinois State Government,* a book much like this one, in order to provide new state agency heads with some sense of their duties, the cycles of their jobs, and the web of interests that surrounds them. That book has served its purpose. Several times I have been stopped by agency heads who told me that the book had helped them, not to govern, but to understand better the objectives and perspectives of the other players in the game and to anticipate some of the challenges they were to face.

This book can serve the same purpose for you, whether you are a public official, a reporter assigned the local government or schools beat, a teacher, a League of Women Voters activist, or someone who might be thrust unexpectedly into a local government role.

Governing can be tough work. Sure, some posts are more visible and demanding than others. But no matter how a local government is run, there never seems to be enough money to meet the public's demands. The work is always there, and you are always there. Once, at lunch on Capitol Hill in Washington, a congressman told me the toughest jobs in government were at the local level, because you cannot get away from your public, the way a congressman can. No escaping the neighbors and the community.

The chapters that follow comprise a compendium of information about local government. But the chapters do not tell you much about yourself and how to go about making decisions. Presumptuous as it sounds, that is my goal in the next few paragraphs. If, as a result, just one reader avoids a pitfall somewhere along the way, the space taken will have been worth it.

During my service in the Illinois House (1968–72), a colleague and friend was indicted and later convicted for taking bribes. He died in prison, a broken man. Several years later, his son was a student at a university where I was teaching. The son looked me up, to learn about his father. "I was just a child when Dad had his problems," said the handsome young man, the spitting image of his father. "What kind of man was he? Was he a bad man, an evil man?" I replied that his father was a man of goodwill, much liked by his colleagues. His father just was not thinking. He went along and did what some others around him were doing; he thought it was the way things had always been done. It was a difficult conversation for me.

Local government officials handle large sums of money and make many decisions about things of value. Like state officials, they can also get in trouble. Just consider the scores of local road district officials in New York who were indicted in 1987 for allegedly accepting favors in return for doing business. I imagine that many of these officials simply forgot to think and just assumed that that was the way things had always been done.

I do not presume to know better than you what is right or wrong. Nor can I anticipate just what decisions you will be asked to make. I will, however, offer you "Nowlan's practical test for ethical decision making." I suggest you apply the following steps (or others you devise) before making public decisions:

1. Think: Is there any dimension of this decision that could possibly be illegal?

2. Never justify a decision solely on the basis of "this is the way it's always been done." Times and attitudes change.

3. Identify a friend or acquaintance whom you respect for great integrity, who will serve unknowingly as your conscience. Ask yourself, "How would so-and-so see my decision?" Would he or she think it right?

4. How do you want your children to remember you? Ask yourself, "Could this decision conceivably affect the way they will remember me?"

Melodramatic? I do not think so. Each year the Gallup organization surveys the public about its perceptions of honesty and ethical standards for a list of occupations. And each year "local political office holders" rank at the bottom, just ahead of state-level officials and car salesmen. To my mind, these perceptions are not justified, yet they reflect the shadow cast on all public servants by the lapses in judgment of a few.

This book will prove useful. In a few years, there will be a need to make revisions and to print more copies. You can help improve the subsequent editions by telling the editors, Keane and Koch, what information you found most—and least—useful as well as what topics you would like to see covered. Your evaluation will strengthen this book for future local government officials, those who will join the fraternity of citizens who feel the responsibility to practice democracy with all the skill at their disposal.

Preface

One particularly frustrating day in May 1983 we both remarked that it was unfortunate that there was no source of very basic information on local government and its workings. When we held public hearings around the state on pending local government legislation, the one question we heard most often was, "What exactly are my duties as a local official?" It seemed the only training for public service at the local level was on-the-job training.

Two years later, after leaving a meeting of the state comptroller's Local Government Advisory Board, former state senator Bill Morris commented to us, "It's too bad there isn't a book like Jim Nowlan's *Inside State Government* that pertains to local government. I wish I had such a book when I was mayor and doubly so now."

Since that book did not exist, we decided to create it, calling on experts in the field such as Roland W. Burris and Ted Sanders. Our intent was to develop a primer on local government in Illinois—a book that any student, taxpayer, or reporter covering his or her first council meeting could sort through to get a rough idea of what local government is, how it works, and whom it affects. We also wanted the book to be a resource for local officials themselves, whether newly elected or appointed officials or veterans of public service. The book is designed to provide an understanding of local government and of the roles and responsibilities of today's local government official.

It was not our intent to provide a lot of detailed, technical information; for that the reader must look elsewhere. Although most chapters of this book contain tables, figures, appendixes, and references for further study, we attempted to provide a broad background on local government in as simple and readable a manner as possible. This book covers only the major aspects of local government and its management. In the following chapters we have tried to include information that is of the widest interest and of the greatest importance to the most readers.

This book is divided into five parts: introduction; units of government; legal aspects and finance; support services, media, and community relations; and future trends. We felt that dividing the book into segments would help categorize subject matter for the reader and simplify the process of finding needed information. In this respect, we hope that the book will be used as a resource, time and again, instead of simply being read once and placed on a shelf.

Over the years we have found local officials to be hard-working, conscientious, and dedicated to the betterment of their community and the people they serve. Local officials possess integrity, common sense, and a good sense of humor. Unfortunately, local officials are often maligned and misunderstood. If this book provides a better understanding of the complexities of local government and the difficult roles local officials assume, or if the book helps make their jobs a little easier, we will be more than satisfied.

This book would not have been possible without the help and support of many people. The respective authors of the chapters in this book comprise a veritable "Who's Who" of local government in Illinois. We are proud to have been associated with them and to have had their participation in this project.

We would specifically like to thank Jim Nowlan for his direction and support. Without *Inside State Government* as a basis to work from, this book would not have been possible. We are grateful to Bill Morris for his idea and to former cartoonist and now syndicated columnist Bill Campbell for sharing his humor with us and allowing us to reprint his cartoons. For advice on financial aspects of government, we would like to thank Loren Iglarsh, economist for the state comptroller, Richard Haas, CPA, Richard Loman, CPA, and Gerry Fink, CPA with Arthur Anderson. We would also like to thank the Illinois Department of Revenue for its statistical information, as well as Dave Bennett, executive director of the Illinois Press Association; Beth Johnson, government liaison for the IPA; Ray Long, bureau chief for the *Peoria Journal-Star;* Pat Coburn, managing editor of the *Springfield State Journal-Register;* and Bob Best and Tom Philips, past president of the IPA, for their time and advice regarding the media. Paul Green, director of the Institute for the Public Policy at Governors State University, Carolyn Kleamenakis, director of local government for State

Comptroller Burris, and Tom Pekras, director of cemetery care for the comptroller, contributed valuable editorial suggestions. We also want to acknowledge Sharon Dunkel, Linda Taylor, Joan Parker, and Pat Campbell for their dedicated performance of countless editorial, typing, and other clerical tasks. Finally, we are indebted to Alice and Valerie for allowing us time to complete this project.

Local government is important. It affects all of our lives in ways we may not comprehend or even realize. If we can develop a little better understanding and respect for it and the people who administer it, we will all benefit. That is our goal and, we hope, yours as well.

PART ONE

Introduction to Local Government

I.

You Have Been Elected!
What Now?

WILLIAM B. MORRIS

The most difficult campaign for office pales when compared to the responsibility of serving in that office. The exhaustion of the final days of the campaign, the fear of losing a cliffhanger because of some small detail forgotten in the rush toward election day, the hours that seem like weeks as the votes are counted all pass into joy when the results are announced and you are declared the winner. Now you are going to "make the difference." You have thought about and expressed your goals often during the campaign. Implementing them will be easy. With your new-found "clout" you will make the system work as no one before you has been able to.

For the first few days after the victory you are sky-high. You thank your volunteers and accept greetings from friends, neighbors, and people you did not even know before. Even though the election was close, you soon are led to believe that everyone voted for you. Then it hits you like a one-two punch from a heavyweight champion. Reality! You are now in office and you will be making literally hundreds of decisions that affect the lives of your family and your neighbors. This is responsibility with a capital R and you begin to wonder if you are up to the task. That is okay. You should be nervous. To perform well in public office, you must simply channel that nervousness into your job.

The night I was elected to the Illinois Senate in an upset victory, I was sure I had all the answers. An issue-based campaign had worked well, and the time to deliver was at hand. Shortly thereafter the realization that Illinois is one of the largest states in the country and that decisions I made would impact on school children, senior citizens, and others six hundred miles from my house hit me. You will realize soon after election that you represent many more people than you originally thought.

The first project, once the "joy of victory" wears off, is to take a more intimate look at the day-to-day workings of your constituency. Once you are elected to office, doors open more easily. Utilize the "honeymoon" period given to you by the public and the press to learn as much about the "nuts and bolts" operation of your government as possible. Limit your public statements to positive reflections on your campaign and discuss your goals in very general terms. Since your focus was on getting elected, you now need to take a close look at the process and rules and learn the system well enough to initiate your programs. Clearly a most frustrating aspect of being a newly elected official is the slowness of implementing your goals. Government by its sheer size is slow to change and adjust. Like almost everyone, government workers naturally resist change. Often the bureaucracy will put hurdles in your path that are much more difficult to jump than those presented by your opponent during the campaign. An example of this might clarify my point.

My first campaign for mayor was based on four major issues: discussion of the city's budget crisis and my claim that I could solve it; the promise of substantial changes in the philosophical direction of all major city departments; a desire to institute a professional, nonpolitical personnel system; and finally, the stated goal to "revive the spirit" of the community. The campaign was well structured and successful. The problem, upon election, was a failure to control a majority of the members of the city council in order to support my agenda. In fact, just three days after my victory, word reached me that targeted department heads would not resign and that my agenda was politically unacceptable to a majority of the city council.

Thus, campaign promises would be difficult to keep. The first steps became obvious. First, reach out to the opposition with the branch of peace. Second, read and understand the statutes governing your community to determine the extent and limit of your powers (most Illinois communities are considered weak mayor–strong councils). Third, develop a plan of action and a calendar to implement your agenda. Finally, initiate contact with incumbents and those newly elected to open discussions and seek common ground.

If you will be functioning in a legislative body such as a city council, you should obtain a copy of *Robert's Rules of Order*.[1] Read it over and understand its value for the conduct of public business. Some bodies have their own set of rules and it is imperative that you understand these rules as well and as soon as possible.

1. Robert, Henry M., *Robert's Rules of Order* (Chicago: Scott-Foresman, 1981).

Now is not the time to become timid. To get elected you asked friends, neighbors, and people you did not even know to work and vote for you. This takes a certain level of self-confidence and courage. Now that you are a winner you need to maintain that level of self-confidence to ask questions, to gather information for making sound, fair decisions. If you maintain your self-confidence and natural curiosity, you have many sources of information to help you become oriented to your new position. A valuable source are the people currently working within the government. Most are proud public servants and will be happy to share their information with you. There are also valuable outside resources available. It is your task to seek out these sources, evaluate what they tell you, and develop your agenda.

Most governments belong to state and national associations. Feel free to contact these organizations for information on your new role. Most offer seminars for newly elected officials. Make sure you attend one or two as early as possible. Also, state universities usually have on their faculties professors specializing in local government who can recommend helpful books. In many areas, you can look to the political science department of your local community college or technical school for people and resources. Another excellent source is the local newspaper. A quick rereading of old issues (go back six months to one year) will help you focus on pressing issues facing the city. Local reporters are also helpful if you simply ask them. Special interest groups are good sources of information, but you must remember that they are trying to "sell" you their special point of view. Listen closely and weigh their suggestions carefully. The best source of information, however, stems from the collection of ideas which the voters of your district expressed during the campaign. One of the best features of the competitive election system is the opportunity for Joe and Jane Q. Public to share their thoughts with candidates during a campaign. Check your notes to help bring people's concerns into focus on your agenda.

You must realize that the wheels of government move slowly. Changes you want to make are important but will inevitably take longer than you plan. You must learn "how to count" to make your suggestions reality. Share your ideas with other elected officials. Listen carefully to their reactions and make notes of their suggestions. Often a minor change or two will make your suggestion acceptable to a majority of the other elected officials. When you have enough votes in support of your ideas, continue to work on those whose support you do not have. If you are not able to get them to support you, try to "soften" their opposition.

There is some truth to the old adage of "being seen and not heard." This is especially true if you are a newcomer with a majority of your colleagues being holdovers. However, it is vital that you speak out on issues of importance to you and your constituents. It is wise to test the waters prior to speaking publicly. You can do this by simply asking your colleagues for their support prior to the public meeting.

An important "rule" is not to embarrass your colleagues. In most cases, members of a city or village council or legislative body begin to like and respect each other as individuals after the first several weeks. This is the result of working together on common interests that develop over time. However, if one member embarrasses another, especially with members of the public or media present, the damage will be long-lasting and retribution is possible.

Always debate issues, not personalities. It is imperative that public business be conducted in a professional manner. In public discussions, an effort should be made to avoid informality. It is always better to refer to a colleague as "the gentleman from the first ward" or "the lady from district Z" rather than by first names.

It is illegal, under the Open Meetings Act, for a majority of elected officials to meet secretly, but it is a good practice to keep each other informed. No elected official likes surprises. Mayors or village presidents need to encourage department heads and others to keep the council members informed of community events, complaints, and concerns. When requests are going to be made of the council, it is a good idea to "touch base" with individual council members to brief them and seek their support ahead of time.

It is also advisable to become an expert on one or two areas of the government's operation. You cannot be an expert in all areas, but by narrowing your focus you can build a good base of knowledge. However, when an issue develops with which you are unfamiliar, do *not* be afraid to ask questions. Without the information gained by asking questions you cannot make good decisions.

The late state senator Dan Doughery gave me some of the best advice I received as a rookie in the Illinois Senate in the midseventies. After a lengthy committee session, he pulled me aside and complimented me for a series of questions I had asked witnesses. I had feared that some were pretty "dumb" questions. Yet the veteran Doughery told me that there was no such thing as a dumb question. In fact, he said the failure to ask a question for fear of embarrassment is a "dumb" act. He was so right. Those of us fortunate enough to be elected to office have an obligation to make the most informed decisions possible. However, during campaigns we learn to project confidence and knowledge, thus reducing our willingness to be inquisitive once we take office. We can all benefit by Senator Doughery's advice.

It is often said that politics is the art of compromise. Fortunately all individuals hold some views that they consider moral issues and thus not open to compromise. When this occurs, you must respect your colleague's position even if you do not agree with it. Probably 90 percent of the decisions made by elected officials are not controversial but rather general "housekeeping" measures. As a result most votes are unanimous and devoid of discussion or controversy. That does not mean that you do not have to do homework. Usually, elected officials receive the meeting agenda three to five days before the meeting. Set aside thirty minutes to read it over and make notes on issues you want more information on. Call the key departments to get answers. This preparation will make your job easier when tough issues arise.

An elected official has three jobs, all of which are of equal importance:

1. to make decisions for your neighbors on issues and the day-to-day business of the community

2. to serve the needs of your neighbors. This involves everything from cutting "red tape" to making sure city services are delivered properly. Never forget that often something a constituent is concerned about may not seem important to you in light of the issues you are debating, yet to that person it might be his or her only contact with government and thus a high priority.

3. to serve as an educator

Often the issues before government are very complex and do not lend themselves to simple cut-and-dried decision making. Occasionally, the elected official's access to detailed and complex information will result in the official making a decision that seems contrary to the public's position. In these cases, the elected official needs to provide information to the public to explain the reason for a decision. In order to make our system of representative democracy work, we cannot hide from the public when difficult and possibly unpopular decisions are made. Rather, we must educate the public about the reasons for the decision. This can be done through holding ward or district meetings, by publishing newsletters, and so on. The elected official must become an educator. Leadership is not always easy. A good leader recognizes that and is willing to stand up and make the right decisions, even if they are not always the popular decisions. I found that facing up to seemingly unpopular decisions in public forums often results in the public gaining respect for the decision maker.

Reality indicates that the techniques described in this chapter will not always work. One only has to reflect back on the "council wars" of the Chicago City Council from 1983 to 1987. Only history will judge the impact of these confrontations. However, it seems clear that the often bitter campaign leading to the election of my Illinois Senate colleague Harold Washington as Chicago's first black mayor set the stage for battle. Political philosophy, race, and power ignited the fuse, which took four bitter years to burn out. Both sides deserve the blame for the battle. In the end, Mayor Washington defeated one of his most outspoken opponents and was re-elected. At the same time, Washington supporters and candidates neutral in the bitter battle won a majority of the city council seats, reversing the numbers of the previous four years. Government, as a result, was less confrontational in Chicago.

I experienced a similar problem upon being elected mayor of Waukegan in 1977. After winning the mayor's office, I did not have supportive majority on the city council. The imbalance was thirteen to three. Following most of the techniques outlined in this chapter, including a breakfast with all sixteen aldermen prior to taking office, I was successful in narrowing the numbers to nine to seven or eleven to five on most issues. Although this was difficult, it did allow me, as mayor, to utilize the veto power as a negotiating tool and win a consensus majority on most issues. Many of the opposition aldermen seemed more interested in confrontation than progress. Unfortunately, I often took the bait, and the first fifteen months were quite painful. Problems were aggravated by the fact that supporters on both sides encouraged the rigid positions held by both sides.

By eventually recognizing my role in the problem, I instituted a strategy change. Simply stated, the strategy was to refuse to be drawn into unnecessary public debates. Combined with that was a full-time public education campaign that focused on issues and goals and did not reflect on personalities. The results were quick. Within months, a citizen-based petition drive utilized state law to change the form of government, forcing all members of the city council to forfeit their seats. In the subsequent election, I received a solid four-to-four city council (the council size was cut in half), which made my tie-breaking vote quite powerful. A few weeks after the new council was seated, most votes were unanimous, with debate focused on issues, not personalities. This finally allowed me to realize my four major campaign goals.

One great problem facing a newly elected official is the tendency to become overwhelmed by the demands of the office. This leads to significant scheduling problems. Often a small group of people, both in and out of government, can dominate the officeholder's time. One must learn to schedule time efficiently. Conscious efforts must be made to set aside time for family relationships. This is quality time necessary for all people. Finally, steps must be taken to keep the elected official accessible to the public. Especially with a mayor, there is a real danger of becoming "office-bound," making decisions others could and should be making. On top of that, there is a great desire by subordinates to seek access and push decisions up the "chains of command" to avoid errors and win favor from the boss. Since this builds the leader's ego, he or she may have a tendency to spend too much time on this phase of the job. Early on, the elected official should establish a system to communicate views to subordinates and delegate properly.

There are not really any decisions I would change from my three years in the Illinois Senate or eight years as mayor of a city of seventy thousand people. I wish I had been a better time manager when first elected and clearly would have set aside more time within the first three to four months to learn the basic day-to-day tricks of administrative management. This could have been done by visiting successful business and corporate managers, as well as by enrolling in a few seminars at local universities. A key ingredient in my training to run a city with nearly five hundred employees and a $30 million budget was the need to structure and manage two campaigns as an underdog. I learned a great deal in the campaign for the state senate and, again, in the campaign for mayor.

Ideally, all newly elected officials will wear all three hats of elected leadership well. They are decision makers, ombudsmen for their neighbors, and educators. If they wear these three hats and keep debate on the issues instead of on personalities, everyone will benefit. They must remember that leadership is difficult, but rewarding. Popularity does not always result in good government or good decisions.

2.

Local Government: The Big Picture

ROLAND W. BURRIS

The strength of free people resides in the local community. Local institutions are to liberty what primary schools are to science; they put it within the people's reach.

—*Alexis de Tocqueville*

Local government has long been and continues to be the backbone of Illinois. The richness and diversity of our people is exemplified in the number and variety of our local governments. Illinois has 6,621 local governments—about 1,300 more than the next closest state, Pennsylvania (see tables 2-1, 2-2).[1] As a means of comparison, Lake County, located in the northern part of Illinois, has more local governments within its borders than the states of Alaska, Hawaii, Nevada, or Rhode Island.

Local government affects almost all aspects of a person's life. Because of such a preponderance of units of government, one would expect a rigid adherence to a strict set of guidelines. Yet, quite to the contrary, Illinois local governments are a crazy quilt of personalities, attitudes, and practices. Local officials are traditionally a very independent lot and do not like to be told how to do their job.

There are two reasons for the large number of local governments. First, they historically evolved over a long period, based on the needs of the early settlers. Geography, climate, and agricultural growing conditions all helped

1. *Census of Governments: Government Organization,* vol. 1 (Washington: Bureau of the Census, 1982), 1.

Table 2-1.
Number of Local Governments in Top Five States

	Local Governments	Counties	Municipalities	Townships	School Districts	Special Districts
1. Illinois	6621	102	1274	1436	1063	2745
2. Pennsylvania	5247	66	1015	1549	581	2036
3. Texas	3884	254	1066	—	1138	1425
4. California	3807	57	413	—	1109	2227
5. Kansas	3726	105	625	1449	327	1219

Source: U.S. Bureau of the Census

Table 2-2.
Number of Local Governments in U.S. and Illinois

	Total	Counties	Municipalities	Townships	School Districts	Special Districts
United States	79,913	3,042	18,862	16,822	15,174	25,962
Illinois	6,621	102	1,274	1,436	1,063	2,745
%	8	3	7	9	7	11

Source: U.S. Bureau of the Census.

develop our current system of counties, municipalities, and townships. Our local governments are thoroughly English in origin because settlers based their government on what was familiar to them. Second, a result of early constitutional limits on borrowing encouraged the formation of new units of government for each local task. For this reason, we have separate library, park, fire protection, mosquito abatement, sanitary district, water conservation, airport, hospital authorities, and so on.

Illinois's system of local government, while not necessarily unique— though some would argue that it is—certainly stands out. As outlined by the Illinois Commission on Urban Area Government two decades ago, local government in Illinois has three very different responsibilities.

1. As an artificial body created by the state, it administers and regulates local concerns of the population living in the area embraced within its corporate limits in matters particular to that place and not common to the state or any other government.

2. It performs duties not strictly local—serving as an involuntary

political and civil subdivision of the state to deal with administration of matters too tedious for the state.

3. It owns and maintains properties and provides services for a fee. In this respect, local government operates much like a business with the main goal of earning a profit.[2]

The duties of local governments and of the officials that administer them are far-ranging but generally fall into four distinct categories: regulatory, service, geopolitical, and corporate.[3] Regulatory functions are those duties of a government that help maintain order within the government's boundaries and among its people. Such functions include fire and police protection; planning, zoning, building, construction, and land use controls; pollution controls; health regulations; animal control; urban rehabilitation; and licensing of businesses, trades, and occupations.

Services provided by local governments take many forms but are generally offered to citizens because the latter are unable or unwilling to provide them for themselves. Services funded from general revenue can include police and fire protection, refuse collection and disposal, health services, public libraries, parks and playgrounds, cultural activities, public welfare, public and community buildings, roads and bridges, weed and insect control. Services usually furnished on a fee basis include public utilities, water supply, sewage disposal, recreational facilities, public housing, hospitals and other medical care institutions, and cemeteries.

Geopolitical functions are the duties of local governments performed as the territorial arm of the state. Local governments serve as a political grouping for other levels of government such as legislative and congressional districts, judicial districts, and so forth. They give an identity to a "group" of people, protect their interests from other groups, and provide the means whereby representatives are chosen to serve at other levels of government. Finally, corporate functions of a local government are carried out from the legal rights it shares with the private sector: to use a corporate name and seal; to sue and be sued; to enter into contracts; to own, maintain, buy, sell, and lease property; to acquire rights and liabilities; and to hire and fire employees.

Local government is a dominant political force. It is the source of political life for elected state officials. Influences and pressures exerted by local governments form and direct much of state and federal policy.

2. *The Structure of Local Government of Illinois* (Springfield: Illinois Commission on Urban Area Government, 1969), 2–3.

3. *The Structure of Local Government of Illinois* (Springfield: Illinois Commission on Urban Area Government, 1969), 6–8.

Types of Governments

There are four basic types of local government: county, municipality, township, and special district. [*Ed. note:* School districts, because of their size and number, will be discussed individually in chapter 8 instead of chapter 9 on special districts.] While some of the boundaries and duties overlap, each type of government performs distinct functions and services for the people it serves.

Counties in Illinois vary greatly in size, population, and function. The scope of government activities in Cook County, with roughly half the state's population, is obviously quite different than in Pope County with approximately four thousand people. Yet the nature of the functions performed is quite similar.

Counties can only perform functions granted to them by the state constitution and general assembly. These functions include:

• fiscal responsibilities, such as appropriation of funds, approving budgets, and levying taxes
• providing law enforcement
• administering elections
• providing assistance to the poor, blind, and elderly
• maintaining public records, such as deeds, mortgages, and wills
• administering justice at the local level for state government

Municipalities in the state include cities, villages, and incorporated towns. There are 1,274 of them (or 7 percent of the U.S. total).[4] Hawaii, by comparison, has one municipal government. Municipalities provide a wide range of services such as building and maintaining public hospitals. In larger municipalities, traffic control and recreational areas are important functions of the municipal government.

Most townships in Illinois are small units, with populations under one thousand; yet they provide services to two-thirds of the state's residents. Functions provided by townships include general assistance, maintenance of sewer and water systems, social services for the poor and elderly, activities for children, libraries, hospitals, mental health programs, and, in some cases, police protection.

Special districts are the most common type of government found in Illinois and in the nation. They are generally limited to one or, at most, a few functions. They can cover areas of less than a square mile or areas with

4. *Census of Governments: Government Organization,* vol. 1 (Washington: Bureau of the Census, 1982), 4.

thousands of square miles and millions of people. Special districts are usually established for one or more of the following reasons: if there is a need for a special service (water, sanitation, mosquito abatement) that no existing government can fulfill; if a local government is willing to pay for a service it needs; if a demand exists to remove a particular issue from politics; or if there is a desire to evade constitutional restrictions on taxing or borrowing powers.

Our system of local government is heavily borrowed from the English political system. In England, the shires, parishes, and boroughs developed almost at random, without planning or forethought. Each local unit appointed its own officials, levied its own taxes, and went its separate way. Officials were chosen at different times for different terms of office through very different methods of voting. Qualifications were uneven or nonexistent. The result was a country with overlapping jurisdictions, territorial conflicts, and confusion of duties.

Counties in Illinois are derived from the English shire. The county is as old as statehood and originally was the main form of government in the state. In New England states, towns served as the basic form of local government. Towns were grouped together for judicial administration. Later, as other needs and functions grew, county government developed into an important institution. Yet it never matched the town in terms of power and influence. The opposite held true in the southern states. The strength of the county system there controlled the legislature and other state activities. Again, borrowing from the English, southern counties combined the role of the shire and the parish. Justices were chosen from the aristocracy of plantation owners, and they controlled county administration. As the population grew, towns and villages were created, but as governmental entities, they did not have the strength or authority of the county.

These two different systems converged on Illinois as settlers from both regions brought with them the types of government they were familiar with and established new governments based on their own experiences. Today, the New England system of weak counties is found in most of Illinois, while the southern system is maintained in seventeen southern (commission) counties.

Municipalities have been around since the ninth or tenth century. Formalized in charters by Edward I and Henry II, municipalities became a corporate form in 1439. In America, municipalities developed in the midseventeenth century as a result of the population concentration of the Industrial Revolution. Municipalities originally were independent of the legislature. Charters were considered a form of contract not subject to revision without the consent of the incorporated place. Functions were limited with power given to a relatively small number of officials.

Townships existed in ancient Germany, and the concept was brought to England during the Anglo-Saxon invasion. The Pilgrims later brought the idea to America. At the time, a township was an area of land occupied by people inhabiting a fenced homestead or farm or village surrounded by an enclosure. Experts believe that our political structure grew out of the township experience and that it is the basis for our overall system of government in America.

The special district, although again owing a debt to the English, is largely an American invention. Very simply, it is a government created by people to meet needs unmet by other governments or by the private sector. In most cases, special districts evolved as a substitute for existing government.

The American adventure proves that local government works, and works well. Even during the American Revolution, there were few calls for change in local government. People were satisfied with their government because a large percentage of the population participated in it. That continues today, especially in Illinois, as it has been estimated that there is one local official for every two thousand citizens in the state.

According to a recent survey by the Advisory Commission on Intergovernmental Relations, local government is judged as doing the best job for the money. When asked, "From which level of government do you feel you get the most for your money—federal, state, or local?", 33 percent favored local government, 32 percent responded federal government, 22 percent answered state government, and 13 percent had no preference. The survey also asked people to choose what they thought would be the best way for their local government to generate new revenue. Forty-nine percent favored user fees, 26 percent opted for local sales tax, 9 percent responded with local income tax, and 7 percent believed property tax was the best means to raise more money.[5]

Sources of Revenue

The property tax remains the primary local government tax source. While some local governments, particularly municipalities, are able to supplement the property tax with a variety of revenue sources, others, such as

5. Illinois Municipal League, "ACIR Poll Finds Local Government Lead in Public Esteem," *Illinois Municipal Review* (Nov. 1987): 14.

school districts, continue to rely almost exclusively on the property tax for tax revenues (for an analysis of the taxing districts in Illinois, see table 2-3).

Illinois local governmental units received $8.673 billion in total tax revenues in the fiscal year 1985. Property tax revenues of $5.736 billion accounted for two-thirds of local tax revenues. Among other locally levied taxes, local sales taxes of $1.104 billion accounted for 12.7 percent of tax revenues, local public utility taxes of $379 million and other local taxes of $377 million each accounted for 4.4 percent of tax revenues. Shared revenues are taxes levied by the state but shared, usually in proportion to the amount collected, with local governments. Among shared revenues, corporate personal property replacement tax distributions of $519 million accounted for 6 percent of local tax revenues, revenue sharing to local governments from the regular state income tax of $246 million accounted for 2.8 percent, and distribution of state motor fuel tax receipts of $312 million accounted for 3.7 percent of tax revenues.

However, the relative share of local government revenues in Illinois derived from the property tax has been declining in part because of the elimination of personal property from the tax base and its replacement by the corporate income and invested capital taxes that comprise the corporate personal property replacement taxes. In a similar study of local government tax revenues prepared with fiscal year 1973 and fiscal year 1974 data, the property tax accounted for 81.1 percent of local tax revenues, while local sales taxes accounted for 7 percent, local utility taxes for 2.4 percent, other locally levied taxes for 1.8 percent, shared state income tax revenue for 2.5 percent, and shared state motor fuel tax revenue for 5.2 percent.

Counties

Of the $970 million in tax revenues reported by counties in fiscal 1985, $609 million, or 62.8 percent, was from the property tax. Among locally levied taxes, $39 million, or 4.0 percent, was derived from sales taxes. County sales tax revenues should increase in coming years based on revenues received from the new supplemental sales tax, which allows counties to levy a .25 percent tax on all sales occurring in the county. Cook County, which as the only home-rule county has greater latitude in its taxing options, reported $126 million in other taxes including wheel, new vehicle, alcohol, gasoline, and cigarette taxes. Among shared revenues, $47 million, or 4.8 percent, was derived from replacement tax distributions, 3.7 percent from state income tax revenue sharing, and 11.7 percent from the state motor fuel tax.

Table 2-3.
Number of Taxing Districts in Illinois

Counties	Total in each county (Omit these counted in other counties)	Townships or Road Districts	Municipalities	Total Schools	Elementary	Unit	High and Non-High	Junior College Districts	Total Special Districts	Fire Protec.	Park Dists.	Sanitary Dists.	Library Dists.	Hospital Dists.	Airport Dists.	Mosquito Dists.	Multi-Twp. Dists.	All Other Dists.
Statewide	5,879 / 7,063	1,530	1,275	1,045	434	448	124	39	1,927	780	324	150	121	23	27	20	360	122
Adams	69 / 77	23	14	6	—	5	—	1	25	11	3	3	—	—	—	—	7	1(1)**
Alexander	12 / 18	1	4	2	—	2	—	—	4	2	1	—	—	—	—	1	—	—
Bond	28 / 43	9	7	2	—	2	—	—	9	3	1	2	—	—	1	—	2	—
Boone	26 / 32	9	3	2	—	2	—	—	11	5	1	—	—	—	—	—	2	3(2)
Brown	17 / 21	9	4	1	—	1	—	—	2	—	—	—	—	—	—	—	2	—
Bureau	101 / 116	25	23	22	11	6	5	—	30	17	2	—	2	—	—	—	9	—
Calhoun	15 / 21	1	5	3	1	1	1	—	5	4	—	—	1	—	—	—	—	—
Carroll	43 / 48	12	7	4	—	4	—	—	16	7	1	1	1	—	1	—	3	2(3)
Cass	27 / 34	11	5	4	—	4	—	—	6	—	1	1	—	—	—	—	4	—
Champaign	107 / 119	30	23	18	8	7	2	1	35	19	4	2	—	—	—	—	7	3(4)
Christian	53 / 68	17	13	9	—	9	—	—	13	5	2	1	—	—	—	—	4	1(5)
Clark	35 / 40	15	4	5	1	3	1	—	10	4	2	—	—	—	—	—	2	2(6)
Clay	31 / 41	12	6	3	—	3	—	—	9	4	—	1	—	—	—	—	4	—
Clinton	60 / 71	15	13	12	8	2	1	1	19	12	1	—	—	—	1	—	4	1(3)
Coles	40 / 52	12	6	4	—	3	—	1	17	8	3	—	—	—	1	—	4	1(3)
Cook	511 / 551	30	119	152	115	2	27	8	209	38	90	27	38	—	—	4	—	12(7)
Crawford	37 / 42	10	6	5	—	4	—	1	15	6	2	1	—	1	1	—	3	1(6)
Cumberland	20 / 33	8	4	2	—	2	—	—	5	1	2	—	—	—	—	—	2	—(6)
DeKalb	67 / 92	19	12	10	—	9	—	1	25	10	6	1	—	—	—	—	5	3(8)
DeWitt	36 / 55	13	7	4	—	4	—	—	11	5	—	1	—	—	—	—	5	—
Douglas	29 / 43	9	9	4	—	4	—	—	6	4	—	—	—	—	—	—	2	—
DuPage	171 / 207	9	29	46	32	6	7	1	86	25	33	7	8	1	—	5	—	7(9)
Edgar	40 / 51	15	8	5	—	5	—	—	11	6	1	—	—	—	—	—	5	—(6)
Edwards	28 / 32	15	4	1	—	1	—	—	7	4	1	1	—	—	—	—	—	1(3)
Effingham	44 / 56	15	10	5	—	5	—	—	13	6	2	—	—	—	—	—	4	1(10)
Fayette	48 / 61	20	7	5	—	5	—	—	15	4	2	1	—	1	—	1	5	1(3)
Ford	42 / 57	12	9	4	—	4	—	—	16	6	1	—	—	1	—	—	5	3(3)
Franklin	50 / 57	12	14	14	8	2	3	1	9	1	2	1	1	—	—	1	3	—(6)
Fulton	89 / 99	26	20	12	5	6	1	—	30	14	6	3	—	—	—	—	7	—
Gallatin	24 / 29	10	7	3	—	3	—	—	3	—	—	—	—	—	—	—	3	—(6)
Greene	34 / 40	13	9	3	—	3	—	—	8	3	—	—	—	—	—	—	4	1(1)
Grundy	51 / 72	17	13	13	8	2	3	—	7	4	—	1	—	—	—	—	2	—
Hamilton	20 / 31	12	5	1	—	1	—	—	1	—	—	—	—	—	—	—	—	—(6)
Hancock	74 / 82	25	15	8	—	8	—	—	25	8	7	—	1	—	—	—	9	—
Hardin	6 / 8	1	3	1	—	1	—	—	—	—	—	—	—	—	—	—	—	—(6)

County																				
Henderson	29	44	11	8	2			2		7	3			1				3		—
Henry	78	97	24	15	10	1	1	9	1	28	12	3	4	1		1		6		2(3)
Iroquois	97	116	26	21	14	3	3	9		35	20	2	2	1				9		1(6)
Jackson	49	54	16	11	10	5	1	4		11		3	1			1		3		—(6)
Jasper	25	34	11	7	1			1		5	2							3		1(6)
Jefferson	53	68	16	9	18	13	3	7		9	2		1		1			3		
Jersey	27	35	11	6	1			1		8	3		1					5		
JoDaviess	54	65	23	10	7		2	1		13	3		1	1				3		
Johnson	17	24	1	7	7	5		7		1								6		
Kane	90	109	16	20	11			9	2	42	20	3	3	6		2				3(11)
Kankakee	74	84	17	16	14	5	2	6	1	26	14	8	1	2		1		3		2(12)
Kendall	32	50	9	6	6	2	1	3		10	5	3	2	1				1		
Knox	68	86	21	14	7		1	6	1	25	11	1	6			1		8		1(13)
LaSalle	172	189	18	44	52	35	11	5	1	57	17	17	9	1		1		9		
LaSalle	124	146	37	23	35	22	7	5	1	28	16		2	1		1		3		—(6)
Lawrence	26	28	9	5	2			2		9	4			1				7		1(3)
Lee	62	88	22	12	6	2		4		21	9	3		1				10		
Livingston	90	115	30	14	19		2	7		26	12		1					7		2(1)
Logan	61	77	17	10	9	8	8	3		24	10		2	1				10		
McDonough	58	68	19	10	5	5	5			23	6		1					1		3(14)
McHenry	96	113	17	24	22	12		5		32	15	2	2	6	1	1		7		3(15)
McLean	102	112	31	21	13	1	1	11		36	18	5	1	1		1		4		7(16)
Macon	70	85	17	12	9			8		31	11	4	2					5		
Macoupin	74	84	26	26	9		1	9	1	12	5	1	3	2	1			1		3(17)
Madison	119	132	24	26	16	2	2	12		52	31	5	8					6		1(3)
Marion	64	70	17	14	14	8		3		18	8	2	2					3		1(1)
Marshall	37	59	12	8	6	1		4		10	4	2						5		
Mason	46	50	13	9	6			6		17	8	2						3		2(18)
Massac	14	18	1	3	4	1		1		5	1		1							2(3)
Menard	29	38	13	5	3			3		7		1	3					10		
Mercer	53	63	15	10	5			5		22	7		1							2(19)
Monroe	29	34	10	6	3			3		9	5	2						6		
Montgomery	58	77	19	20	5			5		13	3	1	5					3		
Morgan	36	47	15	10	5			5		5	3	3	5		1			9		2(20)
Moultrie	29	42	8	6	4			4		10	5	2	4	1	1			4		4(21)
Ogle	76	92	25	12	12	4	4	7	1	26	10	3	7	1	1					
Peoria	84	89	20	14	19	9	9	9	1	30	11	3	9	1				3	3	1(13)
Perry	35	42	14	6	9	5		2	2	5	4		2					9		1(22)
Piatt	28	39	8	7	4			4		8	7		4					4		2(23)
Pike	69	74	24	18	7	1		5		19	6	2	5							
Pope	10	13	3	3	1			1		2			1					10		1(5)
Pulaski	11	15	4	7	2			2					1							1(10)
Putnam	20	25	4	6	2	1	1	1		7	4	1	2					1		—(6)
Randolph	32	37	4	13	8	2	2	5	1	6	1	2	1		1	1			4	3(24)
Richland	22	29	9	5	2			2		5	2	1	5		1	1		2	3	4(25)
Rock Island	71	79	18	15	10	4	4	4	2	27	15	5	8					2	5	1(6)
St. Clair	119	136	22	28	29	16		8	1	39	25	3	4	1	1	1		2	5	
Saline	35	36	13	7	5			4		9			4					4	3	

Table 2-3. Number of Taxing Districts in Illinois (*continued*)

Counties	Omit these counted in other counties	Total in each county	Townships or Road Districts	Munici- palities	Total Schools	Elementary and Combination			Junior College Districts	Total Special Districts	Fire Protec. Dists.	Park Dists.	Sani- tary Dists.	Library Dists.	Hos- pital Dists.	Airport Dists.	Mos- quito Dists.	Multi- Twp. Dists.	All Other Dists.
						Elementary	High and Non-High	Unit											
Sangamon	100	115	27	25	12	—	—	11	1	35	24	1	1	—	1	1	—	6	2(26)
Schuyler	27	40	13	4	1	—	—	1	—	8	2	—	—	—	1	—	—	4	—
Scott	19	23	7	7	2	—	—	2	—	2	1	1	—	1	—	—	—	8	—
Shelby	61	76	24	11	9	2	2	5	—	16	8	—	—	—	—	—	—	3	—
Stark	27	33	8	4	5	2	1	2	—	9	4	2	—	—	—	—	—	3	1(1)
Stephenson	58	70	18	11	6	—	—	5	1	22	10	4	2	2	1	—	1	4	3(27)
Tazewell	97	109	19	16	22	13	4	4	1	39	20	8	—	2	—	—	—	4	4(28)
Union	19	26	1	6	6	3	—	2	1	5	—	—	—	1	—	—	—	—	2(29)
Vermilion	78	88	19	20	16	2	2	11	1	22	11	1	2	2	1	1	—	3	1(6)
Wabash	18	23	6	4	2	—	—	2	—	5	3	—	—	—	—	—	—	5	—
Warren	38	47	15	5	5	—	1	5	—	12	4	2	1	—	1	—	—	5	—
Washington	52	65	16	12	8	6	1	1	—	15	5	1	3	—	1	—	—	5	—
Wayne	49	63	20	9	8	5	—	2	1	11	5	1	1	—	1	—	—	4	—
White	33	41	10	9	6	1	—	5	1	7	2	—	1	—	1	1	—	3	1(22)
Whiteside	68	82	22	11	12	4	1	6	1	22	17	3	6	3	1	1	1	7	4(30)
Will	137	166	24	24	30	19	3	7	1	58	21	15	6	10	—	1	1	1	—
Williamson	29	41	1	15	6	—	—	5	1	6	1	2	—	—	—	1	1	—	—
Winnebago	68	74	14	11	12	4	—	6	1	30	13	2	4	5	—	1	1	2	3(31)
Woodford	62	75	17	15	9	3	1	5	—	20	11	3	—	1	—	—	—	4	1(1)

*Non-High School District.

**Numbers in parentheses refer to these districts:

(1) Street Lighting. (2) Conservation and (2) Street Lighting. (3) Cemetery District. (4) Public Health Dist. (5) Conservation District. (6) River Conservancy Dist. (7) Forest Preserve; T.B. Sanitarium; (2) Public Health; River Conservancy; and (5) Mass Transit. (8) Cemetery; Forest Preserve; Street Lighting. (9) Forest Preserve; (2) Street Lighting; (4) Surface Water Protection. (10) Water Authority. (11) Forest Preserve; Surface Water Protection. (12) Cemetery and River Conservancy Dist. (13) Forest Preserve. (14) Conservation and (2) Cemetery. (15) Street Lighting and (2) Cemetery. (16) (5) Cemetery; (2) Conservation. (17) Water Authority and (2) Street Lighting. (18) Public Health Dist.; Water/Flood Dist. (19) Cemetery; Street Lighting. (20) Forest Preserve; River Conservancy. (21) T.B. Sanitarium; Cemetery; Street Lighting; Mass Transit. (22) Water Flood. (23) (2) River Conservancy. (24) Forest Preserve; Mass Transit; River Conservancy. (25) Public Health; (2) Street Lighting; Surface Water Protection. (26) Auditorium Authority; Mass Transit. (27) Surface Water Protection; (2) Mass Transit. (28) (2) Surface Water; (2) Water Flood. (29) Cemetery and Conservation. (30) Forest Preserve; (3) Street Lighting. (31) Forest Preserve; (2) Street Lighting.

Municipalities

In the fiscal year 1985, Illinois municipalities reported $2.777 billion in tax revenues. Of all types of local government in Illinois, municipalities are least dependent on the property tax. They can levy local sales and utility taxes; in addition, other tax options are available to home-rule municipalities. Further, because state income tax revenue sharing is distributed to municipalities based on their share of the state population (grants to counties are based on the share of the state population living in their unincorporated areas), the bulk (85.4 percent in fiscal 1985) was distributed to municipalities. The motor fuel tax distribution formula also steers the largest portion of motor fuel grants to municipalities.

In fiscal year 1985, municipal property tax revenues of $968 million accounted for 34.9 percent of municipal tax revenues. Among other sources, local sales tax revenues accounted for 25.8 percent, public utility revenues accounted for 13.6 percent, other locally levied tax revenues accounted for 9.0 percent, replacement revenues accounted for 3.7 percent, income tax revenue sharing accounted for 7.6 percent, and state motor fuel tax distributions accounted for 5.4 percent.

Township and Road Districts

Of the $258 million in tax revenues reported by townships and road districts, including state motor fuel tax monies distributed to counties for townships and road districts, $194 million, or 75.2 percent, consisted of property tax receipts. The remainder consisted of $15 million from personal property replacement tax distributions and $49 million (19.0 percent) from state motor fuel tax distributions.

School and Community College Districts

School and community college districts rely solely on property and replacement taxes for their tax revenues, but also receive significant grants-in-aid from both state and federal government. For fiscal 1985, $3.530 billion in tax revenues received by schools was divided between $3.234 billion (91.6 percent) from the property tax and $296 million (8.4 percent) from corporate personal property tax distributions.

Special Districts

Of the $1.138 billion in tax revenues reported by special districts in fiscal

1985, $731 million, or 64.2 percent, was from the property tax, 30.7 percent was from sales taxes, and 5.1 percent was from corporate personal property replacement tax distributions. Among special districts, revenues of $272 million were reported by sanitary districts, $298 million by park districts, and $352 million by mass transit districts or authorities. Most districts rely on property and replacement tax distributions for their tax revenues as almost all of the local sales tax receipts ($342 million) were derived from the Regional Transportation Authority sales tax.

Property Tax Trends

Between the 1975 and 1984 tax years, property tax extensions (billings) increased $2.477 billion (69.3 percent) from $3.572 billion to $6.049 billion. The extension figure for 1984 taxes paid in 1985 excludes governments that do not report to the state comptroller on a timely basis.

The increase in extensions during the decade reflects both growth in the total assessed value of Illinois property, despite several major reductions in the tax base, and higher tax rates. With the elimination of corporate personal property from the tax base for the 1979 tax year, property that accounted for $10.2 billion, or 15.5 percent, of total equalized assessed property values in 1978 was removed from the tax base.

The 1970 Illinois constitution provided the authority to grant homestead exemptions (exemptions that apply to the value of owner-occupied homes). Presently, four homestead exemptions are offered: the general exemption, the senior citizen exemption, the disabled veteran exemption, and the homestead improvement exemption. The general exemption has allowed the homeowner to reduce his or her equalized assessed valuation by up to $1,500 for 1978, $3,000 for 1979 through 1982, and $3,500 beginning in 1983. For the 1984 tax year, the general homestead exemption reduced property tax valuations by $7.3 billion (or 8.4 percent).

Extensions increased modestly in 1983 and 1984, but tax rates have increased because there has been little increase in the total assessed value of taxable property. Extensions increased $215 million (3.8 percent) for the 1983 tax year and $217 (3.7 percent) in 1984. These percentage increases in extensions were lower than the increase for seven of the prior eight years. (The exception was 1979 when extensions declined 5.7 percent because of the removal of personal property from the tax base.) Despite the modest growth in extensions, the tax rate increased from 7.07 percent for 1982 to 7.57 percent for 1984 because the total valuation of property declined $411 million for the 1983 tax year and only increased $820 million for the 1984 tax year. In contrast, the tax rate dropped in 1980 and 1981 when the total valuation increased $8.4 billion (13.9 percent) and $7.1 billion (10.4 percent), respectively.

Municipalities, counties, and townships lost $202.7 million in revenue from the recently eliminated federal revenue sharing program in fiscal 1985, including $129.6 million reported by municipalities, $43.3 million by counties, and $29.8 million by townships. According to data gathered by the Commission on Intergovernmental Relations, although townships received the smallest revenue sharing allocation, federal revenue sharing accounted for 9.6 percent of township general revenue, compared with 2.9 percent for municipalities and 2.7 percent for counties.[6]

Local Government Concerns

Charles Adrian, in his book *State and Local Governments,* recognizes two issues of concern to local governments today: first, local government boundaries drawn up in the nineteenth century are often unsuitable today, and second, the role and structure of local governments often do not meet contemporary needs.[7] This has led more than one critic of local government to propose the idea of consolidation or, in some cases, complete elimination of some government units. "We ought to do away with all city and village governments and our patchwork of school districts. We should eliminate townships, fire protection districts, park districts, sewer districts, airport districts, and all the other collage of separate little bailiwicks."[8]

While good arguments can be made for both sides of this issue of consolidation/abolition of some units of local government, certain problems affecting all local governments cannot be overlooked. These include:

1. *Lack of professional staff.* Although many larger local governments in Illinois employ professional staff to handle all aspects of their government, these are far from the norm. Seventy-five percent of the local governments in the state are small and have little or no staff support of any kind. The

6. On 21 July 1988, the Sales Tax Reform Act was signed into law. Over a two-year period, this law will convert many of the local sales taxes in Illinois to shared revenues. The state sales tax rate will increase from 5 percent to 6¼ percent, while the municipal, county, and supplemental county sales taxes will be eliminated. The incremental revenue from the increased sales tax rate is to be divided among local governments by a formula that replaces the lost sales tax revenues. Home-rule units, the Regional Transportation Authority, and some additional specified units of local government can continue to levy local sales taxes within statutory limits.

7. Charles R. Adrian, *State and Local Governments* (New York: McGraw-Hill, 1976), 170.

8. Ed Armstrong, "Let's Have One County-Wide Government," *Springfield State Journal-Register,* 16 Feb. 1987, p. 5.

officials themselves are part-time employees with little formal training for the position they hold.

2. *Increased costs.* People want more services; they do not want snow on their roads, potholes, burglaries, or delayed trash pickup. However, they do not want to pay more for them.

3. *Lack of cooperation.* Local governments and the officials administering them are fierce protectors of their turf. They are traditionally conservative, loathe change, and do not welcome intrusions by other governments, especially at the state or federal level. As a result, there is little sharing of information, equipment or services.

4. *Duplication of services.* Because of the abundance of local units in the state, much equipment and many facilities are not used to their full capacity because so many governments have their own. Some equipment is not cost-effective if it is not being used all the time. The same can be said for facilities such as sewage disposal and water filtration plants. Intergovernmental agreements that would consolidate expenditures and services at a cost savings for all involved are used too rarely.

5. *Lack of services.* Again, because of great differences in size, population, and budgets of local governments, the number of services provided varies greatly, as do the costs. Key services affected include street maintenance, water supply, street lights, garbage collection, and sewage disposal.

Easy answers to these problems do not exist. However, the first step to a solution is better communication between officials and the citizens they represent, their own staffs, the media, and other levels of government. One would think that in a state with so many units of government, a state with more governments than most countries, we would have learned to communicate with each other pretty well by now. Unfortunately, that is not always the case.

Local officials know that communication involves a great deal more than attending meetings, answering letters, and returning phone calls. Elected officials, appointed executives, supervisors, and employees of local governments spend enormous amounts of time communicating with each other, with citizens of the community, the media, and others. The volume of messages received and sent and the quantity of information available today are unprecedented. How well we communicate can often determine the success or failure of our actions. If local officials make a conscious effort to sit down with representatives from business and labor, the media, and the public, no problem is insurmountable. With better communication, local governments in Illinois will continue to be a strong, vibrant resource for the almost twelve million people they serve.

3.

Intergovernmental Cooperation

JOHN LATTIMER

The federal nature of the American intergovernmental system is derived from a combination of constitutional provisions, laws, political institutions, and customs. The framers of our Constitution settled upon federalism as a compromise between state supremacy and a strong central government. Traditionally, it has been viewed as dual federalism, with functions being divided between the state and national governments and with each level remaining autonomous in its own area of responsibility. Local governments, although not mentioned by the Constitution, historically have been considered creatures of the state. Given the nature of federalism, it is inevitable that tensions should arise among the various levels of government in the United States.

The modern era of intergovernmental cooperation in Illinois is the product of a long history of changing relationships among our federal, state, and local governments. The nature of federal aid has changed from infrastructure development in the 1860s, to the Great Society programs of the 1960s, to general revenue sharing and block grants in the 1970s, to shifts of federal aid from local governments to states in the 1980s. During the 1960s and 1970s, local governments in Illinois took on increased powers and duties with the expanded revenues provided by increased state and federal aid and, more importantly, new state constitutional authority. The 1980s, however, find those same local governments facing unprecedented financial difficulties. Those financial difficulties make intergovernmental cooperation more important than ever before.

The year 1970 was a watershed for intergovernmental cooperation in

he state's newly adopted income tax provided new funds for local
:nts, helping to further the expansion of local programs begun during
at Society." A new constitution and a newly reapportioned legislature—one more attuned to growing urban and suburban needs and no longer
dominated by rural interests—modernized state government and fundamentally changed the relationship between the state and its local governments.

The new constitution provided for a continuous state legislature and a
governor with expanded executive powers. But more importantly, the new
constitution nullified "Dillon's rule" and gave home-rule powers to the
state's municipal governments serving twenty-five thousand or more people and any county with an elected chief executive officer (Cook County). It
also gave local governments a sweeping grant of authority in article 7,
section 10. This "intergovernmental cooperation" section of the constitution allows any unit of local government in Illinois to contract or associate
with any other unit of government "to obtain or share services and to
exercise, combine or transfer any power or function, in any manner not
prohibited by law." This was an innovative attempt to provide an alternative
to special districts. Another innovation in the new constitution provides
that "the state has the primary responsibility for financing the system of
public education." This provision has created much heated debate on the
state's fiscal relationship with school districts.

Although the new constitution gave many new powers to local governments, it omitted any provision to address one of the most important of
today's intergovernmental issues—that of state mandates on local governments. On any survey of local officials, state mandates head the list of
intergovernmental problems. It was not until 1979 that a state mandates act
was passed by the general assembly in an attempt to address this issue.

Intergovernmental Cooperation

Intergovernmental cooperation is just what it sounds like. It occurs when
two or more governments agree on a course of action that is mutually
beneficial. Local governments cooperate with the federal government,
with the state government, and with each other, but the characteristics of
cooperation vary considerably with the level of government. Most federal–
local cooperation takes place when local governments accept and agree to
the terms of federal grants. State–local cooperation is more broad-based.
Because historically local governments have been considered creatures of
the state, they may be required to carry out state-mandated policies with
or without compensation. This "forced" cooperation is sometimes made

more palatable with grants-in-aid. States also share taxes with local governments, providing that certain requirements are met. Cooperative ventures between local governments tend to be voluntary and take place when they appear to benefit all concerned. Mutual aid and cooperative service delivery are the most common kinds of interlocal cooperation.

The Role of Federal Aid

Federal aid to state and local governments came initially in the form of land grants and periodic distributions of budget surpluses. Ultimately, these gave way to limited grants and finally to the wide range of categorical and block grants that we know today.

In the immediate postwar period, a preoccupation with rebuilding the deteriorated infrastructure and promoting growth gave rise to a number of federal programs. These included urban renewal, the FHA and VA housing programs, as well as programs designed to build highways, airports, and water treatment systems. These categorical grants were largely implemented through the private sector, with the federal government providing substantial inducements for participation. The programs proved popular and participation was high. In the early 1960s, the thrust of federal programs changed. A preoccupation with bricks and mortar gave way to a concern for social welfare issues.

A combination of persons and events combined to bring about a remarkable change in the number and kinds of federal grants that were available as well as the way in which they were administered. Rural poverty was highlighted in the Democratic primary of 1960. Urban riots later in the decade caused the Johnson administration to make combating urban blight a high priority. Federal programs were introduced to provide health care, housing, and recreation to the disadvantaged. It was the era of medicaid, medicare, model cities, and the war on poverty. Two programs, however, were directly responsible for changing the scope and administration of federal aid and ultimately for the vigorous attacks on the federal aid system: the Voting Rights Act of 1964 and the Equal Opportunities Act of 1964 were implemented not by local governments but by community action groups. The intention was to avoid the interference of racism, but that did not calm the outrage of local officials everywhere. The fact that urban rioting brought about massive increases in federal aid funneled through these same irregular channels did nothing to improve the situation. Attempts to remedy the problem occurred late in the Johnson administration with the passage of the Green Amendment and initiation of the Model Cities program, but major changes did not come until well into the administration of Richard Nixon. In the meantime, the proliferation of intergovernmental grants engendered a certain amount of overlap and confusion that led to the passage of the Intergovernmental Cooperation Act of 1968. The hope was that some sort of order could be imposed on rapidly developing inter-governmental relations.

New Federalism

The transition to the New Federalism period was marked by the election of Richard Nixon in 1968. With regard to intergovernmental aid, his adminis-tration aimed to provide more flexibility to the system and to remove the debate about programs from Washington by distributing monies according to formula. These goals were carried out in two major programs: general revenue sharing and community development block grants. General reve-nue sharing was an idea that had been formulated by reformers and backed by big-city mayors and others. They argued that the federal income tax was a more elastic source of revenue than any they could tap on the local level and that it made sense for the federal government, which was eroding their tax base, to share that source with them. With the passage of the State and Local Assistance Act of 1972, that program came into being. It met the requirement of the Nixon administration by distributing funds according to formula and it had no strings attached. Both conditions tended to take the management of grants out of the hands of Washington politicians and place it into the hands of local officials. To be sure, Congress could still debate the formula, but it had little to say about how the money was spent.

The community development block grant program initiated by the Hous-ing and Community Development Act of 1974 was somewhat more struc-tured, but it nevertheless provided more flexibility for local officials. It combined seven categorical grants into a single grant program that was distributed by formula. The uses for the grants were limited, but choices within that range were made on the local level. Moreover, because the public participation requirement could be met with as little as an annual public hearing, decision making remained firmly in the hands of local officials rather than groups. One effect of the new distribution formula was to take away the big-city bias that had been prevalent with the old categorical grants. The grantsmanship that enabled them to obtain a large share of the categorical grants was no longer a prerequisite. In 1974, prior to consolidation, 974 communities were receiving categorical grants; by early 1979, there were 3,305 approved community development block grant communities.

In the Wake of New Federalism

The Carter administration proposed no major new initiatives, but the rule changes that occurred did reflect a more liberal point of view than that which prevailed during the Nixon or Ford years. More redistributive strings were added to block grants. There was also a change in the formula by which community development grants were distributed. In the original formula, three factors, including population, formed the basis on which funds were distributed. The loss of population by northern cities to the Sunbelt resulted in substantial losses in grant money and gave rise to a plan that permitted cities to use one of two formulas, whichever benefited them the most. The second formula, which included "population growth lag," proved to be more satisfactory for northern industrial cities. The new strings put added pressure on local governments to employ planners and administrators. The cost to local governments was high, but many had become dependent upon federal aid and found it impossible to get along without it.

The main thrust of the Reagan administration was the attempt to wean local governments from as many federal programs as possible. The desire to turn back a number of large programs to state and local governments has, however, failed. Moreover, efforts to cut some grants for highways and clean water were not successful. Reagan did, however, succeed in changing the clean water grant program to a loan program, with the federal government providing seed money for state revolving funds through 1991. Ironically, one of the few federal grant programs to disappear was general revenue sharing, which by all accounts met the president's requirements for a good program.

In retrospect, there have been dramatic changes in the federal system during the course of the twentieth century. Much of this change has come about as the result of the expansion of the intergovernmental grant programs. Most domestic service is intergovernmental in that few state or local programs are ineligible for federal aid. The most dramatic increases in federal grants-in-aid came during the period from 1960 to 1979 when federal grant payments went from $7 billion to $82.8 billion. During the same period, federal aid as a percentage of state and local expenditures increased from 14.7 percent to 25.8 percent. By contrast, during the period from 1950 to 1960, federal grants increased from $2.2 billion to $7 billion, with the percentage of local expenditures going from 10.4 percent to 14.7 percent (see table 3-1).

The changes in the intergovernmental system as a result of the large increase in federal grants have been attributed to a number of factors; the

Table 3-I.
Grants-in-Aid as a Percentage of State and Local Expenses
(in millions of dollars)

Year	Total Grants-in-Aid	% of State & Local Expenses
1950	2,253	10.4
1955	3,207	10.1
1960	7,020	14.7
1965	10,904	15.3
1970	24,014	19.4
1975	49,834	23.1
1979	82,858	25.8

Source: Office of Management and Budget, Special Analyses Budget of the United States Government, 1981 (Washington: U.S. Government Printing Office, 1980).

most important of these are the decline of political parties, the use of public interest groups, and the increasingly interdependent nature of the system. In the 1800s, political parties fought over federal aid for "internal improvements," and it was not until the Republicans gained control of both the presidency and the Congress after the Civil War that federal lands and funds were given to states for development of the public infrastructure, a policy viewed by the Democrats as an intrusion on states' rights. In the twentieth century the parties have also battled over the nature of federal aid—with Republicans more attuned to infrastructure or general grants (without federal "strings") and the Democrats more interested in social programs with a heavy emphasis on federal oversight.

As the power of political parties has declined, these distinctions have blurred. Republicans as well as Democrats are more willing to listen to the pleas of special interest groups requesting categorical aid for their particular constituency. Democrats are just as eager to vote for internal improvements—particularly if those improvements are made in their districts. The power of these special interest groups has made it nearly impossible to change the existing categorical grant system. The administration has been limited to merely reducing them on the margin and halting their ever-increasing funding.

Many observers believe that the costs of this federal largess have been substantial, because federal grants frequently require matching monies that require an annually increasing proportion of state and local budgets. Also, since many of the grants are for social programs, money previously devoted to traditional municipal concerns such as police, fire protection, and sanitation has been diverted to the new, federally funded social programs. The most important problem has been the development of overlapping and duplicative programs. With the reduction in federal funding under the Reagan administration, state and local governments were then forced to look for ways to integrate similar federal, state, and local programs. In fact, program integration (with stringent assessment systems built in for better program accountability) will be the next phase of federal, state, and local intergovernmental cooperation.

Because revenue sources and administration have become both interdependent and overlapping, policy changes take place only after extensive intergovernmental bargaining; and that requires time and diminishes the control of elected officials. As elected officials begin to assert control over these programs during times of fiscal stress, there is no doubt that they will no longer tolerate overlapping or duplication. They will insist that programs be held accountable and that assessment systems be put in place to check their effectiveness.

Federal Aid to Illinois Local Governments

In general, federal funding of local programs draws more criticism than does state funding, probably because most federal grants come with "strings attached." Moreover, those "strings" may require that at least a certain proportion of the grant go to disadvantaged groups. State aid, on the other hand, is more likely to take the form of shared taxes. That is not to say that there are no state mandates on local governments or that they are not resented, but simply that strings are not generally tied to state aid.

In Illinois, federal aid to local governments increased from $474 million in 1975 to $1.3 billion in 1984 ($200 million in general revenue sharing has now been eliminated). During that period, it grew as a percentage of total general revenue from 13 to 14 percent, reaching a peak of 19 percent in 1981. While dollar amounts of federal aid are expected to increase slightly, this kind of aid will certainly decline as a percentage of total general revenue. Over the past several years, the top six federal programs providing aid to local governments in Illinois have been general revenue sharing, urban mass transit capital and operating grants, urban mass transit capital improvements, the community development block grant entitlement, wastewater plant construction, and job training (see table 3-2).

Table 3-2.
Top Six Federal Programs to Illinois Local Governments,
FY 1983–1985
(in millions of dollars)

Program	FY 1983	FY 1984	FY 1985	% Change
General Revenue Sharing*	213.5	210.1	210.7	−1.3
UMTA-Capital & Operating	28.4	127.3	188.3	563.0
UMTA-Capital Improvements	206.5	101.6	142.0	−31.2
CDBG-Entitlement	191.8	150.7	134.2	−30.0
Wastewater Plant Construction	125.4	196.5	133.4	6.4
Job Training	184.3	107.5	109.1	−40.8

Source: Illinois Commission on Intergovernmental Cooperation, Local Government Financial Assistance Database.

*Amounts shown differ from Census Bureau amounts listed in the text because the Census Bureau reports on a local fiscal year basis and this table reflects federal fiscal year reporting.

State and Local Government Relations

Because local governments are creatures of the state, state–local relationships are different from national–state or national–local relationships. State governments as a result of their superior constitutional position have the power to regulate virtually every facet of local government activity, from incorporation to financial administration. Their tendency to do so has ebbed and flowed with events. In the late 1800s and early 1900s, a wave of municipal bond defaults caused many states to institute rigorous regulation of municipal finances. Another round of regulation occurred in the mid-1970s in response to New York City's financial crisis. The tax revolts of the late seventies caused some state governments to place severe limitations on property tax rates. At the same time, there has been a movement to ease up on regulation by permitting home rule for local governments.

In Illinois, the 1970 constitution provided for automatic home rule for all municipalities with populations over twenty-five thousand and for Cook County. It also contained provisions for other municipalities and counties to become home-rule entities. Home rule has greatly expanded the authority of local governments to tax, borrow, regulate, and license—indeed, to exercise any local power not denied to them by the state. Non-home-rule governments, by contrast, may exercise only those powers explicitly given them by the state. The taxing and borrowing provisions are among the most

BOYHOOD HOME

important home-rule powers. They permit local officials to levy property, sales, and motor fuel taxes at any rate they choose and without statutory limits on their use. They also permit home-rule entities to borrow without going to the voters and without regard for statutory debt limitations, as long as the obligation does not extend beyond forty years.

Home rule has been relatively successful in Illinois. At the time of ratification, sixty-seven cities and villages and one county became home-rule entities. Since then, thirty-four villages and cities have adopted home rule by referendum and four by population growth. Four cities have lost their home-rule status and no counties have adopted home rule, although there have been eleven referenda. The lack of taxing and borrowing restrictions has been a two-edged sword. It has given local governments more taxing and borrowing options, but it has also raised citizen concern about the application of these powers. Most observers believe that fear of almost unlimited taxing authority has been at least partially responsible for the failure of the eleven county referenda and for the loss of home rule in the four municipalities. It would appear that there are some cases in which the public wishes the state to stand between them and the power of their local government.

Other instances of state intrusion into local affairs are viewed with less enthusiasm. State mandating on local governments, for example, has been a contentious issue for the past decade. While the increasing use of state mandates has broadened the scope of local government activities, it has also curtailed their autonomy and made them more dependent upon the state and the federal government for both resources and policy choices. Moreover, in spite of increased state and federal revenues, mandates place a financial burden on local governments. This view was echoed in a study conducted by the Illinois City Management Association and the Illinois Municipal League. They found that nearly half the property tax revenues collected by cities and villages in Illinois were used for state-mandated programs. Since property taxes provide the single largest source of discretionary funds for those entities, many found that they faced the unpleasant choice of cutting their own programs or raising taxes.

As local protest became more vocal, Illinois joined about forty other states in passing a state mandates act. The Illinois act specifies that three categories of mandates be reimbursed at the 50–100 percent level and that a catalog of past mandates be published and reviewed to determine whether the mandates still meet state goals. Since the enactment of the Illinois State Mandates Act, approximately one hundred technically reimbursable

AN' TAR-BABY DON'T SAY NOTHIN'

mandates have passed the Illinois General Assembly. Not one has been reimbursed. Approximately half were excused from reimbursement by amendments to the mandates act. The catalog of past mandates so far has not been published.

Local government officials report that among the most disturbing mandates are those that provide tax exemptions. Indeed, many local officials concede that they could live with other kinds of mandates if only their tax base was not eroded by state action. That is not to say that they do not find other kinds of mandates a burden. Personnel and retirement mandates are seen as troublesome both by general purpose governments and school districts because they are imposed without regard to an area's ability to pay. School districts also report difficulty with some service mandates imposing substantial costs, particularly those dealing with asbestos removal.

Counties in particular are affected by "due process mandates" which are not currently covered under the State Mandates Act. Recent actions, such as driving under the influence (DUI) legislation, the consolidated elections law, child support enforcement, as well as a measure providing for the housing of state prisoners in county jails, have imposed substantial new costs on counties.

In general, all local governments would like to have mandates more consistently reimbursed. Counties would also like to have "due process mandates" fall under the provisions of the State Mandates Act. [*Ed. note:* For further information on state mandates, see chapter 10.]

State Aid

State aid to general purpose governments has declined over the past ten years. In 1975, it represented 16 percent of their total general revenue, but by 1984, that proportion had dropped to 11 percent. There are two basic types of intergovernmental transfers from the state to local governments: grants and shared taxes. Shared taxes make up the largest proportion of these transfers (78 percent in 1984, up from 56 percent in 1975). The shared taxes that provide the greatest amount of revenue to local governments are the motor fuel tax, the local government distributive fund, and the personal property tax replacement fund.

Motor Fuel Tax

The motor fuel tax is a flat tax that is paid by distributors and suppliers, who pass the cost along to consumers. It was instituted in 1927 at a rate of 2 cents per gallon. By 1969, the rate had been increased to 7.5 cents, where it remained until 1983. During the late 1970s and early 1980s, declining gasoline sales resulted in lower revenues from the motor fuel tax. In 1983, the legislature sought to remedy this shortfall with a 5.5-cent increase to be implemented in stages over a two-year period ending in 1985 with a tax of 13 cents per gallon. From 1975 to 1984, the motor fuel tax declined as a percentage of total state aid from 36 percent to 28 percent. The new revenues resulting from the recent tax increase should help to reverse this trend.

Local Government Distributive Fund

The local government distributive fund (LGDF) was established in 1969 to provide financial assistance to local governments. It is funded entirely out of state income tax revenues with one-twelfth of total collections being set aside for that purpose. Fund monies are then distributed to counties and municipalities on the basis of population. A number of attempts have been made to change both the dollar allocation and the allocation formula itself, but all have failed. Neither an early effort to increase the fund by appropriating one-eighth rather than one-twelfth of income tax collections, nor a later attempt to cap the fund at some predetermined dollar level passed the general assembly.

Over a ten-year period from 1975 to 1984, LGDF disbursements to local governments increased from 19 percent to 26 percent of total state aid. There were, however, periods of fluctuation. From 1979 to 1981, the fund actually declined as a percentage of state aid from 25 percent to 21 percent, reflecting economic declines in the state. Moreover, the rapid increase of the fund from 22 percent to 26 percent of total state aid between 1983 and 1984 was the result of the one-year income tax surcharge. Like the income tax itself, the LGDF is extremely sensitive to economic factors as well as modification of tax law. The federal income tax reform, which will permit fewer deductions, will result in the reporting of higher adjusted gross income. That will result in higher collections for the state income tax and for the LGDF.

Personal Property Tax Replacement

The 1970 constitution abolished the personal property tax as of 1 January 1979. The personal property tax replacement (PPTR) was established to restore lost funds to local governments. PPTR is funded from the corporate income tax, the tax on partnerships, and the tax on the invested capital of utilities. From 1980 (the year it was instituted) until 1984, PPTR allocations

Table 3-3.

Major Sources of Illinois Local Government Revenue

	1978	1979	1980	1981	1982	1983	1984	1985	1986
Own Source Revenue (%)									
Property Taxes	29	28	26	24	24	24	27	27	26
Other Taxes	18	17	16	18	19	19	19	18	20
Charges & Misc.	18	20	21	21	23	23	23	24	25
Intergovernmental Transfers (%)									
Federal Aid	17	19	19	19	17	17	14	12	10
State Aid	13	13	13	13	13	13	11	13	14
Other Revenue (%)	5	3	5	5	4	4	4	6	5
Total (%)	100	100	100	100	100	100	100	100	100
Total ($ in millions)	$4,995.5	$5,766.0	$6,539.2	$7,613.7	$8,113.9	$8,685.2	$9,123.8	$9,649.9	$10,201.6

Source: Calculated from U.S. Bureau of the Census, *Governmental Finances* in (Year).

to local governments went from 31 percent to 21 percent of total state aid.
The decline was caused by a reduction of the PPTR portion of corporate
income taxes from 2.85 percent to 2.5 percent.

State aid to general-purpose local governments has grown in dollar
amount, but as a percentage of total general revenue it has declined steadily
from 1975 to 1984. With the end of the federal general revenue sharing
program and additional attempts to cut the federal domestic budget, the
state government may find new requests in the coming years to increase aid
to local governments.

Conclusion

In the late 1970s, Illinois local governments attemptenjoyed a steady
growth in federal aid as a percentage of total general revenue. By the 1980s,
however, that trend had begun to reverse itself. The decline in federal fiscal
conditions resulted in cutbacks and in the termination of one of the most
popular federal programs, general revenue sharing. While the dollar
amounts of federal aid to local governments will remain relatively high, it
will continue to decline as a percentage of total local revenue (see table 3-3).

State aid during the late seventies and early eighties declined steadily.
No doubt the state will be under some pressure to replace lost federal aid,
but it seems unlikely that there will be an influx of new state monies to local
governments. There may, however, be additional revenues from income-
tax-supported state programs (LGDF and PPTR) as the result of the new
federal tax code.

In general, local governments will be forced to rely on their own sources
of revenue. In the recent past, other taxes, charges, and miscellaneous fees
have grown rapidly in importance, but it appears that the property tax may
once again be increasing as a proportion of total local revenue (see fig. 3-1).
It remains to be seen whether local governments can produce the necessary revenues from their existing sources without causing a tax revolt.

Interlocal Government Relations

In recent decades, the growing demand for local services has exposed
inadequacies in the diverse organization of local government. Jurisdictional
boundaries do not always correspond to natural service areas because
many local units were geographically created in a haphazard manner in
response to various public needs. It is extremely difficult, if not impossible,
to reduce the number of units of local government by combining them or

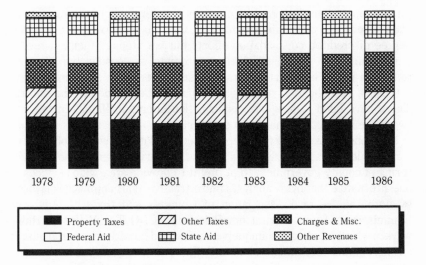

Figure 3-1. Major local government revenue sources, FY 1978–1986.

transferring authority of special-purpose governmental units to counties, municipalities, or the state. Consequently, intergovernmental cooperation can be used to solve problems and provide services in a more efficient, economical, and orderly way.

Illinois leads the nation in the number of governmental units. The 1970 Constitutional Convention and the general assembly have recognized this fact and sought to encourage cooperative agreements by establishing broad, permissive provisions for intergovernmental authority. The following brief summary reviews the history of these provisions and examines certain legal obstacles that still inhibit intergovernmental cooperation.

Consolidation Attempts

In the past, consolidation was seen as the best solution to the problem of fragmented local governments. It was believed that local services could be provided more economically and efficiently if overlap and duplication were eliminated. The earliest attempts at consolidation were made around the turn of the century by reformers who saw fragmentation as one of the major problems confronting urban government. While reformers have continued to push for consolidation, they have been joined by other groups with different agendas. The white residents of large cities, for example, sometimes support consolidation with counties in order to dilute the strength of black voters who outnumber them in the city. These efforts have to some degree discredited consolidation efforts but not stopped them. A recent study found that of the sixty-eight attempts at consolidation through referenda in the last thirty years only seventeen were successful. Nevertheless, consolidation referenda continue to be put before the voters. There have been at least six consolidation efforts in Illinois in the last twenty years, but none has been successful.

Many observers believe that there are better solutions than consolidation to local problems, particularly urban service delivery problems. The restructuring of county government to permit it to provide area-wide services is one alternative that many analysts find attractive. This approach is favored by both the National Association of Counties and the U.S. Advisory Commission on Intergovernmental Relations (ACIR). The ACIR sees three ways in which counties are uniquely qualified to deal with urban problems in a coherent and cost-effective manner. First, counties exist in forty-seven states and are accountable through the electoral process. Second, most counties include a certain amount of urbanized territory and have a broad enough tax base to allow for economies of scale. Finally, most counties have had a great deal of experience with intergovernmental relations.

A number of studies have been done on the cooperative efforts of municipalities in metropolitan areas. They all found that some services such as schools, water, police, and waste disposal can be administered more economically and more easily when they are dealt with on an area-wide basis. Whether that is done seems to depend upon a number of factors. Most formal cooperation takes place in the areas of police protection, public works, fire protection, and utilities. Little cooperation takes place in socially sensitive areas such as parks, recreation, planning, or housing.

In Illinois, the 1970 constitution removed existing barriers to interlocal cooperation in the expectation that such cooperation would stem the proliferation of special districts. Case studies suggest that most cooperative ventures are of a noncontroversial variety—police and fire mutual aid pacts, service agreements, and so forth. Politically sensitive arrangements appear to come about only with the intervention of an outside force. An example is the package of cooperative ventures between Bloomington and Normal that was negotiated by the state in an effort to attract the Diamond Star Company to Illinois. The interest in economic development may well spur similar efforts and perhaps even resurrect an interest in consolidations. One such consolidation is at least being considered in the Quad Cities area. Given the political difficulties of such a move it seems doubtful that it will become the wave of the future.

The Pre-1970 Legal Situation

Prior to the adoption of the 1970 constitution, the basic constitutional doctrine relating to local government powers in Illinois, as in most other states, was Dillon's rule. This doctrine, first stated by Justice Dillon of the Iowa Supreme Court in 1868, held that "municipal corporations owe their origin to, and derive their powers and rights wholly from, the legislature." When applied to proposed intergovernmental cooperation, Dillon's rule meant that unless the power to cooperate with other units was expressly provided by statute, local governments could not undertake, except in unusual circumstances, intergovernmental and associational activities.

Statutory Provisions

In view of the application of Dillon's rule to local powers, recognized by Illinois courts, the general assembly enacted statutes granting local governments the power to cooperate in many areas. A survey of the Illinois statutes in 1969 found over one hundred sections dealing with intergovernmental cooperation. These provisions are still in effect and provide specific statutory authority to engage in many types of cooperative activities. In fact, in a survey of intergovernmental endeavors in 1975, one commentator noted that almost all of them would have been permitted by pre-1970 statutes.[1] With a liberal interpretation of local government powers, that might be true, but experience with Dillon's rule argues persuasively otherwise. Even concerning section 1-1-5 of the Illinois Municipal Code, which follows, the authority for other governmental units to cooperate with municipalities is not clearly stated.

> The corporate authorities of each municipality may exercise jointly, with one or more other municipal corporations or other governmental subdivisions or districts, all of the powers set forth in the Code unless expressly provided otherwise. In this section, 'municipal corporations or other governmental subdivisions or district' includes, but is not limited to, municipalities, townships, counties, school districts, park districts, sanitary districts, and fire protection districts.[2]

At the Illinois Sixth Constitutional Convention, the Committee on Local

1. Martin Korn, "Intergovernmental Cooperation: Does the 1970 Illinois Constitution Give Units the Green Light?" *John Marshall Journal of Practice and Procedures* 8 (Winter 1975): 295–325.
2. Ill. Rev. Stat., ch. 24, sect. 1-1-5, Ill. Municipal Code.

Government reviewed this statutory provision and found it inadequate. The committee report stated:

> There are at least two factors which make this seemingly generous grant a limited and exceptive one. The first of these is the persistence of the psychology of Dillon's Rule among officials of local government in Illinois. Because of legislative actions and judicial interpretations, the belief persists that unless specific authorization can be found in the statutes, local governments may not engage in an activity. The second factor inhibiting intergovernmental cooperation can be found in the statutes themselves. . . . These grants of statutory authority do not provide needed flexibility with respect to financing intergovernmental undertakings.[3]

Two other deficiencies in the municipal code provision for intergovernmental cooperation should be mentioned. First, the provision applies only to the specific non-home-rule powers listed in the code. Second, it seems to allow only joint efforts, not service contracts. For example, it is arguable that two cities may jointly provide garbage collection service, but one city cannot pay another to provide such service and no prudently operated governmental unit would likely commit substantial funds to a project under such circumstances. Although no specific provision is made for intergovernmental fiscal power, the power to borrow money by issuing bonds is one of those mentioned in the code and could, arguably, be exercised jointly. Clearly, however, the certainty in the laws needed to encourage intergovernmental cooperation was lacking.

The 1970 Constitution

The most significant provision in the new constitution dealing with local government is article 7, section 6, which concerns the powers granted to home-rule units. This section reverses Dillon's rule to the extent that it applies to home-rule units and, by itself, would constitute authorization for these units to engage in many varieties of intergovernmental cooperation. It is not entirely sufficient for two reasons. First, many intergovernmental agreements involve some governments that are not home-rule units, including cities, counties, townships, school districts, and special districts. Second, to carry out some types of intergovernmental activities, even home-rule units might need authorization to exercise their powers extra-territorially. For these reasons, and others, the drafters of the new

---

3. Committee on Local Government, *Committee Report* (Springfield: Constitutional Convention, 1970), 57–58.

constitution saw fit to supplement the home-rule provisions with a separate section covering intergovernmental cooperation.

Article 7, Section 10

The committee reports and transcripts of the debates of the Sixth Constitutional Convention concerning article 7, section 10, provide important clues to its potential application. In addition to intergovernmental cooperation, the Committee on Local Government considered several other approaches to solving the structural problems of local units, including metropolitan government. The members recognized that certain proposals to combine or do away with special-purpose units of local government might result in the political defeat of the new constitution. The committee concluded, therefore, that expanded authority for intergovernmental cooperation could provide certain benefits, including economies of scale in the provision of services; the ability to undertake large-scale projects beyond the capacity of single governmental units; and elimination of the need for more special-purpose governments (Sixth Constitutional Convention, committee proposals).

The committee believed that three forms of cooperative arrangements would be needed to obtain these benefits:

1. A single local government performs a service or provides a facility for one or more other local units.

2. Two or more local governments perform a function or operate a facility on a joint basis.

3. Two or more local governments assist or supply aid to one another in emergency situations, such as a large fire or serious riot. (Sixth Constitutional Convention, committee proposals)

In order to secure these benefits and authorize the variety of intergovernmental possibilities the delegates envisioned, the section on intergovernmental cooperation was added to the constitution. In its final form, as approved by the voters, it reads as follows:

Section 10. Intergovernmental Cooperation

(a) Units of local government and school districts may contract or otherwise associate among themselves, with the state, with other states and their units of local government and school districts, and with the United States to obtain or share services and to exercise, combine, or transfer any power or function, in any manner not prohibited by law or by ordinance. Units of local government and school districts may contract and otherwise associate with individuals, associations, and corporations in any manner not prohibited by law or by ordinance. Participating units of government may use their credit, revenues, and other resources to pay costs and to service debt related to intergovernmental activities.

(b) Officers and employees of units of local government and school districts may participate in intergovernmental activities authorized by their units of government without relinquishing their offices or positions.

(c) The State shall encourage intergovernmental cooperation and use its technical and financial resources to assist intergovernmental activities.[4]

Section 10 remedies many of the defects found in earlier statutory grants of power. By authorizing units of local government and school districts to "contract or otherwise associate . . . in any manner not prohibited by law or ordinance," it reverses Dillon's rule as it applies to numerous intergovernmental activities. That this was the intent of the delegates is clear. The committee proposal states, "It will not be necessary for local units to seek statutory enactments before beginning an intergovernmental activity." The role of the general assembly is changed from one of granting powers when it believes local cooperation should be restricted.

In the case of financing intergovernmental activities, the constitutional provision is similarly liberal. "Participating units of government may use their credit, revenues, and other resources to pay costs and to service debt related to intergovernmental activities." This provision clearly authorizes each local unit to incur debt to pay for intergovernmental activities. It may also be interpreted to mean that local units may jointly incur and service debt, since it states that units "may use *their* credit" rather than "each may use its credit." As one commentator has noted, the provision may also authorize local units to jointly issue revenue bonds serviced by the revenues resulting from the intergovernmental activity. "The revenues produced from an intergovernmental activity, allocated and paid to each participant under the agreement, arguably are the revenues of the participant. These conceivably may be used to service the revenue bonds. Bond attorneys would probably be reluctant to approve such revenue bonds, without clearer statutory authority."[5]

The apparent reluctance of bond counsel to approve certain intergovernmental debt issues is understandable. Under Illinois law, any debt which a municipality incurs illegally is void. "There is not power in the municipal corporation to pay the debt—even if it wanted to and was financially able.

4. 1970 Illinois Constitution, art. 7, sect. 10.

5. Illinois Department of Commerce and Community Affairs, *Intergovernmental Cooperation in Illinois*, 1976.

. . . Given the risks involved and the hesitancy of the courts to liberally construe non-home rule units powers and functions in the face of conflicting laws, bond counsel and lenders will most probably require test cases in this order before they will favorably respond to local intergovermental programs involving taxation and joint bonding debt."[6]

The Intergovernmental Cooperation Act

Although article 7, section 10, is self-executing, the delegates to the Sixth Constitutional Convention recognized that the general assembly might wish to pass legislation "to supplement and render more effective this device" (verbatim transcripts). Accordingly, in 1973, the Intergovernmental Cooperation Act was passed, giving the general assembly's stamp of approval to the principle. Basically, the act stipulates that any power or powers, privileges, or authority exercised, or which may be exercised, by a public agency of this state may be exercised jointly with any other public agency of Illinois, any other state, or of the United States to the extent that existing laws of other states do not prohibit it. "Public agency," as used here, means any local government, school district, community college district, the state of Illinois, any agency of the state government or of the United States, or any other state or political subdivision of another state. Section 7 of the act clarifies its relationship with the constitutional provision. "This Act is not a prohibition on the contractual and associational process granted by Section 10, Article VII of the Constitution." As the Chicago Home Rule Commission noted, the legislation was passed "apparently on the theory that if it did grant new authority, it was helpful, but that if it did not grant new authority, at least it would not limit the constitutional scope of intergovernmental authority."[7]

The act, which is patterned on the Model Interlocal Cooperation Act of the Advisory Commission on Intergovernmental Relations, recognizes two varieties of intergovernmental cooperation: intergovernmental agreements and intergovernmental contracts. These are described in sections 3 and 5, respectively. Intergovernmental agreements refer to joint exercise of powers by two or more units while intergovernmental contracts refer to situations where one or more entities agree to furnish a service for one or more others. In actual practice, the difference between the two is "superficial and purely procedural."[8] Two procedural requirements are mentioned

6. Illinois Department of Commerce and Community Affairs, *Intergovernmental Cooperation in Illinois*, 1976.

7. City of Chicago, Home Rule Commission, *Report and Recommendations*, 1972.

8. Marc Towler, "The Illinois Intergovernmental Cooperation Act," *Law Forum* 3 (1974): 498–513.

in section 5 which apply to contracts but not agreements. The first of these is that the "contact shall be authorized by the governing body of each party to the contract." The attorney general has suggested that the adoption of the contract as an ordinance by each of the contracting parties would fulfill this requirement. The second of these is that the contract "shall set forth the purposes, powers, rights, objectives, and responsibilities of the contracting parties."

Section 5 apparently does not require sharing of powers. That is, it does not require that all of the parties to the contract possess the power to perform the function specified by the agreement. If one of the parties has the power, that is sufficient. "Any one or more public agencies may contract with any one or more public agencies to perform any governmental service, activity or undertaking which *any of the public agencies entering into the contract is authorized by law to perform.*"[9] This provision has the potential to greatly expand the possibilities for intergovernmental cooperation and seems to be authorized by the constitutional provision allowing local governments to "transfer any power or function." In adopting this section, the general assembly specifically rejected provisions in the model law which would have required mutuality. However, the attorney general has followed a conservative line of reasoning in this regard and has generally held that a unit must be authorized to conduct an activity singly before it may do so cooperatively.[10] Section 9, which was added to the act as an amendment in 1979, clarifies the problem of mutuality as it applies to counties.

Section 4 implements the constitutional provision that "participating units of government may use their credit, revenues, and other resources to pay the costs and to service debts related to intergovernmental activities." Section 4 was amended in 1980 to allow municipalities to create municipal joint water action agencies with the power to borrow money by issuing bonds and notes. Section 6, which provides for joint self-insurance, has been interpreted by the attorney general to include retirement and disability pension liabilities as insurable areas as well as other risks.[11]

The provisions of the model act which were omitted by the general assembly also give some insight into legislative intent. These include a requirement that each party to the agreement pass a resolution or ordinance specifying: the duration of the agreement; the precise organization

9. Ill. Rev. Stat., ch. 127, sect. 741–48.
10. Martin Korn, "Intergovernmental Cooperation: Does the 1970 Illinois Constitution Give Units the Green Light?" *John Marshall Journal of Practice and Procedure* 8 (Winter 1975): 295–325.
11. Marc Towler, "The Illinois Intergovernmental Cooperation Act," *Law Forum* 3 (1974): 498–513.

and nature of any separate administrative body created; the purpose of the agreement; the manner of financing and budgeting for the activity; and the method of terminating the agreement and disposing of any jointly owned property. The model act also required that any local units contemplating an intergovernmental agreement secure the approval of the attorney general and the state officer or agency having statutory or constitutional authority for the area or function covered by the agreement. A copy of the agreement was to be filed with the keeper of public records and the secretary of state. Evidently, by omitting these sections of the model act, the general assembly intended to leave these procedural questions to the discretion of local officials.

Judicial Interpretation

Since the ratification of the 1970 constitution, no case involving substantial questions concerning the intergovernmental cooperation provision has been brought before the supreme court. However, *Connely v. Clark County*, a 1973 Illinois Appellate Court decision, did address article 7, section 10, in some detail. In that case, Clark County was operating a gravel pit to maintain county roads. In addition, it sold gravel to other local governments such as municipalities and townships at cost. Suit was brought by a private gravel pit operator challenging the right of the county to engage in this activity.

Although the court recognized that the 1970 constitution nullified Dillon's rule as far as intergovernmental cooperation was concerned, it interpreted article 7, section 10, very narrowly and concluded that it applied only to cases where two or more governments formally agreed to perform a function jointly. The court held that the Clark County gravel pit was not a true case of intergovernmental cooperation. The court then relied on Dillon's rule, and, finding no statutory provisions specifically authorizing counties to sell gravel, enjoined the county from selling gravel as it has been doing.

The decision is regarded by many legal scholars as erroneous and inconsistent. As one put it, "The majority lost sight of the fact or did not comprehend the effect of the abrogation of Dillon's rule. The abrogation means that the courts must now look for a clear statutory *prohibition* which prevents units of local government from cooperating rather than looking for a *grant* of power which allows units to cooperate."[12] In addition, the court failed to cite the Intergovernmental Cooperation Act, which had become

12. Martin Korn, "Intergovernmental Cooperation: Does the 1970 Illinois Constitution Give Units the Green Light?" *John Marshall Journal of Practice and Procedure* 8 (Winter 1975): 295–325.

effective two months before the case was decided and specifically authorized local governments to contract for services among themselves as well
as perform functions jointly. Whatever the merits of the court's decision, it
established a precedent which makes bond attorneys and local officials
cautious in approaching cooperative arrangements.

The Role of the General Assembly

The 1970 constitution changed the role of the general assembly in intergovernmental cooperation from one of granting local units of government
the power to cooperate and associate to that of prescribing the power in
cases where it felt such action was inappropriate. In spite of this change,
the general assembly has, from time to time, passed permissive legislation
authorizing cooperation. This has taken the form of amendments to the
Intergovernmental Cooperation Act itself. Such legislation, unless well
analyzed, may be counterproductive since it may encourage the courts to
continue to rely on specific statutory enactments rather than on the
constitution in deciding cases involving intergovernmental cooperation. By
singling out municipal joint water agencies for special mention, the amendments may have diluted local authority to engage in similar cooperative
activities without special enactments.

Intergovernmental cooperation is a potentially valuable tool for local
government. It can offer significant advantages to urban and rural counties,
municipalities, and special districts. Such governmental units might use
cooperation to deal with a variety of problems, including: (1) the need to
utilize expensive technology; (2) fragmentation of service delivery and
responsibility; (3) overlapping of jurisdictions; (4) lack of rationalization
over boundaries; (5) uncoordinated and conflicting planning and implementation; (6) unpredictability of annexation; and (7) the need for economies of
scale or increased purchasing power.

Before entering into an intergovernmental agreement, local governments must follow some basic steps: (1) clearly define the need for
cooperation, (2) understand the practical issues in designing and negotiating the agreement and meet the defined needs, and (3) develop a good
budget that clearly outlines financial responsibility and sources of all
revenues.

Intergovernmental arrangements develop in response to particular needs
and circumstances. As these change, agreements are altered and renegoti-
ated. Any potential party to an intergovernmental agreement should, at a
very early point in the negotiation process, consult an attorney concerning
legal aspects of the contemplated agreement.

Most local officials who have served during the past twenty years understand the need for intergovernmental agreements quite well. The problems they cite include:

1. The fragmentation of responsibility caused by over six thousand units of local government that impedes adequate response to local problems.

2. Increased demands for government services coupled with losses of revenue and taxing power

3. Rapid migration of people to rural and suburban areas

4. Important but costly services that are often deferred until a crisis exists

5. The formation of special districts to circumvent debt limits

6. Public service needs that cross jurisdictional boundaries

7. Annexation laws which make it difficult to plan the location, size, and timing of facilities and services

8. Local governments service areas that do not develop on the basis of logic

In their handbook entitled *Intergovernmental Cooperation in Illinois*,[13] the State Department of Local Government Affairs (now the Department of Commerce and Community Affairs) and the Northeastern Illinois Planning Commission divide the various needs for cooperation into six program areas of major concern to local governments.

1. General administrative services and facilities: General management and personnel utilization, data processing and purchasing, and other general administrative topics

2. Transportation and public works: Roads and streets, mass transit, waste disposal and drainage, water supply, and other public works

3. Recreation and culture: Parks, recreation, and culture

4. Community development: Planning, physical development, economic development, and human resources development

5. Health, fire protection, and emergency services: Health planning services and facilities, civil defense, disaster emergency, ambulance and rescue services, and fire protection

6. Law enforcement and the courts: Planning and mutual aid; law enforcement—police services, court-related services; and innovations in public safety and the criminal justice system

These categories are useful in defining the areas of need for intergovernmental cooperation. But the structure of the agreement must also be decided. Intergovernmental agreements can take four different forms:

13. Illinois Department of Local Government Affairs, *Intergovernmental Cooperation in Illinois*, 1976.

1. One local government or more performs or provides a service or facility for one or more other governments.

2. Two or more local governments jointly perform a function or jointly operate a facility.

3. Two or more local governments mutually assist one another in emergency situations.

4. There exists a permanently formed organization whose main function is to address common problems and needs.

Conclusion

In today's rapidly changing world, an intergovernmental agreement offers a comprehensive solution to the problems of overburdening demand, overlapping jurisdictions, inadequate services and facilities, and inadequate resources at the same time that it maximizes local control.

Through the terms of an agreement, accountability can remain in the hands of local leadership. Local government decisions and the decision-making process remain close to the people whose lives are directly affected by them. Instead of the cumulative, crazy-quilt pattern which adds layer upon layer of governmental units, cooperative agreements can reverse pyramiding. Existing governments can make agreements and in the process provide a more rational response to the needs of their constituencies. More importantly, high-cost governmental services can be provided more efficiently through economies of scale and increased or improved services and facilities. Such services as police and fire protection, data processing, recreation, planning, and transportation can be handled more efficiently and effectively with intergovernmental cooperation.

The use of intergovernmental agreements offers advantages in the nonmetropolitan areas as well as the metropolitan areas. In the nonmetropolitan areas, the primary value is the ability to pool resources and utilize facilities jointly. In the metropolitan areas, the primary value lies in the ability to deal effectively with multi-jurisdictional problems and to coordinate related planning and service systems. This is especially important in areas where there are overlapping jurisdictions.

Some of the issues that transcend municipal or county boundaries include: (1) rationalization of land use and boundaries; (2) annexation policies; (3) services to be provided to newly developed areas; (4) benefits from increased tax revenues; and (5) development and maintenance of open space and recreational facilities.

Intergovernmental agreements may create forums in which long-standing mutual concerns over jurisdictions can be addressed and, perhaps, resolved. The initial needs addressed by a cooperative arrangement, and, accordingly, the purpose and scope of an agreement, may be relatively minor and uncomplicated. The progress of intergovernmental cooperation, however, is often incremental. As participants perceive the benefits of cooperation and perceive cooperation as workable, the willingness to expand such relationships may increase. This willingness is also made more likely by the need for greater efficiency in providing local services — a need which will increase as local service demands, labor costs, and general inflation continue to escalate.

PART TWO

Units of Local Government

4.

Municipal Government

STEVE SARGENT

Illinois is a large and diverse state, with important geographic, historic, and economic differences. Our municipalities represent the same distinctions. Illinois has 1,287 units of municipal government ranging in size from the city of Chicago with over three and one-quarter million population to the village of Time with twenty-seven citizens. Municipal government in Illinois, as elsewhere, is primarily service-oriented. Cities and villages exist to provide the necessary and convenient regulation and facilities desired or required when a number of people reside in close proximity. They were historically created by the legislature at the request of residents as they established settlements in or near watercourses or other transportation or employment facilities.

The scope of an individual municipal government's operations depends on a number of factors including size, type, expectation of quantity and quality of service, and economic vitality. This chapter will attempt to provide a thumbnail sketch of how our cities and villages developed both historically and legally; what forms of organization are permissible and the roles of various elected and appointed officials; how they function both formally and informally; and the municipality's role in our overall system of government. Chicago will be considered only in passing, as the focus will be on other cities and villages.

Municipal government is the level of government most visible to the public. It initiates most modernizations and innovations that streamline public service. It is the level of local government that is the training ground for future state and federal political leaders. It is also the government that offers the best possibility for an individual to serve in the political system.

History

During the late 1600s and into the mid-1700s, Illinois developed along its navigable waterways. Early settlements were French-oriented, usually located near existing Indian villages. They were established to provide protection for trading and religious activities. Probably the first genuine community in Illinois was founded in Cahokia in 1699.[1]

Most of the early Illinois settlements were located in the Great American Bottoms, the fertile strip along the east bank of the Mississippi River in what are now Madison, St. Clair, and Monroe counties. Several of these communities such as Cahokia, Kaskaskia, and Prairie du Rocher still exist in the vicinity of their original founding. During the French period, the non-Indian population of the Illinois area probably never exceeded fifteen hundred to two thousand individuals.[2]

Migrations in the 1700s and early 1800s were primarily from the southeastern states of Virginia, Kentucky, North Carolina, and Tennessee. This influx of frontiersmen into southern and south-central Illinois soon clashed with the older French Catholic settlers and within a very short time dominated the villages. Settlements began to develop along the Ohio River at places like Shawneetown and Massac. A trading post first developed at Chicago Portage around 1700, later became Fort Dearborn, and by 1812 had sixty residents.[3] The somewhat later general development of northern Illinois saw settlers coming primarily from the northeastern areas of America. The not-so-subtle differences between northern and southern Illinois developed early in our history.

Migration to Illinois boomed after statehood in 1818, first by men of the soil seeking fertile farmland and later by merchants, craftsmen, businessmen, and miners drawn by the swelling population and the geographic, transportation, and commercial advantages of the state. Later, large groups of European immigrants rapidly expanded the population of northern and parts of central Illinois. More recent shifts in population are continuing to affect our cities as well. These migrations include: (1) the early World War II movement of southern rural whites and blacks to industrial centers; (2) the post–World War II rush of central city residents

1. Robert P. Howard, *Illinois: A History of the Prairie State* (Grand Rapids, MI: William B. Eerdmans, 1972), 36–37.
2. Robert P. Howard, *Illinois: A History of the Prairie State* (Grand Rapids, MI: William B. Eerdmans, 1972), 39.
3. Robert P. Howard, *Illinois: A History of the Prairie State* (Grand Rapids, MI: William B. Eerdmans, 1972), 90.

to the suburbs; and (3) the continuation of foreign immigration in recent years of people from Asian and Spanish-speaking countries into our central cities.

The overall Illinois municipal population shows very modest to stable growth. Currently, of the 11,500,000 Illinois citizens, 79 percent are residents of incorporated communities. The pattern of change indicates great variance between individual cities, with some population losses in rural convenience communities and some central cities.

Illinois's first constitution had no specific reference to the operation or establishment of municipal governments. Municipalities were instead creatures of the legislature. They were created by special acts of the general assembly referred to as charters. The constitution of 1848 continued this practice. The charters were rather specific and detailed the size, scope of authority, and taxing powers of a particular unit. In total, 394 Illinois towns were fashioned through special charter. A handful still operate under charter today.[4]

The constitution of 1870 prohibited the passage of special legislation. This provision deleted legislative authority to charter additional town governments. In its place, the legislature passed a general law concerning the creation, organization, financing, and operation of municipal government. When a developing area desired to organize a city or a village, it looked to the general municipal law for the procedures to follow. The body of law developed for this purpose is referred to as the Illinois Municipal Code. This practice continues today under the constitution of 1970 with one important exception: home rule, which will be discussed at a later point. The code forms the legal basis under which non-home-rule cities and villages, not under special charters, must act. It also forms the legal basis for home-rule municipalities unless contrary government actions are taken consistent with home-rule powers.

As a practical matter, pure general law that is intended to apply the same terms and conditions to hundreds of municipal governments throughout our diverse and complex state cannot work. This impracticality has led to classification. Differing powers or degrees of authority are given to municipalities based on form, population, or some other set of circumstances. An experienced and clever statutory draftsman can phrase the general language of an amendment so as to isolate one city and permit a legislative solution to that city's problem without impacting other units. Regardless of the shortcomings of classification, something akin to it is necessary.

4. Jim Edgar, *Illinois Counties and Incorporated Municipalities* (Springfield: State of Illinois, 1986), 4–26.

Scope of Municipal Operations and Services

A number of factors affect the quality and quantity of services rendered by a municipal unit. Key elements include its size and related wealth, its purpose and location, and, most importantly, the expectations of its citizenry. The Illinois Statutes require municipal governments to do little or nothing. Cities are not required to have streets, police or fire protection, zoning, drinking water, or employees. This seeming lack of requirements or standards is illusory. Municipalities are organized because people want some or all of the above services; thus these or other services are provided. Once these functions are established by a local unit, the state and federal governments often mandate standards and costs.

Cities developed for a variety of reasons. In today's milieu, we can readily identify certain general types of units. The more important types are the central city, the suburban village, and the rural convenience community. There are others, but most cities can be reasonably placed in one of these three categories. The central city is usually large and provides a full range of municipal services. It most often develops as a result of transportation convenience such as a waterway, railroad facility, and/or highway. In many instances, it is the county seat, the center of commerce, and, more than likely, an educational and industrial community. It may very well have initially developed as the result of the location of a relatively large commercial, industrial, or transportation complex, such as a mine, railroad section point, or plant. For the purposes of municipal government, this type of unit will most likely have full-time employees and broad-ranged programs.

It should also be recognized that central cities exist within the larger metropolitan areas. These "suburban central cities" are most often historic, full-service communities that originally were miles from the central city but became contiguous as suburbs grew, particularly after World War II. Examples of this type of unit would be Elgin, Aurora, Joliet, and Waukegan. A few full-range units withstood the reorganization of the central city itself, examples being Oak Park, Evanston, Cicero, and Berwyn. In addition, a recent phenomenon that seems to be discernible is the growth of new suburban central cities built upon industrial and commercial migration from the older central city.

The suburban municipality is, in Illinois, most often thought of in terms of the northeastern metropolitan counties making up "Chicagoland" and the east side of the St. Louis metropolitan area. In fact, suburban towns surround most of our principal cities. Suburban-type communities are also found in the Peoria and Quad Cities area. They can be divided into several types of municipalities: central-type units, bedroom communities, new cities, and old cities.

Rural convenience communities exist in great profusion throughout the state. They are usually older units; many of them have declined to a point of little or no municipal functioning. On the other hand, there are many that continue to prosper and retain the extreme loyalty of their citizenry. Their scope of services is determined by their size and available dollars. The citizenry generally requires basic services only and volunteerism is important.

Forms of Municipal Government

Except for a few municipalities operating under pre-1870 charters as incorporated towns, all municipalities in Illinois are either cities or villages.[5] Most municipalities operate under a standard aldermanic-city form or trustee-village form. There are simple variations possible under these standard forms, such as the number of members of a legislative body, the terms of office, and minority representation. State statutes also provide more complicated variations that may be adopted by cities or villages desiring the possible advantages which each has to offer. These variations are the "commission form," the "manager form," the "administrator form," the "special-charter form," and the "strong-mayor form." Each form provides its own rules for the selection and type of officers, their powers and responsibilities, and the general operations of government. Some rules are common to a number of governmental forms, while others can be achieved in only a single form.

Aldermanic City

Under the aldermanic-city form of government, the legislative body ordinarily consists of two aldermen from each ward elected for a four-year term. Their terms are staggered so that half are elected every two years.

5. The following discussion of forms of municipal government is based on digest research by noted Illinois municipal attorneys Louis Ancel and Steward Diamond. Louis Ancel and Steward H. Diamond, *Illinois Municipal Handbook* (Springfield: Illinois Municipal League, 1986), 3–8.

The number of aldermen elected depends upon the population of the city. It can be changed by referendum to provide for one alderman for each ward or a combination of an at-large alderman plus one for each ward. A referendum may be used to provide for minority representation in the council or to shorten aldermanic terms to two years.

The mayor is the chief executive officer of the municipality, and he or she is elected at large to a four-year term, as are the city clerk and city treasurer. A provision exists, however, by which the term of all elective officers may be reduced to two years. Unless specifically provided otherwise by statute, other offices and vacancies are filled by appointment from the mayor with the advice and consent of the council, although it may be provided by ordinance that these offices be filled by election.

Trustee Village

In villages, the trustees are the legislative body. There are six trustees, generally elected from the village at large. The number of trustees does not vary with the size of the municipality. Villages with a population of over twenty-five thousand may have each of the six trustees elected by district instead of from the village at large. A recent change in state law allows the opportunity to elect trustees by district in villages with populations over five thousand.

The village president and clerk are elected at large, but the village treasurer is appointed. The term of the president, trustees, and clerk is four years, unless reduced to two years by referendum. As with the mayor in the aldermanic-city form, the appointments to all nonelective offices, unless specifically provided otherwise by statute, are made by the president with the advice and consent of the board of trustees. If the village collector is appointed, the village board may provide by ordinance that the elected village clerk also hold the office of village collector.

Commission

The commission form of government is limited to cities or villages with fewer than two hundred thousand residents. Under this form, the voters elect at large a mayor and four commissioners, who serve as the council. At the first regular meeting after an election, the council, by majority vote, designates each member to be either the commissioner of accounts and finances, public health and safety, streets and public improvements, or public property. The mayor serves as commissioner of public affairs. The council may elect the clerk and treasurer, as well as all the other officers whose appointment is not delegated to one commissioner. Each commissioner is given executive control over such administrative departments as may be assigned to him. By referendum, the electors may provide for the election of commissioners to specific departments.

The commission form of government was much in favor in the early years of this century, but since 1920, the number of municipalities using it has steadily declined. There are presently approximately fifty commission-form municipalities in Illinois. This form may have the disadvantage that all of the elected commissioners may reside in the same section of the city and that each commissioner has near-absolute power over the department he or she heads. As government becomes more complex, municipalities require greater coordination between departments, which is not easily achieved under the commission form.

Manager

The manager form of government is available to all municipalities with a population of less than five hundred thousand. Currently, approximately eighty cities and villages operate under the statutory manager form in Illinois. In addition, a large number of municipalities operate under a variation of this form on a voluntary ordinance basis. A municipality may retain its governmental structure as an aldermanic-city form, trustee-village form, or commission form while adopting the features of the manager form. The voter is given a variety of choices in adopting this form. If the voters elect not to choose aldermen or trustees from wards or districts (i.e., to elect them on an at-large basis), then in cities of less than fifty thousand, the council consists of a mayor and four councilmen. In cities of more than fifty thousand and less than one hundred thousand population, the council consists of a mayor and six councilmen. In cities of more than one hundred thousand, but not more than five hundred thousand, the council consists of a mayor and eight councilmen. A city or village adopting the manager form may elect to continue to choose its aldermen or trustees, as the case may be, from wards or districts, in which case the number of aldermen may range anywhere from six to twenty, depending on the size of the municipality. Any city or village with fewer than one hundred thousand residents may elect only one alderman from each ward; and their terms must be staggered.

Under this form, the power of the council or board is purely legislative, except that the board is empowered to approve all expenses and liabilities of the municipality. The manager is the administrative and executive head of the government for some purposes. If the city or village was governed by article 3 of the Illinois Municipal Code at the time of the adoption of the manager form, the manager appoints and removes all officers not required to be elected. The appointment to most boards, commissions, and other municipal agencies resides in the mayor or president, subject to council or board confirmation, or any other appointing authority established by law. The city manager is appointed for an indefinite term; however, he or she may be removed at any time by a majority vote of the members of the council or board. The manager does not need to live in the municipality at the time of his appointment.

Administrator

This "form" of government is not specifically sanctioned by statute but is in use in a number of municipalities. It may be used in all but the manager form of government. It is not really a "form" of government but rather a legislative device adopted by municipalities which seek a full-time administrator without the permanency of the manager form of government.

Under this system, a municipality creates by ordinance the office or employment of "administrator" and endows that office with certain administrative powers. The administrator may be made the administrative head of all departments and may be given any power not specifically granted to another person by statute. The administrator may be appointed for a term or hired by contract; his or her employment may also be for an unspecified period. In any case, he or she may be removed like any other officer or employee subject to the payment of any valid remaining portion of his or her contract. This system of government allows for a full-time administrator to conduct the day-to-day operations of a community armed with as much or as little power as the corporate authorities may provide.

Special Charter

Special-charter municipalities, which include all incorporated towns, retain the governmental structure set up by the acts creating them, except that each special-charter village now elects its president and clerk.

Strong Mayor

This form of government has an elected mayor, clerk, and treasurer and, depending upon the size of the community, from eight to twenty aldermen elected from wards. The terms of elected officials are four years. The mayor is given the power, without council approval, to appoint and remove

his administrative assistants, the budget and finance director, the heads of all departments, and all other officers of the municipality, and members of commissions, boards, and agencies, except those covered by civil service. The powers of the council are purely legislative. The strong-mayor form, on an informal basis, had been in practical use in many Illinois communities before it received legislative blessing. It is available to municipalities with populations from five to five hundred thousand and may be adopted only after a referendum.[6]

Revenue

This discussion will use generalities and averages, but please remember that the revenue sources of individual units will vary dramatically. A bedroom suburban town with limited commercial activity will have little sales tax revenue. A city with a large regional shopping center may have sufficient sales tax revenue to abate most of the property tax levies. The

6. Louis Ancel and Steward H. Diamond, *Illinois Municipal Handbook* (Springfield: Illinois Municipal League, 1986).

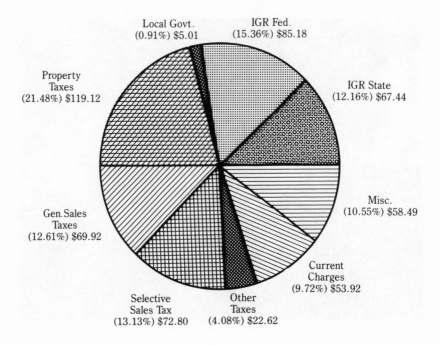

Figure 4-1. Average per capita Illinois municipal revenues, 1984–1985.
Source: U.S. Bureau of Census Government Finances, 1984–1985.

statewide mix of municipal revenue sources is illustrated in figure 4-1. The
principal sources of Illinois municipal government revenue include: property tax, sales tax, shared state–local taxes, local utility tax, other sources
like service charges and fees, and grants.

Property Tax

Total local government property tax revenue is awesome. In the most
recent data year, the total state-wide property tax was an amount equal to
the entire revenue produced by the regular state income tax and about 70
percent of the state sales tax. Of the property tax levied by local governments, municipalities levy about 17 percent. Education levies amount to
approximately 60 percent.

Municipalities particularly since the late 1950s have widened their

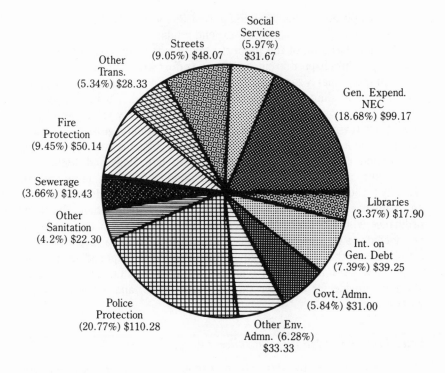

Figure 4-2. Average per capita Illinois municipal expenditures, 1984–1985. Source: U.S. Bureau of Census Government Finances, 1984–1985.

revenue base and have reduced reliance on the property tax for operational activities. As a rule, property tax remains the primary source of funding for infrastructure improvement, maintenance, and pensions. For the data year cited above, municipalities extended a total property tax of $984,950,670. Of that amount, $147.6 million went for bonds and interest, $199.5 million for pensions, $85.7 million for libraries, and $494.9 million for all other purposes. A number of observers and practitioners consider the property tax to be unfair. Legislation in recent years has reduced the property tax base through homestead provisions for the elderly, disabled, and veterans.

Non-home-rule municipalities must have specific statutory authority to impose a property tax, usually for a specific purpose. The exception is the general corporate fund. Revenues from this fund may be used for general operational purposes. As noted in figure 4-2, there are a large number of purposes for which municipalities expend funds.

The administration of the property tax is extremely complex. For the purposes of this chapter no comprehensive effort will be made to define the terms of the property tax cycle. In order to have a basic grasp of municipal property tax funding, a few generalities will be stated. The tax is levied by the city council or village board on the basis of property values developed usually by township government, collected by county government, and spent by the levying municipality. For example, taxes levied in 1987 were spread and collected in 1988 and spent in late 1988 and 1989. The municipality will determine the dollars needed from the property tax (usually through an appropriation ordinance) and levy those dollars through an ordinance. After certain waiting periods and publication, this levy ordinance will be delivered to the county for collection. A taxing authority also includes a rate limitation. This is often referred to as a "peg limit" and simply means that it is the maximum rate that can be imposed against the property value. It is an effective limit on the dollars a unit can raise. Most statutes provide for a higher rate by referendum, and a few rates are without limit.

Sales Tax (Illinois Municipal Retailers Occupation Tax)

Cities are authorized by statute to impose up to a 1 percent local retailers occupation tax on sales made within their municipality. This tax must be imposed by the local corporate authority with notification to the state. The state enforces and collects this levy and returns it to the appropriate city on the basis of point of sale. The state charges a fee for this service.

Sales tax revenues are generally the second most important source of municipal revenue; the most recent year produced $631.8 million state-wide. Its impact on individual communities varies drastically. Those with large central business districts or regional shopping centers may receive sufficient revenues from this source to completely or substantially eliminate property tax levies, while others have very little revenue from sales taxes.

State Income Tax Sharing

Municipalities receive one-twelfth of the net revenue of the state income tax for general municipal purposes based on a per-capita basis. In the most recent year, this amounted to $22.50 per capita per year. These funds are transmitted to the local unit on a monthly basis.

State Motor Fuel Tax Sharing

Municipalities receive major revenues through the sharing of the state tax on motor fuels (about $16.69 per capita per year). The use of these funds is restricted to statutory purposes relating to maintenance and construction of transportation and related facilities.

Municipal Utility Tax

Municipalities are authorized without referendum to impose a utility tax of up to 5 percent on the use of water, electricity, telephone, and natural gas. This tax is collected locally through the utility company. About 250 Illinois municipalities have opted to impose this tax although they tend to be selective on the utilities covered and on the amount of the tax rate. For those cities that impose the tax, it is a very substantial source of revenue.

Other Sources

Other often used but not generally large revenue sources include: wheel tax, license fees, liquor licenses, parking meter fees, fines, and building permits. It should be noted that revenues received from municipal utilities such as water or electric are generally restricted to the operation of the utility, although certain limited transfers to general government are permissible.

Intergovernmental Grants

Federal and state grants and loans, while drastically reduced in recent years, still are an important source for specific infrastructure and human service programs.

Where Municipalities Spend Their Money

Municipalities are service-oriented; thus their largest single expenditure is uniformly for personnel-related costs. Salaries, wages, fringe benefits, and pensions account for over 50 percent of all but the smallest villages' budgets. Smaller municipalities will spend the largest portion of available funds on public works, usually street maintenance, mostly through contractual arrangements since they have few employees.

As cities become larger their scope of functions increases. In all but isolated instances, public work, police protection, and fire protection are the largest outlays and will account for a substantial portion of available funds. The major exception to this pattern is the use of volunteer or mostly volunteer fire departments. This is particularly true in moderate-sized suburban towns and rural communities. Other functions that usually require substantial funding would include: libraries and recreation (when municipal as opposed to special district), health services in larger cities, code enforcement including building, zoning, and subdivision control, traffic control, refuse disposal, insurance, legal costs, and general administration.

Many Illinois municipalities operate utilities, particularly water and sewer. Some municipalities operate electric and/or natural gas systems. These operations are conducted separately from the traditional governmental services, with surpluses being used for bond principal and interest retirement. Most municipal attorneys believe that funds in amounts related to overhead costs can be transferred to the general fund of the city or village. Bond covenant provisions will usually control the use of these funds, including rates for the service. In less sophisticated units, equipment purchased by utility departments (e.g., computers and heavy vehicles) will also be used by general government and in fact offset the need for such expenditures by the other departments.

A municipality will often fund its needs for capital expenditures through issuing either revenue or general obligation bonds. Revenue bonds are repaid through revenues produced. For example, parking meter revenues both on street and off street are used to pay bond costs on the construction of a parking ramp, or water revenues will be used to finance the upgrading of a water distribution system or a sewer improvement. Environmental programs require huge future outlays by local government. Generally, non-home-rule units can issue revenue bonds subject to a backdoor referendum and general obligation bonds (G.O. bonds) only after referendum approval. G.O. bonds pledge the full faith and credit of the municipality in repayments of principal and interest. They are supported by a property tax rate although the levy can be abated if other sources of funding become available. The backup of property tax will result in lower interest costs. Home-rule units may issue either revenue or general obligation debt without referendum. Non-home-rule municipalities are subject to a constitutional debt limit.

Municipalities in Illinois are not required to adopt an operational budget although the overwhelming number do function through a budget mechanism. Budgeting is usually provided for by the terms of the local administrative ordinance. The appropriation ordinance (or budget document in those units operating under the Optional Budget Officers Act) has an important role in the expenditure of funds. No monies may be spent unless a prior appropriation exists. The possibility of unexpected needs or revenues causes most municipalities to overappropriate substantially.

All Illinois municipalities, except those with fewer than eight hundred residents or with bonded debt or a utility, must have an audit each year that is conducted by a certified public accountant. Smaller units must annually submit a financial statement to the state comptroller. These audits and statements are reviewed by the comptroller and are available for public inspection.

Officers and Employees

An officer of a municipality is the individual who occupies a position created by statute or ordinance; all others are employees. Some officers are elected, others are appointed. In the aldermanic-city form, the clerk and treasurer are elected. In the village form, the clerk is generally elected, but the treasurer is appointed. In the commission form, the clerk and treasurer are appointed. The managerial system usually follows the pattern of government in effect immediately prior to the change to the manager system, that is, if the voters elected to change the form of government from aldermanic-city to manager, the clerk and treasurer would be elected. The strong-mayor system provides for the appointment of all officers by the mayor. Recent changes in state law permit smaller municipalities to choose to appoint rather than elect the clerk. The 1970 constitution permits changes in government form through a referendum process.

Duties of certain officials are provided by statute, either directly or indirectly (see appendix 4-1). These statutory duties are not detailed and are those functions usually associated with such offices. For example, the clerk must keep minutes of meetings and is responsible for maintaining many records. The treasurer is the custodian of funds and maintains financial records.

The statutes also provide that municipalities may provide for the election or appointment of other specific officers, such as collector, marshal, superintendent of streets, corporation counsel, and any other officers considered necessary. These offices are created by ordinance. Officers under the aldermanic and village forms are appointed by the mayor or president with consent of the council or board. In the managerial form, most officers are appointed by the manager and do not require confirmation.

Municipalities have broadly used their power to designate officers by ordinance. Some of the more typically ordinance-created offices would be finance officer, code enforcement officer, and city engineer. However, the statutes provide limits on the appointment of officers. The more important limitations include: officers must be residents, except where special skills are involved; officers cannot be debtors to the unit; and they cannot have their compensation raised or lowered during their term in office. Moreover, in those units that have adopted the Civil Service Law, some officers could be covered by its tenure provisions. Police and fire personnel in municipalities with more than five thousand residents are under the provisions of a separate state tenure plan. The chiefs and high-level police officers may or may not be included in these provisions, subject to council or board action. These tenure programs are administered by boards or commissions appointed by the chief executive.

Some of the officers found in Illinois municipalities are: police chief, fire chief, superintendent of streets and alleys, city engineer, city attorney or corporation counsel, building inspector or code enforcement officer, purchasing officer, finance officer, and health officer. The titles of most of the officers listed above are descriptive of their duties. Larger and more sophisticated communities have more types of officers than smaller villages. Often the duties of two or more officers will be combined in one individual. For example, the responsibilities of building inspector, zoning officer, electrical inspector, and plumbing inspector may be performed by a code enforcement officer. The finance officer is often also the purchasing officer. Relatively few Illinois municipalities employ full-time attorneys or engineers. The moderate and smaller units will contract with private law and consulting engineering firms for those professional services. Municipalities with utility services will have specialized staffs of water plant operators, sewer plant operators, engineers, and specialized engineering personnel. In a few instances, the state law requires some officers to have specialized training or certification; these positions include police chief (including all police officers), water plant operators, and sewer plant operators. Engineering and legal officers must be authorized to practice.

Employees are not officers. The corporate authority may provide the manner in which employees are hired or fired and may delegate such power to some person other than the mayor or president. The major exception is where civil service or tenure systems have been adopted or are in effect. In the managerial system and the strong-mayor organization this power is vested with the manager or the mayor, respectively. Municipalities will sometimes create a tenure system by ordinance which will provide a personnel plan. Such systems are usually administered by a personnel officer.

1988 Municipal Calendar of Statutory Duties for Municipal Officials

Municipal officials are required by law to perform certain duties at specified times, and non-home rule municipalities must comply with those statutory requirements. However, home rule municipalities must only comply with statutory requirements until such time as they may otherwise provide by ordinance, unless the home rule power has been preempted by the legislature. In some instances requirements are related to the fiscal year as in the case of the adoption of the appropriation ordinances which must be passed during the first quarter of the fiscal year. Some requirements, however, are set according to the calendar year. For example, a certified copy of the tax levy ordinance must be filed with the county clerk by the second Tuesday of September of each year.

For the purpose of this calendar we have assumed the fiscal year to begin on May 1, as it does in most cities and villages (by statute, the fiscal year in Chicago is the calendar year.) For those municipalities that have adopted another date for the commencement of the fiscal year (Chapter 24, paragraph 1-1-2) this calendar must be adjusted for those duties that must be performed at times related to the fiscal year.

In addition to those duties that must be performed at specific dates, there are many things that must be done by city and village officials at non-specified times during the year.

These include, for example, recording all deeds or conveyances of property to the municipality with the Recorder of Deeds. In addition, the county clerk should be specifically notified of each acquisition of property, by conveyance, annexation, condemnation or otherwise, so that the property will be placed on the tax-exempt list.

Annexation and disconnection ordinances should also be recorded, as should all plats or other documents dedicating or vacating streets; and the county map department should be notified of all changes in street names. At the time an annexation takes place the municipality must file a "document of annexation" with the county clerk and county authority.

When a municipal plan is adopted, it should be filed with the county clerk.

The bonds for members of the council in commission form cities are to be filed with the county clerk.

When an ordinance for a general obligation bond ordinance becomes effective, a copy thereof should be filed with the county clerk in time for inclusion in its next tax levy. If a tax is to be abated for any reason, notice must likewise be given to the county clerk in time to exclude it from the next levy.

For reporting data in connection with the Federal Equal Employment Opportunity Act reference should be made to the rules and regulations of the E.E.O. Commission.

References to the requirements of municipal officials in connection with elections have been eliminated from the calendar because of the passage of the "Election Consolidation" Act. The duties of the municipal clerk in connection with elections have been greatly reduced. Information concerning this election should be obtained from your local county clerk and the State Board of Elections, 1020 S. Spring Street, Springfield, IL 62704 or phone (217) 782-4141.

Two requirements relating to the filing of economic interest statements are contained within the calendar and should be carefully considered by each municipal officer. Paragraph 45 requires candidates for offices to have a currently effective economic interest statement on file at the time they file for nomination for an office. Certain counties have adopted varying interpretations of whether the requirements of chapter 127, paragraphs 604A-105(a) refers to the preceding year (last twelve months) or preceding calendar year. To avoid confusion and potential disqualification, individuals filing nominating petitions should contact the county clerk to determine the interpretation adopted by the local county clerk. This requirement is distinguishable from that contained in item 55 which requires persons subject to the Governmental Ethics Act to file an economic interest statement on or before May 1 unless the officer has already filed a statement in relation to the same unit of government during that calendar year. Under these two requirements, an individual filing a nominating petition and filing an economic interest statement at the time of filing for nomination would not subsequently be required to comply with the May 1st deadline. However, it is possible that a person who had previously filed an economic interest statement and did not file at the time of nomination would be required to file to comply with the May 1st deadline.

Statutory References are to Illinois Revised Statutes.

Performance Required Annually

1. The mayor or president shall annually, and from time to time, give the council or board information relative to the affairs of the municipality, and shall recommend for their consideration such measures as he may deem expedient. (Chapter 24, paragraph 3-11-6.)

2. Section 3-13-2 of the Illinois Municipal Code requires that the salaries of elected officers shall be fixed at least 2 months prior to the general municipal election at which voting is held for such offices.

3. A bank may be selected as the municipal depository; this designation remains in force without need for renewal until a new depository is named. (Chapter 24, paragraphs 3-10-3; 4-5-22.)

4. The annual account of the treasurer shall be made within six months of the end of the preceding fiscal year and published by the clerk. (Chapter 24, paragraph 3-10-5.1.)

5. A copy of the treasurer's annual account, with a certificate of publication, shall be filed with the county collector, within six months of the end of the preceding fiscal year. (Chapter 24, paragraph 3-10-5.2.)

6. The American flag must be displayed and flown each day of the week from each City Hall or Village Hall and Village Square and at the principal entrance to all public parks. (Chapter 1, paragraph 3305.)

7. Corporate authorities of each municipality having a population of 800 or more or having a bonded debt or operating a utility plant must have an annual audit of all Municipal Accounts, made by auditors

authorized to practice in this state. Such audit shall be made as soon as possible, but not more than six months after the close of the fiscal year. (Chapter 24, paragraphs 11-130-11; 8-8-3).

8. A financial report of the operation of any municipal utility must be available for distribution each year. (Chapter 24, paragraph 11-117-13.)

9. Municipalities of less than 800 population which do not own public utilities and do not have bonded debt shall file a financial report with the State Comptroller. (Chapter 24, paragraph 8-8-3.)

10. Two copies of the municipal audit shall be given to the corporate authorities who shall send one copy to the State Comptroller. (Chapter 24, paragraph 8-8-7.)

11. In addition to any audit report required, all municipalities, except municipalities of less than 800 population which do not own or operate public utilities shall file annually with the State Comptroller a supplemental report on forms devised and approved by the Comptroller. (Chapter 24, paragraph 8-8-3.)

12. Annual audit must be made of books of commission form cities regardless of size, and results published in the manner prescribed at the end of the fiscal year. (Chapter 24, paragraph 4-5-16.)

13. A report showing the financial status and results of operation of any municipally owned street railway shall be printed and published annually; and the accounts of any such company shall be audited at least once each year. (Chapter 24, paragraph 11-122-5.)

14. The council or board shall cause to be printed and published an annual report of the operation of any municipal coliseum; and the accounts pertaining to such coliseum shall be audited at least once each year. (Chapter 24, paragraph 11-67-9.)

15. The council or board shall cause to be printed and published an annual report of the operation of any municipally owned or operated utility; and the accounts pertaining to such utility shall be audited at least once each year. (Chapter 24, paragraph 11-123-14.)

16. The council or board shall cause to be printed and published an annual report of the operation of any municipal convention hall; and the accounts pertaining to such

convention hall shall be audited at least once each year. (Chapter 24, paragraph 11-65-9.)

17. The art commission of any city or village shall make an annual report to the mayor or president concerning its services. (Chapter 24, paragraph 11-46-5.)

18. The board of police and fire commissioners shall file an annual report of its activities at such times as may be required by the board or council. Board also shall submit an annual budget request to the municipal governing body. (Chapter 24, paragraph 10-2.1-19.)

19. Housing authority to make annual report of its activities. (Chapter 67½, paragraphs 8-9 and 8-11.)

20. An annual audit of revenue from a sewer system must be available for inspection. (Chapter 24, paragraph 11-141-8.)

21. The board of directors of any city owned hospital must make an annual report of its activities. (Chapter 24, paragraph 11-23-8.)

22. Those municipalities that have elected to place their employees under social security must send in their contributions at such times as may be designated by the State Social Security Agency.

23. Contributions to the Illinois Municipal Retirement Fund must be deducted each pay period from covered employee's pay and remitted to the Retirement Board along with the contribution of the municipality. This requirement is mandatory for municipalities over 5,000 population where Social Security is not provided, and elective for others. (Chapter 108½, paragraphs 7-132 and 7-172.)

24. Any playground and recreation board that operates a community building must report annually to the corporate authorities the amounts needed for the coming year. Board shall also make a full report of all receipts and expenditures. (Chapter 24, paragraph 11-63-11.)

25. Delinquent special assessments must be reported each year to the county collector. (Chapter 24, paragraph 9-2-85.)

26. Municipalities must deposit each year that amount determined by an actuarial report to be necessary for current funding of the Police Pension Fund. (Chapter 108½, paragraph 3-127; and paragraph 22-503.1.)

27. Municipalities must use an enrolled actuary employed by the Illinois Department of Insurance or by an enrolled actuary retained by the pension fund or municipality when determining the actuarial requirements of pension funds. (Chapter 108½, paragraph 4-118.)

Performance Required
Every Six Months

28. Chapter 95½, paragraph 1-102.01, requires municipal ambulances to be safety tested every six months in the same manner as trucks are tested.

29. All officers, except members of the council, receiving fees or other emoluments of office shall file a semi-annual report with the mayor or president, showing all such receipts. (Chapter 24, paragraph 3-13-1.)

Performance Required Monthly

30. Federal Revenue Sharing has been abolished.

31. Every person, other than the treasurer, receiving money for the municipality shall keep a triplicate record thereof; one copy shall be delivered to the treasurer and one to the board or council. Such person shall deliver all money to the treasurer not later than the middle of the following month. (Chapter 102, paragraph 20.)

32. A copy of all receipts given by the treasurer shall be filed with the clerk each month. (Chapter 24, paragraph 3-10-1.)

33. The municipal treasurer shall render an account to the Council or Board, or an officer designated by them, on a monthly basis, or more often if required, showing all moneys received into the treasury together with all amounts paid by the treasurer. On the date that the account is rendered, all warrants paid by the treasurer shall be delivered to the municipal clerk for filing in the clerk's office. (Chapter 24, paragraph 3-10-2.)

34. Each month the council in commission form municipalities of over 15,000 population shall cause to be printed in pamphlet form a summary of its proceedings, including a detailed itemized statement of the receipts and expenses of the village or city during the preceding month; and in commission form municipalities of less than

15,000 this report is to be made annually. (Chapter 24, paragraph 4-5-16.)

35. The board of directors of any municipal tuberculosis sanatorium shall make a monthly report to the council or board of trustees, showing their activities during the preceding month and pay to the municipal treasurer any donations received by the board. (Chapter 24, paragraph 11-29-10.)

36. The council in commission form municipalities shall meet at least twice in each month. (Chapter 24, paragraph 4-5-12.)

37. If the corporate authorities refuse to act upon final plats within sixty days and if the failure to act is willful, municipality becomes liable in damages. (Chapter 24, paragraph 11-12-8.)

38. Annual appropriation ordinance must be passed within the first quarter of each fiscal year. (Chapter 24, paragraph 8-2-9.)

Performance Required Weekly

39. The city or village collector shall turn over to the treasurer at least once each week all money collected by him. (Chapter 24, paragraph 3-11-25.)

40. Municipalities in Cook County must furnish copies of building permits to the township assessor and the county assessor within fifteen days after the issuance of such permit. (Chapter 24, paragraph 11-39-1.)

Performance Required Daily

41. Collected municipal funds which are not needed for immediate disbursement must be invested within two working days at prevailing interest rates or better. (Chapter 102, paragraph 34.)

Performances Required at Specified Times

Where the fiscal year is some period other than May 1–April 30, the items mentioned under the month of May having to do with the fiscal year takes place during the first month of the particular fiscal year.

January

42. League Membership Dues—Approve payment of annual membership dues of your municipality in the Illinois Municipal League.

43. A quarterly statement shall be submitted by the board of inspectors of houses of correction to the comptroller and council or board of trustees. (Chapter 24, paragraph 11-4-5.)

44. An annual statement shall be submitted by the board of inspectors of each house of correction to the city council or village board, and to the Governor of the State. (Chapter 24, paragraph 11-4-5.)

45. Candidates for offices who are subject to the filing requirements of the Illinois Governmental Ethics Act must file a statement at the time of filing for nomination, unless they have filed such a statement within the preceding year. (Chapter 127, paragraph 601-101.)

February

46. Economic Disclosure Statements— Clerk's Certified List—The "Governmental Ethics Act" requires the municipal clerk to provide the Secretary of State with a list of those persons required to file statements of economic interest. The list must be certified not less than 60 days before the May 1 due date for filing the statements. This requirement is found in chapter 127, paragraph 604A-106, which provides in pertinent part as follows:

"Not less than 60 days before the due date for filing such statements, annually, (1) the State Comptroller shall certify to the Secretary of State a list of the names and mailing addresses of the persons described in item (f) of Section 4A-101, and (2) the clerk or secretary of each school district, unit of local government, special district or other governmental entity described in items (g), (h) and (i) of Section 4A-101 shall certify to the Secretary of State a list of the names and residence addresses of such persons described in these items (g), (h) and (i) as are required to file because of their relationship to the entity represented by the clerk or secretary. In preparing such lists, each such clerk or secretary shall set out the names in alphabetical order, by county of residence, and shall file a copy of such list with the appropriate county clerk."

March

47. In every city and village which has a zoning ordinance, the zoning map must be published by March 31st, of each year if there has been any change in the boundaries of a district or if a new district has been created. (Chapter 24, paragraph 11-13-19.)

48. Members of the Board of Police and Fire Commissioners are to be appointed by the Mayor (President) where the Act has been adopted, at least thirty days prior to the expiration of the term of the Mayor or President. (Chapter 24, paragraphs 10-2.1-1; 10-2.1-2.)

April

49. The annual report of the collector is to be made between the first and tenth of April and is to be published by the clerk. (Chapter 24, paragraph 3-11-26.)

50. The municipal fiscal year begins on election day unless otherwise provided by ordinance. (Chapter 24, paragraph 1-1-2.)

51. Commission form councils must meet and appoint officers and assign departments at the first meeting after their election, or as soon as practicable thereafter, except where candidates for Commissioner are required to run for a specific office. (Chapter 24, paragraphs 4-5-3; 4-5-4.)

52. Elections for members of boards of trustees of the police pension funds in cities and villages between 5,000 and 500,000 in population, shall be held biennially on the third Monday in April. (Chapter 108½, paragraphs 3-103; 3-128.)

53. Members of the board of trustees of firemen's pension fund (all municipalities between 5,000 and 500,000 population) are to be chosen the third Monday in April in each applicable year. (Chapter 108½, paragraphs 4-103; 4-121.)

54. The quarterly report by the board of inspectors of the house of correction must be made and filed with the corporate authorities. (Chapter 24, paragraph 11-4-5.)

55. A person subject to the filing requirements of the Illinois Governmental Ethics Act must file a statement on or before May 1 of each year, unless he has already filed a statement in relation to the same unit of government in that calendar year. (Chapter 127, paragraph 601-101.)

May

56. The Annual Appropriation Ordinance must be passed during the first quarter of the fiscal year. In municipalities over two thousand in population, the corporate authorities shall make available for public inspection the proposed appropriation ordinance not less than ten days prior to the adoption and shall hold at least one public hearing on the proposed ordinance. Notice of the hearing shall be published in a newspaper published in the county and having a general circulation in the municipality at least ten days prior to the time of the public hearing.

Prior to the adoption of the annual appropriation ordinance, the corporate authorities of municipalities over 2,000 in population at least 10 days prior to such adoption shall make such proposed appropriation ordinance or formally prepared appropriation document upon which the annual appropriation ordinance will be based conveniently available to public inspection and shall hold at least one public hearing thereon. Notice of this hearing shall be given publication in one or more newspapers published in the municipality, or if there is none published in the municipality, in a newspaper published in the county and having general circulation in the municipality, at least 10 days prior to the time of the public hearing. Such notice shall state the time and place of the hearing and the place where copies of the proposed appropriation ordinance will be accessible for examination. Subsequent to the public hearing and before final action is taken on the appropriation ordinance, the corporate authorities may revise, alter, increase or decrease the items contained therein. (Chapter 24, paragraph 8-2-9.)

57. The annual appropriation ordinance, as well as an estimate of revenues, certified by the Chief Fiscal Officer, by source, anticipated to be received by the municipality in the following fiscal year must be

filed with the County Clerk within 30 days of the adoption of the appropriation ordinance.

58. The tax levy ordinance must be passed and a certified copy thereof filed with the county clerk on or before the second Tuesday in September. (Chapter 24, paragraph 8-3-1.)

59. Within thirty days after the expiration of the fiscal year of the city or village, the library board shall submit to the council or board of trustees and the Illinois State Library an annual statement of liabilities including those for bonds outstanding or due for judgments, settlements, liability insurance or for amounts due under a certificate of the board. (Chapter 81, paragraph 4-10.)

60. Every public officer who receives or disburses money and who does not file a report with the board or council shall within 30 days after the expiration of the fiscal year, cause to be published an account of all money received and spent and shall file the same with the county clerk. (Chapter 102, paragraphs 5 and 6.)

61. The comptroller (or clerk) shall make out an annual report and estimate of expenses and submit it to the council or board of trustees on or before the fifteenth of May. (Chapter 24, paragraph 3-11-24.)

62. The treasurer of the police pension funds—all cities and villages between 5,000 and 500,000 population—shall file an annual report with the trustees and council on the second Tuesday of May. (Chapter 108½, paragraph 3-141.)

63. The term of office of the inspectors of the house of correction, appointed by the Mayor, begins the first Monday in May. (Chapter 24, paragraph 11-4-2.)

64. Trustees of the police pension fund are to be appointed before the second Tuesday in May. (Chapter 108½, paragraph 3-128.)

65. Conference attendance resolution— approve resolution authorizing delegates from your municipality to attend the annual conference of the Illinois Municipal League, usually held in the fall—advance notices of the place and date will be sent to you.

June

66. The annual appropriation ordinance must be passed during the first quarter of the fiscal year. (Chapter 24, paragraph 8-2-9.) In municipalities over 500 population the ordinance must be published in a newspaper of general circulation in the municipality or in pamphlet form; if less than 500 population it may be posted in 3 prominent places in lieu of publication.

67. The tax levy ordinance must be passed and a certified copy thereof filed with the county clerk on or before the second Tuesday in September. (Chapter 24, paragraph 8-3-1.)

68. The annual report of the board of directors of municipal tuberculosis sanatoriums must be filed with the council or board of trustees on or before the second Monday in June. (Chapter 24, paragraph 11-29-11.)

69. The directors of the municipal tuberculosis sanatorium are to be appointed by the Mayor or President before July first. (Chapter 24, paragraph 11-29-4.)

70. The directors of municipal coliseums are to be appointed by the Mayor or President before the first of July. (Chapter 24, paragraph 11-66-5.)

71. Library directors in cities are to be appointed by the Mayor before July first. (Chapter 81, paragraph 4-1.1.)

72. The board of directors of hospitals in cities of less than 100,000 population shall make a financial report to the city council on or before the second Monday in June. (Chapter 24, paragraph 11-23-8.)

73. During the month of June of each calendar year, municipalities must investigate and ascertain the prevailing rate of wages to be paid for work on public works and post or keep available its determination of such prevailing wages as well as file a certified copy thereof in the office of the Secretary of State in Springfield. (Chapter 48, paragraph 39s-9.) Note: Pursuant to paragraph 39s-4, a municipality may request the Department of Labor to ascertain the prevailing rate of wages.

July

74. The Annual Appropriation Ordinance must be passed during the first quarter of the fiscal year. In municipalities over two thousand in population, the corporate authorities shall make available for public

inspection the proposed appropriation ordinance not less than ten days prior to adoption and shall hold at least one public hearing on the proposed ordinance. Notice of the hearing shall be published in a newspaper published in the county and having a general circulation in the municipality at least ten days prior to the time of the public hearing.

75. Quarterly report of the inspectors of the house of correction must be made. (Chapter 24, paragraph 11-4-5.)

76. The annual report of the inspector of weights and measures—in municipalities with a population of 25,000 or more—is to be made to the Director of Agriculture on July first. (Chapter 147, paragraph 119.)

77. A report of delinquent special assessments and special taxes is to be made on or before August first. (Chapter 24, paragraph 9-2-82.)

78. The Truth in Taxation Act (Ch. 120, Par. 866) provides that at least 20 days before any taxing body makes its tax levy it must determine how many dollars in property tax extensions will be necessary. If the amount determined is more than 105% of the previous year's extensions, an additional notice published in the newspaper and a public hearing are required before the levy can be adopted. The notice must state the amount of the previous year's property tax, the amount of the current year's property tax, the percentage increase and the date, place and time of the public hearing.

The notice must be no less than one-eighth page in size, and the smallest type used must be twelve point and must be enclosed in a black border no less than ¼ inch wide. It cannot be published in the legal notices or classified section of the newspaper. The public hearing must be held between 7 and 14 days after the notice is published in the newspaper.

August

79. The tax levy ordinance must be passed and a certified copy thereof filed with the county clerk on or before the second Tuesday in September. (Chapter 24, paragraph 8-3-1.)

80. Nominations for the board of trustees of the Illinois Municipal Retirement Fund are to be made between August first and September fifteenth. (Chapter 108½, paragraph 7-175.)

NOTE: All cities and villages having a population of over 5,000 come automatically under the Act (Chapter 108½, paragraph 7-132) and each may nominate and vote for a member of the seven member board of trustees which manages the Fund for the entire State. (Chapter 108½, paragraph 7-175.)

81. In counties other than Cook County, · the collector shall advertise delinquent special assessments, preparatory to sale after August fifteenth. (Chapter 24, paragraph 9-2-84.)

September

82. The tax levy ordinance must be passed and a certified copy thereof filed with the county clerk on or before the second Tuesday in September. (Chapter 24, paragraph 8-3-1.)

83. Return of delinquent special assessments to be made five days prior to date for taking judgment. (Chapter 24, paragraph 9-2-85.)

84. Votes to be cast for trustee of the Illinois Municipal Retirement Fund. (Chapter 108½, paragraph 7-175.)

October

85. For municipalities having a fiscal year which begins on May 1, the treasurer's report for the preceding year must be filed with the clerk by the end of October. (Chapter 24, paragraph 3-10-5.1.)

86. The quarterly statement by inspectors of house of correction is due. (Chapter 24, paragraph 11-4-5.)

November

87. All municipalities with 100 or more employees must prepare an equal employment opportunity report (Form EEO-4) documenting sex, race and salary data for all employees including part-time help. The report is to be submitted to the Equal Employment Opportunity Commission by November 30 each year.

December

88. In Cook County, a certificate that there has been no change in the ownership of property or use thereof must be filed before January thirty-first to preserve the tax-exemption status of municipal property. (Chapter 120, paragraph 500.)

89. At the beginning of each calendar or fiscal year municipality must prepare a schedule of all regular meetings for the coming year and post notice thereof together with time and place of said meetings. Said schedule shall be given to all news media requesting it. Notice shall also be given of special, rescheduled or reconvened meetings. (Chapter 102, paragraphs 41, 42, 42.01, 42.02, 42.03, 42.04 and 43 and Chapter 24, paragraphs 3-11-13 and 4-5-12.)

Source: *Illinois Municipal Review,* December 1987. Prepared by the staff of the Illinois Municipal League.

5.

County Government in Downstate Illinois

LAUREL LUNT PRUSSING

Counties are often viewed as the backwater of American politics. For example, the American Revolution completely bypassed county government. Two hundred years after the adoption of the United States Constitution, most American counties are still bound to the English system with county boards combining legislative and executive functions. The system of checks and balances developed in the U.S. Constitution is common in city and state government. However, counties are just beginning to adopt the American innovation of the separation of powers.

Counties are responding to the need for change. Their archaic structure makes them ill-equipped to wrestle with the toughest issues of both urban and rural America. Reform waves are rippling across a number of states, including Illinois. For example, in 1960, there were only eight counties in the United States headed by an elected county executive. By 1987, there were 361 counties with elected executives.[1] This chapter presents an overview of the history and current state of Illinois counties, other than Cook County, which is covered in chapter 6.

History

Counties in England began over a thousand years ago as local governments called "shires" responsible for justice and public works. The word "sheriff"

1. National Association of Counties, Washington D.C.

comes from "shire," and the office itself is the oldest stemming from England. With the development of central government after the Norman conquest of 1066, shires became counties and sheriffs became the king's local agents and tax collectors.

In the United States, counties developed in colonial times and exist today in all states except Connecticut and Rhode Island. Two county equivalents are the "parish" in Louisiana and the "borough" in Alaska. The over three thousand American counties vary considerably from state to state. Some include cities and are a government level between cities and the state, while others exist side by side with cities and are the local government for unincorporated areas. Still others have been combined with cities. Illinois counties act both as agents for the state and as units of local government. Their duties and structure have changed with each new state constitution and every legislative session. Clyde Frank Snyder's book *Historical Development of County Government in Illinois* traces the history of Illinois counties from 1778 to 1943 through statehood and the constitutions of 1818, 1848, and 1870.

By the laws of its European settlers, Illinois was first a county before it became a state. Illinois County was established by the Virginia legislature in 1778. The large territory, including portions of what is now Illinois, Indiana, Ohio, Michigan, and Wisconsin, was ceded by Virginia to the federal government in 1784. With statehood achieved in 1818, the first Illinois constitution required counties to elect three commissioners, plus a sheriff and a coroner. The commissioners (called the commissioner's court) set county taxes and issued licenses for ferries and taverns. The first general assembly created the county offices of recorder, treasurer, circuit attorney, and clerk of the commissioner's court. These officers were originally appointed by either the governor or the county commissioners, but gradually came to be elected.

The property tax was adopted for state purposes in 1839. The law allowing a state property tax is still on the books but has been unused in recent years.[2] The limit on county property taxes was originally four mills. By 1987, the limit was up to 7.5 mills (75 cents per $100 dollars of assessed valuation). However, tax rates are only roughly comparable since assessment methods have changed drastically in the last 150 years.

A labor tax of five days of work from able-bodied men under fifty (or an equivalent monetary payment) financed highway maintenance. (The labor

2. *Illinois Revised Statutes*, State Bar Association ed., vol 4, sect. 634, par. 153 (St. Paul: West Publishing, 1985), 530.

tax, or "corvee," had been applied to European serfs in the Middle Ages and was imposed on Chinese peasants well into the twentieth century.) Perhaps the last remnant of the labor tax for local government in the United States is jury duty, although jurors are paid a token amount for their services.

The Illinois constitution of 1848 limited the power of the legislature to create new counties and replaced the commissioner's court by a county court consisting of the county judge and two justices of the peace. The constitution also reestablished townships at the option of local voters after their temporary abolition by the legislature. The presence or absence of townships is a key factor in the structure of Illinois counties.

By 1859, all present counties in Illinois had been established. The seventeen which had been first settled by people from the southern states adopted the commission form of government, reflecting the southern tradition of strong county government and the lack of townships in southern states. Three commissioners were elected at large and were responsible for the welfare of the poor among other duties. The remaining eighty-four counties (excluding Cook County), which had been settled by people from New England and New York, adopted township government. In these counties welfare was the responsibility of the township, not the county.

The 1870 Illinois constitution required commission counties to have three county commissioners elected at large with staggered three-year terms. The form of government for township counties was left to the legislature. This evolved into a system of county boards made up of township supervisors with no relationship between population size and representation on the county board. The constitution of 1870 also provided for the election of a number of county officials, including county judge, county clerk, clerk of the circuit court, state's attorney, treasurer, sheriff, coroner, and surveyor, plus a recorder of deeds in counties of over sixty thousand population.

A century later, the 1970 constitution changed the structure of county government again. First, counties under township organization were required to elect a county board on the basis of "one-man, one-vote." This opened county boards to urban people, who had historically been excluded or outnumbered on the rurally dominated boards. Commission-form counties continued to elect three commissioners at large. The 1970 constitution also prohibited counties from keeping 3 percent of the taxes collected for local governments, a major source of county revenue, but a sore spot with other governments.

The Role of Counties

American counties serve both as arms of state government and as local governments. Throughout the United States, counties have responsibility for the judicial system and tax collection. Many are also responsible for schools and welfare assistance. Although students of government have long considered counties obscure and backwards compared with cities, some now believe counties are the governments of the future, because they may be able to cope with urban problems on a regional basis. Notable city–county consolidations include Indianapolis with Marion County, Indiana, and Miami with Dade County, Florida.

There are 102 counties in Illinois. Unlike Illinois cities, most counties do not have home rule with unlimited taxing authority. Only Cook County has home rule. The other counties are creatures of state government and may collect revenue and provide services only as prescribed by Illinois law.

Most Illinois counties play a relatively limited role because they are not as involved in education and welfare as counties in southern states. Their primary mission is to maintain the judicial system at the local level on behalf of the state. They finance courthouses and jails and pay for the operations of the state's attorney and public defender. On behalf of all local governments and special districts, such as schools, counties maintain the property tax system and collect court fines. Counties also conduct most elections. Counties act as a local government in unincorporated areas by providing law enforcement by the sheriff's department. They construct and maintain county roads and bridges and act as trustees for township road and bridge funds. Illinois counties may operate county hospitals and nursing homes. In Champaign County, for example, what began as the county poor farm has evolved into a nursing home financed mainly by patient fees.

Other optional responsibilities include: operating a county hospital, regional planning commission, mental health board, or public health department; planning and preparing civil defense measures; zoning; and licensing cable television and weather modification. Many of these functions can only be performed after a public referendum.

County Officials and Their Duties

Elected Officials

1. *County Board:* Although the duties are detailed at great length in Illinois law, the essence of the county board's responsibility is to obtain the real and personal property needed to provide county services and to pass the annual

budget and tax levies needed to pay for those properties and services. The county board also has the authority to approve most, but not all, county expenditures.

2. *Sheriff:* The primary responsibilities of the sheriff are law enforcement and maintaining the county jail. The sheriff also has custody and care of the courthouse.

3. *State's Attorney:* The state's attorney has the duty to prosecute both civil and criminal cases in which the people of the state or county may be concerned. The state's attorney is also the attorney for the county board and for all other county officials acting in their official capacity. The office has great power and responsibility because of the discretion in deciding which cases to prosecute.

4. *County Treasurer:* This office has custody of all county funds and is responsible for investing them. The treasurer is also the county collector; he or she collects and disburses property taxes as well as inheritance tax for the state and drainage taxes and mobile home taxes locally.

5. *County Clerk:* The county clerk is ex officio clerk of the county board and records all minutes and resolutions; he or she issues county licenses for marriages, motels, liquor, and bingo; keeps records of births, deaths, and marriages; conducts elections, maintains voter registration (in counties of less than five hundred thousand population), and maintains the property tax extension system by recording the levies from each taxing district and computing the amounts owed for each property in the county.

6. *Coroner:* The coroner investigates all deaths not attended by a physician, determines cause of death or whether an inquest and/or autopsy is needed to determine cause of death, and performs the duties of sheriff if that office is vacant.

7. *Circuit Clerk:* The circuit clerk keeps all court records, issues court orders, collects traffic fines and distributes them to the proper government, and manages the court-ordered child support system; he or she is an officer of the court rather than a true county official.

8. *County Auditor:* The auditor audits all claims against the county and recommends payment or rejection to the county board. He or she conducts a continuous internal audit of the county and reports the county's financial condition; in counties with 275,000 or fewer residents, the auditor is the general accountant of the county. In counties of 75,000 population or less, a county auditor may be appointed by the county board; in counties of 75,000 to 3,000,000 population, the auditor is elected.

9. *Recorder:* The recorder records and maintains permanent public records of all real estate transactions. Documents recorded and indexed include deeds, mortgages, mortgage releases, affidavits, plats, mechanic

liens, corporation papers, surveys, and military discharges. He or she also collects fees for the county and the state.

Appointed Officials

1. *Supervisor of Assessments:* This official instructs and assists elected township assessors, has legal power to make assessments, maintains the property tax assessment system, publishes assessments in the newspaper, sends notices of changes to taxpayers, and works under the rules of the Illinois Department of Revenue. He or she serves as clerk of the board of review and may be elected if approved by voters at referendum.

2. *Board of Review:* This body assesses all property omitted by the assessor, reviews written assessment complaints, may change any assessment, equalizes assessments between townships by applying a multiplier, and delivers assessment books to the supervisor of assessments and to the county clerk so they can proceed with their responsibilities in the property tax cycle. In township counties of under 150,000 population, the board of review is appointed by the county board; in township counties of 150,000 to 1,000,000, the board of review may be elected; in nontownship counties, the County Board of Commissioners constitutes the board of review.

3. *Superintendent of Highways:* The superintendent supervises construction and maintenance of county highways and bridges, plus township motor fuel tax and bridge funds.

4. *Public Defender:* The public defender is appointed by judges of the circuit court and is required in counties with 35,000 or more residents; the office may be created in smaller counties. The public defender acts as attorney for indigent persons accused of crimes.

Revenue

Property Tax

The largest single source of revenue for counties is the property tax. This is followed by state-shared revenue (income tax and state reimbursements for salaries and specific state-encouraged projects) and the local sales taxes. A property tax levy is a sum of money to be raised by a local government to provide a specific service or group of services. The amount of the levy should be the amount needed to provide that service during a budget year in the opinion of the taxing district's governing body.

Counties have a variety of separate property tax levies. The number was reduced in 1986 by the consolidation of several old levies into a newly enlarged general corporate levy. Other major levies include highway, bridge, mental health and/or public health (if adopted by referendum), Illinois municipal retirement fund, social security, and tort immunity (liability insurance, workers' compensation, and unemployment insurance). Most levies have rate limits with the exception of those for retirement funds and tort immunity. Since each levy is for a specific purpose, it should be accounted for in a separate fund and the money only spent for that purpose.

Until 1988 cities were required to set their levies by the second Tuesday in September; counties are required to set their property tax levies "at the September session." This language creates a legal loophole which allows counties to recess their September meeting and delay setting the levies. In 1986, the Champaign county board recessed its September meeting month after month and finally set the tax levies in January 1987. In the meantime, new county board members had been elected in November, considerably stretching the concept of a "recessed meeting." One reason for having a September deadline is accountability to the taxpayers. If taxes are set before the November election, then voters have a chance to express their views. This link between performance and election is broken if the levies are set after the election. Schools have lobbied successfully to have their deadline in December.

Illinois law requires counties to mail out tax bills by 1 May to property owners. Tax bills in 1987, for example, were based on tax levies established in the fall of 1986 and on equalized assessed value as of 1 January 1986. Payment is due in two installments: 1 June and 1 September. Tax bills are mailed out by the county treasurer. If tax bills are sent late, it creates a hardship for every local government in the county. The expense of borrowing for cash flow falls on the local taxpayer.

Only a few counties meet the statutory deadlines. Last-minute changes in the law by the Illinois legislature have frequently caused delay at the local level. However, a number of Illinois counties do not follow the law because of sheer lack of organization. Of seventy-three township counties responding to a recent survey, only nine met the statutory time limits for tax bills.[3] Champaign County eliminated delays by having all individuals involved sit down and work out a coordinated schedule for getting tax bills out on time.

Levies are set by the governing body of each unit of government and sent to the county clerk. Tax rates are computed by the county clerk for each

3. Local Government Audit Advisory Board, *A Review of the Illinois Real Estate Tax Cycle 1986* (Springfield: State of Illinois, 1986), 31ff.

taxing district based on the levy divided by the assessed valuation. Rates are then applied to individual properties for all the taxing districts in which the property is located in order to compute the total tax due.

Property is initially assessed by elected township assessors at one-third the market value as of 1 January. The assessor's books are turned in to the county supervisor of assessments by 1 June. In commission counties, the initial assessment is performed by the supervisor of assessments. The board of review by law should apply individual township multipliers to equalize assessments among townships. If this is not done, inequities will be magnified by a county-wide multiplier imposed by the state. The Illinois Department of Revenue analyzes the work of the board of review and may assign a county-wide multiplier to bring the entire county into line with other counties throughout the state.

Taxpayers may appeal to the board of review if they feel their assessments are too high. Many taxpayers focus only on their assessment and forget that tax levies set by their elected representatives are the main determinants of their tax bills.

Sales Tax

For many years, counties have had the option of adopting a one-cent sales tax in unincorporated areas. A major drawback was that the tax base disappeared as cities annexed land. In 1985, counties were faced with a bleak fiscal outlook. The Illinois Supreme Court ruled as unconstitutional a law permitting counties to keep the interest on taxes collected for other local governments but held briefly by counties prior to distribution. Federal revenue sharing was cut and farm assessments were dropping. At the same time, expenses were growing, particularly for jails since the state had dealt with its prison overcrowding problem by assigning persons convicted of misdemeanors to serve their time in county jails.

A solution approved by the legislature was a new one-quarter-cent sales tax for counties, which would apply throughout the county, including incorporated areas. In exchange, counties would provide property tax relief by combining a number of separate property tax levies in the general corporate fund. For urban counties, this has been a lifesaver. The impact has been smaller in rural counties without large shopping centers. In Champaign County, the one-quarter-cent tax will bring in twice as much as the old one-cent tax. Even though the rate is one-fourth, the tax base is more than eight times as great and grows over time instead of shrinking.

Income Tax

Illinois shares one-twelfth of its state income tax receipts with local governments. The amount that a county receives is based on its population in the unincorporated area. Income tax receipts vary with the ups and downs of the business cycle. The amount that a local government gets depends on total economic activity throughout the state.

Motor Fuel Tax

Motor fuel tax is based on cents per gallon sold and is collected by the state and distributed to counties based on the number of licensed motor vehicles in the county. Distributions to cities are based on population and those to townships are based on miles of road.

Expenditures

The biggest expense of Illinois counties is maintaining the criminal justice system. Counties are often plagued by jail overcrowding. However, county boards historically have had difficulty building new jails because the public does not want to spend the money, and the county board does not feel comfortable taking the responsibility. In an effort to cut costs, counties frequently end up spending far more than necessary.

The similarity of county boards a century ago with those of today is illustrated by the history of the Champaign county jail. In March 1880, grand juries had condemned the county jail for fifteen years as unfit.[4] A committee was appointed to investigate. The committee reported that, although a new jail was desperately needed, it felt the voters should decide. The question of building a new jail was put up for a vote and soundly defeated. After the referendum failure, money was appropriated to add on to the jail and to repair it. However, in 1884, escapes from the crumbling jail were so frequent that another committee was appointed to study the problem. Eventually a new jail was built in 1904.

In 1978, after years of complaints from the sheriff and many grand jury and consultant recommendations, the county board decided to build a new jail. A committee recommended financing it with a building commission. However, county board members, like their predecessors a century earlier, backed off from this decision and wanted the voters to decide by referendum. The 1978 referendum, like the one in 1880, resulted in an overwhelming "no" vote. Then the county board, threatened by lawsuits from the state, decided to build a jail anyway, but a smaller jail than the one proposed to the voters. The new jail had barely begun operations in 1980 when it suddenly became too small.

The state very conveniently dealt with its overcrowding problem by placing prisoners convicted of misdemeanors in county jails. No money was provided to the counties for the extra prisoners. Additionally, the jail population has grown as a result of changes in the legislature's definition of who should be jailed. For example, the cost of new laws requiring the jailing of drunk drivers has fallen on counties.

Standards of what public spending is necessary change over time. In 1899, the Champaign county board reiterated its longtime opposition to "hard" (paved) roads, stating that "the present roads in Champaign County, are with the exception of a few months, in good condition."[5] At other times, civic pride overcomes penny pinching. In 1900, a Champaign County grand jury said that the $50,000 proposed to repair the courthouse was not

4. Minutes of Champaign County Board, Sept. 1877, Dec. 1886, Champaign County Clerk, 167ff.

5. Minutes of Champaign County Board, 1895–1900, Champaign County Clerk, 444.

enough. They wanted to spend $100,000 and provide a facility built to last for the next fifty years. They noted that, with an assessed value of $13 million and a surplus of $40,000 in the treasury, Champaign County could afford to compete with Coles County, which had spent $125,000, and Kane County which had spent $225,000 on their courthouses.[6] The Champaign county courthouse that was built in 1901 is still in use today, although it has undergone extensive remodeling and renovation.

The Budget

The financial health of any government depends on a balance between spending and revenue. Governments, like private citizens, eventually learn, "If your outgo exceeds your income, your upkeep will be your downfall." The federal government has not learned this yet, but county governments should be acutely aware of it. Although the Illinois economy and the national economy have a big influence on county finances, two other factors are important as well: state and federal mandates, and the management skills, or their lack, at the local level. Sometimes, a government can create its own financial crisis, no matter how much money it receives.

Historically, one of the major problems of county governments in Illinois has been caused by state mandates—new services required by the state with no new revenue to pay for them. The State Mandates Act was passed to deal with this problem, but it has become almost meaningless because the legislature has had a tendency to exempt new laws from the State Mandates Act, thereby saving the state money but frequently causing chaos at the local level.

Between 1980 and 1983, Illinois counties were hard hit by legislative action and court decisions. Champaign County, for example, lost almost a million dollars in revenue from: (1) the virtual abolition of the inheritance tax, (2) the elimination of the sales tax on farm equipment, (3) the reduction of farmland assessments, (4) the reduction of residential assessments by the homestead limited exemption, and (5) a court ruling which no longer allowed counties to keep interest earned on taxes collected for other governments. Most Illinois counties became dependent on federal revenue sharing for operating expenses in an effort to make up these losses. Previously Champaign County, for example, had used revenue sharing only for capital improvements.

The federal government has also contributed to financial chaos in local

6. Minutes of Champaign County Board, 1895–1900, Champaign County Clerk, 482ff.

governments. In 1986 alone it (1) raised the cost of borrowing for local governments by removing the tax exemptions from several types of bonds, (2) discontinued the federal income tax exemption for state and local sales taxes, thereby increasing the burden on the local taxpayer and making it more difficult for local governments to raise taxes, (3) required overtime pay for employees of local governments under the Fair Labor Standards Act, (4) required new record keeping for personal use of government vehicles, and (5) required health insurance to be offered to ex-employees and their dependents and also the ex-dependents of current employees. What did Congress do to help pay for all this? It killed revenue sharing.

With the approval of the new quarter-cent sales tax, it seemed that counties like Champaign at last had arrived at financial stability, after years of tight budgets and outright fiscal fright. But the joy was short-lived. Before the first dime had been collected in Champaign County, the county board had managed to spend it all several times over. The University of Illinois asked for $4 million to help finance an airport expansion, and it needed a pledge right away so that the state would provide a grant. The county board was cautioned that it did not have money for the airport. But the board voted for approval, even though several members realized that they lacked not only the $4 million, but probably also the legal authority to make a long-term commitment, since the county does not have home rule. Nevertheless, the board agreed to pay the university $600,000 a year for ten years. This includes $2 million in interest which the university tacked on since the county was unable to come up with the $4 million up front. The payment each year is subject to annual appropriation.

Why would a group of elected officials vote to give away money they do not have? Some thought they could get assistance from the cities of Champaign and Urbana later, since both mayors urged the county to give the university the money in the name of economic development. Subsequently, however, both cities turned a deaf ear on the county's requests. Like a number of other Illinois cities, they have heavily invested in promoting tourism and are searching for new money to cover the loss of revenue sharing. Most county board members were awed by the university president actually attending their meeting and were unable to say no to any project sold as promoting economic growth and tourism.

Money for the airport became available only after the board dropped a proposed jail expansion after spending $500,000 on plans. The board managed to waste more money on the jail project than several years of state mandates had cost the county.

Forecasting revenues such as sales tax and income tax amounts to first understanding the nature of the revenue, keeping careful records of receipts, calculating growth rates, and keeping abreast of legislative and economic changes affecting future revenues. Although one cannot pinpoint future inflation and economic growth, one can make reasonable revenue estimates. Allowing large deficits and depending on "economic growth" is not recommended. The gleam is off supply-side economics.

Setting appropriations is deciding how the pie will be divided. Appropriation requests should originate with department heads. The appropriation is a legal limit on spending. Although the accounting system may have quite detailed accounts, one can specify in the budget resolution the legal level of control. Counties should use general categories such as personnel, commodities, services, and capital outlay.[7] Actual expenditures will probably be less than appropriations. The budget for each fund should be approved by the county board only after it has compared the total requested with estimated revenues and estimated fund balances.

It is helpful to have historical information on the percent of appropriations that are actually spent. In Champaign County, for example, about 94 percent of the general corporate fund budget is actually spent. In expenditure estimates, a figure of 95 percent is used to be on the safe side. In a $10 million budget, each percent that is not spent is $100,000. One should also look at what amount historically has been added to the budget during the year. This must be strictly controlled or else the real budget is being done during the year instead of during a formal budgeting process.

It is not easy to decide the right level of spending. If a government feels that a particular service is vital it may be willing to raise taxes to pay for it. Naturally, some expenditures are mandatory. One must feed prisoners in the jail, for instance. However, the number of prisoners in the jail is not merely a function of the crime rate and the number of arrests. It also depends on sentencing policies. Recent overcrowding in the Champaign county jail was reduced by cooperation between the state's attorney and the public defender in deciding which people should be incarcerated. Before this, the county board had decided to add on to the new jail at a cost of $4.5 million. It spent nearly $500,000, primarily on architects' fees, and dropped the project when the bids came in at over $6 million. Now it looks as if overcrowding might be dealt with by boarding prisoners in other counties. However, no one really knows if such space will be available when needed.

In a fund supported completely by the property tax, the levy should be set so that money is available to cover projected expenditures in a timely fashion. This means that the fund balance should be adequate to cover cash

7. Neil Hartigan, Illinois Attorney General, Attorney General Opinion 84-003, 4 Apr. 1984.

flow needed before the taxes are paid. Any lower balance would require the issuance of tax anticipation notes or warrants and the payment of interest for the borrowed money. Fund balances that are too high, that is, far above what is needed to allow for reasonable cash flow, indicate that the public has been taxed in excess of what is really needed and that a tax cut can be made. It is not legal for counties to salt away money for future projects without a referendum.

Funds that have other sources of revenue, such as the general fund, should have the levy set to make up the difference between total expenditures and the total of all revenue sources other than the levy, allowing for adequate cash flow during the year. A chart comparing month-by-month projected expenditures and revenues will indicate if cash flow problems will arise.

In order to set a levy, one needs to have an estimate of equalized assessed valuation and also know the tax rate limit. The levy divided by the assessed value gives the tax rate. If the estimated rate is above the legal maximum, one will need to reduce the levy, and either cut expenditures or find other sources of revenue. If the increase in the levy total, excluding election expense, exceeds 5 percent over the taxes extended by the government the preceding year, the Truth in Taxation Law requires that a notice be published in the newspaper and a public hearing be held.

Whoever does the county's accounting should provide monthly budget reports on actual revenues and expenditures and how they compare to the budget. At the end of the year, counties are required to have an audit prepared by an independent auditor to verify that accounting records and annual reports conform to generally accepted accounting principles for government.

Structure of County Government

The structure of Illinois's township counties was fundamentally changed in 1972. County boards had previously consisted of township supervisors. In some counties, the old board of supervisors had more than fifty members. The new law required county boards in township counties to consist of no fewer than five and no more than twenty-nine members.

After the 1972 reorganization mandated by "one-man, one-vote," new faces appeared on Illinois county boards. All fifty members of the Champaign county board of supervisors had been white males, who met in a small room clouded in cigar smoke. The new twenty-seven-member county board sworn in in 1972 included the first three women elected since the county's founding in 1833. One local newspaper ran the headline "Faculty Wives Sweep Incumbents from Office." Several years later, the first black representatives were elected. Both the first women and the first blacks elected were Democrats in a once solidly Republican stronghold.

Commission counties still consist of three members elected at large with staggered terms. According to a recent survey by the Illinois Comptroller's Local Government Audit Advisory Board, the commissioners spend an average of ten hours per month hearing property tax appeals as part of their job on the board of review. Although the commissioners favor continuing the present system, a majority of the supervisors of assessments believe that a separate board of review would be an improvement.[8] Also, in recent court cases involving both the city of Springfield and the city of Danville, courts have ruled that the commission form of government excluded minority representation. This could become an issue in commission-form counties.

County Issues

According to a long-term DuPage county board member, "The elected officials make the job of the County board difficult, because the County Board has no control over the operations of the elected officials."[9] Illinois law is clear. The county board has power over the budget, but not over the internal operations of elected and appointed officials, who have the power to run their offices within budgetary limits. However, county board members have invested much time and energy in trying to run offices not under their jurisdiction. Large boards especially tend to get mired in details of administration over which they have no legal authority (e.g., salaries of employees, especially in the offices of elected officials) while ignoring the policy issues they should be dealing with. In 1978, for example, Winnebago County officials won a lawsuit, and a court ordered the county board to stop trying to set salaries in the offices of elected officials. The tension is obvious between elected officials and the county board about who is in control, but the law is clear on the duties of each. Unfortunately, those who have sworn to uphold the law sometimes fail to do so and neglect to learn and perform their own job.

A frequent argument is that officials should be appointed rather than elected, because then their qualifications could be assured. The elective process may be cumbersome and less than perfect, but the appointive process may be no better since the quality of appointments depends on the

8. Local Government Audit Advisory Board, *A Review of Illinois Real Estate Tax Cycle: Commission County Supplement* (Springfield: State of Illinois, 1987), 3.

9. Minutes of DuPage County Task Force on Structure of County Government, 25 June 1987, 1.

quality of those doing the appointing—frequently elected officials. It is impossible to guarantee competence, independence, or nonpartisanship by appointment or by election. There is no evidence that "nonpartisan" elections are better than partisan elections or that appointment is intrinsically superior to election. Those who disdain the squabbling of politics and political parties overlook that that is how the work of governing gets done—not smoothly, but with arguments, conflicts, mistakes, and corrections. Other forms of government seem to have a worse record than democracies with open partisan politics. The real question to be asked is whether it is valuable to have any particular office be independent of the county board and directly accountable to voters. Also, if an office is well run by an elected official, there would seem to be no reason for the position to be appointed purely on theoretical grounds.

Under the present Illinois constitution, the state's attorney, sheriff, treasurer, and county clerk may not be abolished, but the offices of recorder, coroner, and auditor may be abolished by referendum. So far, referendum attempts to eliminate these offices have generally failed, although the auditor's office in Lake County was eliminated in 1980 after the county board had stripped the office of many duties and the incumbent had died. The duties of county auditors are now mandated by law, no longer at the option of the county board.

One of the main weaknesses of county government historically has been its lack of central authority. The structure frequently consists of a large county board trying to act as both a legislative and executive body, in addition to numerous independent elected officials. The lack of central executive authority and responsibility often has contributed to inefficiency, waste, and a lack of accountability to taxpayers.

A modern response has been the development of the county executive form of government, giving counties a separation of powers like that found in cities and states. New York state has been a leader in the creation of county executive government, generally in larger urban counties. In some counties, referendum efforts failed as many as seven times before voters finally adopted the county executive reform. The fastest-growing reorganization of county government has been the adoption of the elected county executive. The number of counties with elected county executives has grown from 8 in 1960 to 253 in 1979, and 378 in 1988. Three states— Kentucky, Tennessee, and Arkansas—now require an elected county executive. [10]

10. Governmental Research Institute, *Reorganizing Our Counties: A Catalog of County Government Reorganization in America* (Cleveland, Sept. 1980), 97.

In Illinois, the creation of the county executive was first linked to home rule. However, early efforts to establish home rule by referendum failed in nine counties which tried it shortly after adoption of the 1970 constitution. Two of these counties tried and failed again in 1976. In 1985, a new law gave counties the option of creating a county executive without home rule. Referendum efforts failed in both Winnebago and Champaign counties in 1986. In 1988, Will County became the first Illinois county to adopt the elected executive. The same measure was defeated narrowly in Champaign County on the second try and by a two-to-one margin in Lake County on the first try.

Large county boards are often cited as hindrances to effective government. An Illinois law limited county boards after 1972 to a maximum of twenty-nine members. The old county boards of supervisors decided the size of the new county board. Many chose large new boards to keep as many old board members as possible. Since 1980 a movement has developed in Illinois to reduce the size of county boards. By law, Illinois county boards must reorganize every ten years. Some county boards have cut their own size; for example, the McLean county board reduced itself in 1980 from twenty-seven to twenty. There is also a growing movement of citizens cutting county boards. A 1984 referendum in Fulton County approved reducing the county board from twenty-seven down to nine. In Macon County, the Chamber of Commerce recommended reducing the county board to fourteen.[11] Similarly, a task force in DuPage County recommended establishing a county executive and cutting the county board to sixteen.[12] The League of Women Voters in Peoria County successfully spearheaded a 1986 referendum to cut the county board from twenty-seven to nine. However, the Peoria county board contended that a referendum is not binding. The Illinois Supreme Court in a split decision ruled that the Illinois constitution does not give voters the right to change the size of county boards. Only county boards can change their size every ten years when they decide the number of board districts and the members per district. The legislature could change the law, however, or the constitution could be amended.

Conclusion

I have attempted to describe Illinois county government. There is no substitute for actual observation, however. If you are a candidate, a

11. Metro. Decatur Chamber of Commerce, *Macon County Governmental Review* (June 1987): 12.
12. Minutes of DuPage County Task Force on Structure of County Government, July 1987.

potential candidate, or simply an interested citizen, the best way to learn
about your county government is to attend county board and committee
meetings, visit county offices, and talk with the participants. Members of
the majority political party on the county board will emphasize their
successes, while the board's minority party will present a different view.
Other elected officials may tell you of their utter frustration in trying to
deal with the cumbersome county board.

To really understand any government requires a working knowledge of
its financial condition. Read your county's budget and annual financial
report and do not hesitate to ask questions.

If you are a newly elected official, you will find it helpful to do the
following. First, you should read the law in the Illinois Revised Statutes
defining your duties. Then attend meetings of your state association so that
you can learn from the experience of others. And finally, get acquainted
with state legislators—they write the rules and will listen to your point of
view.

Bibliography

Advisory Commission on Intergovernmental Relations. *Profile of County
Government.* Washington: U.S. Government Printing Office, Dec. 1971.

Beam, Dave R., ed. *County Home Rule in Illinois.* DeKalb: Center for
Government Studies, Northern Illinois University, 1977.

Government Research Institute. *Reorganizing Our Counties: A Catalog of
County Government Reorganization Experience in America.* Cleveland,
Sept. 1980.

Illinois Revised Statutes, 1985. State Bar Association ed. Vol. 1–4. St. Paul:
West Publishing, 1986.

James, Owen C. *Governing Metropolitan Indianapolis.* Berkeley: University of California Press, 1985.

League of Women Voters of DuPage County, Illinois. "Survey of 16 Reor-
ganized Counties," 1987.

Marando, Vincent L., and Robert D. Thomas. *The Forgotten Governments.*
Gainesville: University Press of Florida, 1977.

Metro. Decatur Chamber of Commerce. *Macon County Governmental
Review* (June 1986).

Wilson, Thomas D., ed. *County Alternatives: The Structure, Functions, and
Management of Illinois Counties.* Chicago: 1976.

6.

Cook County Government

MICHAEL IGOE

Cook County is unique within Illinois in that it not only has the largest population of any county within the state, but in many instances state laws exist which apply exclusively to Cook County. This is the result of the unique urban setting and large population of Cook County. This uniqueness may be diminishing, however, as DuPage and the other collar counties increase in population. Cook County is the only home-rule county in the state. These home-rule provisions went into effect on 1 July 1971, when the 1970 constitution became effective. As a result, Cook County has all of the home-rule rights and privileges extended by the 1970 constitution. (A more complete description of home rule is provided in chapter 11.)

Government Structure

County President

The president's duties are broad and have grown more complex with the growth of Cook County government. He or she presides at the county board meetings and, in general, is the executive leader of Cook County. The president appoints the heads of all departments in county government as well as members of a number of county offices. This is done with the advice and consent of the county board. The president of the county board also appoints members for most committees, either permanent or temporary, established under the auspices of the county board.

One of the more important responsibilities of the president is to prepare the county's budget and present it to the county board for its approval. This provides the president with a great deal of control over county government in comparison to non-home-rule counties. The president can not only participate and vote on matters before the council, but he or she also has the power to veto an ordinance, resolution, or appropriation passed by the board. The board must override the veto by a four-fifths' vote of all members elected to the board. Thus, the president's veto powers are among the strongest in any government.

County Board Members

There are seventeen members of the county board, with ten being elected from Chicago and seven elected from suburban Cook County. As noted earlier, the president of the county board is a voting member and presiding officer. The board is not only the governing body of Cook County but is also a governing body for a number of other entities, such as the Forest Preserve Commissioners of Cook County, the Cook County Board of Health, and the Cook County Planning Commission.

The board acts as a legislative body, levies and collects taxes, maintains roads and bridges, approves purchases, and for a variety of issues holds hearings through the board's nine standing committees. The permanent standing subcommittees of the board deal with finance, public service, zoning, building, roads and bridges, rules, legislation, personnel and civil service, intergovernmental affairs and welfare. The board may also set up such temporary committees as it deems necessary.

State's Attorney

The Cook County state's attorney is the lawyer for the county board and all county officers. His or her responsibilities are similar to those of the Illinois attorney general but limited to Cook County. The state's attorney represents county officers and the county board in court actions. He or she is elected for a term of four years and handles all criminal and civil matters that involve county matters before the circuit court.

Sheriff

The sheriff is also elected for four years and basically has four separate responsibilities. First, the sheriff is responsible for law enforcement in the unincorporated areas of Cook County. In unincorporated areas, the sheriff provides basic and primary police services. In incorporated areas, he or she generally works with the local police and sometimes assumes responsibility for specific police action. Second, the sheriff serves county-wide as a peace officer. Third, the sheriff is responsible for the criminal courts building, other county buildings, as well as the county jail. In this function, he or she is not only responsible for the custodian duties and maintenance of buildings but also for the care and feeding of all prisoners. Finally, the sheriff is an officer of all the courts of the circuit court. He or she is responsible, through a representative, for attending each court session, seeing to the safety and security of the court system, as well as serving judicial writs and carrying out judicial mandates.

County Clerk

The county clerk is elected for a four-year term. He or she is responsible for preparing transcripts of the proceedings of the county board and is keeper of the seal for the county. The county clerk is required to maintain vital statistics including the recording of births, marriages, deaths, and any other ongoing statistics that he or she may be directed to maintain by the county board. He or she is also responsible for the conduct of elections within Cook County outside of Chicago.

One of the most important responsibilities of the county clerk is to extend the taxes by applying the state equalized factor to all assessments. In this process, the clerk determines the amount of money that local tax bodies are levying against property within their taxing districts. This has become an ongoing and growing responsibility of the clerk. In addition, the clerk is responsible for collecting tax bills, delinquencies, providing certificates of sale for property sold at tax sales, and handling the funds received from such sales.

Treasurer

The treasurer's basic responsibility is to mail out tax bills and collect those revenues not only for the county but for all units of local government within the county. Upon collection of funds the treasurer distributes appropriate amounts to the units of local government within the county. The treasurer, who is elected for four years, is also required to keep the proper records of revenues and expenditures and make financial reports to the county board.

County Assessor

The Cook County assessor also is elected to a four-year term. He or she is responsible for determining the value of real property within the county.

The valuation is used by the clerk for the purposes of levying taxes. The assessor is assisted by township elected assessors, who generally report new construction and assist taxpayers within their township in understanding the tax and assessing process.

Board of Tax Appeals

If a taxpayer does not receive satisfaction from the assessor regarding the valuation that the assessor has attached to real property, he or she may appeal to the Cook County Board of Tax Appeals. This two-member elected board is responsible for reviewing assessments either at the request of a taxpayer or the assessor. Should the board of appeals find a need for change, it orders the assessor to make appropriate corrections or revisions. Both members of the board are elected to four-year terms.

Recorder of Deeds

The recorder of deeds, also elected for four years, can be considered the archivist of Cook County. He or she is responsible for keeping records of legal documents, most importantly, those involving real estate ownership. The recorder of deeds is statutorily required to maintain certain records. Cook County has adopted the Torrens system of land title registration, in which the recorder is the registrar.

Superintendent of Educational Service Region

This position is an elected four-year term, and to be eligible to run for the office, one must have an educational background, a master's degree, hold a supervisory or administrative certificate issued by the State Board of Education, and have four years of teaching experience. The superintendent's main duties lie outside of the city of Chicago. One of the major tasks of the superintendent is the distribution of state and federal education funds to school districts within Cook County.

Circuit Court

The Cook County Circuit Court has two major departments, the county department and the municipal department. The county department deals with such divisions as the chancery, county, criminal, divorce, juvenile, law, and probate. The municipal department provides court services to geographic districts within Cook County. Generally, it handles minor issues.

Chief Clerk of the Circuit Court

This elected official is responsible for servicing the circuit court of Cook County. The chief clerk of the circuit court is elected for four years and in general provides administrative support services to the court.

Fiscal Structure

The major fiscal difference between Cook County and other county governments in Illinois is that Cook County, as the only home-rule county in the state, has a much broader potential for new revenue sources and new types of taxes than the other counties within Illinois. It is only limited in its taxing capacity to those specific types of taxes prohibited home-rule units by the 1970 constitution. As in other counties, property tax is the basic revenue source in Cook County. Since home rule was adopted, the sales tax has also become an important source of revenue. The county's responsibility in the tax cycle is for the assessor to determine the value of real property, and once that is done, the county clerk extends the levies of county and local governments against those evaluations after the clerk has computed the state multiplier. Once the clerk has extended the levies of units of local government, the county treasurer sends out tax bills. After these revenues have been collected, they are distributed to the units of local government.

Cook County's fiscal year runs from 1 December through 30 November of the following year. As noted earlier, the budget is an executive one. The board holds hearings and deliberates on the budget in October, and it is required to pass a balanced budget, not to exceed the estimated revenue.

7.

Township Government

GEORGE MILLER

Of all the forms of government in existence in this country today, township organization is probably the most basic in structure and should be the easiest to understand. However, its very simplicity makes it difficult for the unaware individual to comprehend. Recently, an editor of a central Illinois newspaper reading a report on an annual town meeting inquired as to the proprieties taken there. His words were, "it's so simple and easy to understand, it just can't be government at work."

This problem may be partly caused by the use of the word "township." There are two kinds of townships. The civil township, which is a unit of government in Illinois and twenty other states, is different from the congressional township, which is a measurement of area and is used extensively in the Atlantic states and the Midwest for functions such as measurements and evaluations.

History

As a unit of government, the township dates back to the Anglo-Saxon era in England and the groups or clans that fought in units and descended from common ancestors. Each clan governed itself through public meetings and customs which slowly evolved through the centuries. Each of these clans settled in a separate village. The early village was surrounded by a hedge or a ditch that was called a "tun." As much land as could be seen from the tun was the "tunscipe" ("seen from the hedge"). The people in the village lived by farming the tunscipe, and the village and land so farmed, taken together, were then the smallest unit of civil government. Today we call it a township.

The township was one of the earliest forms of government in North America, established in March 1629. There are some who consider the charter of 1629 the most important document in the history of this country. It provided for the governance of the affairs of the Massachusetts Bay Company by a general court of all the free men in the company and for the election by them of a governor, a deputy governor, and a court of assistance. Various types of charters were granted to other companies. One of these was that of Providence, Rhode Island, when Roger Williams established the town of Providence in 1636 as a self-governing municipality or village, tailoring the form of government we call township today.

In most of the southern colonies, the county became the dominant form of government and in certain states, the county continues to be the primary source of government. In the northern Atlantic states, between 1630 and 1640, towns were established in Boston, Rocksbury, Dorchester, Waterton, Newton, Medford, and Saugus, and all of the Massachusetts Bay colonies. These communities of settlers, except for the first few years, did not necessarily function as early town governments. The first town with regular meetings appears to have been Dorchester, where the inhabitants agreed in October 1633 to hold weekly meetings.

An important fact that should be recognized, however, is that 140 years before the American Revolution, town or township government was an established, functioning unit of government in almost the same form in which it operates today. Thirty-eight of the fifty-six courageous men who signed the Declaration of Independence had grown up and lived under, and received the benefits of, township government before Philadelphia existed. Is it little wonder that when this new nation began to move west, the concept of township government went with them?

Over the years, the roles of the township government and township officials have been adapted to meet local needs. In some states, such as Michigan, Pennsylvania, and Wisconsin, townships are granted almost total municipal powers. In other states, such as Illinois, Minnesota, and Ohio, townships have fewer municipal functions to perform. The mandated functions of townships vary from state to state. The fact that they perform their duties at the direction and with the direct input of the taxpayer in the same manner established nearly 350 years ago causes some to consider township government archaic.

For the last sixty years, students of government have predicted the demise of the township as a unit of government. Despite these predictions, township government remains entrenched in the scheme of local government and especially so in Illinois. In fact, in Illinois, the powers of the township and its functions have expanded tremendously in the last ten years. There are those who believe that today an Illinois township has greater powers than either city or county government.

Illinois History

Although township government was not formally established in Illinois until 1848, the Illinois Statutes contained references to township government and to functions to be performed by township officials as early as 1827. In the 1827 *Book of Laws of Illinois,* we find that, effective 30 December 1826, the general assembly provided for the establishment of districts in each county for purposes of electing two justices of the peace per district, except in those districts in which the county seat was located, which would have three justices. Each county was required to have not more than eight of these districts as provided by the Eighth General Assembly. The same provisions concerning justice of the peace also applied to the election of two constables from each district to four-year terms.

Also in the *Book of Laws of Illinois* for 1827, there is a reference to the appointment of road supervisors in each district in a county. The appointed road supervisors oversaw the work on the local roads. Moreover, there is a reference regarding workfare, under a different name. The county commissioners could appoint or designate people on public aid or relief programs to work out the grant by working on roads. A later reference, effective 1 March 1833, mentions townships administering poor-relief, despite the fact that this was still fifteen years away from township government in the state.

The development of Illinois as a state really began with the opening of the Erie Canal in 1825 and the settling of Indian lands in northern and central Illinois in 1833. Settlers in large numbers poured into Illinois from the New England states. They bought with them the tradition of the New England town as the primary unit of local government. In response to their demands, the 1848 constitution directed the legislature to provide an option for civil townships to be created as subdivisions of county government. In counties choosing this organizational form, townships provided county services locally and some municipal services for unincorporated areas.

At the time the 1848 constitution was approved, only 99 of Illinois's current 102 counties were in existence. Kankakee County was formed in 1853 and Douglas and Ford counties in 1859. The initial response to organizing townships was rapid. In 1849, the first year that counties could adopt the township form of government, 24 counties adopted it and organized in that fashion. In the next ten years, 25 more counties adopted the township form of government. Williamson County was the last county to be organized under the township form of government in December 1907.

Williamson County and Johnson County later abandoned townships and reverted to a commission form of government in which three county commissioners determine policies for the county.

Macoupin County organized under township government in 1870 because of a million-dollar courthouse built by the three county commissioners during the Civil War. The electors of the county felt that far too much money had been spent, perhaps improperly, on the courthouse in Carlinville. Owing to voter anger over this issue, they abolished the commission form of county government and adopted the township form. Both the townships in Macoupin County and the million-dollar courthouse still remain effective and functioning today.

The largest Illinois township today is Thornton Township in Cook County, with a population of 191,359 residents. The least populated township is Cincinnati Township in Pike County with a population of 85 residents. The township with the largest equalized assessed valuation is York Township in DuPage County at $2,038,368,942. The smallest township valuation is Ripley Township in Brown County with an equalized assessed valuation of $378,635.

Services

Townships provide the most direct services to unincorporated areas of a county. In the urban and heavily populated counties, their direct services are less recognizable, but still important. The township, urban or rural, fills the gaps and provides the services that sometimes are missed by other units of local government. This is especially true in the general assistance function that is a mandated responsibility of all townships. Illinois townships in the last few years have provided approximately 10 percent of total public aid payments through the township general assistance program. Funds are provided by local real property taxes, and the payouts are issued by the township supervisor, subject to the policies and standards set locally by the town board of trustees.

Certain townships receive reimbursement of funds from the State Department of Public Aid. These townships are referred to as receiving units and are subject to State Department of Public Aid regulations, standards, and guidelines. A receiving unit is created when a township expends in excess of the equivalent of a ten-cent levy against all property valuations in the township and applies to the state for reimbursement of the excess amount.

All townships in Illinois carry the burden of three mandated respon-

sibilities. First, the administration of general assistance programs (already mentioned). Second, in all townships having road districts, the maintenance and construction of roads and bridges in unincorporated areas is the mandated function of the township road or highway commissioner. His or her jurisdiction does not include roads under any other governmental jurisdiction. Finally, with the exception of Cook County, the township assessor is the primary source of property assessment or appraisal. In Cook County, the office of township assessor is a constitutional office; however, the office serves in the capacity of deputies of the Cook County Assessor's Office. In all counties organized under the township system, excluding Cook, the township tax assessors' evaluations are used for determining the levy for taxes or for developing the tax receipts for the varying taxing bodies that include the county itself, school districts, municipal taxes, fire protection, and district taxes (park districts, and so on). All depend on the appraisals established by the township tax assessor. In all counties organized under the township system, except for Cook and St. Clair counties, there is a county supervisor of assessments, who may challenge, and in fact, with the board of review, change the figures submitted by the township assessor.

Recent Township History

During the sixties and seventies, townships had, in addition to the three principal mandated functions, about thirty optional services they could provide. More recently, additional powers were granted to township officials, and they now include about forty separate permissive functions. Some of these require action of the electors at the annual town meeting; others may be undertaken by the authorization of the board or the highway commissioner.

For example, townships are authorized to establish zoning for counties where there is no county zoning. Also, by contract, they may furnish police protection to unincorporated areas. They may establish committees for youth and senior citizens and fund them either with tax dollars or money from other sources. They may keep public wells in good repair. They may even establish, fund, and maintain township comfort stations. They may provide housing for the custodian of the comfort station. With the approval of the electors, townships may provide for fire protection in unincorporated areas, again either through direct funding or contracting with another fire protection district.

Township funds may be spent for the use of a historical society or for preservation of records. Township funds can be spent for planting trees or for developing and maintaining open space areas. They may be used to establish township parks, cemeteries, and libraries. One of the largest libraries in Illinois is the Schaumburg Township Library. Township governments are also permitted to operate and maintain community buildings. They may provide for hospital care and, with the direction and approval of the electors, provide for housing for senior citizens. With referenda approval, they may establish, maintain, and operate sewer systems, water systems, or combined sewer and water systems.

The electors are the corporate authority of the township, and they may provide for the purchase and sale of property and regulate the use of that property. No township or road district property may be sold without the prior approval of the electors of the township. Electors of a town have, in fact, ordered the disposal of township and/or road district property without the endorsement of the township officials. Only at the township level do the electors have such a strong influence.

The electors of the township may exercise their authority in such mundane functions as to determine what is a lawful fence or to prevent animals and livestock from running at large, or they may make such important decisions as establishing new taxes for the township and/or road district. They may also increase existing taxes or adopt new tax rates. The electors also control the transfer of surplus funds into the road and bridge fund. The board of trustees must maintain the funds and must follow the directive of the electors.

Intergovernmental Relations

Since the termination of the Federal Revenue Sharing Act in 1986, townships have little relationship with the federal government. However, there are still a few federal programs in which townships are eligible to participate. The relationship between townships and state government, on the other hand, is considerably stronger. The township, by constitutional provision, is a local government provided for in the constitution and subject to constitutional limitations. Local governments in Illinois operate under what is commonly referred to as Dillon's rule. According to this rule, local governments only have those powers specifically provided by law. The general assembly provides all local governments with the power to undertake certain projects or functions. The relationship with the state, therefore, is very close.

Township relations with county government, while still close, are not the same as they were prior to 1970. At one time, each county's governing body was the county board of supervisors. Every elected township supervisor was an ex officio member of the county board. That system has since changed. The township supervisor does not automatically serve as a member of the county board. Supervisors may serve as members of the county board in all township counties except Cook County. The Cook County system was changed with the constitution of 1870, which prohibits the township supervisor from serving as a member of the county board.

During the early seventies, when the "one-man, one-vote" ruling was being interpreted, it was determined that township supervisors could not be elected for more than one office. A person holding the office of township supervisor could not at the same time hold the office of county board member. Conversely, no county board member could hold the office of township supervisor simultaneously. But in 1976, the general assembly provided that both offices of township supervisor and county board member could be held concurrently. That provision continues today.

The state legislature has determined that in counties of less than three hundred thousand population, a township assessor and/or a township highway commissioner may seek and hold simultaneously the office of member of a county board. In counties of less than one hundred thousand population, a township trustee may also simultaneously be a member of a county board.

Legal Deadlines

Generally speaking, the fiscal year for most townships and road districts in Illinois begins 1 April and ends 31 March. At the present time, the budget and appropriation ordinances for township and general assistance, and road purposes must be adopted not later than by the end of the first quarter of the fiscal year. This has been changed by Public Act 85-853.

The statutes provide that each year the township's board of trustees shall hold a public hearing on the budget and appropriation ordinance for all funds. The tentative budget and appropriation ordinance must be on file with the township clerk thirty days prior to the public hearing. At the public hearing or immediately thereafter, the board of trustees shall adopt a budget and appropriation ordinance in total. Prior to adoption, however, the board of trustees has the authority to make changes in the tentative budget and appropriation ordinance.

Certificates of levy for town general assistance and road purposes must also be certified to the county clerk. In the case of the road district, they must be certified no later than the first Tuesday in September and, in the case of the town and general assistance funds, no later than the second Tuesday in September. State law provides that all official notices of the township be published in a newspaper in the township's jurisdiction and if no such newspaper exists, then in one published in the county in which the township is located. If there is no such newspaper, the publication must then appear in a newspaper of general circulation in that particular township.

According to state law, all funds of the township must be audited six months after the close of the fiscal year. The audit is required to be filed with the office of the Illinois comptroller. In those townships appropriating more than $200,000 per year, exclusive of road and bridge funds, the audit shall be performed by a licensed or certified public accountant. In townships appropriating less than $200,000 per year, exclusive of road funds, the annual audit shall be performed by three electors of the town unrelated to members of the town board, who are competent in accounting procedures. The same provision applies to road and bridge funds either in excess of or less than $200,000 annually. The electors at the annual town meeting may order an independent audit by a licensed or certified public accountant for any year and in every case at the end of each supervisor's term of office.

Other deadlines that appear on the township calendar include the Tuesday preceding the annual town meeting when the supervisor is required to file a full statement of the financial affairs of the township with the township clerk. On the Wednesday preceding the annual town meeting, a single township highway commissioner is to make a report to the board. Two days prior to the annual town meeting each year, the town clerk is required to post a copy of the financial statement at the place where the annual town meeting shall be held.

If township government were a religion, and to some people it is, the annual town meeting would be the highest of all holy days. On the second Tuesday in April each township holds its annual town meeting, at which time every qualified elector of the town is entitled to participate in all discussions and actions concerning the business of the township. They act and cast their votes as the corporate authority of the township. The annual town meeting is prescribed by statute to be held at 2 P.M. on the second Tuesday in April, except if this date falls during the celebration of Passover. In that case, the town board of trustees may change the date of the annual meeting to the first Tuesday after the last day of Passover. The electors or the board of trustees may select a time other than 2 P.M. for the convening of the annual meeting.

The township budget and levy cycle for townships is somewhat different than for other units of local government. For example, the township levy is certified to the county clerk the first Tuesday in September for road purposes, the second Tuesday in September for town and general assistance purposes. Though the levies are certified and filed in September of one calendar year, the funds generated by those levies are appropriated and budgeted in the new fiscal year, which in most cases begins the following 1 April.

Within thirty days after the end of the fiscal year, for the township road district, the treasurer of the road district funds is required by law to submit a sworn statement of itemized account to the road commissioner. Other requirements and deadlines are not clearly defined in the statutes. The majority of townships have the elected officials convene as a board at least once a month. Payroll requirements and other provisions for payment of bills almost necessitate a monthly meeting of the town board. The board, however, must meet prior to approving payment of elected officials' salaries and for any other expenditure of the township with a few exceptions, such as payments for social security, insurance coverage, employees' salaries, and/or payments for general assistance claims. The approval of the town board of trustees is required prior to payment of any bills (Public Act 85-526). The town board of trustees must audit all warrants issued by the road commissioner for road purposes prior to their being paid. These requirements generally require monthly meetings.

"AW, WE DON'T BOTHER MUCH WITH THAT STUFF... SOMETIMES WE COUNT ANIMALS AT FEEDIN' TIME ... WHEN WE GET AROUND TO FEEDIN' 'EM."

Township Officials and Their Duties

The *supervisor* is an elected official and by statute is the chief executive officer of the township. He or she is treasurer of all town funds, ex officio treasurer of the road and bridge fund, supervisor of general assistance, and a member of the town board of trustees. Additionally, the supervisor serves as a member of the electoral board of the township and as a member of the canvass board of the township.

The *town clerk,* also elected, is keeper of all records of the township, including general assistance records that are dormant or have been dormant for at least one year. The clerk is a member of the electoral board of the township and is chairman of the canvass board of the township for township elections. The clerk is ex officio clerk for the road and bridge district and also keeps a record of all transactions made by or on behalf of the township road district commissioner. The town clerk is not the secretary for either the town board or the road district commissioner. The clerk is responsible for the placement of all advertisements and notices for township and road district purposes. The clerk advertises for bids on behalf of the township and for the road district and must be present at bid openings for both the township and the road district. An exception may be made in the clerk's responsibility for placing notices and for being present at bid openings if a bid is accepted by the county superintendent of highways on behalf of all road commissioners and road districts in the county. The clerk convenes the annual town meeting, and, until the moderator is chosen at the annual meeting and elected from the delegates present, the clerk is the only township official who has a formal function at the meeting. All other officials attending the annual meeting do so in the capacity of electors of the town and not in their capacity as township officers.

Each township has four *trustees* elected at large every four years along with the other township officials. They comprise the legislative body of the township. The four trustees and the supervisor are the five regular voting members of the town board.[1] The clerk, also a member of the town board of trustees, has no vote except in the case of a tie when filling vacancies by appointment (Public Act 85-694). Generally speaking, the board of trustees makes the policy for the township. The clerk and supervisor, who are administrators of the township, carry out the directions of the town board. If the electors at an annual or special town meeting have given the board of trustees or any other township official specific directions provided by statute, the officials carry out those directives as well.

The township *highway commissioner* is an elected official and is in charge of all roads and bridges in the road district, except in those townships having less than four miles of road. In townships having less than four miles of road, the town board collectively acts as the commissioner of highways and oversees the functions of the road district in lieu of an elected highway commissioner. There are approximately forty or forty-five townships that have no elected road district commissioner.

The road commissioner annually submits the tax levies for the following year. They are submitted to the town board of trustees so that they may be certified and filed no later than the first Tuesday in September. The certificate of levy so submitted by the highway commissioner may not be increased or decreased in any way by the town board of trustees. It must be certified to the county clerk in the amount determined by the highway

---

1. The senior trustee (with longest period of services) also serves as a member of the township's electoral and canvass boards (Public Act 85-1178).

commissioner. Each spring, thirty days prior to the adoption of the budget and appropriation ordinance for road purposes, the highway commissioner must submit to the clerk and to the town board a tentative budget and appropriation ordinance. This budget shall be available for public inspection for thirty days prior to final action. At any time before final adoption of the budget and appropriation ordinance for road purposes, the town board has the statutory power to amend, alter, increase, or decrease line items in any way that the town board deems necessary. However, when adopting the budget and appropriation ordinance, the town board must adopt a total budget and appropriation ordinance. The board is prohibited from adopting a budget and appropriation ordinance in bits and pieces. Once the budget and appropriation ordinance for road purposes is adopted, the road commissioner has the statutory power to expend those funds according to the line items established in the appropriation ordinance itself.

A township road district is in many aspects a separate government. Neither the town board of trustees nor the township supervisor has any jurisdiction or authority over the road commissioner and/or employees of the road district. The employees of the road district are subject to the directions and requirements set forth by the highway commissioner, not the town board. However, it has been demonstrated clearly that where the highway commissioner, the supervisor, the clerk and the town board work in harmony the taxpayer usually benefits.

Another official elected at large in most townships is the township *tax assessor*. The function of the assessor is to place values on particular parcels of property. All taxes in the township are levied against these values. The title of property assessor is actually misleading. The assessor neither levies taxes, nor is he or she responsible for those taxes being levied. The assessor, who should more properly be called a property appraiser, establishes property values against which other government representatives levy their taxes.

In 1980, legislation was enacted providing for multitownship assessing districts. Any township having a population of fewer than one thousand persons was required by that legislation to become part of a multitownship assessing district with one or more contiguous townships in order to meet the minimum population of one thousand people. There are 673 townships that fall into this category. These townships have formed approximately four hundred multitownship assessing districts by merging with other townships of equal or much larger size.

The day-to-day operation of the office of assessor is immune to direct control of any township official other than the township assessor. Once the budget for the office has been approved by the town board and included with the budget and appropriation ordinance for other town expenses, the assessor may hire the employees he or she sees fit and may spend the monies according to the allocation. The assessor is the only official required by statute to have formal training. Assessors in townships with more than twenty-five thousand residents must meet stipulated requirements before even seeking office. In smaller townships, they must successfully complete a training course before the end of their first year in office. For that matter, any township or multitownship assessor, either elected or appointed to fill a vacancy, is required to successfully complete the prescribed training courses within the first year of holding office; otherwise, he or she must forfeit the office at the end of the first year. Assessors are required by law to maintain sixteen hours per year or forty-eight hours' training over a three-year period in order to maintain their certified designation. The courses are established by the Illinois Department of Revenue (DOR) and are administered by the DOR or by the Illinois Property Assessment Institute located in Bloomington.

The assessor is required to maintain a set of property record cards and may at the request of the county supervisor of assessments duplicate them for the county's use. The township assessor or multitownship assessor is also required to maintain a constant record of all changes in properties during each calendar year and to attend a meeting of the county supervisor of assessments every December. By law, assessors are to receive the property assessment books by 1 January of each year and should update and return the books no later than 15 April of each year.

Although township assessors have been accused of being responsible for delays in the tax cycle, in most instances delays are caused by the tardy distribution of the assessment books by the county supervisor of assessments. There have been cases on record in which the books to be returned by the township assessor by 15 April had not even been distributed to the township assessor by the end of June.

In five Illinois counties—Cook, Madison, Peoria, Sangamon and Will—there is also an elected township *tax collector*. Township collectors are prohibited in counties of less than 150,000 population. In counties of more than 150,000 population but less than 3,000,000, the office of township collector may be abolished by referendum at a general election. The township collectors are very active in Peoria and Sangamon counties. In Peoria County, township collectors collect the majority of taxes prior to 1 September of each calendar year. The same holds true in Sangamon County, where township collectors collect about 80 percent of the tax payments. The tax collectors are less active in Madison County and inactive in Will and Cook counties. Despite a Supreme Court decision concerning the Peoria County township tax collectors, Cook County courts still prohibit the Cook County township tax collectors from functioning or from receiving the collection books. In Will County, the county treasurer in coordinated efforts with some town boards has refused to permit the tax collectors to function. In Madison County, collections at the local level only take place in about half the townships, despite aggressive activity on the part of some township collectors in the early 1980s.

Prior to 1970, the township collector was permitted by law to levy a 2 percent charge on all funds collected by the township. In Cook County this 2 percent collection fee funded all township programs prior to 1970. The 1970 constitution abolished all fee offices in the state; as a result, the township collectors could no longer levy or assess their 2 percent collection fee. This provision resulted in lawsuits by several groups to abolish the office of township collector in Cook County. At that time, it was determined that the township collector had to be elected. He or she, however, was not permitted to obtain the collection books and therefore was unable to perform the historical duties of collector.

In addition to elected officials, there are appointed officeholders such as general assistance caseworkers and social workers, who examine applications, interview applicants, and make recommendations to the supervisor. Other appointed officers and/or groups include township youth committees, committees for senior citizens, mental health committees, and handicapped or disabled citizen committees. Many of the larger townships now find themselves deeply involved in the social service area. Schaumburg Township in suburban Cook County, for example, was the recipient of an award for providing services to disabled citizens in a national contest held in 1986. Other committees that may be established by townships are for parks, the administration of cemeteries, the administration of hospitals, and the administration of housing for the poor and the elderly.

Types of Townships

As mentioned earlier, there is a difference between civil and congressional townships. Civil townships are the governmental units that we generally refer to as townships today. A congressional township is a rectangular gridlike system for the United States. Since the system was established without boundary considerations, congressional townships often overlap political jurisdictions as well as states. Civil townships, on the other hand, have been established according to geographical boundaries. Although a congressional township in some cases serves as the base for a civil

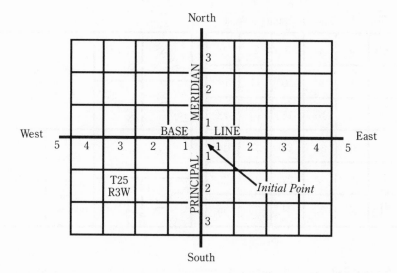

Figure 7-I. Township grid (rectangular survey system). Source: Illinois Department of Revenue, *Illinois Real Property Appraisal Manual.*

township, they more often than not are organized along geographical features such as creeks, rivers, and lakes.

The congressional township is used throughout Illinois for property assessments and tax purposes. Figure 7-1 shows surveys of the rectangular grid system or congressional township located with respect to an initial point of origin, usually a prominent geographic feature through which pass true meridians and parallels of latitude. Townships are approximately six miles square as shown in figure 7-2. Each six-mile division, either north or south of the baseline is called a township north or township south.

Coterminous townships, which have the same boundaries as a municipality, account for only 20 of the 1434 townships in Illinois. Coterminous townships were created when entire townships were incorporated into municipalities. Prior to August 1986 unincorporated areas in adjacent townships were automatically disconnected from that township and made part of the coterminous townships when annexed by the city. Legislation enacted in 1986 made the disconnection process subject to voter approval. The structure of the 20 coterminous townships varies according to when they were organized. Most of them were organized after 1911 though and are governed by the city council, which serves as the township board of trustees. The general assistance functions, however, are performed by the township supervisor of general purpose townships. The city clerk is the ex

Township 2 South, Range 3 West   Section 14

6	5	4	3	2	1
7	8	9	10	11	12
18	17	16	15	Sect. 14	13
19	20	21	22	23	24
30	29	28	27	26	25
31	32	33	34	35	36

NW¼NW¼   NE¼NW¼

SW¼NW¼   SE¼NW¼

Northeast quarter (NE¼)

N½SW¼

Lot 1

Lot 2

Lake

West half of south-east quarter

E½SE¼

Figure 7-2. Subdivision of a township (rectangular survey system). Source: Illinois Department of Revenue, *Illinois Real Property Appraisal Manual.*

officio clerk in a coterminous tonship. The elected township assessor, however, serves as the ex officio city assessor.

In Oak Park Township in Cook County, which was organized under different provisions, the township governing body is totally independent from that of the Village of Oak Park. The Village of Oak Park elects a village president, trustees, and other village officials. Oak Park Township also elects a township supervisor, who performs the same duties as township supervisors in noncoterminous townships. The board of trustees for the township is elected at large and independently from the trustees of the village. The township clerk and township assessor are also independent of the village government. They do provide different services throughout the same areas as the village. In Oak Park Township, as in other Cook County townships, the township collector is elected and subject to applicable statutes concerning township collectors. However, since coterminous townships are wholly comprised of municipal areas, there is no provision for electing highway commissioners in these townships.

In addition to some of the obvious differences between coterminous townships and single townships, there are differences in the way coterminous townships function. While the structure and duties of officials are spelled out either by municipal and/or county ordinance or by statute, day-to-day functions may vary from one coterminous township to another. For example, when the city council or village board in a coterminous township sits as the township board of trustees, in some cases the mayor or village president presides. In others, the township supervisor will preside over that portion of the meeting. In some cases they meet separately, and in others the township boards meet as part of the proceedings of the city council or village board of trustees. In any case, the annual town meeting, at which time the electors act as the governing body, is held in an identical manner.

Effectiveness of Townships

The two questions most often asked about township government are: Isn't it true that township government only provides a duplication of services already rendered by city, county, or state government? And couldn't the city, county, or any other government provide these services more efficiently and more economically than the townships? The answer to both questions, generally speaking, is no. There is no duplication of services, nor could another layer of government provide any of the township services more economically or more efficiently. There may be, though, some individual township administrations cited by advocates for the abolition of township government owing to direct duplication of services and possible savings by merging services under one unit of government.[2] Critics often cite the ability of the county to administer the general assistance more efficiently. Figures provided by the Illinois Department of Public Aid prove conclusively that this is not the case. Examples of the additional costs, to the people, of administering general assistance according to state standards is exemplified in some of the larger jurisdictions that receive state aid. For example, a receiving township whose general assistance budget and appropriation ordinance exceeds $3 million a year receives the large majority of that money from the state. Because it is a "receiving unit," that township is required to meet all state guidelines regarding rentals, levels of payment, the number of employees the township shall have for general assistance purposes, the salaries those people shall be paid, the amount of office equipment and office space, and so forth; all of these are covered by the state, local conditions notwithstanding. Because of state guidelines and requirements, again, all units of government are categorized with all other similar governments, regardless of size, location, or local needs.

There are others who advocate the consolidation of townships and/or transfer of functions and duties, such as road construction and mainte-

2. The duplication, however, is due to individuals, not the system or governments.

nance, because of the savings involved. They cite the savings in machinery as the big item. This might be true, if all township road districts were purchasing new machinery at one time. However, the total cost of maintaining and constructing roads is most economical at the township level when compared to municipal, county, state, or federal jurisdictions. This is due partially to the type of road construction utilized by townships. Even in rural counties having similar low-volume roads, the cost per mile generally is lower in township road districts using comparative road construction techniques and materials. Further, townships generally operate with the elected road official being the principal employee as well as administrator of the road district. Because of their usually conservative outlook, these road commissioners generally try to make do with what they have. It is not at all unusual to find a township road commissioner operating machinery twenty or more years old.

Other criticisms concern the thistle commissioner and the fence viewer. The office of thistle commissioner, now abandoned, was created to determine the location of noxious weeds in a township and arrange for and oversee their extrication or elimination. There is still the need for that type of service. However, the township road commissioner has the authority to eliminate weeds either at his own discretion or in cooperation with the county superintendent of highways. The role of the fence viewer has remained unchanged since the 1870 constitution. Fence viewers were chosen by each person disputing a fence line. Each person involved in the dispute would choose one member of the board of trustees to represent him or her in the fence viewing. After a study was made and the report filed with the township clerk, property owners could either accept the decision of the fence viewer and comply with his or her recommendations, or they had the opportunity to seek relief through the civil court system. Recently, the fence viewer's salary, which is paid by the person seeking the viewing service, was increased from $1.50 per day to $15.00 per day. This was the first change in this office since 1870.

Direction of Township Government

In the late 1960s, there was a strong move to abolish township government. The League of Women Voters, one of the most vocal of all the antitownship groups, succeeded in gaining some support for its position—not enough, however, to prevent townships from being included in the 1970 constitution as a unit of local government, a status they had not been privileged to have prior to this constitution. Prior to 1970, townships were creatures of the state legislature and could be abolished at the will of the state legislature. Being recognized as a constitutional local government permits the abolition of townships only by referendum of the voters in a given township or on a county-wide basis.

The legislature, however, continues to have the power to consolidate the functions of township officials as it did by creating a multitownship assessing district in 1980. The same could happen for township road districts and township general assistance programs. However, there seems to be little inclination for this to be done. The general assembly can abolish the functions of specific township officers, but there seems to be little movement to accomplish this. It was rarely proposed that townships in rural parts of the state be abolished. Even the strong antitownship groups recognized that in rural areas, township government is the only unit of government available to many of the residents and does provide vital and often essential services to communities.

When the federal revenue sharing program was established in the early 1970s, it included township governments as fund recipients. If a township provided four of ten separate functions, it was eligible because it was categorized as a general-purpose government. Township governments in Illinois met the criteria. The infusion of federal dollars gave new purpose particularly to those townships in urban areas. Revenue sharing dollars provided additional funds without local taxation to the townships in areas such as Cook, Lake, and DuPage counties. These areas established many new programs intended to provide previously unmet needs. The revenue sharing program gave new life to senior citizen programs within townships. Programs begun with revenue sharing dollars also included police protection in unincorporated areas, as well as youth committees and mental health programs in both incorporated and unincorporated townships. Programs providing ambulance service and fire protection to unincorporated areas were started. Transportation for the poor, needy, and elderly was established.

In 1986, when the federal revenue sharing program was terminated, some townships were considered "unnecessary." But they have proven themselves most adept and efficient in providing services to their communities and constituents. In numerous advisory referenda conducted in the last two years, urban townships have asked the electors, "Will you pay more tax dollars in order to retain these particular services?" The answer has been an almost unanimous yes! The townships providing these services are now doing so with taxpayers' dollars.

To improve delivery of services, the Township Officials of Illinois (TOI), in conjunction with Governors State University, the Office of Public Policy and Administration, and the Department of Commerce and Community

Affairs, developed a training program solely for township officials. This program was first held in the spring of 1981 in three different locations around the state, and approximately 350 township officials attended. The program was repeated in 1982 and continues today, addressing more people and providing answers and new direction each year. The 1987 series, held in five locations was the most widely attended in the seven years of the program. In 1987, one session alone was attended by more delegates than had participated in the entire first series held in 1981.

The training program, the largest of its kind in the Midwest and possibly in the country, has been recognized and favorably reviewed by the media and academics from all parts of the country. The real catalyst and propelling force has been provided by the elected officials themselves. In addition to showing new interest in their government, they have demonstrated a real desire to learn more about the office that they may hold. They want to learn how to function more efficiently and more economically and how to do the best job possible for their constituents.

In addition to offering this training program, the Township Officials of Illinois (TOI) in 1976 participated in founding the National Association of Towns and Townships (NATAT) with headquarters in Washington, D.C. In 1976, the TOI hosted the first organized meeting of leaders of township organizations from ten states. That first meeting was attended by about fifty people and became the nucleus for the National Association of Towns and Townships, which now represents nearly forty states and seventeen thousand units of government.

Armed with the ammunition and knowledge provided by their state organization and the National Association of Townships, township officials are actively seeking the authority to conduct even more programs and to undertake greater responsibilities. Township officials are asking for the power and ability to tackle and resolve problems of drainage districts, street lighting districts, forest preserve districts, park districts, and emergency service disaster agencies. They look forward to the opportunity of giving a good return for the tax dollars they collect. Through the assumption of additional responsibilities, townships can utilize their administrative abilities and governmental structure already in place to provide the additional services with lower total tax impact.

Additional Information

Information about township government is in short supply. There are a few books and pamphlets available. Most, however, are either outdated or no longer available. The 1977 League of Women Voters published an excellent pamphlet, "Anatomy of a Township." In 1975–76, Lee Ahlswede, formerly editor of the *Illinois and County Township Official* magazine, published a book, *Township Government Today.* The Chicago Public Library has two copies available. In 1982, to commemorate its seventy-fifth anniversary as an organization, the Township Officials of Illinois published, in paperback form, a book entitled *Grassroots Democracy,* which is a very basic history of township government, predominantly in Illinois. It contains several hundred contributions made by township officials and other interested parties. Some of these are historical documents dating back to the earliest days of township governments and before townships became an established unit of government in Illinois. The Department of Commerce and Community Affairs also provides some information regarding township government. The principal source of township information and township law is TOI. This organization currently represents approximately 95 percent of the eleven thousand elected officials from Illinois's 1,434 townships.

8.

Public School Districts

TED SANDERS

Created by the general assembly, public school districts are administrative agents of the state which establish and maintain public elementary and secondary schools. Based on the Tenth Amendment to the United States Constitution, the control and direction of education are clearly vested in the states. Article 10 of the Illinois constitution further sets forth the state's current obligation to provide to its citizens free public education through the secondary level. As agents of the state, school districts do not have sovereign power(s) to operate their districts as they deem appropriate. Thus, although school districts exercise a large degree of local control of education, authority over the operation of the districts remains vested with the state. A school district can be described as an agency of the state which is created to operate, in accordance with state laws and rules, one or more schools, serving pupils who reside within a specified geographic area. School districts are not uniform in size, shape, or population.

History

The historical basis for public education in Illinois was provided by the Continental Congress through the passage of the Northwest Ordinance of 1787. Under the terms of the ordinance, a section of every township in the Northwest Territory was dedicated to the maintenance of common schools. A "section" is one square mile of land and is the basic unit of measure used in the township system of land survey. Upon the elevation of Illinois to statehood, Congress also provided that 3 percent of the net proceeds of all public land sold within the state after 1 January 1819 would be deposited in the common school fund and used to support public education.

Characterized by some as the most farsighted public school legislation of the time, the Free School Act was enacted by the Illinois general assembly in 1825; it provided for the creation of a free school system state-wide. However, the provisions of the act were considered so socially revolutionary that it was repealed by the general assembly in 1827. The Free School Act of 1827 allowed local communities to establish free schools if they chose to do so and included a provision that a property owner could be taxed to support the local school only with his or her consent. The practical effect of the act of 1827 was to delay establishment of a state-wide system of free public schools until 1855.

The foundation for the current system of free schools was laid with the passage in 1846 of an "Act to Establish and Maintain Common Schools." This act made the secretary of state the ex officio superintendent of public instruction and provided for the establishment of school townships and districts throughout the state. Although this act provided the structure for a state-wide system of common schools, it did not provide sufficient motivation to encourage the state's citizens to begin full-scale operation of such a system. However, the Common School Laws of 1855, following the creation of the full-time post of state superintendent of public instruction, represented the watershed in achieving a state-wide system of free schools and brought to fruition the seed originally planted in 1825.

After the introduction of school district structure, public education flourished throughout the state. The report on the condition of schools filed in 1848 by the secretary of state showed a total of 2,002 school districts in fifty-eight of the ninety-seven counties, with 2,317 schools and 51,447 students. By 1857, two years after passage of the Common School Laws of 1855, there were a total of 8,386 public schools operated by 6,709 school districts in the ninety-eight counties reporting, and these schools served a total of 365,407 students.

The function of the first school districts, which generally consisted of one school building, was to provide an elementary education to those living within areas encompassing approximately four square miles of land. Boundaries of the districts were determined by township school trustees. The size of the early school districts was intended to provide for administrative units that were large enough to assure adequate financial support for the school, but were also small enough so that a neighborhood group could determine its preferred level of educational expenditures.

The public demand for common school education beyond the eighth grade developed from a perceived need for formal educational programs beyond those then available and a desire to keep pace with advances in other states. This eventually gave rise to the creation of high-school districts encompassing areas sufficiently broad and economically diverse to support the added expenses of serving additional pupils and providing expanded educational programs. Although some urban areas, having adequate populations and resources, provided for secondary education earlier, legislation enabling the formation of community or township-based high-school districts dates back to 1857. The first township high-school district was formed in Princeton in 1867.

In 1942, there were 12,027 school districts operating in Illinois, including over 11,000 elementary districts. By 1952, as a result of reorganization primarily encouraged through state financial provisions, the number decreased by more than 8,600 to about 3,600 school districts. Ten years later, consolidation had further reduced the number to 1,548, of which 928 were elementary districts. This trend toward consolidation of public school districts has continued to the present date. At the beginning of the 1987–88 school year, 983 school districts (424 elementary, 400 unit, and 119 high-school) were providing educational services to the approximately 1.8 million students attending Illinois public elementary and secondary schools. Illinois, while ranking fifth nationwide in population, twenty-fourth in total land area, and eleventh in population density, ranks third behind Texas and California in the number of its public school districts.

The scope of school district responsibilities has greatly expanded over the years. Between 1909 and 1911, the general assembly passed legislation authorizing local school districts to establish and maintain kindergartens, establish and maintain special classes or schools for certain groups of handicapped children, and secure high-school education for eighth-grade graduates by paying the tuition of indigent children to allow their high-school attendance. In 1917, the general assembly approved legislation authorizing school districts to offer adult education and provide tuition-free public high-school education. Acceptance of the Smith-Hughes Act of 1917 by the governor implicitly authorized school districts to establish and maintain vocational education programs, and in 1946 legislation was passed to authorize school districts to establish nursery schools.

Since 1946, the system of public education in Illinois has expanded to encompass a broad array of educational programs and services. A listing of the major educational programs and services (i.e., in addition to the basic academic subjects) that districts could make, and in some cases had to make, available to students in 1987–88 is given below to illustrate this point.

vocational education
special education

gifted education
bilingual education
driver education
consumer education
foreign language(s)
transportation
early childhood education
remedial education
sex education
conservation education
guidance and counseling
adult education
school lunch/breakfast

Organization

Since 1825, literally thousands of public school districts have been incorporated in Illinois under one of the many general school laws passed by the general assembly over the years. The geographic shape and size of school districts have changed frequently in Illinois during the past century. Particularly during the earlier periods of the century, it was observed that

oftentimes these changes have been made without justification other than local feeling due to misunderstandings and quarrels. At times, lines have been extended one way or another in order to include big taxpayers who might help pay school costs. At other times, taxpayers themselves manipulated the running of the district lines in order to spare themselves from a tax burden they believed too heavy. Such matters as the purchase of a school site or location of a school building have frequently been the cause of a change made in district lines.[1]

In 1837, the state auditor filed a report with the general assembly showing that there were 366 public schools scattered throughout thirty counties in the state. In 1857, two years after the passage of the Common School Laws in 1855, Superintendent of Public Instruction William H. Powell reported that a total of 6,709 school districts existed. The trend since 1950 has been to enhance the quality and expand the number and type of educational services available to students. This has been done largely

1. Neil F. Garvey, *The Government and Administration of Illinois* (New York: Thomas Y. Crowell, 1958), 270.

through consolidation of existing districts in order to better fund the educational system and form larger, more educationally challenging groupings of students.

School district reorganization methods are provided by law. Generally, each of the methods involves agreements among local school boards, citizens' committees, regional superintendents, regional boards of school trustees, and the state superintendent of education. These procedures permit changes of district types, boundary changes, and consolidation of districts to form new districts. As populations shift and demands placed on elementary and secondary schools increase, this process of school district reorganization will continue to occur.

Public school districts in Illinois are generally classified into three major types based upon the grade ranges of their student bodies. *Elementary districts* provide instruction from prekindergarten through eighth grade. Districts offering instruction spanning kindergarten through twelfth grade are called *unit districts*. Districts offering ninth-grade through twelfth-grade instruction are called *high-school districts*. Additionally, school districts are categorized in eight subclassifications which further differentiate operational authority among the three basic district types. Table 8-1 displays the number of districts of each type in operation in 1957 and at the end of the 1985–86 school year, along with the date when the particular district type was first authorized by the general assembly.

Different types of school districts were created at different times in history to address perceived educational needs of the period. Frequently, funding limitations caused by existing forms of school district structures produced a new organizational form that responded to the particular problems. Over time, many of the differences among the district types have been eliminated. However, some operational differences, specifically those that permit differing access to local revenues, continue to exist among the three major types of school districts.

Varying and changing philosophies persist regarding the most appropriate type of school district organization. As a consequence, the laws governing certain facets of school district operations change frequently. For example, in 1945, as part of the legislation authorizing the community unit form of organization, the state provided an incentive for the formation of unit districts. Community unit districts were allowed less taxing authority than the combined authority of elementary and high-school districts, which, since it meant lower taxes, was a means of gathering taxpayer support in dual districts for the unit organization. In subsequent years, this taxing authority has been changed several times in attempts to achieve differing organizational purposes.

Table 8-I.

Numbers and Types of Illinois School Districts, 1957–1986

District Type	Date Authorized	1957 Totals	1986 Totals
Elementary			
Common (CSD)	1855	745	255
Consolidated (CSD)	1917	99	23
Community Consolidated (CCSD)	1919	377	150
Charter (Charter)	1819–1870	4	2
		1225	430
Unit			
Old Type (UD)	1855	29	26
Charter (Charter)	1818–1870	10	10
Community (CUSD)	1947	294	398
Community Consolidated	1919	11	10
(CCUSD)		344	444
High School			
Charter (Charter)	1867	1	1
Community (CHSD)	1917	160	66
Township (THSD)	1872	101	48
Consolidated (CON)	1917	12	6
Protectorate	1917	1	0
Non-High (NHSD)	1917	6	1
		281	122
TOTAL		1850	996

Elementary Districts

Enrollment in the 429 elementary districts operating in Illinois during the 1985–86 school year was 420,633, or 23.1 percent of the student population. Elementary districts varied in enrollment from a minimum of 22 to a maximum of 14,737 students, with a median enrollment of 511. They collectively covered an area of 9,518 square miles, or 17.1 percent of the 55,771-square-mile area of the state, and varied in area from three-quarter square miles to 162 square miles with a median of 11.5 square miles. They encompassed a tax base of $36.25 billion, or 44.1 percent of the total property wealth of the state. They varied in wealth (property wealth per pupil enrolled) from $12,041 to $945,208 and taxed themselves at rates ranging from a minimum of $0.614 per $100 of assessed value to a maximum of $6.36 per $100 of assessed value. The median wealth among elementary districts was $67,424.80 while the median tax rate was $2. 328 per $100 of assessed value.

Unit Districts

In the school year 1985–86, 444 unit districts were in operation in Illinois, enrolling 1,181,414, or 64.8 percent of the total student population of 1,823,275. Enrollment varied from a minimum of 96 to a maximum of 433,978, while the median enrollment was 806. Unit districts encompassed an area of 46,252.5 square miles, or 82.9 percent of the 55,771 square-mile area of the state. They varied in area from 2 square miles to 461 square miles, with a median of 92 square miles. They encompassed a tax base (real property) of $45.95 billion, or 55.9 percent of the total property wealth of the state. They varied in wealth (property wealth per pupil enrolled) from $5,386 to $502,666 and taxed themselves at rates ranging from a minimum of $1.05 per $100 of assessed value to a maximum of $5.53 per $100 of assessed value. The median wealth among unit districts was $38,716.40 per pupil, while the median tax rate was $3.39 per $100 of assessed value.

High-School Districts

In 1986, Illinois had 122 high-school districts, enrolling 221,228, or 12.0 percent of the student population. Enrollment varied from a minimum of 46 to a maximum of 13,051, with a median enrollment of 1,002. High-school districts collectively encompassed an area of 9,518.21 square miles, or 17.1 percent of the 55,771 square-mile area of the state. They varied in area from 2.5 square miles to 325 square miles, with a median of 55 square miles. They maintained a tax base of $36.25 billion, or 44.1 percent of the total property wealth of the state. (This is a duplicate of the elementary district tax base since, in the aggregate, both types of districts are coterminous in their boundaries.) They varied in wealth from $38,254 per pupil to $1,671,058 and taxed themselves at rates ranging from a minimum of $0.596 per $100 of assessed value to a maximum of $3.405 per $100 of assessed value. The median wealth among high-school districts was $130,476, while the median tax rate was $1.915 per $100 of assessed value.

As a general rule, the extent to which each of these characteristics varies among district types (that is, the number of students served, area encompassed, and taxable local wealth) is representative of the operational problems that each type must address. Unit districts are required to serve approximately two-thirds of the student population, supported by slightly over half the available local tax base. Compared to elementary and high-school districts, unit districts have relatively greater needs for external financial assistance and have potentially greater costs associated with transporting students to and from school.

Financing

The financing of public school districts in Illinois is a shared responsibility of the federal and state governments and of each local school district. Article 10, section 1, of the state constitution provides that the state has the primary responsibility for financing the system of public education. Although the 1970 constitution established that the state has the responsibility for being the primary provider of funds for elementary and secondary education, the courts have ruled that the state's "primary responsibility" role is a goal and not a fixed target such as the provision of at least 51 percent of the funds.

Local, state, and federal contributions to funding education have greatly varied over time. For example, in fiscal year 1968, the state furnished only 27.13 percent of the total funds for the operation of elementary and secondary education, while the federal government contributed 5.03 percent and school districts provided the remaining 67.84 percent. The closest the state has come to achieving the 50 percent or more funding goal was in FY 1976 when the state's percentage was 48.36. However, since that time, the state's relative share has fallen. In FY 1988, the local, state, and federal contributions were 52.7 percent, 39.35 percent, and 7.95 percent, respectively.

Local Participation

The vast majority of local funds for education are generated through local taxes on real property in the school district. School districts may levy taxes to be deposited in as many as nine separate funds for up to nineteen separate purposes, including education, transportation, tort immunity, facility replacement, bonds, capital improvements, operations, rent, summer school, and others. Most major funds derive their revenues from tax rates up to a maximum legislatively established permissive tax rate which can be levied without voter approval. Higher tax rates can be approved in many funds by voter referendum in each school district, although there are also statutory maximums for voter-approved rates. For example, effective fiscal year 1989, elementary and high-school districts may levy taxes for their respective education funds at a rate of up to 0.92 percent per hundred dollars of equalized assessed valuation of the district without voter approval. Unit school districts may levy a tax up to 1.84 percent (the combined rate of elementary and high-school districts) without referendum. With voter approval the maximum rates, respectively, are 3.50 and 4.00 percent. For tax year 1985, approximately $3.3 billion was generated by public school districts from local property taxes.

A second source of local revenue stems from funds received from corporations as a result of the abolition of the tax on corporate personal property. These corporate personal property replacement revenues, which are generated by a special state tax on corporate income, are distributed by the state to the affected districts in proportion to the corporate personal property tax the districts had received in the base year. The base year is 1976 for Cook County and 1977 for all other counties. In 1985, the corporate replacement dollars distributed totaled $300.7 million.

A third, much smaller, source of local revenues for education comes from fees charged directly to the student and tuitions paid for educating students who live outside the district. While not all school districts charge student fees, some districts obtain part of their revenues from this source. These fees may include such items as textbook rental, driver education, lock and locker rental, laboratory fees, fees to participate in interscholastic athletics, and parking fees.

A fourth source of money is generated by donations. Donations can take the form of funds designated for a specific purpose, for example, for volunteer workers employed in summer programs. They enhance school programs and provide "extras" which schools may otherwise have to do without. Organizations supporting art, music, and athletics, as well as the general education program, raise funds and provide volunteer support to their specific area of interest. Beginning in the 1980s, communities and school districts have begun establishing tax-exempt foundations as a major means of raising donations from both individual and corporate sources. Parent organizations, such as the PTA, remain a popular service and fundraising mechanism.

State Participation

In 1986–87, $2.985 billion was appropriated by the general assembly for the operation of elementary and secondary education. Of this total, general state aid, the largest state funding program, amounted to $1.819 billion. General state aid is unrestricted aid provided to school districts to be used in meeting any legally authorized expense. Categorical aid programs were funded at approximately $546 million. Reform programs (i.e., new programs created through the "Education Reform Act," Public Act 84-126 et al. in 1985) received approximately $90 million in state funds. State funds provided for categorical aid programs and reform programs are related to the specific programs for which the funds were appropriated. An additional source of state resources for school districts is available through grants provided through the Capital Development Board for acquiring school sites, buildings, and equipment to meet the needs of school districts unable to provide such capital assets. In addition to school construction project grants, school districts can receive funds for capital planning assistance, debt service, and improvement of school grounds.

The primary sources of state revenue are the state income tax and the state sales tax, which in FY 1988 were $4.161 billion and $3.509 billion, respectively. Additional sources of state revenue for education include taxes on motor fuels, public utilities, tobacco products, alcoholic beverages, investment incomes, inheritances, estates, and hotels, in addition to collections from license fees, insurance taxes and fees, realty transfers, and the state lottery. Total state revenues for FY 88 were $9.103 billion.

State moneys for education are appropriated primarily from state general funds, made up primarily of the common school fund and the general revenue fund. Twenty-five percent of the state sales tax receipts not earmarked for other funds, lottery proceeds, and lottery investment income are earmarked for the common school fund. A portion of driver's license fees and fines is earmarked to support the driver education program. General state aid and teacher retirement systems are funded from the common school fund, while categorical programs are primarily funded through the general revenue fund. Generally, state moneys are obtained when a local public school district files a claim or an entitlement through a regional superintendent to the Illinois State Board of Education. Once the claim has been approved, the state superintendent of education submits a voucher to the state comptroller, who processes payment to the respective regional superintendent for the school district.

GENERAL STATE AID   General state aid in Illinois is designed to assure that school districts with less property wealth per pupil receive proportionately more financial support from the state. School districts receive general state aid based on one of three formulas. In practice, general state aid is calculated under each of the three formula options and districts receive the greatest of the three calculated amounts. Most school districts (over three-fourths of them) receive general state aid funds under the provisions of the special equalization formula. Under this formula, each district has access to a guaranteed wealth base as measured by the

equalized assessed value of real property and computed corporate personal property replacement assessed valuation per student. This guaranteed tax base is determined for each of the three district types (elementary, unit, and high-school) and is based on a per-pupil support level (frequently referred to as a foundation level), which is determined by the amount of the annual appropriation. A district's entitlement is computed by obtaining the product of the pupil count and the difference between the state guaranteed tax base per pupil and the district's tax base per pupil times the applicable calculation rate. Elementary districts with an operating tax rate at or above 1.28 percent have a formula calculation rate of 1.90 percent, unit districts taxing at or above 2.18 percent have a calculation rate of 2.76 percent, and high-school districts taxing at or above 1.10 percent have a calculation rate of 1.10 percent. An operating tax rate is a combination of rates districts tax in different fund categories to raise funds for the operation of schools.

Each district's entitlement is based in part on the number of pupils served. A district's pupil count, currently used by the state as the measure of district need, is based on average daily attendance and includes weightings, which are added values intended to reflect higher costs incurred in serving pupils with special needs. For example, students in grades K–6 have a weighting of 1.00, while students in grades 7–8 are weighted at 1.05, and students in grades 9–12 are weighted at 1.25. The pupil count also includes weightings for pupils from low-income families, with a maximum weighting of .625. The level of low-income weighting is based on the district's proportion of low-income students compared to the state-wide average proportion. In addition, districts are allowed to use the greater of the prior one-year attendance count or the prior three-year average upon which to claim general state aid. Of the 994 districts operating in FY 1987, 758 received general state aid under the special equalization formula.

A second formula, the alternate method, is applied to those districts whose property wealth per student is greater than or equal to 87 percent of the state guaranteed tax base for that type of district. These districts receive a maximum of 13 percent of the per-pupil support level described above. In FY 1987, 179 districts received general state aid based on the alternate formula calculations. School districts that do not qualify for general state aid under either of these distribution formulas, because their property wealth per student exceeds the state guaranteed tax base, are provided a flat grant of 7 percent of the per-pupil support level. Flat grant districts (57 in FY 1987) have relatively greater local property wealth than districts receiving general state aid under the special equalization or alternate formulas.

CATEGORICAL AID   Categorical aid differs from general state aid in both its emphasis and application. Categorical aid programs are used to distribute to public school districts and other local educational agencies (special education joint agreements, nonpublic schools, and so forth) specific state and federal funds to meet the needs of students. This funding process frequently accompanies mandates by the state that certain programs such as special education, school foods, and driver education can be established and provided in accordance with state and federal laws. Other categorical programs, such as adult education, are permissive in nature, that is, school districts are not required by law to provide the program for students served by the district.

There are more than four dozen mandates and permissive categorical funding programs. Categorical programs which were created as a part of the education reforms of 1985 included preschool education, reading improvement programs, truant/dropout optional education, summer school for gifted and remedial students, and educational service centers. In fiscal year 1987, appropriations totaled approximately $332 million for special education programs, approximately $101 million for regular and vocational transportation, $41.5 million for vocational education, and approximately $9 million for gifted education. The total reform program appropriations in FY 87 amounted to $88.3 million, with approximately $50.3 million going to preschool education and K–6 reading programs. The driver education program received $20.4 million.

Federal Participation

Federal funds for elementary and secondary education are, for the most part, appropriated by the general assembly and distributed to districts on a grant or reimbursement basis through the Illinois State Board of Education. (A small portion of federal funds is granted directly to school districts in limited categorical areas, e.g., impact aid, bilingual programs.) Federal funds are provided as categorical aid through approximately twelve granting programs, earmarked for specific purposes.

Federal support in Illinois public school districts was $464 million in FY 87, which, as noted earlier, amounted to slightly over 7 percent of the total revenues in Illinois for elementary and secondary education. Of this amount, $211 million was provided under the Education Consolidation and Improvement Act which included Chapter 1 (educationally disadvantaged— $190 million) and Chapter 2 (block grants—$20 million). Other major federal categorical support areas were school foods ($158 million), handicapped students ($58 million) and vocational education ($30 million). The federal government also provides support in areas such as civil rights, math/science, sex equity, adult education, and job training.

Administration

The local governing body of each school district in Illinois is the school board (board of education), which is the legal body through which the will of the people is translated into educational programs at the local level. A board of education is a legal entity separate and distinct from the municipality of government which includes the school district within its boundaries. In all Illinois school districts it is the board of education that operates the schools in accordance with statutory provisions enacted by the general assembly. In all school districts except those with a population over 500,000 (Chicago), the seven board members are elected; in Chicago an eleven-member board is appointed by the mayor.

Illinois school board elections are held on the first Tuesday after the first Monday in November of each odd-numbered year. Staggered four-year terms of members are structured so that three or four seats are contested at each biennial election. Each board of education is required to elect a president and a secretary, who serve terms of either one or two years, depending on local preference. The president must be a member of the board, but neither the secretary nor the treasurer is required to be a board member. The board president presides at meetings and, along with the secretary or treasurer, signs or acts on all contracts, orders, or agreements approved by the board. The secretary is required to keep full and accurate records of board proceedings, maintain records, official documents, and correspondence, and certify candidates and public policy issues (e.g., referenda, district boundary changes, and so on) to the election authority. In districts located in counties other than Cook County, the board must appoint a school treasurer. As the fiscal officer, the treasurer receives all moneys belonging to the district, makes payments in accordance with board orders, and maintains an accounting of all receipts and expenditures. Township school treasurers serve this function for school districts in Cook County.

Boards of education for public school districts in Illinois have extensive administrative duties, which are set forth in *The School Code* (Ill. Rev. Stat. 1987, ch. 122). School boards also have considerable discretionary powers that they exercise to carry out assigned duties. Perhaps the broadest duty school boards are required to fulfill is the mandate (article 10, paragraph 20.5 of *The School Code)* that they "adopt and enforce all necessary rules for the management and government of public schools of their district." Although many of the duties set forth in the statutes are quite specific as to the action to be taken within specified periods, the latter directive grants the school boards discretionary power to operate their districts. Many statutes establish general requirements, such as maintaining records, selecting textbooks, and determining the curriculum, but they allow school boards the discretion to implement these laws in various ways. The popular phrase "local control" arose, in part, from these facts.

Often state law specifies what school boards are required to do, but does not address how these functions are to be performed. For example, school boards are required to appoint teachers and set salaries, but, with few exceptions, the law is silent regarding required rates of pay, the number and types of teachers to employ, and so forth. Similarly, boards are required to direct "what branches of study shall be taught and what apparatus shall be used," but again, with few exceptions, state law does not fully specify what is to be taught in public schools. Thus, school boards have rather wide discretion in determining the full scope and depth of the educational delivery system for the population they serve.

School board responsibilities span all phases of the day-to-day operation of school districts. School boards are required to employ a superintendent, principal(s), other administrators, and teachers (who must hold certificates, issued by the state and appropriate to their positions), approve the school calendar, maintain records to substantiate claims for state aid and/or federal assistance, levy property taxes to provide the revenue necessary to maintain district schools, determine the textbooks to be used and the subjects and grade levels to be taught, designate attendance center (school) boundaries, and furnish each school with a flag and flag staff. School boards also have the authority to borrow money, build, repair, or improve school buildings, suspend or expel students, and dismiss teachers for certain causes. This listing, incomplete as it is, serves to illustrate the extensive authority and responsibility of local school boards.

The Role of the District Superintendent

As noted earlier, the district superintendent is hired by the local school board. Except for those districts with only one school and fewer than four teachers, state law requires districts to employ a superintendent to administer the schools under the discretion of the board of education or board of directors. District superintendents are responsible to their respective boards for managing the school district.

Some of the superintendent's administrative duties as chief executive officer are specified by law. These include making recommendations to the board regarding budget, building plans, selection of employees, textbooks, instructional materials, and courses of study. In addition, school boards typically perform their executive functions by adopting policies that delegate those functions to the superintendent. The superintendent generally serves as an ex-officio member of all committees of the board. In this capacity, the superintendent is expected to contribute to the board's deliberations by furnishing reports, information, and recommendations for action. Other duties include representing the school district before the public, informing staff and the public as to the activities, needs, and successes of the school district, and maintaining personnel, pupil, and fiscal records as prescribed by law and the policies of the board of education.

Principals, Teachers, and Other Staff

Schools having four or more teachers are required by law to be supervised by a principal. The principal, like all district staff, is hired by the school board based on the superintendent's recommendations. The principal is responsible for the planning, operation, and evaluation of a school's educational program. The principal is also required to make recommendations concerning the appointment, retention, promotion, and assignment of all personnel. Many districts employ one or more assistant principals. If a principal is absent because of extended illness or leave of absence, an assistant principal may be assigned to fulfill the principal's duties for up to sixty days. In the 1986–87 school year, a total of 4,204 principals and assistant principals were employed in Illinois public school districts.

Teachers are, of course, the centerpiece of the local educational system. In the 1986–87 school year, 104,609 teachers were employed in Illinois' public elementary and secondary schools. Of the total, 54,427 were elementary, 30,254 secondary, and 16,027 were special education teachers (teachers of handicapped students). Illinois ranks fifth among all states in the total instructional staff employed. State laws and regulations specify minimum qualifications for those who can legally be employed as teachers or administrators, but school boards have the authority to request additional levels of training and/or experience. With few exceptions, school boards also have the authority to determine the number of pupils each teacher is required to instruct. Pupil-teacher ratios are typically a function of board policy, fiscal resources, and collective bargaining. In the school year 1986–87, the average pupil-teacher ratio in elementary schools was 20.5 pupils per instructor; the average pupil-teacher ratio at the secondary level was 17.9 students for each teacher.

In addition to the school personnel already identified, the effective administration and delivery of school services requires contributions from many other classifications of employees. Depending on the population characteristics and wealth of the district, schools may employ guidance counselors, school nurses, librarians, social workers, psychologists, audiologists, diagnosticians, and others, all of whom must be certified by the state for employment in their respective classifications. Noncertified personnel, including cooks, custodians, bus drivers, secretaries, clerks, teachers aides, and others, provide a broad range of services required to operate a school district. In the 1986–87 school year, school districts employed a total of 63,284 noncertified personnel.

Role of the Federal Government

The responsibility for public education is primarily the concern of the states, but, like all other state activity, its exercise must be consistent with federal consitutional requirements as they apply to individual rights and state actions. Typically, the role of the federal government in public school operations is quite limited. However, there are two situations in which the federal government can exert extensive control. Operation of a school district must be in compliance with the United States Constitution. When federal courts determine that the constitutional rights and privileges of individuals have been violated as a result of school district operation, the federal government has the authority to require the district to make necessary changes in its operations to comply with the law. Attendance center enrollment patterns, courses of instruction, and textbook content are some of the operational concerns that are frequently scrutinized for possible violations of federal laws.

The federal government also determines the framework within which the districts must operate as a condition of receiving federal funds. The federal government's influence over districts' total operations is not pervasive since it is for the most part limited to the structure of the program it funds. Also, when participation in a program is optional, school districts that choose not to provide a federally funded program are not bound by its requirements. Approximately 5 percent of the funds for elementary and secondary education are provided by the federal government and are targeted for such programs as compensatory education, special education, food and nutrition, and vocational education.

Role of the State

As previously noted, the Illinois constitution of 1970 provides the basis for the state's role in public education. The constitution also established the State Board of Education and required the general assembly to determine its structure, duties, and powers. In response to these constitutional mandates, the general assembly has enacted a body of laws generally known as *The School Code*. Among other things, these laws provide for the creation of school districts and boards of education and set forth the broad structure within which they must operate. Included in *The School Code* are laws governing school finance, administrators' and teachers' qualifications, and their general duties and responsibilities, school board selection and governance procedures, certain educational program requirements and staffing patterns, school terms, instructional materials, regional superintendent duties and functions, and the structure, authority, and responsibilities of the State Board of Education.

It is important to recognize that although the general assembly has delegated considerable authority over the operation of local school districts, the state can withdraw or alter the powers granted to local districts at any time. All powers of school boards and administrative personnel at all levels, including the State Board of Education, which is a constitutional body, are delegated to them by the legislature. In tests of its governing authority, the courts have held that the general assembly has absolute power over education, subject only to limits established by the federal and state constitution. The state is constitutionally charged with providing "an efficient system of high-quality public education institutions and services." In response to this, the present school district system was put in place by the legislature, with day-to-day authority over school district operations entrusted to local boards of education.

The laws governing elementary and secondary education are changed in some ways each year, and periodically they are extensively revised to provide for reform of the educational system to produce better-educated citizens. The most current reforms were enacted in 1985. Generally, the "Year of Education" reforms focused on changing the state's emphasis from the inputs of schooling to outcomes for students. The emphasis of school operations was shifted from grades, classes, years, and courses to what students should know and be able to do as a result of their schooling.

The new laws established, among other things, that "the primary purpose of schooling is the transmission of knowledge and culture through which children learn in areas necessary to their continuing development." They further specified the fundamental learning areas to be language arts, mathematics, the biological, physical, and social sciences, fine arts, and physical development and health. The 169 components of the laws in the reform package addressed issues, programs, and personnel that have posed continuous challenges to public elementary and secondary education. Programs were enacted to help prevent truancy and dropouts and to provide special help to children at risk of academic failure through early childhood education programs, remedial programs, and bilingual educational services. The reforms also placed renewed emphasis on the preparation, recruitment, continuing support, and overall quality of teachers and administrators in the public school system. Additionally, eighteen educational service centers were created to help local districts more efficiently and effectively provide programs such as gifted education, computer education, and staff development training. The 1985 laws also more explicitly defined the state's expectation that students should have a full range of basic educational programs and services available to them. Toward that end, there were provisions in the reforms to encourage citizens to examine the structure of schools in their areas to determine if a different organizational structure could better serve the needs of their children.

The State Board of Education, whose seventeen members are appointed for six-year terms by the governor, with the advice and approval of the state senate, is mandated by the Illinois constitution to appoint a chief state education officer (the state superintendent of education). All other powers and duties of the State Board of Education are determined by the general assembly. The state board has the authority to determine the state superintendent's duties and responsibilities. The state board is responsible for educational policies and guidelines for public and private schools, preschool through grade 12, and vocational education. The state board, among other things, is responsible for providing educational leadership to school districts. The state board also assures that schools and school districts meet minimum statutory and regulatory standards for educational programs, personnel, business management practices, and student safety, to name only a few. The board distributes almost $3 billion in state and federal funds and provides various consultant and management services to school districts.

The state board annually gathers information from school districts and other governmental agencies regarding a very wide range of district operations. Based on information received from these sources, the state board submits a report on the condition of elementary and secondary education to the governor by 14 January of each year. The report contains information on education programs, numbers and kinds of school districts, number of attendance centers, personnel, enrollments, absences, local revenues, expenditures, tax rates, and many other aspects of school district operations. The state board uses this information, in addition to research conducted by staff, to recommend desirable modifications in the laws that affect schools.

The administrative structure of the state also features educational service regions. These fifty-seven administrative units are legally constituted units of school government between the State Board of Education and the local school district. The chief administrative officer of these governance units is a regional superintendent of schools, who is elected by the eligible voters in each educational service region (an educational service region typically serves more than one county). Superintendents assist local districts in several ways, including interpreting state laws and regulations, administering the General Educational Development (GED) program, maintaining official maps of school districts, supervising the work permit program for minors, overseeing bonding qualifications and performance of school treasurers, and establishing county- and district-level institutes for staff training. Other duties and services include enforcing standards for school construction and school health/life safety, processing reimbursement claim forms for such programs as the school lunch program, and approving all building plans.

A Typical School Year

Many people think of the school year as generally being the period from September to June when students are attending classes. However, a typical year in the life of a school district is actually a combination of years, that is, state and federal fiscal years, the calendar year, and the academic or school year.[2] The overlapping years create a somewhat confusing array of planning, dissemination, and reporting deadlines. For example, although a district's school year may officially begin on 1 July, most of its budget and program decisions will have been made several months earlier, because state law requires school districts to make most personnel-related decisions at least sixty days prior to the end of the school year. Because the state's appropriations process for elementary and secondary education is not completed until 30 June or later, and because of potential delays in property assessments, tax extensions, and collections, local district staffing and other budget decisions must be based only on estimates of state, local, and federal funding. This necessity tends to ensure that a school district's year usually gets off to a rather uncertain fiscal start.

A district's typical year is a maze of overlapping activities, many of which are prescribed by law, some of which are in response to actions taken in previous years, and a number of which are required to deal with issues that arise somewhat unexpectedly. Districts must annually develop and implement a budget, elect officers and organize the school board (biennially in some districts), establish attendance zones for the school district, develop and approve the annual school calendar, conduct labor relations and staff planning, and make textbook selections and curriculum determinations. To some extent, many of these activities receive almost daily attention from one or more of the district's personnel. A district's budget, for example, is actually the work of many people. Teachers make lists of materials and supplies they will need for the coming year. Principals collect, review, and

2. The state's fiscal year is from 1 July through 30 June; the federal fiscal year is from 1 October through 30 September; the calendar year is from 1 January through 30 December; and the school year is generally as indicated above (Sept–June). For reasons of law and local practice, a school district may be using any combination of these "years" in its operations.

amend these requests and submit them to the district superintendent. The superintendent and his or her staff (which, depending on the size and wealth of the district, could include a business manager, statisticians, clerks, accountants, and curriculum specialists) analyze student characteristics and other data for the purpose of predicting both short-term and long-range student enrollment. A new textbook series or changes in laboratory, shop, or library facilities also require planning and research. Toward the end of eventual replacement, maintenance supervisors periodically assess the operating conditions of school buses, as well as heating, cooling, and other equipment. Legislation which could have an impact upon the district's budget or operations must also be analyzed and monitored during the regular legislative session, the veto override session, and any special sessions that may be called by the governor. All of these activities and numerous others are blended into a tentative recommended budget that the district superintendent submits to the school board for consideration.

To a great extent, the budget reflects the district's values and goals and certainly dictates the scope and depth of educational services to be offered. Most, if not all, activities in a school district are directly related to the district's budget. Meeting state programmatic, administrative, and reporting requirements, satisfying school board pupil-teacher ratio decisions, and negotiating and implementing labor contracts are some of the obvious cost-related activities. Many other activities, including changes in course offerings, athletic programs, facilities and their maintenance and use, district boundaries, property values, tax rates, enrollments, attendance averages, student discipline policies, and liability coverages also can have a dramatic impact upon the district's budget and thereby the quality of education offered in the district.

Fortunately, most of a school district's activities occur annually, and therefore, they can be planned, scheduled, and carried out by school boards and district personnel. However, not all situations or activities lend themselves to a convenient schedule. For example, when facilities suffer damage or are lost because of fires, natural disasters, or vandalism, when litigation is initiated by or brought against the district, or personnel problems such as strikes erupt, they must be dealt with immediately. Activities of this nature tend to be disruptive of district operations and may require changes in curriculum, the school calendar, or site attendance patterns.

One school year in Illinois represents the extension of prior years of legislative, managerial, administrative, and education decision making at the local, state, and national levels. Actions taken during the school year may also affect legislative, managerial, administrative, and educational decision making for a number of years into the future (see appendix 8-1).

Date	Activity	Date	Activity
June 30	Last day of fiscal year.		of schools in the township.
	First installment of property taxes due.	July 31	On this date, federal and state income tax withholding reports must be filed and taxes paid for quarter ending June 30.
	Last day for action by general assembly during regular legislative session requiring only simple majority to pass bills.		
	Effective date of the annual school audit.	August 1	Last day for filing with educational service region superintendent a list of unfilled teaching positions in the district (lists to be updated monthly).
	Last date for filing with the educational service region superintendent state aid claims based on the average daily attendance of the current year.	August 15	School boards required to submit report of funds withheld and make payment of money owed to the teachers retirement system.
July 1	First day of state and local school district fiscal year.	August 20	First day of teacher/staff attendance.
	Clerk or secretary of school board shall report to the educational service region superintendent the names and addresses of students who left school during previous attendance quarter (due on first "school day" of July).	August 23	First day of pupil attendance.
		August 31	Final date for public hearing on tentative school district budget for current fiscal year.
July 10	District claims for reimbursement of allowable costs of transporting students for the prior year are due with regional superintendent of schools.		Final date for educational service region superintendent to file with the state superintendent of education an affidavit showing which treasurers of the school districts are properly bonded.
July 15	Claim for general state aid for the coming school and fiscal year is due with the State Board of Education.	September 15	Second installment of property taxes due.
		September 30	Last date for school district fiscal year budget adoption.
	Final date for submitting to educational service region superintendent a statement of condition for the past year		Last day of the federal fiscal year.
		October 1	First day of new federal fiscal year.

Clerk or secretary of board shall report to the educational service region superintendent the names and addresses of students who left school during the previous quarter (due on first school day in October).

October 15   School districts submit audited report of district finances to educational service region superintendent.

October 31   Last date for filing quarterly federal and state income tax reports and paying taxes due.

November 2–8   General election day; occurs on the first Tuesday following the first Monday of November. (In odd-numbered years, the election is known as the nonpartisan election in which school board members, school trustees, directors of school boards of directors, county boards of school trustees, and boards of school inspectors are elected.)

November 9–15   Within seven days following election of directors or board members, officers must be selected and the time and place of regular meetings established.

November 15   Regional superintendent submits audited reports of district finances to state board.

November 30   First day on which a member of the general assembly can prefile a bill.

Final date for publishing in the appropriate area newspaper the school district's annual fiscal statement.

December 1–15   State board conducts public hearings regarding the state board's budget recommendations for the next fiscal year.

December 25–31   Certificates of tax levy are due at the county clerk's office on or before the last Tuesday in December, reflecting the amounts needed to finance the budget adopted September 30. Tax anticipation warrants may be issued in anticipation of taxes to be received from levy.

January   State Board of Education submits elementary and secondary education state funding recommendations to the governor and general assembly. Although no date is specified by law, by practice the state board submits budget requests by late January for the next fiscal year.

January 2   Final date for school board's clerk or secretary to report to the educational service region superintendent the students who left the district in the previous quarter (due first school day in January).

January 2–31   School district personnel begin development of tentative school district budget for the next fiscal year.

January 8–14   General assembly annually convenes on the second Wednesday of January.

January 31   Final date for filing quarterly federal and state income tax reports and paying taxes due.

February 1   List of tenured personnel in seniority order by position must be established and submitted to employee representative.

February 22–28 (29)   Consolidated primary election (held on last Tuesday of

Date	Activity	Date	Activity
	February in odd-numbered years).	April 1	Notify district superintendents and principals having three-year contracts of nonrenewal of contract (ninety days prior to end of fiscal year).
March 1–7	The governor submits budget recommendations to general assembly (by first Wednesday in March).		Final date for school board's clerk or secretary to report to the educational service region superintendent the students who left the district in the previous quarter (due first school day in April).
March 15–21	General primary election (held third Tuesday in March in even-numbered years).		
March 29	District's tentative budget developed.		
March 30	Notify tenured teachers and principals on one-year contracts of nonrenewal of contracts for coming school year (sixty days prior to end of school term).	April 1–7	Consolidated election (first Tuesday in April in odd-numbered years).
		April 30	Final date for filing quarterly federal and state income tax reports and paying taxes due.
March 31	Educational service region superintendent to complete inspection of all schools in the region.	May 1	Statement of economic interests due with county clerk.

Bibliography

Burrup, Percy B. *Financing Education in Climate of Change.* Boston: Allyn and Bacon, 1977.

Cubberly, Ellwood P. *School Funds and Their Apportionment.* New York: Teachers College, Columbia University, 1906, 1915.

Doyle, Don Harrison. *The Social Order of a Frontier Community.* Urbana: University of Illinois Press, 1978.

Garms, Walter I., James W. Guthrie, and Lawrence C. Pierce. *School Finance: The Economics and Politics of Public Education.* Englewood Cliffs, NJ: Prentice-Hall, 1978.

Garvey, Neil F. *The Government and Administration of Illinois.* New York: Thomas Y. Crowell, 1958.

Illinois Department of Revenue. *The Illinois Property Tax System.* Springfield: State of Illinois, 1983.

Illinois Economic and Fiscal Commission. *Revenue Estimate and Economic Outlook FY 1988.* Springfield: State of Illinois, 1987.

Illinois State Board of Education. *Proposed Budget Fiscal Year 1988.* Springfield: State of Illinois, 1987.

Illinois State Board of Education. *State, Local, and Federal Financing for Illinois Public Schools, 1986–1987.* Springfield: State of Illinois, 1987.

Mace, William H. *A School History of the United States.* Chicago: Rand-McNally, 1918.

Mort, Paul R., Walter C. Reusser, and John W. Polley. *Public School Finance: Its Background, Structure, and Operation.* New York: McGraw-Hill, 1960.

National Education Association. *Report of the Committee of Ten on Secondary School Studies.* New York: American Book Company, 1894.

Pease, Theordore Calvin. *The Story of Illinois.* Chicago: University of Chicago Press, 1965.

Peterson, Leroy J., Richard A. Rossmiller, and Marlrin M. Volz. *The Law and Public School Operation.* New York: Harper and Row, 1969.

Sheppard, Victor H. *A Brief History of the Office of Public Instruction, State of Illinois.* Springfield: State of Illinois, 1957.

State of Illinois. *Biennial Reports of Superintendent of Public Instruction.* Springfield: State of Illinois, 1864–1970.

State of Illinois. *Constitution of the State of Illinois.* Springfield: State of Illinois, 1970.

State of Illinois. *Illinois Revised Statutes.* St. Paul: West Publishing, 1987.

Weber, Oscar F. *Problems of School Organization and Finance.* Urbana: University of Illinois, 1938.

9.

Special Districts

TED FLICKINGER AND PETER M. MURPHY

Park Districts

Illinois has long been noted for its large number of diverse units of local government. These local governments were spawned by Illinois's 1870 constitution, which set debt limitations upon municipal forms of government. The spread of "special districts" resulted from the need to deliver specialized services (for a summary chart of independent and quasi-independent special districts, see appendix 9-1). One of the most predominant of these special districts is the park district. Illinois's prowess in the delivery of local park and recreation services has been recognized nationwide. It is the direct result of having an individual unit of local government responsible for all park, recreation, and open space management within a particular community or within a combination of communities.

The first park districts in Illinois were formed in 1869 when the general assembly enacted legislation that created three park districts in the city of Chicago as units of local government separate from the city government. In 1934, the individual park districts located within the city were merged into what is now known as the Chicago Park District. Legislation to permit the formation of a park district outside of Chicago was enacted in 1893. Since that time, numerous laws relating to the development of park and recreation programs have been enacted and, in 1951, were codified into the *Park District Code* (Ill. Rev. Stat., ch. 105, par. 1-1 et seq. For a summary of special district provisions, see appendix 9-2). There are now more than 332 park districts in Illinois covering a total of 152,000 acres of land. Total agency budgets exceed $676 million, with user fees collectively generating $111.2 million. There are more than 603 local park sites in Illinois, and

151

these agencies employ more than seven thousand full-time, fourteen thousand part-time, and thirteen thousand seasonal employees. Park districts have general taxing and bonding authority, and provide for their corporate and recreational tax levies (see appendix 9-3 for a detailed breakdown of park district and other special district taxation powers).

The charge of Illinois park districts is to preserve natural resources and open spaces, as well as to provide opportunities for the public to participate in structured recreational programs and sport activities. Facilities and activities offered in these parks include indoor and outdoor swimming pools, field houses, gymnasiums, beaches, skating rinks, conservatories, golf courses, tennis courts, museums, aquariums, arts and crafts classes, dance classes, exercise classes, baseball and softball diamonds, preschool programs, senior citizen activities and trips, ski areas, trails for biking and hiking, zoos, botanical gardens, and a host of fine arts activities. A general survey of park districts has produced findings that show a variety of recreational facilities and areas: tennis courts (2,140), softball fields (1,398), and baseball fields (1,287). Eleven park districts have zoos, 14 have conservatories, 26 operate equestrian trails, and 91 have nine-and eighteen-hole golf courses. There are 33 performing art centers, 40 tree nurseries, 44 health/fitness centers, 60 nature centers, 58 arts/crafts centers, and 226 swimming pools. Five parks operate airports. In addition, many park districts operate facilities through intergovernmental agreements with municipalities, schools, and libraries. The list is endless and ever-evolving as Illinoisans look to new and innovative opportunities to meet their growing recreational and leisure time needs.

A park district is created through referendum initiated locally by citizens of a defined area. State statutory authority creating park districts as corporate entities recognizes them as separate and distinct units of local government. Park district boundaries are independent from those of other units of local government and often incorporate more than one community. Most park districts are governed by a five-member board; however, seven-member boards are optional. Park district commissioners are unique in that they receive no compensation, serving typically a six-year term of office. They maintain a close kinship with the community and thus are readily able to respond to community needs and desires. This directness does not come readily in a layered bureaucracy. Park boards keep democracy green at the roots.

There really is not a typical park district in the state in terms of size, staff, programs, or budgets. However, each and every one of these agencies shares the common bond and mission of meeting the recreational needs of the public in Illinois, improving the quality of life and contributing substantially to state and local economies. Local merchants benefit substantially from the sales of recreation and sports equipment and clothing apparel. The state gains valuable revenue from sales taxes on purchased recreational merchandise.

Profile of a Park District: Naperville

Special district status is important, Naperville park director Glen Ekey believes. Historically, park and recreation departments within city or county government tended to take a back seat to streets, police, fire, utilities, and other "mandatory" services when the time came to set or cut budgets and hire qualified personnel. "The advantage to the park district form of government," says Ekey, "is that we can concentrate on our major objectives without having to compete with other city or county departments."

Naperville Park District was approved by city-wide referendum in 1967, after which the city began a gradual process of turning over park facilities to the new district. As executive director, Ekey handles day-to-day administration of the district and reports to the five-member policy-making board of commissioners.

The park district generates 60 percent of its revenues from local property taxes. Due to Naperville's tremendous growth, and the resulting increase in the local property tax base, the park district's tax levy has actually dropped in the 1980s, from a high of forty-five cents per $100 assessed valuation to its current thirty-one cents. User fees and concession sales make up the other 40 percent of total annual revenues, which, Ekey estimates, amounted to $5.8 million in 1986.

The park district also owes much credit for its growth to Naperville's city government. The council passed a land donation ordinance in 1972 which soon became a model for community development legislation nationwide. The ordinance requires that real estate developers donate land—or the cash to buy land—for schools and parks in proportion to the size of proposed residential developments. This ordinance assures that school and park land acquisition will keep pace with the city's development. At the time, some citizens were concerned that the ordinance would drive developers away from Naperville, and they challenged the city's ordinance in court. But it has survived legal tests all the way to the U.S. Supreme Court. The "Naperville Ordinance," as it became popularly known, later served as a blueprint for other cities struggling to keep school and recreation services in step with residential development. This ordinance is the main reason why the Naperville Park District has been able to grow so quickly. Judging by recent census figures, the land donation ordinance probably enhanced rather than harmed the city's development efforts. The city recognized that as a community grows, it not only needs more firemen and police, but also more pools and parks to handle all the people. Developers have found that where they provide those facilities, their properties become more valuable and sell faster.

Despite the doubling of park acreage and near-doubling of the number of parks since 1980, the district's full-time staff has remained constant at thirty-three members. Gaps between manpower and demand are made up, in part, through greater use of part-time employees and the purchase of larger mowers and other more efficient maintenance equipment. Cooperation is also integral to a long-range planning effort currently underway between the Naperville Park District, a community hospital, the two school districts, and a local small college. Together the five agencies are studying how to fund, locate, and build an indoor swimming pool that would best serve the community.

A similar common-sense approach to development pervades the park district's plans to build a second eighteen-hole golf course. "We've been looking at building a second course," Ekey says, "but then we started talking with consultants and developers and found that at least two private developers are looking to build public courses in the area. We said, 'Great, if they can do it, we'll back off.' So we've gone into hibernation for a year to 96give these people an opportunity to get plans made and begin construction. If they don't, then we're going to have to take a look and see if we should go ahead with a second course."

In recent years, the park district has also cooperated with other recreation providers in the city. For example, the district and the local YMCA have combined two marginal summer day camp programs into one successful program. Also, rather than build extensive facilities, the park district offers tennis and racquetball lessons through local racquet and health clubs. "We don't feel the park district has to be all things to all people," Ekey continues. "Even though we're a separate agency, I don't think we can function efficiently without exploring cooperative ventures with other community organizations, the city, and the school districts. We try and go with the best use of resources. As a public agency, we want to be a complement to the private sector. I think by working together, not fighting, we can accomplish the main objective—providing a variety of quality recreation services."

Naperville Park District facilities offer an intriguing blend of the traditional and the unusual. In addition to the golf course, a pro shop and gymnasiums, the district oversees forty playgrounds, thirty athletic fields, seven outdoor ice rinks, seven tennis courts, four outdoor basketball courts, two volleyball areas and two fitness trails. Two of the largest park district facilities are in the center of downtown Naperville. The first, Centennial Beach, qualifies as "the most unusual recreation facility I've ever dealt with in the twenty-some years I've been in the business," says Ekey. At its heart is the fifty-year-old Centennial Beach facility, a limestone quarry. Naperville residents enjoy a 7.5 acre beach-front area complete with a paddle boat marina, rafts, playgrounds, volleyball areas, a sand beach, and a 6.5 million gallon pool for swimming and diving. Centennial Beach improvements are funded from rental fees and concession sales. The facility, in fact, generates a modest revenue surplus each year, with attendance ranging as high as 235,000 in the hottest summer seasons.

Another uncommon development, Riverwalk, is a brick walkway stretching a mile along the banks of the DuPage River, through a once-blighted section of downtown. Picnic shelters, benches, fishing spots, and period lighting complement the picturesque walkway, which has rejuvenated retail development in the downtown area. A citizens' group originated Riverwalk, then later gave it as a gift to the city on its 150th anniversary. To date, more than $3 million has been invested in the Riverwalk development. Ekey says that the project will eventually stretch four to five miles, linking the Centennial Beach facility on one end with a soon-to-be developed five-hundred acre park called Knoch Knolls, situated at the confluence of the east and west branches of the DuPage River. "Frankly, Riverwalk has injected a lot of vitality into downtown that didn't exist before," says Ekey. "Our downtown area was at best a typical small-town downtown. It has made a complete turnaround."

Special Recreation Associations

With the current demand to provide services for all groups and all populations, Illinois, through its legislative process, permits units of local government to join together and create special recreation associations. Illinois continues to be recognized as the national leader in the development of such special recreation program delivery systems for the mentally and physically handicapped citizens of our state. The special recreation associations also provide services to residents of nursing homes, participants and clients of sheltered care workshops, and to community-based special populations. In addition, these associations provide tremendous assistance to many local school districts in their delivery of special education programs. In 1968, Illinois, through the efforts of the Chicago Park District and the Joseph P. Kennedy, Jr., Foundation, hosted the first ever Special Olympics competition at Soldier Field. From that national event, Illinois can boast participation by special athletes in local, area, regional, and state programs in the tens of thousands.

Forest Preserve Districts

The initial legislation authorizing the creation of forest preserve districts passed the Illinois General Assembly in 1913 (Ill. Rev. Stat., ch. 96 ½, par. 6301 et seq.). Under this law, a forest preserve district may be organized and established by referendum whenever any area of contiguous territory lying wholly within a single county contains one or more natural forests, one or more cities, towns, or villages, and at least five hundred voters. A forest preserve district is separate and distinct from any other governmental entity. It is comprised of land within one county and cannot extend beyond the boundaries of that particular county. Thirteen counties in Illinois currently have forest preserve districts: Champaign, Cook, DeKalb, DuPage, Kane, Kankakee, Kendall, Lake, Ogle, Piatt, Rock Island, Will, and Winnebago. Forest preserve districts protect natural areas totaling over 114,000 acres of Illinois land.

Power and authority are granted to forest preserve districts in three main areas: conservation, education, and recreation. The governing authority is the county board with a term of four years. The size of the board can vary from eight to twenty-nine members as set by ordinance. Districts are authorized to acquire land in order to fulfill their mandate to protect and preserve natural resources and the flora and fauna within the forest areas. Forest preserves are outdoor recreation and resource management agencies. Their services, which focus on public awareness and appreciation of natural resources, include nature trails, environmental education centers, interpretive programs, and unstructured recreational activities such as hiking and camping.

When the county and forest preserve district boundaries are coterminous, the entire county board functions as a board of commissioners for the forest preserve district. The commissioners may receive a per diem for their services related to the forest preserve district not to exceed $36 per day for each day worked. They serve a five-year term and many receive as an alternative to a per diem an annual salary of up to $3,000 a year. When a forest preserve district includes only part of a county, the board of commissioners has five members, who are appointed by the county board chairman with the advice and consent of the county board.

Conservation Districts

In 1963, the Illinois General Assembly passed the Conservation District Act (Ill. Rev. Stat., ch. 96½, par. 7101 et seq.), which enables counties either individually or collectively (up to five counties) to establish, by referendum, conservation districts. Currently, there are five conservation districts in Illinois in the counties of Boone, Macon, McHenry, Putnam, and Vermilion. Collectively, they cover approximately eighteen thousand acres of land.

Counties with less than one million population that already have a forest preserve district cannot establish conservation districts. Since suburban and collar counties in the Chicago area established forest preserve districts in 1913, they have not been able to qualify for conservation districts. Therefore, conservation has been created to a greater degree in more rural areas of the state. The functions and purpose of the two types of districts are very similar. The primary purposes of a conservation district is to acquire, develop, and maintain open spaces for public recreational use in a manner that will ensure the preservation of forests, flora, fauna, and other natural resources. Recreational areas and activities include fishing, boating, camping, nature and hiking trails, beaches, swimming and other facilities and areas. Nature and interpretive centers, nurseries, and horticultural areas are available for those interested in conservation and environmental education.

A conservation district is governed by a board of five trustees, who serve five-year terms. They are appointed by the county board chairman with the consent of the county board. The trustees serve without compensation. The board of trustees may levy property taxes up to .10 percent (10 cents per $100 of assessed valuation), broken down as follows: (1) Up to .025 percent (2½ cents per $100 of assessed valuation) for general corporate purposes, including land acquisition and development. This may accumulate from year to year to no more than .075 percent of the assessed valuation of the district. (2) Up to .075 percent (7½ cents per $100 of assessed valuation) for land acquisition. This may also be used for land development, and for general purposes with approval of the Illinois Department of Conservation. The revenue may accumulate from year to year to no more than .25 percent of the assessed valuation of the district.

A conservation district may issue bonds for land acquisition without a referendum and for land development with a referendum. Bonded indebtedness may not exceed .575 percent of the assessed value of taxable property in the district. A district may also accept gifts, grants, bequests, contributions, and appropriations of money and other personal property to be used to further the purposes of the conservation district.

Soil and Water Conservation Districts

Illinois has ninety-eight soil and water conservation districts generally set up on county boundary lines. These units of government are responsible for helping people plan and care for their natural resources. The State Water Quality Management Plan assigned districts the primary responsibility for reducing sediment pollution. Districts develop rapport and working partnerships with land operators through resource information and education, technical assistance, incentives, recognition, and evaluation based on mutually developed goals.

Districts work cooperatively with many other conservation agencies to achieve their objectives, but primary support comes from the Illinois Department of Agriculture and the U.S. Department of Agriculture, with the Soil Conservation Service providing technical assistance. The Agricultural Stabilization and Conservation Service provides farmer incentives, and the Cooperative Extension Service develops educational programs. District employees provide technical assistance, informational programs, and demonstrations.

District directors are direct links to the most important part of the system—land operators. Since districts do not have taxing authority, directors are frequently searching out funds. As in other states, districts have organized themselves into councils and a state association, which helps develop a consensus on regional and state conservation issues. The association emphasizes an action program of assisting soil and water conservation districts to develop local watershed projects. More than thirty local watershed projects with a variety of funding mechanisms are now operating. Many projects have local funds. A state watershed selection committee reviews projects for possible applications of state or federal funds. All projects are geared to meet the soil erosion standards in specific watersheds above affected waterbodies. The districts' arrangements with numerous agencies and organizations are complex, but in Illinois the soil erosion control standards help to unite the conservation family and give it direction and a measurable goal. Soil and water conservation districts have significantly improved water quality and reduced sediment through targeting lake watersheds.

Soil on the Move

One person sized up the soil erosion problem with this suggestion: "Tag your soil with radioactive material. Then, when you quit farming take a Geiger counter, go down to Louisiana, identify your soil and retire on it." A ludicrous suggestion? Of course. Nevertheless, it points out the problem of "traveling soil"—eroding soil. Soil erosion is a natural process, but when it gets out of hand, it scrapes away the most productive soils. Much of the soil winds up in the bottom of streams and lakes; or as the anecdote about traveling soil notes, it can drift down south. According to estimates, 40 percent of Illinois agricultural land is suffering from excessive erosion. In all, an estimated average of 180 million tons of soil erode in Illinois every year and roughly 160 million tons come from agricultural land (see also appendix 9-4).

Illinois has developed a program for bringing erosion under control. It is a step-by-step plan with the ultimate goal of "T by 2000." Essentially, this means that by the year 2000, all farmland in Illinois should meet what is known as the soil-loss tolerance level, or the T value. When erosion exceeds the T value, soil is being lost so fast that its natural productivity is being diminished.

The state's step-by-step plan consists of a series of erosion-control guidelines adopted in 1980 by the Illinois Department of Agriculture. The ninety-eight soil and water conservation districts in Illinois used these guidelines to establish erosion-control standards in their respective areas. Each district had to develop standards that were at least as stringent as the guidelines, which are listed below.

1. By 1 January 1983, soil loss on all farmland cannot exceed 4 to 20 tons of soil loss per acre annually, depending on the soil type. Four to 20 tons equals four times the T value.

2. By 1 January 1988, soil loss cannot exceed 2 to 10 tons per acres per year (2T). However, for land where conservation tillage is enough to solve the problem and the slope is less then 5 percent, the goal is to reduce soil loss to the T value (1 to 5 tons per acre annually).

3. By 1 January 1994, soil loss on all farmland cannot exceed 1½ to 7½ tons per acres annually (1½T).

4. By 1 January of the year 2000, erosion cannot exceed the T value on all Illinois farmland.

During 1981 and 1982, the ninety-eight districts set local erosion-control standards. Sixteen of them opted for more stringent standards than the state's guidelines. These standards went into effect on 1 January 1983.

Fire Protection Districts

Illinois has a complex system of local government organization to provide fire protection. There are more than 1,280 municipalities and more than 701 fire protection districts in Illinois. About 625 of the municipalities have one thousand or fewer residents, and many of those small communities are in fire protection districts. A substantial number of fire protection districts contract with medium-sized or large municipalities or other fire protection districts for service. The fire protection districts are almost evenly divided between urban (SMSA) and rural (non-SMSA) counties. There remain substantial areas in most rural sections of the state which are not covered by fire districts or other jurisdictions with fire protection; three rural counties are without fire districts entirely.

Adding to the complexity of the pattern, some townships provide fire protection or contribute to the support of municipal or district departments in the township. A few county governments cooperate with fire departments in the county in matters of fire safety, code enforcement, fire communications, and public fire safety education. Counties have authority to provide fire protection to an unincorporated area of a township under contract with the town board.

Finally, there are a substantial number of volunteer fire departments which are freestanding; they are not governmental agencies, but are organized as private associations, or as not-for-profit corporations under state law. Altogether, there are approximately 1,300 fire departments operating, mostly with the support of Illinois's network of local taxing bodies. Over forty-three thousand Illinois citizens, mostly volunteers, serve in these fire departments and make the system work.

Official Powers and Responsibilities

The Fire Protection District Act, enacted by the general assembly in 1927, is found in chapter 127½ of the Illinois Revised Statutes. The purpose of districts established under the act is the acquisition, establishment, maintenance, and operation of fire stations, facilities, vehicles, apparatus, and equipment for the prevention and control of fire, protection from fire of persons and property within the districts, and regulation for the prevention and control of fire. Districts have only the powers which are granted by state law. Those powers set the scope and nature of the district's responsibility. The board of trustees of fire protection districts is the corporate authority of the district. It exercises all the powers and controls all the affairs and property of the districts (par. 26). The basic power and duty of the district as exercised by the board of trustees is set out in paragraph 31.

> The board of trustees of any fire protection district incorporated under this Act has the power and it is its legal duty and obligation to provide as nearly

adequate protection from fire for all persons and property within the said district as possible and to prescribe necessary regulations for the prevention and control of fire therein. Consistent with this duty, the board of trustees may provide and maintain life-saving rescue equipment, services and facilities.

Further authority is given to fire protection districts by chapter 127½, according to which a district

1. may borrow money for corporate purposes and issue bonds to an amount not to exceed 5.75 percent, on the value of property as determined by the last assessment for county taxes previous to the incurring of such indebtedness (par. 32);

2. may provide emergency ambulance service, combine with other units of government to do so, or subsidize or contract for the service, upon referendum approval of a proposal to provide the service and levy a tax not to exceed .30 percent (30 cents per $100 of assessed valuation, par. 38.5);

3. may acquire private property by gift, lease, purchase, condemnation, or otherwise within the boundaries and for one mile beyond the district boundaries (par. 30);

4. may adopt and enforce ordinances to protect sources of water supply (par. 30);

5. may build houses for the care of fire-fighting equipment (par. 30);

6. must provide fire protection for public school buildings situated outside the district in accordance with section 16-19 of the *School Code* (par. 31c);

7. may, through its firemen, enter lands of any person, firm, private or municipal corporation, or the state while engaged in preventing or extinguishing fires and shall not be civilly or criminally liable for entering such property.

Library Districts

Created by the general assembly in 1965 (Ill. Rev. Stat. 1987, ch. 81, par. 1-1 et seq.), library districts are a totally independent governmental unit, with autonomous taxing powers and the power to pass their own ordinances. The advantage of library district status is that its boundaries are self-determined at the time of creation and can be enlarged through annexation. Library district borders do not have to be tied to historical or political boundaries.

Creation

A library district can be formed in one of two ways: by creation or conversion of an existing local library. One of the instances in which district libraries may be created is in territories where there are no local tax-supported libraries. In this case, the first step is for one hundred or more voters of the territory to petition the circuit court for creation. District libraries may also be created by municipal, township, or county libraries that have adjacent territory without a local tax-supported library. In this case, either the library board or one hundred or more voters in the municipality, township, or county having the library may petition for creation.

Trustees

The governing body of a district library is called the library board of trustees. They are nominated by a petition signed by fifty voters in the district; the elections are nonpartisan and the winners serve without compensation (but they are reimbursed for their expenses). From their own ranks, the members of the board of trustees elect a president, secretary, treasurer, and another officer, if they wish. The officers serve two-year terms. Generally, as with library directors, their main responsibilities concern all aspects, especially financial, of running and maintaining a library. The board of trustees must meet at least five times a year with a quorum of four members present. A simple majority rules.

Types of Libraries

Municipal Libraries. City and village libraries occupy an unusual position in Illinois local government law. They are independent for most purposes, particularly village libraries, which have an independently elected board. (City library boards are appointed.) They have a catalog of independent powers, including the power to sue and be sued (which by law implies the power to employ an attorney; ch. 81, par. 4-7). However, their tax levies are formally passed by the "corporate authority," the city or village, "in the amounts determined by the (library) board" (ch. 81, par. 3-5). There is a similar provision for approval by the corporate authorities dealing with building bonds and tax anticipation warrants.

The result is a library board with virtually complete independence, but with an unresolved potential for conflict if the corporate authorities do not follow the statute in levying taxes in amounts determined by the library board. City and village libraries are coterminous in their boundaries with the boundary of the municipality. Of the 617 public libraries in Illinois, more than 50 percent are municipal libraries.

Township Libraries. Township libraries are similar in organization to municipal libraries and have the same semi-independence, with powers of taxation shared with corporate authorities. They have the advantage of a fairly large geographical area, but have the disadvantage that annexation by municipal libraries or districts into the township generally results in disconnection of the tax base from the township library. In Illinois there are 104 township libraries.

District Libraries. District libraries are totally independent special taxing units, comparable to school districts, park districts, fire protection districts, sanitary districts, and the like. They may annex surrounding territory by ordinance or referendum. This unlimited annexation ability and a generally high degree of independence have made the district library an increasingly popular legal form. Although only 187 of the libraries in Illinois are district libraries, the number is increasing more rapidly than other forms.

Appendix 9-1

Basic Powers and Taxing Authority of Illinois's Independent and Quasi-Independent Special Districts

Sources: This appendix was prepared from the data contained in *Special Districts in Illinois, Volume I—An Inventory of Special Districts: Powers and Numbers in Existence.* The information in all but the column "Number in Existence" was taken from the Illinois Revised Statutes 1977, the 1977 Supplement to the Illinois Revised Statutes, and certain public acts from the 1978 session of the 80th general assembly. The information in the column "Number in Existence" was drawn from a number of sources, primarily the *Illinois Property Tax Statistics 1975* published by the Department of Local Governmental Affairs and *Statewide Summary of Special District Finance 1975,* published by the state comptroller's offices. Other sources were used for districts which do not levy property taxes, including U.S. census data, state government agency listings, and telephone surveys.

Basic Community Services

Name	Purpose & Powers	Formation	Governing Body	Property Tax Authorization	General Obligation Bond Authorization	Revenue Bond Authorization	¹Dissolution/ ²Consolidation	¹Annexation/ ²Disconnection	Number in Existence 1965	Number in Existence 1975
Fire Protection Districts	To provide for the prevention and control of fires, provide ambulance service.	Contiguous territory in 1 to 5 counties, by referendum. District cannot divide a municipality.	3 member appointed board. Compensation limit varies from $750/yr to $1,500/yr; with 50% more if district maintains ambulance service.	Yes. Corporate rate of .125%, no referendum. Increase to .30% by backdoor referendum. Increase to .40% by referendum. A special tax up to .30% for ambulance by referendum.	Yes. Debt limit of 5% of assessed valuation. Referendum required.	No statutory provision.	1) By resolution or court order (initiated by petition of a municipality) only in cases where a municipality annexes all of a district and takes over its function. 2) By referendum.	1) By referendum and ordinance or by petition and ordinance. 2) By referendum or by court order.	676	785

Public Library Districts	To establish and operate public libraries.	Territory in one or more counties by referendum.	7 member elected board. If district is in more than one county, may change to appointment by referendum. Reimbursement for expenses.	Yes. Corporate limit of .15% unless a higher rate is specified on ballot in referendum creating the district. May increase to .40% by referendum.	Yes. No debt limit. Referendum required.	No statutory provision.	1) By referendum. 2) By ordinance or referendum.	1) By ordinance or referendum. 2) By ordinance or referendum. Automatic disconnection if territory within a district is annexed to a municipality that maintains a public library.	25 97
Local Libraries (semi-autonomous)	To establish and operate public libraries.	Boundaries coterminous with municipality, by ordinance in cities and by referendum in villages, towns, and townships.	Number of members varies. Elected in villages & townships. Appointed in cities. Selection of members' lengths of term varies. No compensation provided.	Yes. In cities under 500,000 pop. Corporate limit of .15% without referendum, unless a higher rate is specified on ballot in referendum creating the district. May increase to .40% by referendum. In cities over 500,000 pop. Corporate limit of .12% without referendum. *Additional tax levies available. *Limits for libraries in home rule units now being contested in the courts.	Yes. Limited to cost of the project. Referendum and approval of corporate authorities required.	No statutory provision.	1) No statutory provisions. However, the powers of the board are suspended while territory is included in a library district. 2) When 2 or more municipalities or townships merge, the libraries also merge.	1) No statutory provision. 2) No statutory provision.	456 476

Basic Community Services *continued*

Name	Purpose & Powers	Formation	Governing Body	Property Tax Authorization	General Obligation Bond Authorization	Revenue Bond Authorization	¹Dissolution/²Consolidation	¹Annexation/²Disconnection	Number in Existence 1965	1975
Housing Authorities	To investigate and make recommendations in relation to housing needs.	Municipalities with over 10,000 people, or county (1 to 5), by petition initiated by governing body, voters or DCCA (Dept. of Commerce and Community Affairs) and DCCA approval.	5 member board, appointed by presiding officers of initiating government unit(s). 5 yr. term. Reimbursement for expenses.	No statutory provision.	No statutory provision.	Yes. No debt limit. No referendum required. Financial undertakings must be approved by local government affairs.	1) Resolution of the board and governing body of the service area, and approval of DCCA. 2) No statutory provisions.	1) No statutory provision. 2) No statutory provision.	110	97
Land Clearance Commissions	To redevelop and improve community areas.	Municipalities with over 25,000 people, or county, with no dept. of urban renewal, by resolution of government unit and approval of DCCA.	5 member board, appointed by municipality or county, with DCCA approval. 5 yr term. Reimbursement of expenses.	No. But the municipality can levy in an amount sufficient to retire G.O. bonds.	No. But the municipality may, by referendum.	Yes. No referendum required.	1) Automatic when municipality establishes a dept. of urban renewal. 2) No statutory provision.	1) No statutory provision. 2) No statutory provision.	5	4
Public Building Commissions	To construct public buildings for lease to government units.	Counties or county seats by resolution. A municipality over 3,000 which is not a county seat by referendum initiated by corporate authorities.	Number of members varies. Appointed 5 year terms. Reimbursement for expenses.	No. But governmental leasee can levy a tax in an amount sufficient to pay the lease, no referendum required.	No statutory provision.	Yes. No referendum required.	1) No statutory provisions on annexation at the initiative of the PBC. However, other units of government may join by resolution. 2) No statutory provision.	1) No statutory provision. 2) No statutory provision	?	30

Recreation and Civic Activities and Facilities

District	Purpose	Formation	Governing Board	Taxing Power	Debt		Dissolution	Creation		
Street Light Districts	To provide street lighting services.	Any area not within a municipality, by referendum.	3 member board appointed by presiding officer of county board(s). Compensation limit of $300/yr.	Yes. Corporate limit of .125% without referendum. 1.00% with referendum.	Yes. No debt limit. Rate limit of .075% included in corporate rate limit.	No statutory provision.	1) No statutory provision. 2) No statutory provision.	1) By referendum. 2) By petition of voters and judicial decision; or automatic by annexation to a municipality providing services.	21	22
Cemetery Maintenance Districts	To maintain public cemeteries.	Territory within a single county, by referendum.	3 member appointed board. Compensation limit of $50/yr.	Yes. Corporate limit of .06%. No referendum required.	No statutory provision.	No statutory provision.	1) No statutory provision. 2) No statutory provision.	1) No statutory provision. 2) No statutory provision.	7	20
Park Districts of less than 500,000 inhabitants	To build and maintain parks and other facilities.	Connected territory under 500,000 inhabitants, by referendum.	General Parks: 5 member elected board, but may change to 7 by referendum or resolution. Township Parks: 3 member elected. All: 6 yr. terms but may change to 4 by referendum or resolution. No compensation provided.	Yes. Corporate limit of 10%. No referendum required. Additional .05% by referendum. Additional taxes available by referendum.	Yes. Debt limit of 2.5% of assessed valuation. May be increased to 5% by referendum. Issuance requires referendum if debt exceeds .5%.	Yes. Variety of authorizations, usually subject to backdoor referendum.	1) By petition of 2/3 of voters and referendum; or by petition and court order. 2) By ordinance of commissioners of each district in proposition.	1) By petition and ordinance; by petition and referendum; or by ordinance alone. 2) By petition and ordinance, by petition and court order, or by referendum.	216	311

Recreation and Civic Activities and Facilities *continued*

Name	Purpose & Powers	Formation	Governing Body	Property Tax Authorization	General Obligation Bond Authorization	Revenue Bond Authorization	¹Dissolution/ ²Consolidation	¹Annexation/ ²Disconnection	Number in Existence	
									1965	1975
Chicago Park District	To build and maintain parks and other facilities.	Former park districts within, and partially within, Chicago in 1933, by statute.	5 member board, appointed by mayor of Chicago. 5 yr. terms. No compensation provided.	Yes. Corporate limit of .60%. No referendum required. Additional .09% for aquariums & museums. No referendum required.	Yes. 2% debt limit of assessed valuation. Referendum required if issuance raises total debt over .75%.	Yes. No debt limit. No referendum required.	1) No statutory provision. 2) No statutory provision.	1) No statutory provision. 2) No statutory provision.	1	1
Downstate Civic Centers (7 acts creating 9 civic center authorities). (Aurora, Decatur, Danville, Peoria, Rockford, Springfield, Bloomington, Waukegan, Joliet)	To provide facilities and activities for civic functions and events, including office space in some cases.	By statute. Boundaries usually co-extensive with city boundaries.	Appointed board except for Springfield. Reimbursement for expenses and secretary and treasurer may receive compensation.	Only for retirement of G.O. bonds except for Springfield and Peoria which have a corporate rate of .05%. Peoria needs referendum to levy.	Yes. Generally no debt limit and referendum is required. Some have limit on tax levied to retire bond.	Yes. No debt limit and no referendum requirements.	1) No statutory provision. 2) No statutory provision.	1) No statutory provision. 2) No statutory provision.	1	9

Metropolitan Fair & Exposition Auth. (McCormick Place)	To provide facilities and activities for public entertainment.	By statute, boundaries coextensive with corporate boundaries of Cook county.	14 member appointed board. Reimbursement for expenses. Secretary and treasurer may receive compensation.	No statutory provision.	Yes. No referendum required.	1) No statutory provision. 2) No statutory provision.	1) No statutory provision. 2) No statutory provision.	1	1
Metropolitan Exposition, auditorium & office building authorities. (General Authorization)	To provide facilities and activities for civic functions and events including public office buildings.	Any county or counties having an assessed valuation of at least $300 million but less than $5 billion, by ordinance or resolution.	9 member appointed board. Reimbursement for expenses. The secretary and treasurer may receive compensation.	No authorization for corporate purposes. Authorized to levy tax sufficient to retire G.O. bonds, with a rate limit of .0005%.	Yes. Authorities under 300,000 population have a debt limit of 2½% of assessed valuation. Referendum required.	Yes. No referendum required.	1) No statutory provision. 2) No statutory provision.	1) No statutory provision. 2) No statutory provision.	0	0
Exhibition Councils	To provide facilities and activities for public entertainment.	Counties between 100,000 and 500,000 and cities between 80,000 and 500,000 by resolution or ordinance.	6 member appointed board. No compensation provided.	No authorization for corporate purposes. Authorized to levy tax at a sufficient rate to retire G.O. bonds.	Yes. No debt limit. Referendum required.	Yes. No referendum required.	1) No statutory provision. 2) No statutory provision.	1) No statutory provision. 2) No statutory provision.	0	2

Transportation

Airport Authorities	To establish and operate public airports and facilities.	Territory with at least 5,000 inhabitants, with at least one municipality and no public airport, by referendum.	Number of board members varies. Appointed. Compensation limit varies from $150/mo. to $10,000/yr.	Yes. Corporate limit of .075%. Referendum required if original rate is less than .075 and the board wants an increase to that maximum.	Yes. Debt limit of 2% of assessed valuation. Referendum required if bonds exceed .75% of assessed valuation.	Yes. No referendum required.	1) By ordinance, subject to backdoor referendum. 2) No statutory provision.	1) By referendum and ordinance; or by petition and ordinance. 2) Petition and court order.	26	27

Transportation *continued*

Name	Purpose & Powers	Formation	Governing Body	Property Tax Authorization	General Obligation Bond Authorization	Revenue Bond Authorization	¹Dissolution/ ²Consolidation	¹Annexation/ ²Disconnection	Number in Existence 1965	Number in Existence 1975
Port Districts (13 separate acts) (Chicago, Joliet, Waukegan, Tri-City, Seneca, Shawneetown, Southwest, Kaskaskia, Havana, Mt. Carmel, White County, Illinois Valley, & Jackson-Union County)	Generally, to establish and operate terminals, port facilities and airports.	By statute, boundaries statutorily defined.	Appointed board, numbers of members and lengths of terms vary. Reimbursement for expenses. The secretary and treasurer may receive compensation.	Chicago regional port district cannot levy taxes. All others have a corporate limit of .05%. Referendum required.	Chicago Regional, Illinois Valley Regional, and White County Port Districts cannot issue G.O. bonds. The others can, with no debt limit and a referendum required.	Yes. No debt limit and no referendum required.	1) No statutory provision. 2) No statutory provision.	1) No provisions for Chicago, Kaskaskia, Havanna, White County, & Illinois Valley Districts. In others: by referendum or, if no voters reside in proposed territory, by unanimous petition and court order. 2) No statutory provision.	7	13

	Purpose	Boundaries	Board	Revenue	Debt Authority				
Urban Transportation Districts	To establish and operate public transportation systems.	Contiguous territory within a single municipality, by resolution and referendum.	5 member appointed board. Compensation is $10,000/yr. Reimbursement for expenses.	Yes. Corporate limit of .10%. No referendum required.	No statutory provision.	1) No statutory provision. 2) No statutory provision.	1) No statutory provision. 2) No statutory provision.	0	0
Local Mass Transit Districts	To establish and operate public transportation systems.	One or more municipalities or counties or combination thereof. By resolution, participating districts, recognizing no county or municipal boundaries, by referendum.	Number of board members varies. Appointed. Compensation limit of $25/day ($100/mo. limit) and reimbursement of expenses.	Yes. District formed prior to 1967: .05% w/o referendum; .25% with referendum. Districts formed after 1967: .25% with referendum or by organizing election.	No statutory provision.	1) By resolution of board and municipality or county which created it. 2) No statutory provision.	1) By petition and ordinance of the board; or by ordinance of the county or municipality and approval of the board. 2) Same as 1) above.	0	6
Regional Transit Authority (RTA)	To control and support public transportion.	Collar counties, by statute, with acceptance by referendum.	9 member appointed board. 5 yr. terms. Compensation for members except chairman is $200/day, limit of $25,000/yr. Chairman's salary by ordinance.	No statutory provision. Available revenue includes retail motor fuel sales tax (5% limit) and motor vehicle parking tax (no limit).	Yes. Debt limit of $500,000,000. No referendum required. (Paid from any revenues).	1) No statutory provision. 2) No statutory provision.	1) By referendum and ordinance. 2) No statutory provision.	0	1'
Metropolitan Transit Authority (CTA)	To acquire, construct, and operate a transportation system.	Boundaries statutorily defined, by statute, with acceptance by referendum.	7 member appointed board. 7 yr. terms. Compensation set by ordinance. Maximum for chairman is $25,000/yr. if otherwise employed.	No statutory provision.	Yes. No referendum required.	1) No statutory provision. 2) No statutory provision.	1) Municipalities within statutorily defined boundaries, by ordinance and referendum. 2) No statutory provision.	1	1

Transportation *continued*

Name	Purpose & Powers	Formation	Governing Body	Property Tax Authorization	General Obligation Bond Authorization	Revenue Bond Authorization	¹Dissolution/ ²Consolidation	¹Annexation/ ²Disconnection	Number in Existence	
									1965	1975
Interstate Bridge Commissions	To construct and operate bridges and approaches.	Created by statute, boundaries statutorily defined.	10 member board (5 from each state) appointed by respective states, terms fixed by legislature. No provision for compensation.	No statutory provision.	No statutory provision.	Yes. No debt limit. No referendum required.	1) No statutory provision. 2) No statutory provision.	1) No statutory provision. 2) No statutory provision.	3	3
Railroad Terminal Authorities	To rebuild and redevelop railroad terminal areas.	By resolution of the city council of any city.	7 member board, appointed by mayor. 6 yr. term. $100/day (max. $5,000/yr.) plus expenses.	No statutory provision.	No statutory provision.	Yes. No debt limit. No referendum required.	1) No statutory provision. 2) No statutory provision.	1) No statutory provision. 2) No statutory provision.	0	0
Capital City Railroad Relocation Authority	To relocate railroad tracks from central area of Springfield.	By statute, boundaries coterminous with capital, Springfield, and Woodside townships.	10 member board. 6 appointed by governor, 3 by city council, 1 by county board. 3 yr. terms. Reimbursement for expenses. Secretary and treasurer may receive compensation.	No statutory provision.	No statutory provision.	Yes. No debt limit. No referendum required.	1) No statutory provision. 2) No statutory provision.	1) No statutory provision. 2) No statutory provision.	0	1

Bi-State Development Agency	To coordinate with Missouri in the operation of transportation facilities.	Bi-State (3 Illinois counties) by statute and interstate compact.	10 member board (5 from each state) appointed by respective governors. 5 yr terms. No provision for compensation.	No statutory provision.	Yes. No debt limit, no referendum required.	1) No statutory provision. 2) No statutory provision.	1) No statutory provision. 2) No statutory provision.	1	1
St. Louis Metropolitan Airport Authority	To coordinate development and construction of airports in the greater St. Louis area.	5 Illinois counties by statute.	5 member board appointed by the governor.	No statutory provision.	Yes. No debt limit, it, no referendum required.	1) No statutory provision. 2) No statutory provision.	1) No statutory provision. 2) No statutory provision.	0	1
Interstate Airport Authority	To construct airports in cooperation with adjoining states.	Cities, counties, or airport authorities of adjoining states, by legislative resolution.	Number of board members set by enabling legislation, appointed by respective governors. No provision for compensation.	No statutory provision.	Yes. No debt limit, it, no referendum required.	1) No statutory provision. 2) No statutory provision.	1) No statutory provision. 2) No statutory provision.	0	0

Health

Public Health Districts	To enforce regulations pertaining to preservation of health.	Any township in a county under township organization or road district in a county not under township organization, with minimum of 75,000 inhabitants, by referendum.	Board made up of officers of member units. No compensation provided.	Yes. Corporate rate limit of .10%, subject to backdoor referendum.	Yes. No limit, by referendum.	No statutory provision.	1) No statutory provision. 2) No statutory provision.	1) A township or road district by referendum. 2) No statutory provision.	5	7

Health *continued*

Name	Purpose & Powers	Formation	Governing Body	Property Tax Authorization	General Obligation Bond Authorization	Revenue Bond Authorization	¹Dissolution/ ²Consolidation	¹Annexation/ ²Disconnection	Number in Existence 1965	Number in Existence 1975
Hospital Districts	To establish and operate public hospitals.	Contiguous territory in one or more counties under 1 million. May not divide municipalities. By referendum.	9 member appointed board. No compensation provided.	Yes. Corporate limit of .075%. No referendum required.	Yes. 5% debt limit of assessed valuation. No rate limit. Referendum if debt limit will exceed 1.5%.	Yes. No debt limit, no referendum required.	1) By ordinance and backdoor referendum. 2) No statutory provision.	1) By referendum. 2) By petition of at least 50% of voters in proposed territory, within 60 days of creation, and referendum.	24	26
Tuberculosis Sanitarium Districts Act of 1937	To provide services for persons afflicted with tuberculosis and other pulmonary diseases.	Any territory lying within one county but outside a municipality which has adopted a tuberculosis tax, by referendum.	Appointed board. In districts of 500,000 or more, there are 5 members. In districts of less than 500,000, there are 3 members. No compensation provided.	Yes. Corporate limit of .075%. No referendum required.	Yes. Debt limit of 5% of assessed valuation. No rate limit, except rate is included within corporate property tax rate. Referendum required if for purpose other than buying land.	No statutory provision.	1) No statutory provision. 2) No statutory provision.	1) No statutory provision. 2) No statutory provision.	2	2
Act of 1939	Same as Act of 1937	Any 2 or more contiguous counties, by referendum.	7 member elected board. Compensation limit of $2,500/yr., and reimbursement for expenses.	Yes. Corporate limit of .25%. No referendum required.	Same as Act of 1937.	No statutory provision.	1) No statutory provision. 2) No statutory provision.	1) No statutory provision. 2) No statutory provision.		

District	Purpose	Composition	Taxing Authority	Bonding Authority		Creation	Dissolution		
Mosquito Abatement Districts	To exterminate mosquitoes and other insects.	Contiguous territory with at least 300 inhabitants, by referendum.	5 member appointed board. No compensation provided.	Yes. Corporate limit of .025%. No referendum required.	No statutory authority.	No statutory authority.	1) By referendum or resolution of the county board. 2) No statutory provision.	1) Board may accept petition, subject to backdoor referendum, or may submit to direct referendum. 2) By court order or resolution of the county board.	18	20
Medical Center District	To operate hospitals or other medical facilities.	A specific area within Chicago, by statute.	7 member appointed board. No provisions for compensation.	No statutory authority.	Yes. No debt limit. No referendum required.	No statutory authority.	1) No statutory provision. 2) No statutory provision.	1) No statutory provision. 2) No statutory provision.	1	1

Sanitation

District	Purpose	Composition	Taxing Authority	Bonding Authority		Creation	Dissolution		
Urban Sanitary Districts— Act of 1917	To provide drainage and sewage disposal.	Contiguous territory containing all or parts of one or more municipalities and area within 6 miles of a municipality. By referendum.	3 or 5 member appointed board. 3 yr. terms. Compensation limit of $3,000 a yr.	Yes. Corporate limit of .083% or limit in effect on 8-2-65, whichever is greater. Additional .083% by referendum. May roll back increase by referendum.	Yes. Debt limit of 5% of assessed valuation. No rate limit. Referendum required, unless acting under EPA (Environmental Protection Agency) orders.	Yes. By petition and referendum, or backdoor referendum, unless acting under EPA order.	1) No statutory provision. 2) No statutory provision.	1) By referendum and ordinance; by ordinance and court order; or by ordinance alone. 2) By referendum and ordinance.	128	159
Rural Sanitary Districts— Act of 1936	To provide drainage and sewage disposal.	Contiguous territory in a single county and outside any municipality, by referendum.	3 member appointed board. By referendum, may change method of selection to election. 3 yr. terms. Compensation limit of $3,000/yr.	Yes. Corporate limit of .25% or rate in effect on 8/4/65, whichever is greater. May increase to .50% by referendum. Increase may be rolled back by referendum.	Yes. Debt limit of 5% of assessed valuation. No rate limit. Referendum required unless acting under EPA order.	Yes. By petition and referendum; or by backdoor referendum, unless acting under EPA order.	1) By referendum. 2) No statutory provision.	1) By referendum and ordinance; by ordinance and court order; or by ordinance alone. 2) By referendum and ordinance.	(Act of 1917) and (Act of 1936)	

Sanitation *continued*

Name	Purpose & Powers	Formation	Governing Body	Property Tax Authorization	General Obligation Bond Authorization	Revenue Bond Authorization	¹Dissolution/ ²Consolidation	¹Annexation/ ²Disconnection	Number in Existence 1965	Number in Existence 1975
Chicago Metropolitan Sanitary District	To provide drainage and sewage disposal.	By statute, boundaries statutorily defined.	9 member elected board. 6 yr. terms. Max. salaries of following: Pres. — $32,500/yr. Vice pres. — $30,000/yr. Finance chrmn. — $27,500/yr. Others — $25,000/yr.	Yes. Corporate Limit of .46%. Special tax, with a limit of .260%. No referendum required.	Yes. Debt limit of 5% of assessed valuation. For corporate purposes. Referendum required. Debt limit of 3% for special purposes. No referendum required.	Yes. No referendum required.	1) No statutory provision. 2) No statutory provision.	1) By statute. 2) By petition and court order.	1	1
Sanitary District 1907 Act. (East Side Levee)	To provide drainage and sewage disposal.	Any contiguous territory within two counties. Having at least 2 municipalities, and a population of at least 3,500, by referendum.	5 member elected board. Compensation limit of $2,000/yr. for president, $1,000/yr. for others.	Yes. Corporate limit of .20% or the rate in effect on 7/1/67, whichever is greater. No referendum required.	Yes. Debt limit of 5%. No rate limit. Referendum required.	No statutory provisions.	1) Districts with $100,000,000 valuation or more may dissolve & reorganize under "Metro-east Sanitary District Act of 1974"; by referendum. 2) No statutory provision.	1) Territory being served by ordinance. 2) No statutory provision.	1	1

District	Purpose	Formation	Governing Board	Corporate Tax	Debt		Dissolution	Creation		
North Shore Sanitary District Act — Act of 1911	To provide drainage and sewage disposal.	Contiguous area within a single county, having at least 2 municipalities, which procure water from Lake Michigan, by referendum.	5 member elected board. Compensation limit of $7,500 a year for president, $5,000 for others.	Yes. Corporate limit of .083% or rate limit in effect on 8/2/65, whichever is greater. Can go to .35% by referendum.	Yes. Debt limit of 5% of assessed valuation. No rate limit: referendum required.	Yes. Subject to backdoor referendum, unless acting under EPA order.	1) No statutory provision. 2) No statutory provision.	1) By petition, election and ordinance; by petition and ordinance, or by ordinance alone. 2) Under certain conditions, by referendum and ordinance.	1	1
Metro-East Sanitary District	To provide drainage and sewage disposal.	Districts created under 1907 act may dissolve and form under this act by referendum.	5 member board, appointed by county boards. Per diem pay, rate set by county boards.	Yes. Corporate limit of .20%, or the limit in effect on 7/1/67, whichever is greater. No referendum required.	Yes. debt limit of 5% of assessed valuation. No rate limit. Referendum required.	No statutory provision.	1) No statutory provision. 2) No statutory provision.	1) No statutory provision. 2) No statutory provision.	0	0
Solid Waste Disposal Districts	To collect solid waste and to establish facilities for disposal, treatment or conversion of such.	1 to 5 adjoining counties (excluding Cook) or 1 to 5 adjoining townships, by referendum. Multi-unit districts must have EPA approval.	5 member appointed board. Reimbursement for expenses.	Yes. Corporate limit of .05%. No referendum required.	Yes. Debt limit of .5% of assessed valuation. Referendum required. Rate included in corporate tax rate.	Yes. No referendum required.	1) No statutory provision. 2) No statutory provision.	1) No statutory provision. 2) No statutory provision.	0	0

Drainage and Resource Conservation

District	Purpose	Formation	Governing Board	Corporate Tax	Debt		Dissolution	Creation		
Drainage Districts	To construct or repair drains or levees.	Land in the same natural drainage area by petition and court order; by referendum; by user; or by mutual agreement.	3 member board. Methods of selection differ. Compensation limit of $20/day and reimbursement of expenses.	No statutory provision, however, annual maintenance assessments based on benefits received may be levied.	Yes. Debt limit of 90% of amount of assessment, but may go higher with court approval. No referendum required.	No statutory provision.	1) By petition (initiated by either landowners or commission) and court order if special conditions are met. 2) By referendum.	1) By petition (initiated by either landowners or commission) and court order. 2) Petition and court order.	?	814 (Active) 1,500 (Total)

Drainage and Resource Conservation *continued*

Name	Purpose & Powers	Formation	Governing Body	Property Tax Authorization	General Obligation Bond Authorization	Revenue Bond Authorization	¹Dissolution/ ²Consolidation	¹Annexation/ ²Disconnection	Number in Existence	
									1965	1975
Surface Water Protection Districts	To provide for the collection, conveyance and disposal of surface water.	Contiguous territory in one or two counties by referendum or by unanimous consent of all landowners.	5 member appointed board. 5 yr. terms. Compensation limit of $250/yr.	Yes. Corporate limit of .125%. May be increased to .25% by referendum. No referendum required if formed by unanimous consent and all agree.	Yes. Debt limit of 5% of assessed valuation. No rate limit. Referendum required unless district formed by unanimous consent.	No statutory provision.	1) No statutory provision. 2) No statutory provision.	1) By referendum. 2) By petition and court order.	6	7
River Conservancy Districts	To provide for river and flood control, irrigation, conservation and recreation.	Area need not be contiguous. By referendum.	Appointed board. Number of members varies (at least 5). 5 year terms. Compensation limit of $3,000/yr.	Yes. Corporate limit of .083%. May be increased by referendum to .75% in smaller districts, and to .375% in larger districts. Increases may be rolled back by referendum.	Yes. Debt limit of 5% of assessed valuation. No rate limit. Referendum required.	Yes. No debt limit, subject to backdoor referendum.	1) No statutory provision. 2) No statutory provision.	1) By referendum and ordinance. 2) No statutory provision.	9	13
Soil & Water Conservation Districts	To develop plans for the control and conservation of soil and water resources.	25 or more landowners, by petition, approval of the Illinois Dept. of Agriculture, and Election.	5 member elected board. Upon petition of governing body, the Dept. of Agriculture may authorize elections to be held at board meeting rather than at general election. 2 yr. terms. Compensation of $20/day plus expenses.	No statutory provision.	No statutory provision.	No statutory provision.	1) By petition of landowners, referendum and dept. approval. 2) By petition of landowners, referendum, and dept. approval.	1) By petition, dept. approval and referendum; no referendum required under some circumstances. 2) No statutory provision.	?	98

	Purpose	Territory/Boundaries	Board	Corporate Tax	Debt		Creation	Dissolution		
Soil & Water Conservation Sub-districts	To execute projects for the control and conservation of soil and water resources.	Contiguous territory in the same watershed by petition to the parent district and referendum.	5 member elected board. 3 yr. terms. Compensation of $20/day.	Yes. Corporate rate of .125%.	Yes. No debt limit. Tax is included in corporate rate limit.	No statutory provision.	1) Petition of majority or landowners.		1	4
Forest Preserve Districts in counties of less than 3 million	To create forest preserves and develop various recreational facilities.	Contiguous territory within a single county, having a natural forest, and containing one or more municipalities, by referendum.	When boundaries are coextensive with municipality or county, the corporate authorities constitute the board. Otherwise, 5 member appointed board. $36/day compensation, 15¢ mile for travel.	Yes. Corporate limit of .025% without referendum. May be raised to .06% with backdoor referendum. Provisions exist for special purpose taxation.	Yes. Debt limit of 2% of assessed valuation. No rate limit. Referendum required for bonds issued for acquisition of lands in excess of a total 55,000 acres.	Yes. In districts of 100,000 or more inhabitants, may be issued for acquisition, operation and development of recreational facilities. No referendum required.	1) No statutory provision. 2) No statutory provision.	1) By referendum initiated by petition. 2) No statutory provision.	9	9
Forest Preserve Districts of 3 million or more (Cook County Forest Preserve Dist.)	To create forest preserves and develop various recreational facilities.	Area within a single county of 3,000,000 or more by referendum.	The county board constitutes the forest district board. No compensation provided.	Yes. Corporate limit of .06% without referendum. Provisions exist for special purpose taxation.	Yes. Debt limit of .3% of assessed valuation. No rate limit. Referendum required for bonds issued for acquisition of lands in excess of 75,000 acres.	Yes. Can be issued for development, acquisition and operation of recreational facilities. Referendum required.	1) No statutory provision. 2) No statutory provision.	1) By referendum initiated by petition. 2) No statutory provision.	1	1
Conservation Districts	To acquire and manage wildlands.	Contiguous territory, boundaries coextensive with boundaries of 1 to 5 counties, by referendum. Multi-county districts need Dept. of Conservation approval.	5 member appointed board. No compensation, but allows reimbursement for expenses.	Yes. Corporate limit of .1%. District limits for individual purposes. No referendum required.	Yes. Debt limit of .5% of assessed valuation. No rate limit. Referendum required unless bonds are for purchase of real property.	Yes. Referendum required.	1) By referendum initiated by petition. 2) No statutory provision.	1) No statutory provision. 2) No statutory provision.	1	5

Water Supply

Name	Purpose & Powers	Formation	Governing Body	Property Tax Authorization	General Obligation Bond Authorization	Revenue Bond Authorization	¹Dissolution/ ²Consolidation	¹Annexation/ ²Disconnection	Number in Existence 1965	1975
Water Commissions & Water/Sewer Commissions	To operate a water supply and waterworks system. Also sewer system in certain cases.	By vote of boards of member municipalities. Boundaries coterminous with member municipalities.	Appointed board of varying size. Appointed by member municipalities and county board or circuit court judge.	No statutory provision.	No statutory provision.	Yes. No debt limit. No referendum.	1) No statutory provision. 2) No statutory provision.	1) Other municipalities can join under certain circumstances. 2) No statutory provision.	?	16 Water Comm. 2 Water/Sewer Comm.
Public Water Districts	To obtain and distribute water, and to provide for waterworks and sewerage properties.	Contiguous area with not more than 500,000 residents, by referendum.	7 member appointed board. May reduce to 5 or 3 members by resolution and court order. Compensation limit varies from $600 to $1200/yr.	Yes. Corporate limit of .02%, referendum required. Levy limited to 10 years.	No statutory provision.	Yes. For special purposes, no referendum required.	1) By referendum initiated by ⅔ of board members, or under certain conditions, initiated by voters. 2) No statutory provision.	1) By petition (initiated by ⅔ of voters) and ordinance. 2) Under certain conditions, by petition and court order.	?	37
Water Authorities	To regulate use of water and wells.	Contiguous territory, by referendum.	Appointed, but may change to election by referendum. Number of members varies. Compensation limit of $500/yr.	Yes. Corporate limit of .08%. No referendum required.	Yes. No debt limit. No rate limit. Referendum required.	Yes. No referendum required.	1) No statutory provision. 2) No statutory provision.	1) By petition and court order. 2) By petition and court order.	1	1
Water Service Districts	To distribute water.	Area not within a municipality, by referendum.	3 member appointed board. Compensation limit of $50/yr.	Yes. Corporate limit of .125%. No referendum required.	Yes. Debt limit of 5% .075% rate limit, included in corporate rate. Referendum required.	No statutory provision.	1) No statutory provision. 2) No statutory provision.	1) By petition, validated by court order. 2) Under certain condition, by petition and court order.	?	16

Appendix 9-2
Illinois Revised Statutes: Provisions Relating to Special Districts

---

1. Cemetery Maintenance District—Ch. 21, sect. 64.24a et seq.
2. Child Protection District—Ch. 23, sect. 2162 to 2177.
3. Conservation District—Ch. 57½, sect. 101 to 117.
4. Consolidated Township Road District—Ch. 121, sect. 6-1.
5. County Tuberculosis Sanitarium District—Ch. 34, sect. 5216.
6. Drainage District—Ch. 42, sect. 3-1 to 3-31.
7. Fire Protection District—Ch. 127½, sect. 21 to 38.
8. Forest Preserve District—Ch. 57½, sect. 1 to 15a4.
9. Hospital District—Ch. 23, sect. 1251 to 1273.
10. Local Mass Transit District—Ch. 111⅔, sect. 351 et seq.
11. Mosquito Abatement District—Ch. 111½, sect. 74 to 85b.
12. Park District—Ch. 105, sect. 1-1 to 13-9e.
13. Public Health District—Ch. 111½, sect. 1 to 20.4.
14. Public Library District—Ch. 81, sect. 1001-1 to 1008-2.
15. Public Water District—Ch. 111⅔, sect. 188 to 212.9.
16. River Conservancy District—Ch. 42, sect. 383 to 410.
17. Sanitary Drainage and Sewage Disposal District (two or more counties having two or more municipalities)—Ch. 42, sect. 247 to 298a.
18. Sanitary and Sewage Disposal District (one or more municipalities)—Ch. 42, sect. 298.99 to 319i.
19. Sanitary District (area of less than 500,000 population)—Ch. 42, sect. 319.1 to 319.22.
20. Sanitary District (county area outside municipalities)—Ch. 42, sect. 411.99 to 447.2.
21. Soil and Water Conservation District—Ch. 5, sect. 106 to 138.2.
22. Street Lighting District—Ch. 121, sect. 355 to 364.1.
23. Surface Water Protection District—Ch. 42, sect. 448 to 471.
24. Tuberculosis Sanitarium District—Ch. 23, sect. 1701 to 1714.
25. Water Service District—Ch. 111⅔, sect. 213 to 222.1.
26. Water Authority—Ch. 111⅔, sect. 223 to 250.

Other Units
1. Exhibition Council—Ch. 85, sect. 1201 to 1215.
2. Housing Authority—Ch. 67½, sect. 1 to 27e.
3. Land Clearance Commission—Ch. 67½, sect. 63 to 91.

4. Municipal Airport Authority—Ch. 15½, sect. 68.1 to 68.20.
5. Public Building Commission—Ch. 85, sect. 1031 to 1054.
6. Railroad Terminal Authority—Ch. 114, sect. 361 to 389.

Miscellaneous Entities

1. Capital City Planning Commission—Ch. 123, sect. 21 to 39.
2. Northeastern Illinois Planning Commission—Ch. 85, sect. 1101 to 1139.
3. Southwestern Illinois Metropolitan Area Planning Commission—Ch. 85, sect. 1151 to 1189.

In addition to the tax rates on the following pages, many special districts may levy taxes for the purposes set forth below. The cited statutory provisions should be examined to determine their applicability to a specific type of district.

Audit	.005% (.5¢ per $100 of assessed valuation).	Ch. 85, par. 701 & 709
IMRF	No rate limit. Levy not to exceed amount appropriated for municipal contributions to the retirement system.	Ch. 108½, par. 7-105 par. 7-171
Lease from Public Building Commission	No rate limit. An amount sufficient to pay the annual rental.	Ch. 85, par. 1048
Social Security	No rate limit. Levy sufficient to meet the cost of participation.	Ch. 108½, par. 21-108
Tort Judgments General, and Liability Insurance	No rate limit. Amount sufficient to pay insurance premiums, for participation in a joint self insurance association payment of tort judgments or settlements and for creating a reserve.	Ch. 85, par. 9-107
Unemployment Insurance	No rate limit. Amount sufficient to pay insurance for employees' protection under the Unemployment Insurance Act.	Ch. 85, par. 9-107
Workers' Compensation & Occupational Disease Claims	No rate limit. Amount sufficient to pay judgments and settlements or to otherwise provide protection under the Workers' Compensation & Occupational Diseases Acts.	Ch. 85, par. 9-107

Bonds & Interests

Tort Judgments, Settlements or Reserve	No rate limit. Bonds for payment of outstanding tort judgments, settlements, or for creating a reserve.	Ch. 85, par. 9-105 par. 9-107

Airport Authorities

Corporate	.075% (7½¢ per $100 of assessed valuation). Authorized by referendum.	Ch. 15½, par. 68.2c par. 68.13
Bonds & Interest	No rate limit. Referendum if aggregate debt exceeds ¾ of 1% of assessed valuation.	Ch. 15½, par. 68.14a par. 68.14c par. 68.14e

Cemetery Maintenance District

Corporate	.06% (6¢ per $100 of assessed valuation).	Ch. 21, par. 64.24j

Civic Centers; Various Exposition and Auditorium Authorities; Exhibition Council

Exhibition Council

Bonds	No rate limit. Authorized by referendum of voters within city or county which created the Council.	Ch. 85, par. 1209.1

Metropolitan Exposition, Auditorium and Office Building Authorities

Bonds	.0005% (.05¢ per $100 of assessed valuation). Authorized by referendum.	Ch. 85, par. 1373 par. 1374

Aurora Metropolitan Exposition, Auditorium and Office Building Authority

Bonds	.0005% (.05¢ per $100 of assessed valuation). Authorized by referendum.	Ch. 85, par. 1413 par. 1414

Bloomington Civic Center Authority

Bonds	No rate limit. Authorized by referendum.	Ch. 85, par. 1581-14 par. 1581-17

Danville Metropolitan Exposition, Auditorium and Office Building Authority

Bonds	.0005% (.05¢ per $100 of assessed valuation). Authorized by referendum.	Ch. 85, par. 1563 par. 1564

Decatur Metropolitan Exposition, Auditorium and Office Building Authority
Bonds   .0005% (.05¢ per $100 of assessed valuation).   Ch. 85,
               Authorized by referendum.   par. 1563
                                                               par. 1564

DuPage County Metropolitan Exposition, Auditorium and Office Building Authority
Bonds   .0005% (.05¢ per $100 of assessed valuation).   Ch. 85,
               Authorized by referendum.   par. 3413
                                                               par. 3414

Elgin Metropolitan Exposition, Auditorium and Office Building Authority
Bonds   .0005% (.05¢ per $100 of assessed valuation).   Ch. 85,
               Authorized by referendum.   par. 3614
                                                               par. 3615

Illinois Quad City Civic Center Authority
Bonds   .05% (5¢ per $100 of assessed valuation).   Ch. 85,
               Authorized by referendum.   par. 3113
                                                               par. 3114

Jo Daviess County Civic Center Authority
Bonds   .05% (5¢ per $100 of assessed valuation).   Ch. 85,
               Authorized by referendum.   par. 3713

Orland Park Metropolitan Exposition, Auditorium and Office Building Authority
Bonds   .0005% (.05¢ per $100 of assessed valuation).   Ch. 85,
               Authorized by referendum.   par. 3713
                                                               par. 3714

Pekin Civic Center Authority
Bonds   .05% (5¢ per $100 of assessed valuation).   Ch. 85,
               Authorized by referendum.   par. 3213
                                                               par. 3214

Peoria Civic Center Authority
Site   No rate limit. Aggregate of $300,000 over a   Ch. 85,
Acquisition   period not to exceed 10 years. May be levied   par. 1448
and   by city council upon request of Authority.
Development

Corporate   .05% (5¢ per $100 of assessed valuation).   Ch. 85,
               Authorized by referendum.   par. 1448

Bonds   No rate limit. Authorized by referendum after   Ch. 85,
                   consent of city council.   par. 1450

Rockford Metropolitan Exposition Auditorium and Office Building Authority
Bonds   .0005% (.05¢ per $100 of assessed valuation).   Ch. 85,
                   Authorized by referendum.   par. 1343
                                                                     par. 1344

Schaumburg Metropolitan Exposition, Auditorium and Office Building Authority
Bonds   .0005% (.05¢ per $100 of assessed valuation).   Ch. 85,
                   Authorized by referendum.   par. 3913
                                                                     par. 3914

Springfield Metropolitan Exposition and Auditorium Authority
Corporate   .05% (5¢ per $100 of assessed valuation).   Ch. 85,
                                                                     par. 1263

Bonds   No rate limit. Referendum required if aggre-   Ch. 85,
                   gate bonds issued exceed 1.5% of assessed   par. 1263a
                   valuation. If aggregate will not exceed such   par. 1263b
                   limit, ordinance is subject to backdoor refer-
                   endum.

Sterling Metropolitan Exposition, Auditorium and Office Building Authority
Bonds   .0005% (.05¢ per $100 of assessed valuation).   Ch. 85,
                   Authorized by referendum.   par. 3514
                                                                     par. 3515

Waukegan Metropolitan Exposition and Auditorium Authority
Bonds   No rate limit. Referendum required.   Ch. 85,
                                                                     par. 1580-14
                                                                     par. 1580-15

Will County Metropolitan Exposition and Auditorium Authority
Bonds   No rate limit. Referendum required.   Ch. 85,
                                                                     par. 1580-14
                                                                     par. 1580-15

Conservation Districts

Corporate   .025% (2½¢ per $100 of assessed valuation).   Ch. 96½,
                   For general purposes, including land acquisi-   par. 7114
                   tion, may accumulate to not more than .075%
                   of assessed valuation.

Land Acquisition	.075% (7½¢ per $100 of assessed valuation). May accumulate to not more than .25% of assessed valuation. May be used for land development or general purposes with approval of Department of Conservation.	Ch. 96½, par. 7114
Bonds & Interest	No rate limit. Authorized by board for land acquisition. Authorized by referendum for development of real property.	Ch. 96½, par. 7116
Endangered Species	.01% (1¢ per $100 of assessed valuation). For funding research projects involving endangered species of Fauna and Flora, providing facilities and staff and maintenance or to provide for maintenance by a not-for-profit organization. Authorized by referendum.	Ch. 96½, par. 7114.1

County Historical Museum District

Corporate	.004% (4 mills per $100 of assessed valuation). Authorized by referendum.	Ch. 34, par. 6601 thru par. 6619

County Water Commission

Corporate	.055% (½¢ per $100 of assessed valuation) and an additional tax at a rate not to exceed .20% (20¢ per $100 of assessed valuation) for one year only. ¼% sales tax may be imposed by referendum.	Ch. 111⅔, par. 251 thru par. 254
Bond & Interest	No rate limit. Authorized by referendum.	Ch. 111⅔, par. 251 thru par. 254

Fire Protection Districts

Ambulance	.30% (30¢ per $100 of assessed valuation). Authorized by referendum. If a district had authority to levy .25% (25¢) prior to 1-1-78, board may increase maximum to .30% by resolution, subject to backdoor referendum. Exception, a district which lies within a single	Ch. 127½, par. 38.5 par. 38.6

county which has a population between 275,000
and 285,000 or lies within 2 counties with
respective populations between 275,000 and
285,000 and between 655,000 and 675,000
may by ordinance levy a tax not exceeding
.095% (9½¢) for the purpose of providing
ambulance services pursuant to an intergovernmental cooperation agreement with any
other unit of local government and provided no
other tax is levied to provide ambulance services.

Corporate	.125% (12½¢ per $100 of assessed valuation). May be increased to .30% (30¢ per $100 of assessed valuation), by ordinance, subject to a backdoor referendum, and to .40% (40¢ per $100 of assessed valuation) by referendum. In addition to other uses, these funds may also be used to provide emergency ambulance service to area.	Ch. 127½, par. 34, par. 31 par. 38.5
Firemen's Pension or IMRF	No rate limit. A rate which, when added to all other receipts, will be sufficient to meet the requirements of the pension fund, exclusive of all other rates extended.	Ch. 108½, par. 4-118 par. 7-171
Bonds & Interest	No rate limit. Authorized by referendum.	Ch. 127½. par. 32 par. 33

Forest Preserve Districts

Corporate	.025% (2½¢ per $100 of assessed valuation), in districts of less than 3,000,000 inhabitants. May be increased to .06% (.6¢ per $100 of assessed valuation) subject to backdoor refer- endum. In districts of 3,000,000 or more inhabitants, .06% (6¢).	Ch. 96½, par. 6324 par. 6425
Development of Forests & Construction of Improvements	.025% (2½¢ per $100 of assessed valuation) in districts of 100,000 to 3,000,000 inhabitants. In districts of more than 3,000,000 inhabi- tants, .021% (2.1¢ per $100 of assessed valua- tion) for constructing, restoring, recondition- ing and reconstructing improvements and development of forests.	Ch. 96½, par. 6324 par. 6425
Bonds	No rate limit. Referendum is required under certain specified circumstances.	Ch. 96½, par. 6323 par. 6424

Bonds Refunding	No rate limit. To fund payment of existing indebtedness.	Ch. 96½, par. 6551 par. 6552
Bonds Working Cash Fund	No rate limit. Aggregate of bonds allowed to be issued is $7,000,000. Applies to districts in counties of more than 3,000,000 inhabitants.	Ch. 96½, par. 6431
Bonds Zoological Park	No rate limit. Applicable to districts having 150,000 or more inhabitants.	Ch. 96½, par. 6445
Employee's Annuity & Benefit Fund	.00126% (1.26 mills), or rate which will produce $239,000, whichever is higher. Applicable in districts having more than 500,000 inhabitants.	Ch. 108½, par. 10-107
Zoological Park	.0058% (5.8 mills per $100 of assessed valuation) for districts of 150,000 or more and fewer than 3,000,000 inhabitants. .025% (2.5¢ per $100 of assessed valuation) for districts having 3,000,000 or more inhabitants.	Ch. 96½, par. 6801 par. 6802 par. 6444
Botanic Garden	.0048% (4.8 mills per $100 of assessed valuation) for districts over 200,000 and fewer than 3,000,000 inhabitants. .0076% (7.6 mills per $100 of assessed valuation) for districts having 3,000,000 or more inhabitants.	Ch. 96½, par. 6702 par. 6447

Hospital Districts

Corporate	.075% (7½¢ per $100 of assessed valuation).	Ch. 23, par. 1270
Bonds & Interest	No rate limit. Referendum if aggregate debt will exceed 1.5% of value of taxable property.	Ch. 23, par. 1271

Library Districts

Bonds & Interest	No rate limit. Authorized by referendum.	Ch. 81, par. 1005-2 par. 1005-3
Buildings	.0833% (8⅓¢ per $100 of assessed valuation). Authorized by referendum.	Ch. 81, par. 1005-4 par. 1005-5 par. 1005-6

Buildings   .02% (2¢ per $100 of assessed valuation).   Ch. 81,
                     Subject to backdoor referendum each year it is   par. 1003.1
                     levied.

Building   .0833% (8⅓¢ per $100 of assessed valuation).   Ch. 81,
Reconstruction   Authorized by referendum.   par. 1003-8
                                                              par. 1003.9

Corporate   .015% (15¢ per $100 of assessed valuation),   Ch. 81,
                     unless a higher rate is specified on ballot in   par. 1003-1
                     referendum creating the district. May increase   par. 1003-2
                     to .60% (60¢) by referendum.

Working   .05% (5¢ per $100 of assessed valuation).   Ch. 81,
Cash Fund   Subject to backdoor referendum. May be lev-   par. 1003-11
                     ied for no more than 4 years, but the 4 years
                     need not be consecutive.

Mass Transit Districts

Corporate   .05% (5¢ per $100 of assessed valuation).   Ch. 111⅔,
                     Referendum required if district (other than   par. 355
                     district created under p. 353.1) was created   par. 355.1
                     after 7-1-67. May be increased to .25% (25¢)
                     per $100 of assessed valuation) by referen-
                     dum.

Multitownship Assessing District

Assessing   No rate limit. Amount sufficient to meet as-   Ch. 120,
Purposes   sessing costs.   par. 482.3

Mosquito Abatement Districts

Corporate   .025% (2½¢ per $100 of assessed valuation),   Ch. 111½,
                     or the rate limit in effect on 7-1-67, whichever   par. 82
                     is greater.

Park Districts (of Fewer than 500,000 Inhabitants)

Airport   .075% (7½¢ per $100 of assessed valuation).   Ch. 105,
                     Authorized by referendum.   par. 9-2a

Aquarium & Museum	.07% (7¢ per $100 of assessed valuation). Subject to backdoor referendum.	Ch. 105, par. 327
Bonds & Interest	No rate limit.	
Corporate	.10% (10¢ per $100 of assessed valuation) or the rate limit in effect on 7-1-67, whichever is greater. Rates do not include tax for bonded indebtedness and taxes authorized by special referenda.	Ch. 105, par. 5-1
Corporate (Additional)	.25% (25¢ per $100 of assessed valuation). Authorized by referendum.	Ch. 105, par. 5-3
Conservatory	.05% (5¢ per $100 of assessed valuation). Authorized by referendum.	Ch. 105, par. 5-7
Health, Safety Environmental Handicapped Access & Energy	.05% (5¢ per $100 of assessed valuation). To pay for alterations and repairs when insufficient funds not available may not exceed estimate of cost. May be increased to 10% (10¢ per $100 of assessed valuation) by referendum.	Ch. 105, par. 5-10
Paving & Lighting, Streets & Roadways	.005% (.5¢ per $100 of assessed valuation). Subject to backdoor referendum.	Ch. 105, par. 5-6
Playground & Recreation Commission	.09% (9¢ per $100 of assessed valuation). Park District assumes rate being levied by city, village or incorporated town upon a ⅔ vote of the park board and the governing board of the city, village or incorporated town to merge the Playground and Recreation Commission with the Park District.	Ch. 105, par. 5-2a par. 5-2b
Police System	.025% (2½¢ per $100 of assessed valuation). Subject to backdoor referendum. May not be levied by any district not participating under the Police Training Act.	Ch. 105, par. 5-9
Programs for Handicapped	.04% (4¢ per $100 of assessed valuation).	Ch. 105, par. 5-8
Recreational & Community Center	.075% (7½¢ per $100 of assessed valuation). May be increased to .12% (12¢ per $100 of assessed valuation) by referendum.	Ch. 105, par. 5-2
Recreational (Additional)	.25% (25¢ per $100 of assessed valuation). Authorized by referendum.	Ch. 105, par. 5-3a
Working Cash Fund	.025% (2½¢ per $100 of assessed valuation). May be levied for a maximum of four years.	

| | Park Districts that levied this tax in previous years are also limited to a total of four years including back years. | Ch. 105, par. 11.2-2 |
| Public Benefit | .025% (2½¢ per $100 of assessed valuation). Authorized by referendum. | Ch. 105, par. 7-5 |

Bonds & Interest

Airport	No rate limit. But rate for bonds is set off against rate allowed for Airport Fund, unless improvements are required to conform to federal or state standards. If tax exceeds Airport Fund rate, then only rate for bonds will be extended. Authorized by referendum.	Ch. 105, par. 9-2b par. 6-6
Corporate	No rate limit. General obligation nonreferendum debt is limited to .575% per issue. Referendum required if aggregate indebtedness will exceed 2.875% of equalized assessed valuation.	Ch. 105, par. 6-2, 6-3 par. 6-4, 6-6
Playground & Athletic Field	No rate limit. Bonds issued to match grant or donation. If amount of bond issue exceeds $5,000 or .066% of taxable property, referendum must be held.	Ch. 105, par. 255.28 par. 255.29 par. 255.36
Refunding	No rate limit. To repay existing indebtedness.	Ch. 105, par. 6-1 par. 255.19 par. 255.20

Port Districts

Havana Regional Port District

| Corporate | .05% (5¢ per $100 of assessed valuation). Authorized by referendum. | Ch. 19, par. 620 |

Illinois Valley Regional Port District

| Corporate | .05% (5¢ per $100 of assessed valuation). Authorized by referendum. | Ch. 19, par. 828 |

Jackson-Union County Regional Port District

| Corporate | .05% (5¢ per $100 of assessed valuation). Authorized by referendum. | Ch. 19, par. 863 |
| Bonds | No rate limit. Authorized by referendum. | Ch. 19, par. 858 |

Joliet Regional Port District

Corporate	.05% (5¢ per $100 of assessed valuation). Authorized by referendum.	Ch. 19, par. 262
Bonds	No rate limit. Authorized by referendum.	Ch. 19, par. 258

Kaskaskia Regional Port District

Corporate	.05% (5¢ per $100 of assessed valuation). Authorized by referendum.	Ch. 19, par. 528.1
Bonds	No rate limit. Authorized by referendum.	Ch. 19, par. 522.1

Mt. Carmel Regional Port District

Corporate	.05% (5¢ per $100 of assessed valuation). Authorized by referendum.	Ch. 19, par. 717
Bonds	No rate limit. Authorized by referendum.	Ch. 19 par. 711

Seneca Regional Port District

Corporate	.05% (5¢ per $100 of assessed valuation). Authorized by referendum.	Ch. 19, par. 363
Bonds	No rate limit. Authorized by referendum.	Ch. 19, par. 358

Shawneetown Regional Port District

Corporate	.05% (5¢ per $100 of assessed valuation). Authorized by referendum.	Ch. 19, par. 413
Bonds	No rate limit. Authorized by referendum.	Ch. 19, par. 408

Southwest Regional Port District

Corporate	.05% (5¢ per $100 of assessed valuation). Authorized by referendum.	Ch. 19, par. 466
Bonds	No rate limit. Authorized by referendum.	Ch. 19, par. 460

Tri-City Regional Port District

Corporate	.05% (5¢ per $100 of assessed valuation). Authorized by referendum.	Ch. 19, par. 296

Bonds   No rate limit. Authorized by referendum. Ch. 19,
                        par. 291

Waukegan Regional Port District
Corporate   .05% (5¢ per $100 of assessed valuation). Ch. 19,
       Authorized by referendum.   par. 195

Bonds   No rate limit. Authorized by referendum. Ch. 19,
                        par. 186

White County Port District
Corporate   .05% (5¢ per $100 of assessed valuation). Ch. 19,
       Authorized by referendum.   par. 770

Public Health Districts

Corporate   .10% (10¢ per $100 of assessed valuation). Ch. 111½,
       County Clerk must abate from this rate the par. 15
       amount accruing to the district due to extension of rate for county or multiple county health departments. District to be served must be at least 75,000 population. Subject to referendum. In any public health district in which a public health department was established by a referendum prior to 1 January 1970, the Board of Health may, by resolution adopted by ⅗ vote and without subsequent referendum levy at a rate not to exceed .10% (10¢ per $100 of assessed valuation) for any increase in excess of .05% (5¢ per $100 of assessed valuation).

Bonds   No limit. Authorized by referendum. Ch. 111½,
& Interest   par. 20.2
                      par. 20.3 & 20.4

Public Water Districts

Corporate   .02% (2¢ per $100 of assessed valuation). Ch. 111⅔,
       Referendum required. Levy limited to 10 years. par. 192a

River Conservancy District

Corporate	.083% (8⅓¢ per $100 of assessed valuation). May be increased to .75% (75¢ per $100 of assessed valuation) in districts with less than 25,000 population, and .375% (37½¢ per $100 of assessed valuation) in districts with 25,000 or more population, by referendum.	Ch. 42, par. 400
Special Service Area	No rate limit. Tax imposed only in special service area. May not be imposed if objection petition is filed by 51% of electors and 51% of landowners.	Ch. 42, par. 404
Bonds & Interest	No rate limit. Authorized by referendum.	Ch. 42, par. 397 & 398
Special Service Area Bonds	No rate limit. To provide special services, tax imposed only in special service area. May not be imposed if objection petition is filed by 51% of electors and 51% of landowners.	Ch. 42, par. 404

Road Districts

Bonds & Interests	No rate limit. Authorized by referendum.	
Roads & Bridges* **	.125% (12½¢ per $100 of assessed valuation) or rate in effect on 7-1-67, whichever is greater. Applies to single township road district may be increased to .165% (16½¢) with approval of town board.	Ch. 121, par. 6-501 par. 6-504
	.175% (17½¢ per $100 of assessed valuation) or rate in effect on 7-1-67, whichever is greater. Applies to consolidated township road district.	
	.165 (16½¢ per $100 of assessed valuation) or rate in effect on 7-1-67, whichever is greater. Applies to road district in commission county. Must be approved by county board.	
	Any of the above may be increased to .66% (66¢) by referendum.	
Road Damage	.033% (3⅓¢ per $100 of assessed valuation). Approved by the county board in commission counties.	Ch. 121, par. 6-503
Permanent Road Fund**	.167% (16.7¢ per $100 of assessed valuation). Authorized by referendum.	Ch. 121, par. 6-601

Bridge-Joint Construction with County** .05% (5¢ per $100 of assessed valuation). Approval by county board in commission counties. May be accumulated for a specific project. May be increased by referendum to .25% (25¢) for a 10-year period. If surplus is transferred to Road & Bridge Fund, referendum is required to reauthorize levy. Ch. 121, par. 6-508

Equipment & Building** .035% (3½¢ per $100 of assessed valuation). Authorized by referendum. Approval by county board in commission counties. Ch. 121, par. 6-508.1

Unit District Bridge .05% (5¢ per $100 of assessed valuation). Applies to County Unit Road Districts. Ch. 121, par. 6-512

Unit District* Road .165% (16½¢ per $100 of assessed valuation). Applies to County Unit Road Districts. May increase to .33% (33¢) by referendum. Ch. 121, par. 6-512 par. 6-512.1

Bonds & Interest

Road Purposes No rate limit. Authorized by referendum. Ch. 121, par. 6-510

Road Purposes— County Unit No rate limit. Authorized by referendum. Ch. 121, par. 6-513

Refunding No rate limit. Ch. 121, par. 6-514 par. 6-515 par. 6-516

Sanitary Districts

Act of 1907

Corporate .20% (20¢ per $100 of assessed valuation), or the rate limit in effect on 7-1-67, whichever is greater. Ch. 42, par. 247 par. 263

Sewage Treatment .03% (3¢ per $100 of assessed valuation) if required by Pollution Control Board. May be increased to .05% (5¢) by referendum. Ch. 42, par. 263

Bonds— Corporate No rate limit. Authorized by referendum. Ch. 42, par. 262 par. 262.1

Bonds— Refunding No rate limit. Applies to all districts. Ch. 42, par. 298.1 par. 298.2

Act of 1911

Corporate	.083% (8⅓¢ per $100 of assessed valuation), or rate limit in effect on 8-2-65, whichever is greater. Can go to .35% (35¢ per $100 of assessed valuation) by referendum.	Ch. 42, par. 277 par. 288
Sewage Treatment	.03% (3¢ per $100 of assessed valuation) if required by Pollution Control Board. May be increased to .05% (5¢) by referendum.	Ch. 42, par. 288
Bonds— Corporate	No rate limit. Authorized by referendum.	Ch. 42, par. 285 par. 286
Bonds— Refunding	No rate limit. Applies to all districts.	Ch. 42, par. 298.1 par. 298.2

Act of 1917

Corporate	.083% (8⅓¢ per $100 of assessed valuation) or rate limit in effect on 8-2-65, whichever is greater. Additonal .083% (8⅓¢) may be authorized by referendum.	Ch. 42, par. 299 par. 311
Public Benefit	.05% (5¢ per $100 of assessed valuation). Pay district's share of special assessment.	Ch. 42, par. 317d.1
Sewage Treatment	.03% (3¢ per $100 of assessed valuation) if required by Pollution Control Board. May be increased to .05% (5¢) by referendum.	Ch. 42, par. 311
Bonds Corporate	No rate limit. Authorized by referendum.	Ch. 42, par. 308 par. 309
Bonds— Refunding	No rate limit. Applies to all districts.	Ch. 42, par. 298.1 par. 298.2

Act of 1936

Corporate	.25% (25¢ per $100 of assessed valuation) or rate limit in effect on 8-4-65, whichever is greater. May increase to .50% (50¢ per $100 of assessed valuation), by referendum.	Ch. 42, par. 412 par. 427
Sewage Treatment	.03% (3¢ per $100 of assessed valuation) if required by Pollution Control Board. May be increased .05% by referendum.	Ch. 42, par. 427

| Bonds—
Corporate | No rate limit. Authorized by referendum. | Ch. 42,
par. 422
par. 424 |
| Bonds—
Refunding | No rate limit. Applies to all districts. | Ch. 42,
par. 298.1
par. 298.2 |

Metro-East Act of 1974

Corporate	.20% (20¢ per $100 of assessed valuation) or the rate limit in effect on 7-1-67, whichever is greater.	Ch. 42, par. 505-1
Bond— Corporate	No rate limit. Authorized by referendum.	Ch. 42, par. 505-2
Bonds— Refunding	No rate limit.	Ch. 42, par. 298.1 par. 298.2

Soil and Water Conservation Subdistricts
(Watershed Protection and Flood Prevention Act)

| Corporate | .125% (12½¢ per $100 of assessed valuation). | Ch. 5,
par. 131b |

Solid Waste Disposal Districts

| Corporate | .05% (5¢ per $100 of assessed valuation). | Ch. 85,
par. 1668 |
| Bonds &
Interest | Included within corporate limit. Authorized by referendum. | Ch. 85,
par. 1671 |

Street Lighting Districts

| Corporate | .125% (12½¢ per $100 of assessed valuation). May be increased to 2.00% ($2.00 per $100 of assessed valuation) by referendum. Rate to include payment of any bonds issued. | Ch. 121,
par. 364
par. 364.1 |

| Bonds & Interest | .075% (7½¢ per $100 of assessed valuation). Authorized by referendum. Included in corporate rate limit. | Ch. 121, par. 362 par. 363 |

Surface Water Protection Districts

| Corporate | .125% (12½¢ per $100 of assessed valuation). May be increased to .25% (25¢) by referendum, except no referendum required if district was created by petition of all property owners and all property owners agree. | Ch. 42, par. 468 |
| Bonds | No rate limit. Referendum required unless district was created by petition of all property owners and all property owners agree. | Ch. 42, par. 466 par. 467 par. 467a |

Tuberculosis Sanitarium Districts

Act of 1937

| Corporate | .075% (7½¢ per $100 of assessed valuation). Applies to district wholly within one county. | Ch. 23, par. 1714 |
| Bonds & Interest | No specific rate limit, except that this levy is included within the .075% corporate levy limit. Referendum if for purpose other than acquisition of land. | Ch. 23, par. 1714 |

Act of 1939

| Corporate | .25% (25¢ per $100 of assessed valuation). Applies to district embracing two or more contiguous counties. | Ch. 34, par. 5216 |
| Bonds & Interest | No specific rate limit, except that this levy is included within .25% corporate levy limit. Referendum if for purpose other than acquisition of land. | Ch. 34, par. 5216 |

Water Authority Districts

| Corporate | .08% (8¢ per $100 of·assessed valuation). | Ch. 111⅔, par. 228 |

Bonds   No rate limit. Aggregate total not to exceed   Ch. 111⅔,
                     .5% of assessed valuation.   par. 228

Water Service Districts

Corporate   .125% (12½¢ per $100 of assessed valuation).   Ch. 111⅔,
                                                                    par. 222

Bonds &   .075% (7½¢ per $100 of assessed valuation).   Ch. 111⅔,
Interest   Authorized by referendum. Included in corpo-   par. 221
                     rate rate limit.

* NOTE: One-half of the road fund tax levied under section 6-501 or 6-512 on property lying
   within a municipality, where streets and alleys are under care of municipality, must be
   turned over to treasurer of the municipality. (See ch. 121, par. 6-507, par. 6-512, Ill. Rev.
   Stat.)

** Referendum may be held at the annual town meeting or special town meeting.

Appendix 9-4
Soil Facts

- One hundred and eighty-eight million tons of soil are eroded from all Illinois land—enough to fill Chicago's Sears Tower building 73 times.
- Thirty-five thousand acres of Illinois farmland are converted each year to housing developments, shopping centers, highways, and airports.
- Over 8,300 square feet of reservoir capacity are lost annually, and replacing that capacity will cost over $3 million for each year it continues.
- Of over twenty-five million tons of soil dumped into the Illinois River annually, fourteen million tons settle to the bottom.
- The public cost of removing sediment from reservoirs and rivers is approximately $5–10 per ton while erosion prevention typically costs the public less than $1 per ton.
- In 1986 an estimated $7 million was spent for removing sediment from road ditches.
- About $12 million of state and federal funds are being used annually in Illinois to administer the point sources (factories and sewage treatment plants) pollution control program (which relies on regulation). Tens of billions of taxpayers' dollars have been used to clean up these sources, but very little has been devoted to nonpoint source (farm) cleanup.

Source: Association of Illinois Soil and Water Conservation Districts.

PART THREE

Law and Finance

10.

The Law and Local Officials

MICHAEL E. POLLAK

The laws governing local officials are extremely diverse. The Illinois Municipal Code alone covers five volumes of the Smith-Hurd Annotated Statutes. Many laws affecting local officials are contained outside the Illinois Municipal Code. To sort through the maze of legalities, this chapter deals with laws regulating the conduct of the local official as well as the conduct of the local government. To the unknowing there are so many laws restricting conduct that it seems difficult to do anything without restricting actions. There are laws governing ethics disclosure and conflict of interest, as well as how meetings must be conducted, what local officials and governments are mandated to do, and what information and documents must be made public. There is even a law which establishes temporary locations for seats of government in an emergency and regulates who can exercise governmental powers in a crisis due to enemy attack. These laws restricting the conduct of local officials take the form of both disclosure and prohibition. Any action in violation of these laws could result in a crime being committed.

Ethics

Our current ethics law has as its genesis the Illinois constitution of 1970. Article 13, section 2, requires that all candidates and holders of state offices must file a statement of economic interest. The constitution further adds that the general assembly may impose a similar requirement on candidates for, and holders of, offices of local government units. The general assembly has followed this recommendation by adopting the "Illi-

205

nois Governmental Ethics Act".[1] The act is a disclosure law for local as well as other governmental officials. It requires the local official to disclose his or her economic interest and that of his or her spouse. The economic interest form is printed in the statutes and is made available to the local governmental official by the respective county clerk or the Illinois secretary of state. The form is required to be filed by 1 May of each year in the county clerk's office in the county in which the local official resides. The law as amended in 1985 provides that if the disclosure form is not filed by 1 May, the county clerk with whom the form is to be filed must mail notice to the local official of the failure to file. The local official has until 15 May to file the statement of economic interest along with a $15 late filing fee. In the event filing is not made by 15 May, the local official is subject to a $100.00 per day fine for each day after 16 May that the form is not filed.

A severe penalty, forfeiture of office, is provided in the event the economic interest statement is not filed by 31 May. Prior to 1985, the penalty for failure to file the economic interest statement by 1 May of each year was forfeiture of office. When the mayor of Chicago failed to file his economic interest statement by 1 May 1987, the opposition party in the Chicago City Council filed a lawsuit to have the office declared vacant. The courts ruled that forfeiture was too severe a penalty for any public official who inadvertently failed to file on time. After this incident, the Illinois General Assembly responded by providing for a system of notification, late filing fees, and fines before forfeiture. The 1985 amendments provide for the following action if a local official fails to file an economic interest statement by 1 May of any year:

1. The county clerk with whom the statement is to be filed shall notify the local official within seven days after 1 May of the failure to file.

2. If the statement is filed with the county clerk between 1 May and 15 May, a late filing fee of $15 is imposed.

3. If the economic interest statement is not filed by 15 May, the local official is subject to a penalty of $100 for each day the statement is not filed after 16 May.

4. Failure to file by 31 May could result in forfeiture of office by the local official.

The statements of economic interest are intended to disclose financial interests which could be deemed a conflict of interest. The statements are available for public inspection and copies are provided upon request. Each person examining a statement must first fill out a form identifying the

1. Ill. Rev. Stat., ch. 127, par. 601-101 et seq.

examiner by name, address, and telephone number and also give the date and reason for examination. The information is then sent to the public official whose statement was examined.

This notification provision was included in the Illinois Ethics Act because elected officials were concerned that their statements were being reviewed anonymously by their would-be opponents. Accordingly, a provision in the law was inserted to require the examiner to provide the information prior to examining a statement of economic interest. As always, however, where there is an action, there is a corresponding reaction. Most of the reviewers of the statements have fictitious names, are "students" and need to review a statement for "research" purposes. Incredibly, the statements find their way into the hands of the elected official's would-be opponent.

The financial and economic interests required to be disclosed are:

1. any professional practice with which the local official is involved, in which income in excess of $1200 per year was derived during the preceding calendar year;

2. the nature of any professional service and the nature of entity to which they were rendered if fees exceeding $5000 were received in the preceding calendar year;

3. the identify of any capital asset from which a capital gain of at least $5000 was realized in the preceding calendar year;

4. the name of any unit of government which has employed the official other than the unit of local government of which he is an official;

5. the name of any entity from which a gift or honorarium valued in excess of $500 was received during the preceding calendar year;

6. the name of any entity owned by the local official doing business with the unit of local government of which the person is an official, if the ownership interest of the local official exceeds $5000 or if dividends or income in excess of $1200 were received in the preceding calendar year;

7. any request to a unit of local government for any license, franchise, or permit for annexation, zoning, or rezoning of real estate during the preceding calendar year, if the ownership interest in the property for which the request is made exceeds $5000 or if income or dividends in excess of $1200 were received from the property during the preceding calendar year.

The penalty for filing false or incomplete statements is a class A misdemeanor, which is punishable by up to one year in jail and not more than a $100 fine. The state's attorney in the county where the statement is required to be filed is charged with the responsibility of enforcing the Illinois Governmental Ethics Act.

Conflicts of Interest

Other laws, with certain exceptions, prohibit a public official from having a financial interest in any contract where he or she may be called upon to act or vote. "An Act to prevent fraudulent and corrupt practices in the making or accepting official appointments and contracts by public officers" is one of these.[2] Similarly, a provision in the Illinois Municipal Code[3] prohibits a public official, with certain exceptions, from having an interest in a contract in which the price is paid out of the municipal treasury or from any assessment levied by any statute or ordinance.

The provision in the act to prevent fraudulent and corrupt practices specifically provides that no person holding office may be interested directly or indirectly in any contract or the performance there of upon which the officer is called upon to act or vote. In addition, the local official may not represent or act as an agent of such if he is called upon to act or vote. This law has a narrow application; unless the public official is called to act or vote on the contract, the law would not be violated. There are two exceptions to this which allow the official to supply materials, merchandise, labor, or services even if the public official must act or vote on the contract. In both exceptions, which are described below, all of the circumstances must be present before the exemption is available. In order for the first exception to apply

1. the public official must have less than a 7½ percent ownership interest in the contracting party;

2. the public official must disclose the nature and extent of his or her interest prior to or during deliberations concerning the proposed award of the contract;

3. the local official must abstain from voting on the matter (he or she may be counted in the quorum);

4. the award of the contract must be approved by a majority of those members presently holding office (this is a larger than normal majority required to take action);

5. the contract must be awarded after sealed bids have been taken if the contract amount exceeds $1500 (if the contract amount is less than $1500, sealed bids are not necessary);

6. the award of the contract must not cause the aggregate amount of all such contracts awarded to the local official or his firm to exceed $25,000 in the same fiscal year.

2. Ill. Rev. Stat., ch. 102, par. 3
3. Ill. Rev. Stat., ch. 24, par. 3-14-4.

The second exception deals with contracts that do not exceed $1000. Materials, services, and labor may be supplied to the municipality by the local official if all of the following conditions are met: (1) the award is approved by a majority vote of the governing body, provided the local official shall abstain from voting; (2) the award of the contract would not exceed $2000 awarded to the local official or his or her firm in the same fiscal year; and (3) the public official discloses his or her interest prior to or during deliberations of the proposed award. Any violation of the above law is considered a class 4 felony (punishable by up to three years in the penitentiary and up to a $10,000 fine); upon conviction of such a violation, the local official forfeits his or her office.[4]

The Illinois Municipal Code provision which prohibits financial interest in contracts is much broader in coverage than those provisions concerning fraudulent and corrupt practices. The municipal code provides that a local official may not directly or indirectly be interested in any contract or in the sale of any article to the municipality if the consideration is paid from either the treasury or by any assessment levied by any statute or ordinance. This covers any payment from any tax or fee levied or charged by the municipality. The code further prohibits the local official from directly or indirectly purchasing any property which belongs to the municipality and which is sold for taxes or assessments or which is sold as a result of a court order. The exceptions to the prohibited actions under the Illinois Municipal Code as well as the penalties for violations are identical to those of the act concerning fraudulent and corrupt practices.

The law also makes bribery a class 4 felony and requires the forfeiture of the office held by the local official.[5] No local official may take or receive or offer to receive, directly or indirectly, any money or other thing of value as a gift or bribe as a means of influencing his or her vote. Other sections of the law provide that upon conviction the officer shall be ineligible to continue in his or her office.[6] If the conviction is reversed during the term of office, however, the official shall be reinstated. The actions previously discussed have been enacted to prevent obvious conflicts of interest. Other laws require disclosure as a means of dealing with conflict of interests situations, and bribery statutes provide for stiff penalties in order to provide a deterrent to the taking of money to perform or influence an official action.

A little-known law designed to prevent an opportunity for dishonesty was enacted by the legislature in 1973. This act applies to all public officials and

4. Ill. Rev. Stat., ch. 24, par. 3-14-4(e).
5. Ill. Rev. Stat., ch. 102, par. 3, 4.
6. Ill. Rev. Stat., ch. 102, par. 120.

provides that no official shall specify or suggest that a check for payment of any fees be payable to a named person. In other words, it is illegal for a local official to specify or request a check for a dog license to be made payable to "John Doe" if he happens to be village clerk when it should be made payable to "Village of Dog Patch." The drawing of the check payable to the individual creates conditions for the account. This method of misappropriation seems so obvious that it is hard to believe that a law is necessary to specifically prohibit it. However, some time ago an official whose responsibility it was to collect fees for the state died and a substantial amount of cash was found among his personal effects and in shoe boxes. While the official was never charged with doing anything illegal or with obtaining cash illegally, there were rumors that the funds could have been accumulated from checks made payable to the individual. The legislature acted to prevent any atmosphere where such action could take place and adopted "an Act in relation to payments for governmental services, fees, or taxes."[7]

Open Meetings Records

Disclosure not only is used as a means of dealing with conflicts of interest situations, it is also a means of making government open and responsible to the governed. Disclosure of a government's actions is mandated by requiring meetings of all local governmental bodies to be open and available to the public. Openness in government also is required by the Illinois Freedom of Information Act, which requires government agencies to allow the public to inspect and copy public records.

One would think that it is only natural that governmental decisions should take place in an environment that is open to the public, but this is not always the case. Without the Illinois Open Meetings Act,[8] public meetings would not have to be open to the public. Only as recently as 1957, when the "Open Meetings Act" was adopted, was the public guaranteed the right to be present at meetings of its elected and appointed officials. It seems that even now some public officials go to great lengths to hide their deliberations from public view. Public decisions can be tough decisions, and those determinations made under a cloak of privacy can be made anonymously, with no responsibility.

An old joke is applicable to the situation in Illinois. Several old men sitting around a table have told their jokes so often that they assigned each joke a

7. Ill. Rev. Stat., ch. 102, par. 37–38.
8. Ill. Rev. Stat., ch. 102, par. 41 et. seq.

number. When a newcomer sits down, he hears someone call out "44," and everybody laughs. Then someone yells out "34," and everybody laughs. Then someone yells out "23," and the good old boys are rolling in the aisles. The newcomer, wanting to participate, shouts "62," and there is stone silence. He is bewildered, so he asks the person next to him what happened. The person replies, "Some people just don't know how to tell a joke!" However, it was no joke when a municipality went to such an extreme as to vote on ordinances by number, having neither distributed copies nor discussed the ordinances prior to a vote.

To shed light on the local governmental decision-making process, the "Open Meetings Act" was adopted. Except for certain enumerated circumstances, all meetings of public bodies must be public meetings. The definition of a public body is all-encompassing. As it relates to local governments, it incudes all executive, administrative, and advisory bodies, all boards, bureaus, committees, or commissions, and all subsidiary bodies of the above, including all those which are supported in whole or in part by those which expend tax revenues. A meeting is defined in the act as any gathering of a majority of a quorum of the members of a public body held for the purpose of discussing public business. Two elements are necessary for a meeting to take place: a minimum number of persons must be present, namely a majority of a quorum; and the purpose of the gathering must be to discuss public business. It is possible for an illegal meeting to take place if the minimum number of members of a body gather informally over coffee and happen to discuss pending official business.

In order to ensure open and public meetings, notice of all regular meetings of a body must be given. There are several ways notice must be given: (1) Each public body must, at the beginning of its calendar or fiscal year, prepare and make available a schedule of its regular meetings for the year. The schedule must list the date, time, and place of each meeting. (2) Notice shall also be given by posting a copy of the notice at the main office of the body or at the building in which the meeting will be held. (3) Copies of any notice must be given to any news medium that has filed an annual request for such notice.

In the event a change is made in the regular meeting dates, a ten-day advance notice of the change must be made by publication in a newspaper of general circulation. The notice must also be posted in the office of the body or where the meeting is to be held and given to all news media which have filed an annual request. Notice of a special meeting or rescheduled or reconvened regular meetings must also be given at least twenty-four hours before the meeting and should include the agenda for the meeting. Notice of emergency meetings should be given as soon as possible before the meeting. Failure of the news media to get any notice does not invalidate any action taken at any meeting. A provision in the act also stipulates that no meeting shall be held on a legal holiday unless the regular meeting date falls on that day. This prevents a meeting from being changed to a legal holiday in order to make the meeting inconvenient for the public to attend. The Open Meetings Act not only requires that most meetings be conducted in public, the act also allows any person to record the proceedings by any means — audio or video tape or film. These provisions may be suspended if a witness refuses to testify before the meeting on the grounds that he or she may not be compelled to testify if a portion of the testimony is recorded.

There are certain exceptions to the requirements that all meetings be public meetings. Generally, the circumstances creating the exceptions would put the local government at a competitive disadvantage or disclose information that may affect the right to privacy. The exceptions are:

1. collective bargaining meetings
2. deliberations concerning salary schedules for one or more classes of employees
3. meetings at which the acquisition of real estate is being considered. However, except in the case of school boards, the selling of real estate cannot be considered behind closed doors.
4. meetings held to discuss pending litigation or a case in which the

action is probable or imminent. A finding of such probability must be entered in the minutes.

5. meetings held to consider information regarding appointment, employment, or dismissal of an employee or to hear testimony lodged against an employee

6. meetings to establish reserves or settle claims under the Local Government and Governmental Employees Tort Immunity Act if the claim or potential claim might be prejudiced

7. meetings to consider the appointment to fill a vacancy on the body holding the meeting

If a meeting is called for several purposes and one of those to be discussed is to be discussed in secret, only the consideration of those matters permitted to be discussed in private may be considered at the closed portion of the meeting. The rest of the meeting must be open to the public. In order to close a meeting or a portion of it, at least a majority vote of the quorum present must be in favor of closing the meeting. The vote of each member must be recorded in the minutes and a reference to the specific exception in the law which authorizes the closing of the meeting must also be set forth. While certain matters may be permitted to be discussed under the cloak of secrecy, no final action on those matters discussed may be taken in the closed portion of the meeting. Any action or vote must be held in public.

What happens if a meeting is illegally closed or if a prohibited action is taken at a closed meeting? The Open Meetings Act provides for both civil and criminal sanctions. The state's attorney in the county where the local government is located or where the meeting is held has the general responsibility for enforcement. However, a civil action may be filed by any person. A civil action may even be brought before the meeting is held if there is probable cause to believe that the provisions of the act will not be complied with. At the hearing of the case, the court may order such action as it deems in the best interest of the parties, including: (1) requiring the meeting to be open; (2) granting an injunction against future violations; (3) ordering the body to make public the minutes of the portion of the closed meeting; and/or (4) declaring null and void any final action taken in violation of the act. In addition to the civil sanctions, the act provides that any person violating the law is guilty of a class C misdemeanor, with a penalty of up to thirty days in jail and a fine of not more than $500.

The Freedom of Information Act is the latest step in guaranteeing the public's right to know about government. This comprehensive legislation, which took effect 1 July 1984, was finally enacted after several attempts. It balances the interest of the public policy of openness in government with the right to maintain privacy of one's individual and property rights. However, the Freedom of Information Act was not the first law requiring public access to public records. Certain records are required to be made available for inspection and copying under the Local Records Act.[9] The Freedom of Information Act sets out precisely what records are public records, what records may be exempt from disclosure, what procedure is required for obtaining the records, and what can be done to appeal a decision of a local government that refuses to disclose records.

The Freedom of Information Act applies to all public bodies, particularly all local governments. It sets out a threefold requirement for record keeping and disclosure of public bodies: (1) It mandates certain records and information to be assembled and retained. (2) It lists certain records that are included in the definition of public records and states that the definition of public records is not limited to those mentioned. (3) It lists those records which are specifically exempt from inspection and copying.

9. Ill. Rev. Stat., ch. 116, par. 43.101 et. seq.

The act requires every public body to provide some basic information about itself. This information must be displayed at the public body's administrative office, made available for copying, and sent through the mail to any person requesting it. The basic information includes a short description of the organization, including an organizational chart delineating its functional subdivisions; the amount of its operating budget; the number and location of its offices; the approximate number of full-time and part-time employees; the identification and membership of all advisory boards and commissions. Included with the basic information must be directions on how the records and information are to be requested, a directory of those persons to whom the request is to be made, and the fees charged for the copying of the records.

Each public body must categorize all of its records. It must then make available to the public a list of the categories. The records which must be included in categories are:

- with certain exceptions, administrative manuals, procedural rules, and instructions to staff
- final orders and opinions in the adjudication of cases
- substantive rules
- statements of interpretation of policy
- final planning policy, recommendations, and decisions
- factual or inspection reports prepared by or for a public body
- information in any account, voucher, or contract dealing with the receipt or expenditure of funds
- names, salaries, titles, and dates of employment of all employees
- names of all officials and their voting records
- applications for contracts, permits, or grants, except as exempted, and all information relating to such contracts or grants
- all studies and reports prepared for the body

Certain documents are exempt from disclosure. It should be remembered that it is the public policy of the state to disclose and make available for inspection or copying all public documents. Therefore, all exemptions detract from this policy and must be strictly analyzed in light of such public policy. There are twenty-six specific exemptions from the disclosure rules. These exemptions can be divided into six categories.

1. *Privacy.* All documents which, if disclosed, would result in an unwarranted invasion of personal privacy. Examples are records of persons receiving medical services, personnel files containing personal informa-

tion, records regarding professional or occupational registration or licensing, tax assessment and collection records.

2. *Law enforcement.* Examples are investigatory records, criminal history records, manuals on tax collection procedures.

3. *Educational records.*

4. *Legal proceedings.* Examples are those records relating to litigation and privileged communication between a public body and its attorney or auditor.

5. *Internal operations.* Examples are preliminary drafts of memos in which opinions or policies are formulated, minutes of legally closed meetings (closed pursuant to the Open Meetings Act).

6. *Business and financial records.* Examples are certain business and financial records of private persons (including businesses) and public bodies, trade secrets, architects and engineering drawings, records relating to the purchase of real estate while the purchase is pending.

Of course records required to be kept confidential in accordance with federal or other state laws may not be disclosed either.

When a request to review or copy public documents is received must the public body respond? Yes and no. The government may provide the information, request more time to respond, or deny the request. If a written request is received by the public body, it must promptly respond to the request. Promptly in this instance means a response within seven working days of the request. The act allows the local government to charge reasonable fees for the cost of copying records. The fees cannot include the cost of research and must not exceed the cost of reproduction. If the local government determines that a waiver or reduction of fees is in the public interest, the fees can be waived.

In certain circumstances, a local government can extend the seven-day response time. If the response is not made within the initial period and it is not extended as provided in the act, the request is automatically considered denied. The local government can extend the response time for an additional seven working days. For this extension, a written notification to the person requesting the records must be made specifying the reason for delay. This notification must be sent during the initial response period and must set the date at which the records will be produced, or the request will be denied. If the response is not made during the extended period the response will be considered denied. Reasons to extend the initial seven-day response time include:

1. The records are located in another place.

2. The request requires the collection of a substantial amount of records.

3. The request is made in categorical terms.

4. The records have not been found after a routine search.

5. The records need to be reviewed to determine if they are exempt from disclosure.

6. The request cannot be complied with without unduly burdening the operations of the local government.

7. Time is needed to discuss disclosure with another public body which also has an interest in the matter.

Only one extension can be granted. It must also be remembered that there is no limit on the number of records requested. Cost may be a factor, however. A person does not have to request documents by name or subject matter. One can request records falling within the categories made available by the local government. There are certain limitations on categorical requests, however. A request need not be complied with if: (1) compliance would be unduly burdensome, (2) there is no way to narrow the request, and (3) the burden on the public body outweighs the public's right to know.

Before a local government can use one of these reasons for denial of categorical requests, it must give the requestor an opportunity to narrow the request. If after that the request is not narrowed, the public body may deny the request by notifying the person in writing, giving the reason why the request was unduly burdensome. Repeated requests by the same persons for the same records are considered unduly burdensome. It must be kept in mind that the above exception applies to categorical requests only.

If a local government denies any request, it must do so in writing, explaining the reasons for denial. The names of all persons responsible for the denial must also be given in the letter. The letter must indicate that the person may appeal to the head of the public body, and, if the appeal is denied, further appeal may be made to the local courts. The head of the public body has seven working days from the appeal to make his or her decision. All letters of denial must be kept in a central file, indexed by exemption, and be available for inspection.

Critics have repeatedly tried to change the act because governments can draw the extension and appeal process out for a long time and stymie the intent of the law. Another criticism is that it takes too long from the time the initial request is made to the time all administrative avenues for review are exhausted—twenty-one working days. When the appeal is made to the courts, the long and involved legal process comes into play.

Courts, after hearing the case, may require disclosure of the document and award attorney's fees to the party filing the suit. However, fees are awarded only in extraordinary circumstances. A finding must be made that the records were clearly of significant public interest and the public body lacked any rational basis for denial. Critics have pointed to this provision as lacking teeth. (The attorney general's office has published a helpful "Guide to the Illinois Freedom of Information Act." In it are suggestions for implementing the act, an explanation of the law, as well as the text.)[10]

State Mandates Act

Local governments are products of the state. Until the adoption of the Illinois constitution of 1970, which provided for home rule, governments were only empowered to do those things mandated or authorized by the state. The state has mandated open meetings, open records, public access, and ethics disclosure. In fact, the state has a law on mandates, the State Mandates Act.[11] This law determines whether an act is really a mandate or not.

Local officials have been complaining for a long time that the state has been requiring local governments to implement programs without giving them the wherewithal to pay for them. The state has mandated election costs, retirement benefits, 911 emergency phone numbers, health standards, workers' compensation for public employees—the list seems endless. In the middle to late 1970s, a reaction to many of these spending programs became apparent. Tax and spending limitations for state and local governments became popular. California adopted Proposition 13 and Massachusetts adopted its own form of tax and spending limitations. These limitations were arbitrary and did not necessarily take into consideration the needs of the public. To address these spending concerns, Illinois responded with a more reasonable and less arbitrary concept. That concept requires that, if the state is going to mandate that a local government carry out a program, the state should pay for the program. If the state does not provide the funds, the local government should not have to implement the program.

The concept is not new. Congress has attempted to impose these restrictions on itself. Illinois, in response to substantial pressure from local officials, created a commission on state-mandated programs. Its report was

10. Neil F. Hartigan, Attorney General, "A Guide to the Illinois Freedom of Information Act" (Springfield: State of Illinois, 1984).
11. Ill. Rev. Stat., ch. 85, par. 2201 et. seq.

completed in October 1977.[12] The matter was further studied by the legislature, and in 1979, it adopted the State Mandates Act. The act, which became law in November 1979, became effective 1 January 1981. The State Mandates Act concerns itself with any statutory or executive action imposing additional expenditures on local governments or removing taxes from the local tax base. It requires the state to estimate the fiscal impact of legislation on a local government prior to a law's adoption by the general assembly. It further classifies mandates and provides that certain of those mandates are reimbursable by the state unless the mandate is exempt under the act.

A state mandate is "any State initiated statutory or executive action that requires local government to establish, expand, or modify its activities in such a way as to necessitate additional expenditures from local revenues." Court-ordered mandates and federal mandates are exempt from the law.

Mandates are classified as follows:

1. *Service Mandates.* These mandates create or expand local services. Examples include programs in the areas of education, public health, pollution control, solid waste treatment and disposal, and expansion of duties of a public official. Service mandates are reimbursable by the state.

2. *Personnel Mandates.* These are activities affecting local government personnel costs such as employees' salaries, wages, benefits, qualifications, training, hours, working conditions. Personnel mandates are reimbursable by the state.

3. *Tax Exemption Mandates.* These are local tax-relief measures including exemption of business inventory from the property tax base or food and medicine from the local sales tax base. Tax exemption mandates are reimbursable by the state.

4. *Local Government Organizational Mandates.* These are mandates which affect forms of local government, the establishment of multicounty districts, the holding of local elections, the designation of public officers and their duties, and the prescription of administrative practices and procedures. These mandates are not reimbursable.

5. *Due Process Mandates.* These mandates concern the administration of justice, notification and conduct of public hearing, procedures for administrative review, protection of the public from malfeasance, misfeasance, or nonfeasance of local government. Due process mandates are not reimbursable.

12. Commission on State-Mandated Programs, Report and Recommendation to Governor James R. Thompson, Oct. 1977.

Two of the classes of mandates are never reimbursable, but exclusions may also apply to the reimbursable mandates. These allow the state to avoid reimbursement of mandates under certain conditions. They occur if

- the mandate accommodates a request from local governments (this provision has never been tested in court and the question remains open as to whether one local government can request a mandate which makes the mandate nonreimbursable for all other governments)
- the mandate can be carried out by existing staff at no appreciable additional cost
- the increased cost is offset from savings
- the increased cost is recovered from federal, state, or other external aid
- the increased cost is not more than $1,000 for each local government or less than $50,000 in the aggregate
- the legislature specifically exempts a mandate from reimbursement

To receive a reimbursement, the local government must file an application for reimbursement with the Illinois Department of Commerce and Community Affairs (DCCA). In the first year of the mandate, the local government has sixty days after the effective date of the mandate to file the application. Thereafter, the application must be filed by 1 October of each year.

A close reading of the State Mandates Act gives the impression that it is a law of exceptions. Not only are there certain mandates that are not reimbursable, but for the reimbursable mandates the legislature has provided certain exclusions as well. In addition to these exclusions, the rate of reimbursement varies, depending on the type of reimbursable mandate. All of the lost revenue resulting from a tax exemption or the increased cost resulting from increases in salaries, wages, or personnel benefits are fully reimbursed. Between 50 and to 100 percent of the service mandates are reimbursed.

The DCCA reviews all claims for reimbursement, except those relating to education; those applications are made to the State Board of Education. After review, the department determines the reimbursability of the claim and whether it is reasonable and not excessive. If approved, the payment is made in three equal installments during the year. In the event a claim is turned down, the State Mandates Act provides for an appeals procedure. An appeals board consisting of five members appointed by the governor and confirmed by the senate hears appeals of department decisions as to whether there should be reimbursement and how much it should be. If the state fails to appropriate funds for a reimbursable mandate, local governments are relieved from the requirement of carrying it out. The local government may choose to comply voluntarily with the mandated program even though funds are not available.

As always there are exceptions to exceptions when dealing with the spending of state money. The Mandates Act provides for reimbursable and nonreimbursable mandates and exclusions from reimbursable mandates. As noted earlier, where no exclusion has been available, the state legislature on occasion has passed legislation specifically exempting certain laws which create reimbursable mandates. The first of these exceptions was created in 1983, just two years after the law became effective. It deals with exemptions from the real estate tax, a local tax created by state law. In 1983, the legislature wanted to provide tax relief by increasing the homestead exemption and the homestead improvement exemption to the real estate tax act. If the tax-relief measure had been passed without exemption under the terms of the State Mandates Act, the state would have had to reimburse the local government for the loss of revenue. A political dilemma was created. The legislature and the governor wanted to give tax relief but the state could not afford the loss of revenue. The solution was to give tax relief by reducing revenues to local governments. If the legislature creates something, it can exempt it. The measure increasing the homestead exemption contained the following amendment to the State Mandates Act: "The following mandate is exempt from this act. The homestead exemption set forth in section 19.23-1A of the Revenue Act of 1939." With this, the legislature found a new way to create nonreimbursable mandates. Since that time, seven exemptions have been created by the legislature, five in relation to the "Revenue Act of 1939" and two others.[13]

The rapid changes in the law, not only in dealing with mandated programs, make it difficult for local officials to keep abreast of new developments. Most local government associations maintain a strong presence in Springfield, as do several regional organizations. These organizations, along with the local legislators, are the best source of information concerning legislation affecting local government. Furthermore, the speaker of the Illinois House and the president of the Illinois Senate both maintain services to obtain up-to-date information on the status of legislation.

13. Ill. Rev. Stat., ch. 85, par. 2208.1–2208.12.

Constitution of Illinois:
Provisions Affecting Local Government

Article 4 (Legislative Article)

Section 4 prohibits legislative appropriations by private law.

Section 20 forbids the state to pay the debts of, lend money, extend credit to, any public corporation.

Section 22 prohibits local or special legislation on the following subjects:

Laying out, opening, altering, or working on roads or highways

Vacating roads, town plats, streets, alleys, and public grounds

Locating and changing county seats

Regulating county and township affairs

Changing or amending the charter of a city, town, or village

Providing for the election of members of the board of supervisors in townships, incorporated towns, or cities

Opening and conducting of any election or designating places of voting

Creating, increasing, or decreasing fees, percentages, or allowances of public officers during term of office

Chartering or licensing toll bridges or ferries

Remitting fines, penalties, or forfeitures

Granting the right to lay railroad tracks or amending an existing charter for the purpose

Granting special or exclusive privileges, immunities, or franchises

Section 22 also directs that special laws are not to be enacted when general laws can be made applicable on any subject.

Section 23 forbids the general assembly to release or extinguish debts, liabilities, or obligations due to a municipal corporation.

Section 28 forbids the legislature to extend the term of any public officer, elected or appointed.

Section 31 allows the legislature to permit construction of drains, ditches, and levees across lands of others for agricultural, sanitary, and mining purposes, and to permit the establishment of drainage districts with the power of special assessment.

Section 34 relates specifically to local government in Chicago.

Article 6 (Judicial Article)

Paragraph 5(a) of the schedule substitutes the circuit court for local justices of the peace, police magistrate court, city, village, and town courts, municipal courts, county courts, probate courts, Superior Court of Cook County, and Criminal Court of Cook County, but requires election of at least one circuit judge per county.

Article 9 (Revenue Article)

Section 3 permits the legislature to exempt the property of local government from state taxes.

Section 6 forbids the legislature to release or discharge a county, city, township, town or district, or any inhabitants, for their proportionate share of state taxes, once an obligation is incurred.

Section 8 limits the county tax rate to 7.5 mills. Referendum is required for excess taxation.

Sections 9 and 10 allow special assessments for local improvements, forbid the general assembly to tax municipal corporations or their inhabitants for corporate purposes or corporate contracts, require uniformity of general taxation by local government, and exempt private property from sale for satisfaction of unpaid local taxes.

Section 11 withholds public office from any collector or custodian of local funds who is in default.

Section 12 limits local debt to 5 percent of the value of taxable property and limits the term of local debt to twenty years.

Section 13 specifically deals with bonding rights of the City of Chicago.

Article 10 (County Article)

Sections 1 to 3 specify the limitations on the creation of new counties, division of existing counties, and popular referenda.

Section 4 governs changes in county seats.

Sections 5 to 7 provide for the organization of township government, election of county commissioners in unorganized counties, and the election of county commissioners in Cook County.

Sections 8 to 13 regulate the election and reimbursement of county and township officers.

Other Provisions

An unnumbered schedule prohibits capital stock subscriptions, loans, and the extension of credit by local government to railroads and private corporations.

II.

Illinois Home Rule

KURT P. FROEHLICH

Under the present constitution of Illinois, subject to certain exceptions, a home-rule municipality "may exercise any power and perform any function pertaining to its government affairs." Surprising to many is that not all units of local government[1] and school districts have full authority concerning their government and affairs. Yet this is the case for over six thousand units of local government and school districts which are subject to the ability of the general assembly and the governor to understand local problems and concerns and then to devise reasonable and all-applicable solutions.

For municipalities alone this was and continues to be a difficult legislative task. For example, prior to the 1970 constitution of Illinois, the general assembly knew that many of the municipal laws it enacted applied with as equal force to the city of Chicago (pop. 3,005,072) as to the village of Bone Gap (pop. 350). Not surprisingly, the general assembly was rarely able to meet the more complex governmental concerns and needs of the largest municipalities without creating something unnecessarily unwieldy and unworkable for the smallest municipalities. This led to a legislative practice of enacting many laws applicable only to municipalities with a population over five hundred thousand. The generic reference to municipalities having a population over five hundred thousand was necessary because of the requirement in the 1870 constitution of Illinois that all laws had to be of general application. A law limited by reference to Chicago by name would be unconstitutional.

---

1. Section 1 of article 7 of the constitution provides: " 'Municipalities' means cities, villages and incorporated towns. 'Unit of local government' means counties, municipalities, townships, special districts and units, designated as units of local government by law, which exercise limited governmental powers or powers in respect to limited governmental subjects, but does not include school districts." These constitutional definitions will be used in this chapter.

Home Rule: A Dramatic Change

Home rule is a startling and dramatic change in state–local relations from that existing prior to the 1970 Illinois constitution. Home-rule municipalities may design legislative programs unique to their community needs, desires, and requirements. Each home-rule municipality has the power and authority to address its own special concerns, without necessarily having to balance such concerns as large and small, urban and suburban, and agriculture and industry. If a solution does not work as expected, or perhaps there is a better alternative, rarely would a home-rule municipality have to wait more than just a few weeks for another council or board meeting to make changes. The general assembly could never be expected to be so responsive. Citizens can expect their home-rule councils and boards to be that responsive. Such responsibility is not just available; it is an obligation of effective local government. Home rule carries with it the obligation to exercise local power and authority responsively, responsibly, and effectively. The power is great. Home rule includes the ability to consider action where the applicable laws provide no solution, provide an inadequate, incomplete, ineffective, or partial solution, or even provide that the solution may not be used. Home-rule municipalities may act even in the face of many proscriptive laws.

However, home-rule power and authority are not absolute. The constitution itself describes many areas in which even home-rule municipalities may not act or may act only in accordance with general laws. In addition, the home-rule provisions of the constitution describe a mechanism by which the general assembly may deny, declare exclusive to the state, or share almost all local authority which home-rule municipalities may exercise. This ability of the general assembly to take away almost all home-rule authority is generally referred to as "preemption." The result is that home-rule councils and boards are responsible and accountable not only to their citizens and voters, but also to the general assembly, which may take away all home-rule power and authority.

Home-Rule Power and Authority

The councils and boards of municipalities have adopted many thousands of ordinances pursuant to the power and authority of home rule under the constitution of Illinois. The concept of home rule is now relatively well understood by home-rule municipalities, the general assembly, and the courts. Home rule has been available in Illinois since 1 July 1971, the effective date of the present constitution of Illinois. Even in 1971, home rule was available in some form in almost forty of the United States. From the experiences of other states and the experiences in Illinois since 1971, home rule has relatively well defined parameters, well tested in judicial examination.

Two relatively systematic studies have described the exercise of home rule by municipal councils and boards.[2] As systematic as these attempts were, they had to err on the side of omission because of at least incomplete replies, the failure to recognize otherwise unauthorized actions, and changes in local councils, boards, and administrations since 1971. State laws have changed, permitting many local actions that once were not available or of questionable availability. In addition, there is no requirement to label ordinances as "home rule," so classification is often difficult, and there is sometimes a natural reluctance to declare unusual or draw attention to certain actions.

Of the many thousands of home-rule enactments, many have been the subjects of opinions by the supreme and appellant courts of Illinois. Such judicial analysis has resulted in the approval of many types of home-rule actions. Home-rule actions approved by Illinois supreme and appellate courts include:

> *Supreme Court:* cigarette tax; nonreferendum general obligation bonds; tax on retail sale of new motor vehicles; parking tax; creation of new county comptroller office; wheel tax ordinance; unrestricted application of certain tax proceeds; unincorporated area only wheel tax; increasing board size; appointment of clerk; reduction in mandatory fire and police retirement age; employers' expense (head) tax; hearing officer for police disciplinary cases; extraterritorial set-back regulation; retail sale of alcoholic beverages tax; eliminate police captain and create deputy chief; police chief and each deputy chief managerial appointments; admissions tax for racing; reduction in vote for appropriations; transaction tax; demolition procedures; unique commercial urban development program; land dedications, or cash in lieu, for schools and parks; exceed library tax rate limit; zoning for landfill sites; concurrent environmental authority; park district collection of amusement/food tax; amusement admissions tax; revenue act referendum cannot reduce home-rule tax rate; increase in official salaries during term; residential landlord/

---

2. James M. Banovetz and Thomas W. Kelty, "Home Rule in Illinois," in *Illinois Issues* (Springfield: Sangamon State University, 1987), adapted by the authors from a series of eight articles in the Illinois Municipal League's *Illinois Municipal Review* (March–Dec., except July and Nov., 1985), and Kurt P. Froehlich, "Home Rule," in *Illinois Municipal Law*, ch. 24 (Illinois Institute for Continuing Legal Education, 1974).

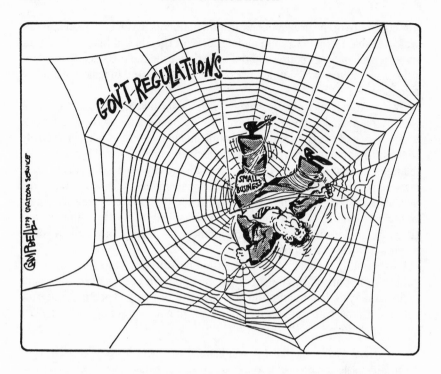

tenant relations; handgun prohibition; prohibition of Cubs night games; boat mooring tax; zoning of park district land.

Appellate Court: municipal intervention in county zoning case; pay toilet ban; zoning vote definition; change from eighteen to twenty-one for drinking age; zoning authority; mobile home park regulation; business license revocations; prohibit unattended unlocked motor vehicles; liquor employment age twenty-one; registration site as basis for wheel tax; tap-on water and sewer fees; prostitution as basis for business license revocations; low-income housing development; retroactive building code application; ten-day notice for lease termination; nonpartisan municipal elections; police eligibility list removal for DUI; negotiated redevelopment real estate sale; require liquor manager to be a resident; self-service gas regulation; abolish detective rank; zoning vote requirements; interim zoning regulation; no publication of interim sign regulations; no need to file three copies of building code book; special use definition; prohibit gas/liquor sales at same location; revoke liquor license for prostitution; chief dismissal of probationary officer; abolish police and fire departments and create public safety department; recall election; equity assurance program; hotel/motel tax; residence as a condition of employment; rule promulgation by personnel commissioner refrigerator trucks; gasoline tax; city to enforce others personnel policies; message tax.

Limits to Home-Rule Application

The debate surrounding the adoption of the constitution of Illinois recognizes that the powers of home-rule units relate to their own problems, not those of the state or nation. Their powers should not extend to such matters as divorce, real property law, trusts, or contracts, which are generally recognized as falling within the competence of state rather than local authorities. The Illinois supreme and appellate courts have recognized some matters that do not pertain to the government and affairs of home-rule units:

> Establishing the number of real estate tax installments; special service area procedures; home-rule intervention does not render prior decisions invalid or validate prior ordinances; county law library fees; adoption of Administrative Review Act; health ordinances conflicting with Environmental Protection Agency; noise regulation; regulation of branch banking; extraterritorial subdivision regulation; school district enforcement of amusement and food tax; municipal quick take condemnation procedures; reduction in veto override vote; regulate county road construction in municipality; unwritten zoning moratorium; reducing officials' salaries; fair employment regulation of noncoterminous school districts; separate mayoral salary as liquor commissioner; department head hiring and firing; personnel director extending probation period; certain penal ordinances conflicting with criminal code; challenge another municipality's zoning; discrimination based upon personal appearance; certain extraterritorial condemnation; disposition of unclaimed property; royalty fees for oil-well drilling; prevailing wage.

A special constitutional home-rule provision governs home-rule county/municipality conflicts. The provision is that when a home-rule county ordinance conflicts with a municipal (home-rule or non-home-rule) ordinance, the municipal ordinance prevails within the municipality's jurisdiction. One Illinois supreme court decision found no conflict when Cook County and several home-rule municipalities imposed a simultaneous tax on the retail sale of motor vehicles. Each was independently exercising an independent power to tax. The possible "double" tax was not a conflict.

Arguably, some of the actions listed above, approved by the Illinois supreme and appellate courts, might have been approved even for non-home-rule municipalities. However, it is questionable. Home rule removes almost all doubt in such cases. The Illinois constitution expressly provides that the powers and functions of home-rule municipalities "shall be construed liberally." This provision for liberal construction of home-rule authority is designed to reverse long-standing rules that local governmental powers are to be narrowly construed. This concept of narrow construction, Dillon's rule, is expressed as follows:

> It is a general and undisputed proposition of law that a municipal corporation possesses and can exercise the following powers, and no others: First, those granted in express words; second, those necessarily or fairly implied in or incident to the powers expressly granted; third, those essential to the accomplishment of the declared objects and purposes of the corporation . . . not simply convenient but indispensable.

Non-home-rule municipalities in Illinois still operate under the restrictions of Dillon's rule. However, when the present constitution went into effect, home-rule municipalities were freed from the traditional methods of interpreting grants of power to local governmental units. The general powers and functions of home-rule and non-home-rule units may be compared by contrasting the home-rule and non-home-rule provisions of the constitution found in appendix 11-1.

Home-Rule Units in Illinois

The Illinois constitution provides that any county which has a chief executive officer elected by the voters and any municipality which has a population greater than twenty-five thousand are home-rule units, and other municipalities may elect by referendum to become home-rule units. The result is that all municipalities and counties may be home-rule units, either by population, form of government, or by election. As of this date, there are over one hundred home-rule municipalities (see table 11-1).

Cook County is also a home-rule unit. The suggestion has been made that DuPage and St. Clair counties might really be home-rule units because their county board chairmen are elected at large and have been given many executive-type powers and functions. The home-rule provisions do not describe what an elected "chief executive officer" is. However, there is a specific county executive form of government provided by law to effect home rule.

Table II-I.
Illinois Home-Rule Municipalities

Municipalities	County Location	1980 Census Population	Municipalities	County Location	1980 Census Population
Addison	DuPage	28,836	McCook	Cook	303
Alton	Madison	34,171	Moline	Rock Island	45,709
Arlington Heights	Cook	66,116	Morton Grove	Cook	23,747
Aurora	Kane	81,293	Mound City	Pulaski	1,102
Bedford Park	Cook	988	Mt. Prospect	Cook	52,634
Belleville	St. Clair	42,150	Mt. Vernon	Jefferson	17,193
Berwyn	Cook	46,849	Muddy	Saline	88
Bloomington	McLean	44,189	Naperville	DuPage	42,330
Bolingbrook	Will	37,261	Naples	Scott	128
Bryant	Fulton	333	National City	St. Clair	70
Buffalo Grove	Cook	22,230	Niles	Cook	30,363
Burbank	Cook	28,462	Normal	McLean	35,672
Burnham	Cook	4,030	Norridge	Cook	16,483
Calumet City	Cook	39,673	Northbrook	Cook	30,735
Calumet Park	Cook	8,788	North Chicago	Lake	38,774
Carbondale	Jackson	27,194	Oak Forest	Cook	26,096
Champaign	Champaign	58,133	Oak Lawn	Cook	60,590
Channahon	Will	3,734	Oak Park	Cook	54,887
Chicago	Cook	3,005,072	Orland Park	Cook	23,045
Chicago Heights	Cook	37,026	Palatine	Cook	32,166
Cicero	Cook	61,232	Park City	Lake	3,673
Countryside	Cook	6,538	Park Forest	Cook	26,222
Danville	Vermilion	38,985	Park Forest South	Will	6,245
Decatur	Macon	94,081	Park Ridge	Cook	38,704
Deerfield	Lake	17,430	Pekin	Tazewell	33,967
DeKalb	DeKalb	33,099	Peoria	Peoria	124,160
Des Plaines	Cook	53,568	Peoria Heights	Peoria	7,453
Dolton	Cook	24,766	Peru	LaSalle	10,886
Downers Grove	DuPage	39,274	Quincy	Adams	42,352
East St. Louis	St. Clair	55,200	Rantoul	Champaign	20,161
Elgin	Kane	63,798	Rockdale	Will	1,913
Elk Grove Village	Cook	28,907	Rock Island	Rock Island	47,036
Elmhurst	DuPage	44,251	Rolling Meadows	Cook	20,167
Elmwood Park	Cook	24,016	Rosemont	Cook	4,137
Evanston	Cook	73,706	Sauget	St. Clair	205
Evergreen Park	Cook	22,260	Schaumburg	Cook	52,319
Flora	Clay	5,379	Skokie	Cook	60,278
Freeport	Stephenson	26,406	South Barrington	Cook	1,168
Galesburg	Knox	35,305	South Holland	Cook	24,977
Glenview	Cook	30,842	Springfield	Sangamon	99,637
Golf	Cook	482	Standard	Putnam	277
Granite City	Madison	36,815	Stickney	Cook	5,893

Table II-I. *continued*

Municipalities	County Location	1980 Census Population	Municipalities	County Location	1980 Census Population
Hanover Park	Cook	28,850	Stone Park	Cook	4,273
Harvey	Cook	35,810	Thornton	Cook	3,022
Highland Park	Lake	30,611	Tinley Park	Cook-Will	26,171
Hoffman Estates	Cook	38,258	Urbana	Champaign	35,978
Joliet	Will	77,956	Watseka	Iroquois	5,543
Kankakee	Kankakee	30,141	Waukegan	Lake	67,653
Lansing	Cook	29,039	Wheaton	DuPage	43,043
Lincolnshire	Lake	4,151	Wheeling	Cook	23,266
Mascoutah	St. Clair	4,962	Wilmette	Cook	28,229
Maywood	Cook	27,998	Woodridge	DuPage	22,322

The municipalities of Lisle, Lombard, and Rockford have elected by referendum not to be home-rule units. Rantoul dropped below twenty-five thousand population and elected to retain home rule. Villa Park similarly lost population and elected not to retain home rule. A special provision in the Illinois Municipal Code preserves home rule until the next election at which a home-rule referendum may be held in those cases in which population has dropped below twenty-five thousand.

Constitutional Limitations

The power and authority available to home-rule units are broad. As noted and illustrated above, a home-rule unit "may exercise any power and perform any function pertaining to its government and affairs." However, that constitutional statement of power and authority is not without limitations. First, the home-rule provisions themselves contain specific limitations. Second, by way of preemption, the general assembly has the power to deny, declare exclusive, or share almost all power and authority available under home rule. Third, other constitutional provisions affect home rule.

The home-rule provisions themselves specify certain things that home-rule units may not do or may do in a restricted way. Those specific provisions are as follows:

- a home-rule unit may not incur debt maturing more than forty years payable from ad valorem property tax receipts
- a home-rule unit may not define and provide for the punishment of a felony
- a home-rule unit requires authority from the general assembly to punish by imprisonment for more than six months

- a home-rule unit requires authority from the general assembly to license for revenue or impose taxes upon or measured by income or earnings or upon occupations (as imagined, because of the impact on taxes and revenue, this limitation has been the most litigated of the home-rule provisions)
- a home-rule unit with referendum approval may adopt, alter, or repeal a form of government provided by law. A home-rule municipality may provide for its officers, their manner of selection and terms of office, only as approved by referendum or as otherwise provided by law

Constitutional home rule in Illinois is in large measure a delicate balance of power between the general assembly and the home-rule units. One or the other has to prevail or have the last word. In almost every feature of home rule, the general assembly potentially has the constitutional power to prevail. Noted above are several specific areas of decidedly local concern that require action or approval by the general assembly. In almost all other areas that pertain to home-rule government and affairs there is constitutional authority for home-rule units to act, subject to the overriding authority of the general assembly to take it all away.

The ability of the general assembly to take away the power and authority of home rule is often called *preemption,* although that specific term is not used in the constitution. The home-rule provisions concerning preemption are expressly in three basic concepts:

1. *Denial.* By a ⅗'s vote of each house, the general assembly may deny or limit the power to tax and any other power or function (with very few exceptions) of a home-rule unit not exercised or performed by the state. The ⅗'s vote requirement affirms a presumption in favor of home-rule authority where the general assembly only wants to deny or limit in areas where the state is not acting. That is, to merely say "no" is more difficult. That that is difficult is shown by the very few ⅗'s vote denials or limitations of home rule. Areas of this type of preemption include: Chicago area regional transportation authority; certain insurance matters; police pensions; fire pensions; ride sharing; postage machines; stock, commodity, and option transactions and sales tax reform.

2. *Declaration of Exclusivity.* By a simple majority vote, the general assembly may provide specifically by law for the state's exclusive exercise of any home-rule power or function except taxation, local improvements, special assessments, and special service areas. This simple majority vote, in contrast to the ⅗'s vote for mere denial or limitation, is to make it easier for the general assembly to provide an exclusive, and perhaps more uniform, exercise of power by or throughout the state. What is not clear

either in the constitution or by judicial opinions is what degree or level of exercise by the state is required to declare such exclusivity. For example, is the mere declaration of a set of regulations considered to be an "exercise by the state" where no state agency or officer does anything?

3. *Concurrent or Shared Authority.* This is perhaps not really a preemption provision, but rather one to clarify home-rule power where the general assembly has not preempted and both the state and home-rule units may overlap in the exercise of power and authority. Home-rule units may concurrently exercise and perform with the state any power or function of a home-rule unit (except as specifically denied or limited or declared exclusive, as described above).

To make certain that inadvertent preemptions do not occur, there is a special enactment concerning home-rule preemption laws. This provision requires a specific reference to section (g), (h), or (i) of section 6 of article 7 of the constitution to allow a preemption. Otherwise, although a supreme court decision requires such specificity, it would be unclear as to the preemptive effect to be given, for example, in the case of a bill that was passed in both houses by at least a ⅗ vote that had some implications for municipal powers.

A number of preemptions have been labeled as "exclusive" and/or "concurrent" exercises in the areas of home-rule municipal or county affairs and government.

> Vehicle code; open meetings; public notices; electrical supply; dangerous drugs; health facilities planning; regulation (real estate brokers, doctors, dentists, nurses, pharmacists, optometrists, physical therapists, podiatrists, veterinarians, psychologists, social workers, public accountants, shorthand reporters, business schools, beauticians, deception examiners, insurance brokers, architects, professional engineers, structural engineers, surveyors, nursing homes, sanitariums, tree experts, well pump contractors, and private detectives); vehicle inspections; public labor relations; pension fiduciaries; police/fire benefits; alcohol abuse; truth in taxation; and real estate time shares.

Preemption provides a dynamic mechanism to balance the local governmental matters of home-rule units with those of the state. Ultimately, the state has the last word, with the first preemption being that home rule is to be given precedence.

Provisions other than in the home-rule section of the constitution affect or limit home rule. No one believes that the United States Constitution is in any way superseded, voided, diminished, or impaired by the home-rule provisions of the Illinois constitution. Similarly, the provisions in the Illinois

Bill of Rights (due process, and so on) should not be set aside by home rule. The Illinois Supreme Court has already rendered opinions to the effect that the environmental, judicial, condemnation, and branch banking provisions of the Illinois constitution are to be given effect over conflicting home-rule ordinances. If a measure impacts on other local governments and on other branches of government it is highly suspect as not pertaining to home-rule government and affairs.

Special Home-Rule Powers

Under the constitution's home-rule provisions, the general assembly may limit the amount and require referendum approval of home-rule municipal debt payable from ad valorem property taxes, but only in excess of percentages of assessed value, as follows:

Population	Assessed Value Percentage
500,000 or more	3.0
25,000–500,000	1.0
25,000 or less	0.5

Debt incurred prior to 1 July 1971, the constitution's effective date, does not count in the percentage computation. This limited power is one that even the general assembly may not take away, except possibly to a ⅗'s vote denial preemption. The interrelationship of these provisions is not clear.

The constitution also provides that the general assembly may not deny or limit the power of home-rule units to make local improvements by special assessment (and jointly with other units of local government having that power on 1 July 1971, unless such power is denied to all such other units). Also, the general assembly may not deny or limit home-rule power to levy or impose additional taxes for special services upon areas within home-rule units in the manner provided by law to pay for such services and related debt. In accordance with a home-rule supreme court decision holding that the general assembly is to be the source of special service area procedures and mechanisms, the general assembly implemented special service area financing. Under the Illinois constitution of 1870, special service techniques were not possible because the entire taxing jurisdiction was required to be uniformly taxed. Under the present constitution the impediment of uniform taxation does not exist (except that within a class there must be uniformity).

The Effect of General Laws

Home rule gives certain municipalities and counties the ability to exercise any power and perform any function pertaining to their governments and affairs. To use this constitutional authority, a home-rule unit must adopt ordinances and resolutions or take other actions that supplement, vary, modify, nullify, diminish, or impair the statutory framework otherwise applicable. A transition schedule in the constitution provides that until such action is taken, all general laws apply. Laws in effect prior to the constitution could not have been enacted with a view to affecting home rule. Therefore, they cannot be preemptive in character. Laws after that date could be, if enacted as preemption measures. In the absence of preemption, or except for activity in an area that does not pertain to its government and affairs or otherwise fails to comply with the specific home-rule provisions, a home-rule unit has many opportunities.

Illinois Constitution Provisions Affecting Home-Rule
and Non-Home-Rule Municipalities

Section 6, Powers of Home-Rule Units, Article 7
of the Illinois Constitution

(a) A county which has a chief executive officer elected by the electors of the county and any municipality which has a population of more than twenty-five thousand are home-rule units. Other municipalities may elect by referendum to become home-rule units. Except as limited by the section, a home-rule unit may exercise any power and perform any function pertaining to its government and affairs including, but not limited to, the power to regulate for the protection of the public health, safety, morals, and welfare; to license; to tax; and to incur debt.

(b) A home-rule unit by referendum may elect not to be a home-rule unit.

(c) If a home-rule unit county ordinance conflicts with an ordinance of a municipality, the municipal ordinance shall prevail within its jurisdiction.

(d) A home-rule unit does not have the power (1) to incur debt payable from ad valorem property tax receipts maturing more than forty years from the time it is incurred or (2) to define and provide for the punishment of a felony.

(e) A home-rule unit shall have only the power that the general assembly may provide by law (1) to punish by imprisonment for more than six months or (2) to license for revenue or impose taxes upon or measured by income or earnings or upon occupations.

(f) A home-rule unit shall have the power subject to approval by referendum to adopt, alter, or repeal a form of government provided by law, except that the form of government of Cook County shall be subject to the provisions of section 3 of this article. A home-rule municipality shall have the power to provide for its officers, their manner of selection, and terms of office only as approved by referendum or as otherwise authorized by law. A home-rule county shall have the power to provide for its officers, their manner of selection, and terms of office in the manner set forth in section 4 of this article.

(g) The general assembly by a law approved by the vote of three-fifths of the members elected to each house may deny or limit the power to tax and any other power or function of a home-rule unit not exercised or performed by the state other than a power or function specified in subsection (1) of this section.

(h) The general assembly may provide specifically by law for the exclusive exercise by the state of any power or function of a home-rule unit other than a taxing power or a power or function specified in subsection (1) of this section.

(i) Home-rule units may exercise and perform concurrently with the state any

237

power or function of a home-rule unit to the extent that the general assembly by law does not specifically limit the concurrent exercise or specifically declare the state's exercise to be exclusive.

(j) The general assembly may limit by law the amount of debt which home-rule counties may incur and may limit by law approved by three-fifths of the members elected to each house the amount of debt, other than debt payable from ad valorem property tax receipts, which home-rule municipalities may incur.

(k) The general assembly may limit by law the amount and require referendum approval of debt to be incurred by home-rule municipalities, payable from ad valorem property tax receipts, only in excess of the following percentages of the assessed value of its taxable property: (1) if its population is five hundred thousand or more, an aggregate of 3 percent; (2) if its population is more than twenty-five thousand and less than five hundred thousand, an aggregate of 1 percent; and (3) if its population is twenty-five thousand or less, an aggregate of .05 percent. Indebtedness which is outstanding on the effective date of this constitution or which is thereafter approved by referendum or assumed from another unit of local government shall not be included in the foregoing percentage amounts.

(l) The general assembly may not deny or limit the power of home-rule units (1) to make local improvements by special assessment and to exercise this power jointly with other counties and municipalities, and other classes of units of local government having that power on the effective date of this constitution unless the power is subsequently denied by law to any such other units of local government or (2) to levy or impose additional taxes upon areas within their boundaries in the manner provided by law for the provision of special services to those areas and for the payment of debt incurred in order to provide those special services.

(m) Powers and functions of home-rule units shall be construed liberally.

Section 7, Counties and Municipalities Other Than Home-Rule Units, Article 7 of the Illinois Constitution

Counties and municipalities which are not home-rule units shall have only powers granted to them by law and the powers (1) to make local improvements by special assessment and to exercise this power jointly with other counties and municipalities, and other classes of units of local government having that power on the effective date of this constitution unless that power is subsequently denied by law to any such other units of local government; (2) by referendum, to adopt, alter, or repeal their forms of government provided by law; (3) in the case of municipalities, to provide by referendum for their officers, manner of selection, and terms of office; (4) in the case of counties, to provide for their officers, manner of selection, and terms of office as provided in section 4 of this article; (5) to incur debt except as limited by law and except that debt payable from ad valorem property tax receipts shall mature within forty years from the time it is incurred; and (6) to levy or impose additional taxes upon areas within their boundaries in the manner provided by law for the provision of special services to those areas and for the payment of debt incurred in order to provide those special services.

12.

Campaigns and Elections

WILLIAM MCGUFFAGE

This chapter will not tell you how to run a campaign and win an election. Raising money, recruiting volunteers, developing issues, targeting voters, buying ads, and building a candidate's image are the responsibilities of a campaign manager and staff. So if you have a clean record, good issues, a pleasing personality, and a professional campaign manager, and your opponent has just the opposite, you should have a fun campaign and an easy victory.

Then why bother reading this chapter? Because your charisma, your opponent's problems, and your campaign manager's skill are meaningless unless you can get your name on the ballot and get all the votes you are entitled to on election day. This chapter will provide you with the "nuts" and "bolts" of elections—the law and procedures you must know in order to protect your candidacy and your votes.

Do you need an attorney to advise you on election law? Probably, if your opponent challenges your candidate petitions or your campaign financial reports. But if you read this chapter carefully and follow step by step the law and procedures laid out, your petitions and reports should be objection-proof and your limited campaign funds will not have to be spent on legal fees. Most lawyers in this state are not considered election law experts, but those who are agree that the Illinois Election Code is a confusing mishmash of technical rules, exceptions to rules, and exceptions to exceptions put there by the party that was in control of the Illinois legislature at the time to frustrate candidates of other parties and independent candidates. Although the federal courts in recent years have declared unconstitutional several state election law provisions which restrict a candidate's right of ballot access, the Election Code is still a legislative maze that could eliminate a candidate from the ballot or cripple his or her campaign. The first part of this chapter will guide you through this maze and help you avoid the traps. Later in this chapter, you will learn how to protect your votes before, after, and on election day.

Candidacies

In most cities, villages, and townships, partisan elections are permitted; that is, a candidate may be affiliated with a political party or may run as an independent with no party affiliation. However, in some cities and villages, the form of government (i.e., commission form, some managerial forms) or a municipal election ordinance may require nonpartisan elections in which candidates are not permitted to run under political party or independent labels. In nearly all school districts, park districts, and other local taxing districts, nonpartisan elections are required by law.

If you are running for office in a city, village, or township where partisan elections are permitted, you must choose a label under which to run. You can run as an established political party candidate, which means that you will have to win nomination in a primary election or party caucus to be eligible to run in the general election. You can run on a new political party ticket or as an independent candidate and avoid a primary or caucus. But you will need substantially more petition signatures than an established party candidate for the same office.

When one thinks of an established political party, one usually thinks of the Democratic party and the Republican party. Except in the city of Chicago, some Chicago suburbs, and some large downstate cities, candidates for municipal or township office never run as Democrats or Republicans. They prefer to concentrate on local issues and not identify with the Democratic or Republican position on national or state issues, which may not be popular in their communities.

However, local political parties other than Democrats and Republicans often become established in a municipality or township because the candidates of such parties always receive more than 5 percent of the total votes cast in each election. Names like the Taxpayer's party, the Better Government party, The Village Voice party, and so forth, are common in municipal and township elections. If such parties have been successful in electing candidates and have become identified with popular positions on local issues, such parties may remain established, hold primaries or caucuses, and nominate candidates who are usually able to win a general election. Therefore, if you are challenging an incumbent who has previously won an election as the local established party candidate and is running again as that party's candidate, you may have a better chance of defeating him or her in a primary than running in the general election as an "outsider" on a new party slate or as an independent. On the other hand, you may have to go the new party or independent route in order to get on the general election ballot if the local established party nominates by caucus. Under the caucus system, party leaders tend to control voter participation and candidates favored by the party leaders tend to win nomination.

Nevertheless, local established parties in municipal and township elections are the exception rather than the rule. Local parties are normally organized for each election. If a local party becomes established by reason of its vote in the last election, it will usually change its name for the next election and become a new party all over again in order to avoid a costly and competitive primary. Thus, the Village Voice party in the last election may become the Village Choice party for the next election; the Better Government party becomes the Good Government party, and so forth.

The bottom line of this discussion is: Confer with your campaign manager and staff and do what is most politically advantageous for you. If the local established party has a good track record, join it and try to get the nomination. If the party in power is "in trouble" with the electorate and changes its name, run against it on a new party ticket or as an independent. If there are no established parties for the next election, form a new party or run as an independent. To form a new party, candidates for *each* office to be filled at the municipal or township election must appear on the petition. To run as an independent, you do not have to team up with candidates for the other offices; just pick your office and file a petition.

Petitions

Whether you are an incumbent seeking another term or a challenger seeking to upset the incumbent, the Election Code requires that you file a petition and accompanying documents to qualify as a candidate. The minimum number of signatures needed on your petition is usually determined by taking a percentage of the vote cast in the last election. Signature requirements differ depending on what office you are seeking and whether you are running as an established political party, new political party, independent, or nonpartisan candidate. You should contact the State Board of Elections in Springfield (217/782-4141) or Chicago (312/917-6440) and obtain the *Candidate's Guide,* which delineates the signature requirements for each elective office in a county, city, village, township, school district, park district, fire protection district, and so forth. Once you determine how many petition signatures are required for the office you are seeking, you will need to know and understand the basic legal requirements for preparing, passing, and filing your petition.

The standard petition sheet is a legal size (8½" by 14") document. Its size is not important (so long as all the petition sheets you file are the same size), but the words that are printed on it are very important. At the top of each sheet must appear the word *Petition,* followed by a preamble which declares the intent of the signers that you shall be a candidate (either a political party or an independent candidate) for a particular office to be voted for at a particular primary or election. After the preamble must be printed three (or four) boxes containing the following information:

1. Name: Print your name exactly as it appears on your voter registration record. If you are registered under the name of John P. Doe, then John P. Doe must be printed in this box and *not* Jack Doe or J. P. Doe. However, you may add a nickname before your last name so long as it is set off in quotation marks such as John P. "Jack" Doe. But you *cannot* add a title before or after your name such as Dr., Ph.D., Esq., and so on.

2. Office: Print the exact name of the office for which you are a candidate. For example: Do not print Village Trustee if the legal name of the office is Trustee of the Village of _____ . Similarly, do not just print Alderman, City of _____ , if you are running from a ward. The ward number must also be indicated.

3. Party: Print the exact name of the political party with which you are affiliated (Democrat, Republican, Taxpayer's party, Good Government party, etc.). If you are running as an independent (no party affiliation), print the word *Independent* in this box. However, if you are a candidate in a nonpartisan election, disregard this box.

Underneath these boxes are twenty signature and address lines. At the bottom of each petition sheet are the circulator's affidavit, the notary's affidavit, and a space for the notary seal. Petition sheets and accompanying documents appropriate to your candidacy may be obtained from the State Board of Elections.

Petition Signers

Persons who sign your petition must be registered voters who are residents of the political subdivision or district in which the election is to be held. A "political subdivision" means a county, township, city, or village, school district, sanitary district, road district, park district, or any other local government which elects officials at large. A "district" means a county board district, city ward, village district, school district unit, or any area within a political subdivision which elects officials to serve only that area. To illustrate: if you are running for mayor of a city, you are running at large in a political subdivision and your petition signers must be registered to vote from a residence inside the city. If you are running for alderman of a ward in that same city, you are running from a district within a political subdivision and your petition signers must be registered to vote from a residence inside the ward.

This is important. Make sure that the circulators of your petition know the boundaries of the area in which you are a candidate. If you are running for alderman of Ward 1, any petition signatures obtained from registered voters who live in other wards are invalid. A good rule to remember is if they cannot vote for you, they cannot sign your petition.

It is more practical and much safer to have your petition circulated door to door in a residential area within the political subdivision or district. Unless you are running for mayor of Chicago and need thousands of signatures, do not circulate your petition at fairs, in shopping malls, outside churches, on street corners, or at any other fixed location where many signers may not be residents of the political subdivision or district. Otherwise, you and your workers will have to spend a lot of time and effort reviewing each sheet of the petition before it is filed, checking signer addresses, striking ineligible signatures, and filling out affidavits for each stricken signature.

Remember that only registered voters can sign your petition. Each of your circulators should be assigned to a precinct and be supplied with a poll sheet for that precinct. All persons whose names appear on the poll sheet are registered voters. As they go door to door soliciting signatures, your circulators should be checking the addresses against the poll sheet. If an address does not appear on the poll sheet, there are no registered voters in that household. However, the circulator should note that address so that someone can go back later and get those folks registered. Also, he or she should note if anyone listed on the poll sheet has moved and get the names of the new residents so they can be registered later on.

Poll sheets can be obtained from the office of the election authority. If you live in the city of Chicago, Aurora, Rockford, Peoria, Danville, Bloomington, Springfield, or East St. Louis or in DuPage County, the election authority is the Board of Election Commissioners. If you live anywhere else in the state, the election authority is the county clerk. Get to know and love your election authority. They will not only provide you with poll sheets but also with forms and information you will need as your campaign progresses.

More importantly, they are the ones who conduct the election and count your votes.

To ensure that your circulators are collecting valid signatures, make sure that they understand the following:

1. The petition signer must *write* (not print) his or her own name as it appears on the poll sheet. If the signer is registered to vote as John P. Doe, he cannot sign as Jack Doe.

2. The petition signer must write or print his or her exact numerical residence address or rural route number on the space to the right of his or her signature. Standard abbreviations may be used (e.g., 100 S. Main St.).

3. The petition signer must print the name of the city, village, or town in which he or she resides and the zip code on the space to the right of his or her address. If you are running for a city or village office so that only registered voters in that city or village can sign your petition, then have the name of the city or village preprinted on the petition sheet.

4. The petition signer must *not* have signed a petition for another candidate for the same office. If you are running for township supervisor and any signers of your petition have previously signed your opponent's petition, those signatures on your petition are invalid.

Petition Circulators

Although the same rules that apply to petition signers apply to petition circulators, the consequences of not following such rules are much more serious. For example: If three signers of a petition sheet are not registered voters or do not live in the political subdivision or district in which you are a candidate, only those three signatures are invalid and the remaining signatures on the sheet are acceptable. Put another way, a few invalid signatures on a petition sheet do not invalidate the entire sheet. However, a nonresident or nonregistered circulator can invalidate an entire petition sheet of twenty otherwise valid signatures. Important rule: If they cannot vote for you on election day, they cannot circulate your petition. Make sure that anyone who volunteers to pass your petition is registered to vote and lives in the political subdivision or district in which you are a candidate. Your opponent will first look at the qualifications of your circulators. The fastest way for your opponent to disqualify you as a candidate is to disqualify your circulators and thereby remove enough signatures to put you below the required minimum number.

In addition, the following restrictions apply to circulators:

1. A petition circulator must *not* have circulated a petition of another

candidate for the same office. Check this out. You certainly do not want someone who was passing your opponent's petition to be working in your campaign.

2. A petition circulator must *not* have circulated a petition for a candidate of another political party or for an independent candidate. For example: If you are the Good Government party candidate for mayor, you cannot have someone passing your petition who is also passing the petition of the Taxpayer's party candidate for city treasurer or an independent candidate (no party affiliation) for city clerk.

3. A petition can be circulated only within the ninety days preceding the last day for petition filing. The time periods for filing petitions are discussed in the State Board of Election's *Candidate Guide*. Remember that you cannot start collecting petition signatures more than three months ahead of the petition filing deadline.

So much for the restrictions. What must a circulator do when he or she has finished collecting signatures? He or she must complete and sign the affidavit at the bottom of each petition sheet he or she circulated, have the affidavits notarized, and bring the sheets back to you. It sounds simple, but this is where problems may arise. Let's look at a classic example. Each of your petition circulators agrees to collect one hundred signatures (five sheets) in two weeks. One of them, Will Pass, waits until the last weekend to start circulating his petition sheets. He spends four hours on Saturday afternoon going door to door in the precinct and collects forty signatures. Knowing that he will have to continue on Sunday, but wanting to get home in time to watch the football game, Will Pass recruits his sixteen- and nineteen-year-old sons to help him out. On Sunday evening, each son returns a fully signed sheet to Pass, who has them complete and sign the circulator's affidavit. He then runs next door and gets his neighbor, Will Seal, to notarize the affidavits. Monday, Will Pass returns four completed petition sheets to your headquarters.

Let us assume that all signatures on the petition sheets are valid. What is wrong with this example? First of all, the sixteen-year-old son is too young to be a registered voter and therefore not qualified to circulate the petition. Second, the nineteen-year-old son, if registered to vote, is a qualified circulator; but he did not complete and sign the circulator's affidavit in front of the notary, as required by law. As circulator, he must personally appear before a notary and swear that the signatures on the petition sheet were signed in his presence and are genuine (i.e., not forgeries). Be aware that anyone who intends to object to your petition will determine whether or not a circulator is a registered voter and also whether or not the circulator was present when his or her affidavit was notarized. In the above example, one petition sheet could be thrown out for defective circulation and one for defective notarization even though each sheet contained twenty valid signatures.

Accompanying Documents

STATEMENT OF CANDIDACY   When filed, your petition must have attached to the front of it a statement of candidacy which

1. states your name and address as they appear on your voter registration record
2. states the title of the office for which you are a candidate
3. states that you are qualified to hold the office, if elected
4. states that you have filed (or will file before the close of the petition filing period) a statement of economic interests, as required by the Illinois Governmental Ethics Act
5. requests that your name be placed on the ballot for nomination or election to the office and must be notarized

Failure to file such a statement together with your petition will disqualify you as a candidate.

You must file a statement of economic interest (ethics statement) with the county clerk and get a time-stamped receipt. This receipt should be attached to your statement of candidacy and filed with your petition. On the ethics statement, you list sources of income other than your salary. If none, you simply print "none" in the spaces provided. The purpose of this statement is to reflect any financial conflicts of interest you may have in relation to the office you are seeking. For example: if you are running for alderman, you should not be an officer or stockholder in a company doing business with the city. Ethics statements are available for public inspection in the county clerk's office. Failure to file an ethics statement and file the receipt for it with your petition will disqualify you as a candidate.

LOYALTY OATH   This is an optional filing. The requirement of a loyalty oath for candidates has been declared unconstitutional. However, if you do not file it, your opponent may accuse you of being a Communist or an Iranian terrorist. Avoid the hassle. Sign the loyalty oath form and attach it to your petition.

CERTIFICATE OF OFFICERS Only if you form a new political party, the petition must have attached a certificate listing the names and addresses of the party officers (i.e., chairman, secretary, treasurer). Usually, the new party officers are the same as its candidates.

Petition Preparation

Several years ago, a candidate, in an appeal from an electoral board decision removing him from the ballot for improper petition filing, was told by a judge that "if you cannot follow the simple requirements of the state election law, you do not deserve to be a candidate for public office." In this case, the candidate was disqualified for filing loose, unnumbered petition sheets. So make sure that before your petition is filed, the sheets are consecutively numbered and securely bound. Use the following checklist:

1. After all of your circulators have returned signed petition sheets to your headquarters, go through them and make sure that each circulator's affidavit is completed, signed, and notarized. For convenience, a notary should be available at your headquarters when the circulators make their returns so they can sign the affidavit and have it notarized right there. Also, if all or most of the signatures on a petition sheet appear to be of the same handwriting, throw out that sheet. You should have more than enough signatures without it. Do not file it! Even if your opponent is unable to find other defects in your petition that would bring you under the minimum number of signatures needed, he or she may make that one forged sheet a campaign issue in order to question your honesty.

2. After you have scrutinized each of the returned petition sheets, number them on the space provided at the very bottom of the sheet (Sheet No. _____). It makes no difference when a sheet was circulated. If you have a pile of ten sheets fully or partially signed, number the first sheet 1, the second sheet 2, and so forth. It is immaterial whether a sheet has only five signatures on it or the full twenty. All valid signatures count.

3. After you number the sheets, arrange them neatly in a pile. Then staple the receipt for the filing of your ethics statement to the bottom left side of your statement of candidacy. Next, place the loyalty oath behind your statement of candidacy and place these documents on top of the pile of petition sheets. Finally, two-hole-punch the entire pile at the top and bind it with a fastener. If you are filing many petition sheets, you may want to bind these documents in a booklet. Now, your petition is ready to be filed.

Petition Filing

Consult the State Board of Election's *Candidate's Guide* to determine when and where your petition must be filed. If you are a candidate for county office, you file with the county clerk. For all other local offices, you file with the clerk or secretary of the political subdivision. However, if you are a candidate for office in a city under the jurisdiction of a board of election commissioners, you file with that board. There are seven days in a filing period; it usually runs from a Monday to a Monday. Important Rule: File your petition in person on the first day of the filing period at the opening hour of the filing office. Even if you have no known opposition, another candidate may unexpectedly appear. The ballot position of candidates is determined by when they file. You will get first ballot position, that is, the voters will see your name at the top of a list of candidates for that office, if you file first and your opponents file later. However, if you and your opponent are in line to file at 8:00 A.M. on the first day, both of you are considered first filed and a lottery will be held after the filing period to determine first and second ballot positions. You may still come out on top.

The only reservation to the "file first" rule is when you are opposed by five or more candidates and all of you show up to file first. Here you must make a decision. If you are the incumbent, go for the lottery. It will not make any difference where you appear on the ballot; the voters will recognize your name. But if you are a challenger who is not exactly a household word, you may be better off filing on the last day just before the closing hour of the filing office and assure yourself of last ballot position. It has been statistically shown that in a field of five or more candidates for the same office, voters look at the first name on the ballot and then look at the last name. You can go for the lottery and you might win first position. On the other hand, you might get sandwiched in third position. Or you can file last and let your opponents take the luck of the draw. In any event, make sure you get a time-stamped receipt for the filing of your petition. Now you are officially a candidate and your campaign can get moving; that is, unless objections to your petition are filed.

Objection and Withdrawal

If you have carefully followed all of the rules for circulating, signing, and filing your petition, you will probably avoid objections. More than likely, your opponent will request and review a copy of your petition soon after it is filed. Your opponent and his or her workers will first check to make sure that the petition is securely bound and the petition sheets are consecutively numbered and that all accompanying documents — statements of candidacy, loyalty oath, ethics statement receipt — are attached. They will count the number of signatures on the petition sheets to see if you have the required minimum. Next, they will examine each petition sheet for obvious defects such as similar handwriting on signature lines (possible forgeries), incomplete or unsigned circulators' affidavits, and unsigned or unsealed notarization of circulators' affidavits. Last, they will look to see if your statement of candidacy is properly filled out, signed, and notarized.

Up to this point, let us assume that your petition is in order. Your opponent will then have to check the registration and residence of signers and circulators in an effort to trim the number of signatures down below the minimum. This means that he or she will have to inspect the precinct registration binders in the office of the election authority in order to (1) determine if each circulator has a registration record and, if he or she does, compare the address and signature on his or her record with the address and signature on the affidavit on the petition sheets that he or she circulated; (2) determine if each petition sheet signer has a registration record and do the address and signature comparison described above. This can be a long, tedious exercise. Your opponent will probably not bother to check the registration of the signers if you have, as I strongly suggest, three to five times more signatures than you need.

So far, so good. You opponent has found few, if any, irregularities on your petitions which would bring the total number of signatures below the minimum. If persistent enough, he or she will send campaign workers out to interview the circulators and find out whether or not they personally circulated your petition and interview the notaries and find out whether or not the circulators personally appeared and signed the affidavit in front of them. Even if your opponent cannot find any basis for filing objections, he or she may nevertheless object just to disrupt your campaign. Do not let this concern you; this can work to your advantage. Publicly criticize him or her for wasting everyone's time with frivolous objections and characterize him or her as a spoilsport or "dirty tricks" candidate. Objections must be filed with the appropriate electoral board within the five days following the close of the petition filing period. There is an electoral board for each political subdivision which hears and rules on objections to petitions. If an electoral board upholds the objections and decides that the candidate does not have enough valid petition signatures or has not otherwise complied with the election law, the candidate will be disqualified from appearing on the ballot. However, the disqualified candidate (or the objector, if his objections are not upheld) may appeal the electoral board decision to the circuit court. You will need a lawyer if objections are filed to your petition. But make sure you get a lawyer who is knowledgeable in election law and is known and respected by the electoral board members and the circuit court. Local electoral boards are composed of elected local government officials. So do not hire your brother-in-law unless he is an election law expert with political "clout."

If the members of the electoral board are your political adversaries (or your opponent's allies), you may have a problem, depending on whether or not any of your opponent's objections are valid. But an unfair and unfavorable ruling can be appealed to the circuit court, which will more objectively weigh the evidence and possibly reverse the electoral board. Once again, make sure you have the "right" lawyer. Also, if one of the members of the electoral board is a candidate for the same office you are seeking, that member has a conflict of interest and is ineligible to serve. Your attorney must assert that member's ineligibility and force his or her removal and substitution. If he or she remains and you lose, the circuit court may reverse the electoral board's ruling.

The bottom line is: You may avoid all this by "objection-proofing" your petition. On the other hand, you will want to examine your opponent's petition. If your opponent has not read this chapter, he or she may have a defective petition. Find enough defects, get the "right" lawyer, and object. If your objections are upheld by the electoral board and on appeal, your opponent will be knocked off the ballot and you will have saved a lot of campaign time, effort, and expense. Also a candidate may withdraw at any time up to sixty days before the primary or general election. This is the date for ballot certification; it is the date when the county clerk sends the ballot containing the names of the candidates for each office to the printer. Withdrawals must be made in writing to the local official with whom the petition was filed.

Campaign Financial Disclosure

Now that you have filed your petition, you can start campaigning. Unfortunately, campaigns cost money. You have to pay for ads, brochures, signs, phones, transportation, volunteer expense, office rent, office equipment, and so on. In other words, you have to raise and spend money. Obviously, you will need a campaign budget and a campaign treasurer who can manage your budget (keep track of the money you raise and the money you spend. This should be a person with accounting experience and, more importantly, a person you can trust. He or she will be responsible for preparing and filing your campaign financial disclosure reports.

There is no need here for a detailed explanation of all the rules and procedures for compliance with the Illinois Campaign Financing Act. Basically, if you raise more than $1000 in campaign contributions from your supporters or if you spend more than $1000 of your own money on the campaign, you are required to file a statement of organization as a local political committee with the county clerk. Once you exceed $1000 in contributions or expenditures you have thirty days to file this statement which must include:

1. The name of your political committee (e.g., Citizens for Will Win)

2. The starting balance in your campaign treasury (e.g., cash on hand, $1000 +)

3. The purpose of your committee. You can state a specific purpose (to elect Will Win the Mayor of _____) or a general purpose (to support the political goals of Will Win).

4. The names and addresses of your committee chairman and treasurer. You can wear the chairman's hat, but you are better off appointing someone else to do this job. You will be too busy campaigning.

5. The name and address of the bank where your campaign funds are to be deposited. You need a separate campaign checking account. Do not put campaign money in your personal bank account; it could lead to problems with the State Board of Elections and even the Internal Revenue Service. Your campaign treasurer should be the only one writing checks. You or your campaign chairman can direct the treasurer to write a check, but he or she should manage the money and should control the checkbook.

6. The disposition of leftover funds if and when your political committee dissolves. If you win the election, you should keep the committee active. It should be a continuing committee that can collect funds while you are serving in office. You can use this money for Christmas cards, birthday gifts, funeral flowers, contributions to charities or local civic groups, contributions to other candidates' campaigns, or any other purpose that will demonstrate your gratitude to political supporters and "build bridges" to the next election. But do not use any of this money to pay off personal debts or buy a new house or car unless you intend to declare it to the IRS and pay taxes on it.

If you should lose and want to fold the committee, you have only three legal options for disposing of leftover money: Give it back to the contributors, give it to charity, or give it to another political committee. The election law does not permit you to give it to yourself. For this reason you are always better off keeping the committee alive. Even if you lose, you may want to run again for the same or another office. Why give the money away?

To illustrate: Back in 1978, a popular incumbent county official decided that he did not want to run for another term. At the time, he had almost half a million dollars in his political "war chest." He has not run for any office since that time, but maintains the fund, pays taxes on the interest, and donates to incumbents who are in a position to do him political favors. In any event, your treasury will probably be tapped out after the campaign and you will owe money. You cannot dissolve the committee until its debts are paid off; at the least, you must keep it alive for deficit fundraising.

Packets containing the forms for filing the statement of organization and the reports, as well as a manual of instructions for preparing the reports, are available at the office of the county clerk. Send your treasurer to the county clerk's office to pick up, read, and digest this packet of information. Do not wait until after you file your petition. As a declared candidate, you probably will raise and spend over $1000. Your treasurer should be ready to file the statement of organization as soon as the campaign reaches the $1000 threshold and prepare the reports that follow.

What has to be reported? Each contribution of more than $150 has to be itemized; that is, the names and addresses of these generous folks must be disclosed. So, if you do not want anybody—especially your opponent—to know where some of your money is coming from, tell supporters whose names you do not want appearing on your report to limit their contributions to $150 and not one penny more. No names are disclosed for contributions of $150 or less. Such amounts are added together and reported as a lump sum. In addition, expenditures over $150 must be itemized. You need not be concerned about anyone knowing how you are spending your campaign funds. Those disclosures only appear in the annual report filed after the election. Remember, however: spend these funds only for political purposes or you may have to answer to Uncle Sam.

Meanwhile, here are several tips for you and your treasurer:

1. Any person, corporation, or labor union can give you a direct donation of $1000 or more out of personal or treasury funds. However, if they go out and solicit $1000 or more from other people on your behalf, they will have to organize as a political committee and file financial reports. None of your big contributors want to go through this drill. Nevertheless, this does not prevent your influential supporters from getting involved in your fundraising effort. The way you can accomplish this is to make them members of your political committee and appoint them to a subcommittee on finance. Then they may solicit and receive contributions from anyone on your behalf.

2. Any campaign contribution in any amount that you or anyone working in your campaign receives must be turned over to the treasurer within five days after its receipt. Failure to follow this procedure could disrupt your

campaign. For example: Someone hands a campaign worker a $200 check just before the end of a reporting period, but it is not disclosed in the report because he or she forgot to give it to the treasurer. Knowing of the contribution, your opponent files a complaint with the State Board of Elections alleging nondisclosure. Then the local news media (who may be supporting your opponent) make it look as if you are hiding a contribution. To avoid such problems, advise all of your campaign workers to forward contribution checks they may receive to the treasurer immediately. You, too, had better get those contribution checks you personally received out of your pocket and into the hands of your treasurer.

3. During the campaign, do not permit mass collections of money at campaign rallies or other fundraising events. Do not let your supporters take up a collection or encourage people to "drop" money in a box. The reason: your treasurer must account for each $20 contribution. Since mass-collected donations are normally in cash, you treasurer will not know who made them and, more importantly, will not know whether anyone donated $150 or more, which requires report itemization and donor identification. Moreover, these are anonymous contributions which are prohibited by state election law.

4. Screen your contributors. Common sense dictates that you do not take money from anyone whose business interests conflicts with your declared position on an issue. For example: If you are running for mayor and one of your key issues is protection of the environment, you do not want a contribution from a local manufacturing firm that dumps its waste all over town. Similarly, if you agree with the majority of people in the community who are opposed to expansion of the local airport, you do not want a contribution from the airlines. You get the picture. On the other hand, you may receive a check for a substantial amount from an individual that neither you nor anyone else involved in your campaign has ever heard of. Beware. It could be a setup. The mystery contributor may be someone affiliated with a group whose endorsement would be the kiss of death to your campaign. Several years ago, a congressional candidate in a southwestern state accepted a sizeable contribution from an individual whom he did not know but who later turned out to be one of the leaders of a group advocating the legalization of dope. As soon as this contribution was publicized, his candidacy was doomed. The rule of thumb is: Do not take a donation over $150 from anyone who cannot be identified by your campaign management staff. It is unwise to have a name appearing on your report that your opponent and the news media can use to embarrass you. You should have a screening committee that examines each check and advises the treasurer of any donation over $150 from a person or group whose name does not

appear on any of your fundraising solicitation lists. If the treasurer cannot find out who the mystery donor is, he or she should send the check back with a "thanks, but no thanks" note. If the treasurer finds out that the donor is respectable, he or she can deposit the check.

5. Be sure that you include the notice "A copy of our report filed with the county clerk is (or will be) available for purchase from the county clerk" on all campaign literature (letters, tickets, and so on) which *solicits money.* However, you do not have to print this notice on any campaign literature (brochures, ads) that only *solicits votes.* Make sure you separate the two. Candidates have had complaints filed against them because their vote solicitation literature contained a one-line request for financial support and did not contain the notice.

6. As mentioned previously, your financial reports are public record when filed. You can inspect your opponent's reports at the county clerk's office and he or she can inspect yours. Sometimes a candidate will look at an opponent's report or the report of a candidate for a different office to find out who the big money contributors are and then solicit these people for donations to his or her campaign, or try to turn off their support for yours. Although it is illegal to use information copied from someone else's report for the purpose of soliciting funds for one's own campaign, it is a pretty common practice. The tip-off is when someone fills out a request for inspection at the county clerk's office and states as the purpose for inspection of your report that he or she is a "student" doing "research." If you check it out, you will probably find that this "student" is one of your opponent's campaign workers. If any of your contributors complain that they are being solicited by your opponent, you should ask the State Board of Elections to investigate.

Voter Registration

Your political committee may qualify as a civic organization for the purpose of appointing deputy registrars to conduct a voter registration drive before the primary (if any) or the election. In other words, your campaign workers can register new voters within the political subdivision (county, city, village, township, school district, and so forth) or district (county board district, ward, village district, school district unit, and so forth) in which you are a candidate.

First, you must apply to the State Board of Elections (on a form they provide) for certification as a civic organization. When approved, you send a written request—together with a list of your campaign workers' names and addresses and the state board certificate—to your election authority (county clerk or board of election commissioners) for appointment of deputy registrars. No legitimate group will be denied civic organization status by the State Board of Elections, and no election authority will refuse to appoint deputy registrars, so long as the people whose names you submit are registered voters. After attending a short training session conducted by the election authority, your workers will be sworn in as deputy registrars and given forms and other materials to take registrations up until the thirty-fifth day before the primary (if any) or the election. The rules and procedures for accepting registrations, completing the registration forms, and making returns of completed registrations will be explained by the election authority at the deputy registrar's training sessions. There are usually several of these sessions at different times and locations so that your workers can be scheduled accordingly.

What is to be gained from a voter registration drive? The answer is simple: new voters—people who have recently moved into the political subdivision or district in which you are a candidate or people who have recently turned eighteen years old and are eligible to vote. Most of these people will forget or not bother to get registered on their own. It is an inconvenience for them to go to the election authority's office or another location to register. Make it convenient and bring registration to them. For this service, they may be your voters on election day.

How do you find out who is and who is not registered to vote? Have your petition circulators do it, as follows:

1. If a circulator obtains signatures from two registered voters at a residence, he or she should ask if anyone else in the household needs to be registered. There may be an unregistered son or daughter or in-law living there.

2. If a circulator observes a residence address that does not appear on the precinct poll sheet, the circulator should make a note of that address. For apartment buildings, the circulator should note any names on the mailboxes at that address that do not appear on the poll sheet. This information should be turned in by your circulators at the time they turn in the signed petition sheets.

By this method, you have identified potential voter registrations in each precinct. Send your registrars out to sign them up. If your registrars sign up one hundred new voters and eighty of them come out to vote on election day, you may get at least sixty of those votes. That is sixty more than you had before.

For any number of reasons, not everyone who is unregistered will want to get registered. Other than non–U.S. citizens, cranks, and "crazies," people do not register because they do not want to get called for jury duty. Your registrars can advise them that jurors are now picked from driver's license lists as well as voter registration lists. If they own a car, they will probably by called anyway; so they should register and exercise their right to vote. Another point: Do not set up registration tables in stores, banks, church lobbies, and so on. Your deputy registrar will wind up registering people who do not live in the political subdivision or district and cannot vote for you. As with petition circulation, it is more productive to go door to door.

Absentee Voting

Some of your voters—people who signed your petition, people who were registered to vote by your deputy registrars, people who told your precinct workers that they intended to vote for you—may be out of town on election day, may be away at college or in the military service, or may be physically disabled and unable to get to the precinct polling place and vote on election day. These people are eligible absentee voters who should be identified and solicited for absentee ballots. Applications for absentee ballots may be obtained from the election authority. While your precinct workers are making their door-to-door visits and urging voters to nominate or elect you, they should have such applications completed by those voters. Set a deadline of at least ten days before the election for your precinct workers to return all completed absentee ballot applications to your campaign head-quarters. One of your reliable campaign workers should deliver the applications to the election authority.

When an application for absentee ballot is received, the election authority will first check to see if the applicant is a registered voter and will then send out an absentee ballot (with voting instructions and a return envelope) to the voter usually within two days after receipt of his or her application. The voter should complete the ballot and return it to the election authority as soon as possible. Your precinct workers should contact their absentee voters and make sure that each voter has received his or her ballot from the election authority, has voted, and has returned it to the election authority. To be counted, it must be received by the election authority *before* the polls close at 7:00 P.M. on election day. *Under no circumstances* should a precinct worker assist an absentee voter in marking his or her ballot or deliver the voter's absentee ballots to the office of the election authority. This is illegal. Just have your workers follow up by phone or personal visit and remind absentee voters to mail or bring their voted ballot in to the office of the election authority. Your workers have made it convenient for such voters to apply for an absentee ballot; so most of them should be grateful enough to vote for you.

Getting your potential absentee voters identified and applied and getting them to vote and return their ballots is a major campaign project, but it is a worthwhile project. Those absentee votes may make the difference between losing or winning a close election.

Vote Protection

Several years ago in a downstate city and township election, I dropped into a precinct polling place around 6:30 A.M. and found that 485 votes had already been cast on one voting machine. To make a long story short, the election judges and a precinct committeeman were arrested and later convicted of vote fraud. As it turned out, these officials were bribed by a candidate and cast the bogus votes before the polls opened. To cover their tracks, they forged 485 applications for ballots using the names of persons who had died, moved out of the city years ago, or never existed and using the addresses of vacant lots, abandoned buildings, gas stations, fast-food franchises, and the city dog pound. Had we not decided at random to visit that particular polling place at that particular time, the vote fraud might not have been discovered and the corrupt candidate, who faced a strong challenge from a reform candidate, might have won a close election. Although fraud is hardly ever as blatant as the incident described above, it can and occasionally does occur in more sophisticated forms in hotly contested local elections.

Another point I want to make with this story is that vote fraud does not occur only in Chicago. The fact is that Chicago elections just receive all of the attention from the news media, law enforcement agencies, and good government groups. While the watchdogs are falling over each other in Chicago polling places trying to catch somebody stealing votes, somebody may be stealing votes in some downstate village or school election way beyond the boundaries of Chicago where no one is watching.

Even if you enjoy a comfortable lead and are confident of victory, your political opponents might be scheming to swipe your votes. Do not get complacent; do not say, "It can't happen here." Start thinking now about vote protection. Start building a defense by recruiting and appointing supporters to serve as your poll watchers on election day. At least two poll watchers should be assigned to each precinct polling place. For example, if there are twenty precincts within the political subdivision or district in which you are a candidate, you will need forty poll watchers. For each precinct, one poll watcher should work the early shift and one should work the late shift. In other words, one will be there when the polling place opens and one will be there when the polling place closes and the ballots are taken to the counting location.

Poll watching is a tedious job, but your poll watchers must be alert in order to spot voting irregularities and must be diplomatic when calling such irregularities to the attention of election judges. To prevent burnout, limit your poll watchers to eight-hour shifts. However, if some of your supporters cannot take a day off from their employment, you may not have a sufficient number of poll watchers to cover all precincts. In that case, concentrate your poll watchers in those precincts where voting irregularities have occurred in past elections and in other precincts where you suspect or have heard that irregularities may occur in this election.

Each poll watcher must submit a credential signed by the party chairman or the candidate to the election judges upon entering the polling place. Such credential authorizes the poll watcher to remain in the polling place and observe the conduct of the election. Poll watcher credentials in whatever quantities you need are available at the office of the election authority two weeks before the election. Your poll watchers must be thoroughly trained in election procedures so they know which procedures are correct and which are irregular. They must know the rules of poll watching, what they can and cannot do in a polling place. The best training manuals are the *Pollwatcher's Guide* published by the State Board of Elections and the *Manual of Instructions for Judges of Election* published by the election authority. You should be able to get a sufficient supply of these publications for distribution at your training session. The name of the game is prevention—preventing an opponent from enhancing his or her vote and diminishing yours. Before election day, your precinct workers should take a poll sheet and spot-check registered voter addresses. Should any of these addresses be vacant lots, abandoned buildings, gas stations, park benches, and so on, or should these addresses be legitimate but the voters listed at such locations long ago died or moved away, turn this information over to the election authority, who will send a first-class, nonforwardable notice to the suspect addresses. If such notices are returned undeliverable, the election authority will hold hearings to remove the "ghosts" from the registration rolls. In addition, you should turn this information over to the state's attorney and the attorney general, who can assign prosecutors to polling places to challenge any "ghosts" who appear at the polls and attempt to vote.

On election day, your poll watchers should make sure that election judges compare the voter's signature on his or her ballot application with the signature on his or her registration record card in the precinct binder. If the signatures do not reasonably match, then the person applying to vote should not be allowed to vote. This procedure is designed to prevent persons from voting who (1) have no registration record, (2) have already voted, and (3) are attempting to vote in someone else's name. At the same time, your poll watchers should make sure that one election judge initials ballot cards before handing them to voters.[1] This procedure ensures that prevoted ballots are not smuggled into the polling place and stuffed in the ballot box (chain balloting). The election judge in charge of the ballot box is supposed to check for the other judges' initials on a voted ballot card before depositing it. Any ballot cards not containing a judge's initials cannot be counted.

Should any of the following irregularities occur, your poll watchers should first call them to the attention of the election judges. If the election judges fail or refuse to take corrective action, the poll watchers should call your campaign headquarters and request that the election authority, the state's attorney, and the attorney general be contacted to investigate the matter. The most common types of election law violations are:

1. *Electioneering:* Campaign workers are prohibited from distributing candidate literature or hustling voters inside or within one hundred feet of the door of the polling place. Voter intimidation and vote buying can be prevented if the electioneering prohibition is enforced.

2. *Authoritarian Precinct Committeemen:* A precinct committeeman (precinct captain in Cook County) is just another poll watcher and has the same rights and limitations as any other poll watcher. He has no authority whatsoever over the conduct of the election. When a precinct committeeman is observed settling voting disputes, handling ballots and other materials on the election judge's table, and giving orders to the election judges, it may be assumed that some or all of the election judges are under his unlawful control.

3. *Illegal Voting Assistance:* No voter is entitled to assistance in voting unless he or she is physically disabled and cannot mark the ballot (i.e., blind, arthritic) or is illiterate (cannot read the English language). Upon completing an affidavit of assistance, such a voter may receive assistance from a friend or relative or from two election judges of opposite party

1. Most election jurisdictions (county clerk or board of election commissioners) have a computer voting system which utilizes punch-card ballots. Very few still have paper ballots (which also require initialing) or voting machines where the ballot appears on the face of the machine and the voter activates party or candidate levers.

affiliation. Whoever renders the assistance may mark the voter's ballot only for the candidates selected by the voter.

The following activities indicate that "controlled voting" or illegal voting assistance is in progress: obviously healthy voters claiming to be disabled or English-speaking voters claiming to be illiterate and requesting assistance from their "friend," the precinct committeeman; whoever renders the assistance telling the voter to mark his or her ballot for certain candidates (a poll watcher can usually determine this if he or she stands within earshot of the voting booth).

Moreover, the continued failure or refusal of election judges to do signature comparison or ballot initialing should be considered a violation of the election law and reported to the election authority, state's attorney, and attorney general. When elections judges are following lawful voting procedures, it will be difficult if not impossible for anyone to perpetrate vote fraud. In fairness, it must be said that the great majority of election judges are honest, dedicated people who work long hours for short pay. But it takes only one corrupt election judge to set a vote fraud scheme in motion.

Recounts and Contests

Your candidate petition was in order and no objections were filed; your financial disclosure reports were properly prepared and filed; your workers registered many new voters and generated a lot of absentee ballots; your campaign was energetic and issue-oriented; your candidacy was well received and you were not victimized by vote fraud. But you lost a close election. Do not give up yet. You may have received enough votes to be within striking distance of the winner. You may be entitled to a discovery recount.

If the official canvass of votes shows that you received votes equal to 95 percent of the number of votes cast for the winning candidate, you may petition for a recount in 25 percent of the precincts of the political subdivision or district in which you were a candidate. Such a recount will cost you $10.00 per precinct and will entitle you to an examination of ballots, ballot applications, and voter affidavits and a test of the vote counting equipment (i.e., computer). You may also request a "redundant count," which entitles you to have punch-card votes for the office counted by hand rather than by the computer, which may have miscounted them in the first place. It is not inconceivable that election judge error or computer error could have cost you the election.

For the recount, choose the precincts where you did worse than expected and precincts where your poll watchers reported election day problems. There is always the possibility that a recount will turn up additional votes for you—votes that were not counted or counted improperly for your opponent. If the result of the recount shows that you would have won instead of lost a close election, then you initiate an election contest, which, in effect, is a lawsuit to overturn the results of the election. Rather than confuse you with an explanation of the legal technicalities and proceedings involved in contesting an election, I suggest at this point that you hire a lawyer—not just any lawyer, but one who is a recognized expert on election law.

There are many examples in past local elections where victory was snatched from the jaws of defeat by the runner-up candidate who pursued a recount and election contest. The most recent example was a few years ago in a city about one hundred miles west of Chicago, where a recount disclosed that the votes for aldermanic candidates were reversed. The losers became the winners due to a programming error on the computer that tabulated the votes. A contest was filed and the results of the election were overturned. Do not walk away from a close election and hope for better luck next time. Pursue the remedies available to you in the state election law.

13.

Financial Reporting

GARY KOCH

The reporting of financial transactions of local governments has been a constant source of debate over the years. Local officials feel that the reports they are required to provide are tedious to research, time-consuming to prepare, and expensive to publish. Newspapers, on the other hand, argue that information provided in such reports is often incomplete and inaccurate and does not adequately inform the taxpayer of what the government is doing with its money.

What exactly is financial reporting? According to *Governmental Accounting, Auditing and Financial Reporting,* commonly known as the "Blue Book," it is the "total process of communicating information concerning the financial condition and financial activities of an entity. Financial reports may be written or oral, formal or informal, and technical or nontechnical."[1] The Blue Book goes on to say that reports differentiate as to their content and purpose. Financial reports are often divided into two groups based on when they are issued—interim or supplemental reports and annual financial reports.[2]

There are many types of financial reports. Some are prepared for local government officials and their staffs; others are designed to aid the citizen in his or her understanding of the fiscal aspects of the particular government or community. These reports may vary considerably in size and content, but their major function is to analyze, interpret, and offer an accurate financial picture of the government's operations (see appendix

1. *Governmental Accounting, Auditing and Financial Reporting* (Chicago: Municipal Finance Officers Association of the United States and Canada, 1980), 22.
2. *Governmental Accounting, Auditing and Financial Reporting* (Chicago: Municipal Finance Officers Association of the United States and Canada, 1980), 22.

13-1 for a glossary of terms). Internal financial reports, which contain detailed information and statistical data, are geared for officials themselves. External reports are used to keep the public informed of government activities.

Financial reporting by local governments serves several functions:

- to bring problem areas to the attention of officials soon enough to make allowances or alterations
- to provide accurate records instead of estimates
- to allow for effective financial planning
- to provide for the investment of idle funds
- to allow for comparisons between types of government (beneficial to the general assembly in reviewing the fiscal impact of certain legislative measures on local governments)
- to keep taxpayers informed
- to provide a check-and-balance system on the efficient administration of government

Financial reports may have several audiences. Among them:

- the media, serving as the public watchdog

- other government officials
- investors and creditors
- service consumers
- taxpayers
- U.S. Census Bureau
- universities and colleges
- local government associations

In Illinois, the state comptroller has the responsibility of administering three laws which pertain to the filing of financial reports by various types of local governments. They are the Illinois Municipal Auditing Law (Ill. Rev. Stat., ch. 24, sec. 8-8-1 through 8-8-9); the County Auditing Law (Ill. Rev. Stat., ch. 34, sec. 2011–2018); and the Audit of Accounts (Ill. Rev. Stat., ch. 85, sec. 701–711), which addresses filing requirements of townships and special-purpose districts (see appendix 13-2).

Filing requirements differ somewhat, depending upon the type of government involved. For example, municipalities having a population of eight hundred or more, or having bonded debt or owning or operating any type of public utility, must be audited annually by a licensed public accountant. This audit plus the comptroller's supplemental report, must be submitted to the state comptroller within six months following the close of the government's fiscal year. Municipalities having less then eight hundred population, no bonded debt, and no public utility must only submit an annual report to the comptroller. The comptroller may grant an extension of sixty days for the filing of the report. Generally, if a request is submitted in writing, and there are no known problems, the extension is granted.

In the event the required reports are not submitted, the comptroller must cause an audit to be made of that unit of government, with the local unit responsible for reimbursing the state for the cost involved. Audits prepared by licensed public accountants must be performed in accordance with generally accepted auditing standards. The reporting should be carried out in accordance with generally accepted accounting principles insofar as possible, for all types of local governments.

All counties must submit an annual financial report to the comptroller. If a county's population exceeds ten thousand, but is less than five hundred thousand, an audit by a licensed public accountant is required as well. Townships and special districts also must file an annual report with the state comptroller. If annual appropriations are $200,000 or more, an audit must be submitted. School districts must prepare financial reports as well, but they are handled a little differently. Each year, the regional superintendent of schools must present, on or before 1 January, a written report to the county board. The report must contain the following information: the balance on hand at the time of the last report; all receipts since that date; sources of the receipts; amount distributed to each school treasurer in the county; and any existing balance. The regional superintendent must also provide a copy of every financial report to the State Board of Education.

Almost twenty years ago, a study of local finance in Illinois by Southern Illinois University reported that

> there is no necessary correlation between the degree of state supervision of local finance and financial reports. That is, states may have financial reporting and little or no state regulation. Illinois is one of the few states in which there is minimal reporting to a state agency by local units. In fact, the basic reporting other than the local property tax statistics on the specialized school district data is by municipalities and counties in accordance with the provisions of . . . municipal and county auditing laws.[3]

Unfortunately, little has changed since the SIU study was undertaken. Article 8, section 4, of the 1970 constitution, which requires systems of accounting, auditing, and reporting of the obligation, receipt, and use of public funds, has never been totally implemented.

The legislative Local Accounting Task Force, created in 1981, was established to study the problem. After reviewing the local government financial procedures nationwide, holding a dozen public hearings throughout Illinois, and sponsoring legislation to address local government finance issues, the task force offered several recommendations in its final report.

1. *A uniform local government budget law should be established.* Such a law is necessary for assuring better decision making, more effective control over expenditures, and greater accountability to the public.

2. *A uniform fiscal year should be established.* All local governments should have a common fiscal year. This would bring uniformity to the budgeting process while allowing for the comparison of fiscal information between local governments. Such a fiscal year could be 1 July through 30 June to coincide with the state fiscal year. An alternative would be to establish uniform fiscal years for local governments by type—municipality, county, township, and so on. Currently, counties across the state employ three different fiscal years; municipalities, twenty-four; and townships, seventeen. However, 93 percent of all counties use the same fiscal year, 82 percent of municipalities share the same year, and 93 percent of all townships have a common fiscal year (see fig. 13-1).

3. Le Cohen, *State Supervision of Illinois Local Finance: Public Policy Background Study* (Edwardsville: Regional and Urban Development, Southern Illinois University, 1969), 4.

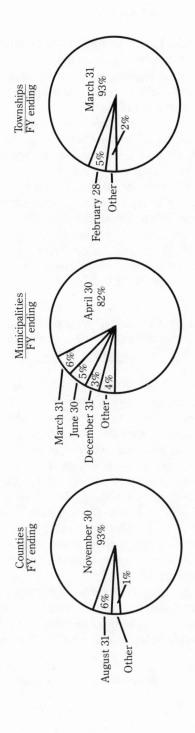

Figure 13-1. Fiscal year for Illinois counties, municipalities, and townships.

3. *Annual treasurer's report requirements should be revised.* A better format for the annual treasurer's report should be developed so that important financial information regarding a local government's activities can be better communicated to the taxpayer. Such a report would benefit the local official, the media, and the citizen.

4. *Local government financial reporting and auditing should be improved.* Local governments should prepare and publish annual financial statements for their individual funds according to generally accepted accounting principals (GAAP). Minimum standards and procedures for local government independent audits should be developed that are sufficient to control both the nature and amount of local government spending.

5. *Financial information collected by the state should be used for research and analysis.* Financial information collected from local governments by the state should be shared with educators, local government associations, and others to be researched and analyzed. Such information could promote greater intergovernmental cooperation.[4]

Of these recommendations, several have been suggested to local governments but only one has truly been acted on—changes in reporting requirements. State law requires most local governments to publish their annual treasurer's report in their local newspaper and to file a copy with the town or county collector of taxes.

In 1985, the state comptroller's office developed legislation to improve financial reporting requirements for local governments. The legislation, Public Act 84-640, extended the period for local officials to file their government's financial statement with the county clerk and publish it in a local newspaper, from ninety days after the end of the fiscal year to six months after the fiscal year end. This was designed to give public officials and accounting firms more time to complete and file the statements. Another important change in the law reduces the amount of information required in the financial report. Under the new law, three things are required: a list of vendors receiving $1000 or more during the fiscal year, and their amounts received; a list of government employees and their salaries; and a summary statement of operations for all funds and account groups of the local government.

As mentioned earlier, the treasurer's report continues to be a battleground between local officials and the media. Government officials still do not enjoy devoting serious amounts of time and money to publishing their financial report in the newspaper because they believe few citizens read it.

4. *Final Report of the Legislative Local Accounting Task Force* (Springfield, 1984), 5.

They recommend: abolishing the report; publishing a notice in the local newspaper that the entire report is available, during regular business hours, at a public site such as city hall, courthouse, or public library; mailing an abbreviated summary of operations with utility bills; and changing the format to show expenditures by account classification rather than by vendors to provide more complete information. Newspapers argue that the only way to make governments accountable to all their citizens is to publish information on the government's activities in the local paper. This "public watchdog" role, newspapers believe, makes government more accountable, and the public does have the right to know.

It has been the position of state government that a better format should be developed for the treasurer's report so that important financial information regarding a local government's activities can be better communicated to the taxpayer. Such a report would benefit the local officials, the media, and the citizens. Looked at another way, what goals should local officials have for their financial reports? What information should they want to communicate? The Government Accounting Standards Board proposes the following objectives:

1. Financial reporting should provide a means of demonstrating accountability to the citizenry and enable the citizenry to assess that accountability by

   a) demonstrating whether resources were obtained and used in accordance with the entity's legally adopted budget (it should also demonstrate compliance with other finance-related legal and contractual requirements), and

   b) providing information about the service efforts, costs, and accomplishments of the governmental entity.

2. Financial reporting should provide information necessary to evaluate the operating results of the governmental unit for the period by

   a) providing information about sources and uses of financial resources;

   b) providing information about how the governmental entity financed its activities and how it met its cash requirements; and

   c) providing information necessary to determine whether the governmental entity's financial condition improved or deteriorated as a result of the year's operations.

3. Financial reporting should provide information necessary to assess the ability of a government to continue to finance its activities and meet its obligations by

   a) providing information about the financial condition, financial resources, and obligations of a governmental entity, and

b) disclosing legal or contractual restrictions placed on resources and the risk of potential loss of resources.

4. Financial reporting should provide information about the governmental unit's physical and other nonfinancial resources having useful lives that extend beyond the current accounting period, including information that can be used to assess the service potential of those resources.[5]

In the spring of 1987, the state comptroller's office simplified its reporting forms for local governments (see appendix 13-3). In the past, each type of local government had a separate form to complete. Now, all local governments file their financial information on a common form. The new form will allow the comptroller's office to prepare various analyses and comparisons among similar types of local government. For the first time, local governments are required to file a balance sheet as part of their report. To make the task as simple as possible, the general format is modeled after the typical general-purpose financial statements included in an annual audit.

For newly elected officials not familiar with preparing financial reports or for veteran officials or staff persons not yet used to the new forms, the following information may be helpful:

1. *Balance Sheet* (pages 3 and 4 of form): The descriptions of the fund types and account groups are from the Governmental Accounting Standards Board. In general, balances for day-to-day operations, including special revenue debt service and capital projects, should be included in the governmental fund type. Activities such as water and sewer operations should have their balances reported in the proprietary fund type. Pension funds and funds for which the particular government has only a trustee responsibility should be classified as a fiduciary fund type. It would not be unusual for certain smaller units (townships and special districts) to report all of their end-of-the-year balances in the governmental fund column.

Small units of government (and some larger ones) that use the cash basis or checkbook method of accounting should list all of their year-end asset balances under cash and investment assets (lines 101 and 102). These and other figures on pages 3 and 4 of the report are year-end balances, not the totals of activity that occurred during the fiscal year. The amounts reported for each column for total assets (line 120) must equal the amounts reported for total liabilities and equity (line 145).

2. *Statements of Receipts and Disbursements* (pages 5–8): Many smaller

---

5. *Governmental Accounting, Auditing, and Financial Reporting* (Chicago: Municipal Finance Officers Association of the United States and Canada, 1980), v.

units of government (townships and special districts) should report all of their receipts and expenditures in the general fund column. The excess of revenue over (under) expenditures (line 301) should equal receipts minus expenditures (line 240 minus line 270). Also, the total of fund balances shown for general, special revenue, debt service, capital project, and special assessment funds (line 310) should equal the total equity (line 142) for the governmental fund type shown on page 4 of the balance sheet.

3. *Changes in Retained Earnings/Fund Balance*: The income statement for the fiscal year for proprietary funds and fiduciary funds is listed on page 9 of the comptroller's annual report form. The total of retained earnings shown for the enterprise and internal service funds (line 348) should equal total equity for the proprietary fund (line 142).

4. *Statement of Operations* (pages 5–9): In years past, small municipalities, special districts, and townships have reported only the combined total of activity for all of their various sources of revenues and expenditures. These governments, in completing the new reporting forms, should allocate the revenue totals for each source (local, state, and so on) and the expenditure totals in the appropriate fund classifications (general, special, revenue, and so forth).

For the first time, some local governments will be reporting their expenditures on the basis of function (general government, public safety, etc.), rather than on expenditure (salaries, contractual services, capital outlay). Functional classifications include the following:

General Government: expenditures for legislative, executive, and judicial branches of a government.

Public Safety: expenditures for protection of persons and property, such as police and fire protection.

Corrections: expenses for confinement and correction of persons convicted, including probation and parole.

Judiciary: costs relating to the courts such as grand jury, public defender, civil and criminal courts.

Public Works/Transportation: expenses for roads and sidewalks, construction, maintenance and repair of bridges and viaducts, and removal and disposal of sewage.

Health and Welfare: expenses for maintaining and improving public health and providing assistance for those who are economically unable to care for themselves.

Culture and Recreation: expenses for cultural and recreational activities for citizens and visitors.

Development: costs related to planning and providing housing, improving economic development of an area.

Debt Service: interest and principal payments on general long-term obligations and interest amounts applicable to other debts.

Other: expenses for miscellaneous activities that cannot be included elsewhere.

5. *Indebtedness*: The indebtedness information on page 10 of the reporting form is pretty much self-contained. Certain amounts in the total column for lines 378 through 386 should agree with the various debt outstanding totals on page 4 of the form. (For more information on how a typical small local government should fill out the reporting form, consult appendix 13-3.)

Where is financial reporting headed? Well, it will continue to be with us as taxpayers; the media and government officials themselves demand more information, and better information, on the operations of government. It is a good guess that reporting standards will continue to improve to reflect better management techniques. Conformity in financial practices of local governments will be stressed, as will implementation of article 8, section 4, of the Illinois constitution. Legislation will be introduced to consolidate existing laws and to promote generally accepted accounting principles to allow for more effective financial management. Ultimately, the issue of financial reporting boils down to the needs of local officials themselves and the public they serve. We all have a vested interest in our local government.

Appendix 13-1
Glossary of Financial Terms

Assets

Cash. Bank deposits that are available (checking accounts, NOW accounts, saving accounts, money market accounts) and currency, coin, checks and money orders on hand, including petty cash and amounts held by fiscal agents.

Investments. Securities (certificates of deposit, Treasury bills, repurchase agreements, etc.) and real estate held for the production of income in the form of interest, dividends, rentals or lease payments. Amounts should exclude real estate used or held for future use in governmental operations as reported in the General Fixed Asset Account Group.

Property Tax Receivables. The uncollected portion of property taxes which a government has levied. Amounts shown should be net of the estimated allowance for uncollectibles.

Accounts Receivable. Amount owed on open accounts from private individuals or organizations for goods and services furnished by a government. Taxes, assessments and amounts due from other funds should not be included in this amount.

Accounts Receivable from Other Governments. Amounts due the reporting government from another government. These amounts may represent intergovernmental grants, entitlements, or shared revenues; or grants, taxes collected for the reporting government by an intermediary collecting government, loans and charges for services rendered by the reporting unit for another government.

Special Assessment Receivable. The uncollected portion of special assessment which the government unit has levied.

Interfund Receivable. Amounts owned to a particular fund by another fund in the same government.

Other Receivables. Amounts owed a government from all other sources including taxes other than property taxes not identified above. Material amounts should be separately disclosed on the balance sheet.

Inventories. Materials and supplies on hand for future consumption or resale.

Prepaid Items. Rent, interest, unexpired insurance, etc., charged into the accounts for benefits not yet received.

Fixed Assets. Land, buildings, improvements and equipment expected to last for more than one year.

Other Assets. Any tangible or intangible asset, the benefit of which will be realized in the future, that has not been described in another account. Material amounts should be separately disclosed in the balance sheet.

Amount Available in Debt Service Fund. An amount which designates the amount of assets available in debt service funds for the retirement of general long-term debt.

Amount To Be Provided for Payment of Long-Term Debt. An account which represents the amount to be provided from taxes or other general revenues to retire outstanding general long-term debt or other long-term obligations.

Liabilities

Accounts Payable. Amounts owed on open account to private persons or organizations for goods and services furnished to a government. This term would also include vouchers payable which have been preaudited and approved for payment but which have not been paid.

Accounts Payable to Other Governments. Amounts owed in connection with judgments payable as a result of court decisions or condemnation proceedings, annuities payable due to retired employees, contracts payable for goods and services furnished to a government and any related retainage percentage held by the government.

Wages Payable. Wages earned by employees but not yet paid.

Interfund Payables. Amounts owed by a particular fund to another fund in the same government.

Other Payables. Amounts owed in connection with judgments payable as a result of court decisions or condemnation proceedings, annuities payable due to retired employees, contracts payable for goods and services furnished to a government and any related retainage percentage held by the government.

Other Liabilities. Amounts for obligations of the government not covered by the above descriptions, such as amounts accrued for judgments, claims, sick leave and vacation. Material amounts should be separately disclosed on the balance sheet.

Customer Deposits. Liability of a utility enterprise fund for deposits made by customers as a prerequisite to receiving services provided.

Deferred Revenue. Amounts for which asset recognition criteria have been met but for which revenue recognition criteria have not yet been met. Under the modified accrual basis of accounting, such amounts are measurable but not available.

Debt Service Payable. Current liabilities for the principal portion of debt instruments of the government such as bonds, notes, leases, installment purchase agreements, other obligations and all special assessment bonds should be shown in their respective funds. Long-term amounts should be classified as long-term liabilities in appropriate fund types or included in the long-term debt account group.

Equity

Fund Balance—Reserved. Segregation of a portion of fund balance representing resources legally restricted for future year payments for matters such as debt service. The segregation can also be a result of a reservation for encumbrances or for an asset held by the government which does not represent available spendable resources such as inventory or prepaid items. Fund balance may also be reserved for the various contribution or actuarial requirements of employee pension plans.

Fund Balance—Unreserved, Designated and Undesignated. Designated unreserved fund balance represents the segregation of a portion of fund balance to indicate tentative plans for financial resource utilization in a future period, such as for general contingencies or for equipment replacement. Such designations reflect tentative managerial plans or intent and should be clearly distinguished from reservations. Such plans or intent are subject to change and may never be legally authorized or result in expenditures. *Undesignated unreserved* fund balance represents the remaining excess of the assets of a governmental fund or trust fund over its liabilities and fund balance reserved accounts. The total of these two amounts should be disclosed as unreserved fund balance.

Retained Earnings—Reserved. Segregation of a portion of retained earnings normally in accordance with the terms of a revenue bond indenture for amounts that should be accumulated in such restricted asset account, less current liabilities for revenue bond principal and interest.

Retained Earnings—Unreserved, Designated and Undesignated. Designated unreserved retained earnings represents the segregation of a portion of retained earnings to indicate tentative plans for financial resource utilization in a future period, such as for general contingencies or for equipment replacement. Such designations reflect tentative managerial plans or intent and should be clearly distinguished from reserves. Such plans or intent are subject to change and may never be legally authorized or result in expenses. *Undesignated unreserved* retained earnings represents the remainder of total unreserved retained earnings of an enterprise or internal service fund which are not reserved for any specific purpose. The total of designated and undesignated unreserved retained earnings should be disclosed as unreserved retained earnings in the financial statements.

Contributed Capital. Permanent fund capital contributed to a proprietary fund by sources such as the general government resources, customers, subdivision developers and builders, or other governments.

Investment in General Fixed Assets. An account in the general fixed assets account group which represents the government's equity in general fixed assets.

Revenues

Property Taxes. Ad valorem taxes levied on an assessed valuation of real property. Do not include nontax revenue, all taxes levied by another level of government, such as a county or state or the Federal Government even when distributed to the municipality, and all taxes levied by the reporting government based on other than general property values.

Sales Tax. Taxes imposed upon the sale or consumption of goods.

Utility Tax. Taxes levied in proportion to gross receipts on public or privately-owned public utilities that provide electric, gas, water or telephone service to resident.

Other Taxes. Represent locally assessed taxes imposed on the sale or consumption of selected goods and services, such as motor fuel, alcohol products, tobacco products, income taxes assessed on either individuals or corporations and any other gross receipts, business taxes on businesses other than public utilities.

Intergovernmental Revenues (State and Federal). Separate amounts should be shown for revenues from other governments for the distribution of state income taxes, motor fuel taxes, replacement taxes, Federal revenue sharing and other forms of grants, entitlements, shared revenues or payments in lieu of taxes.

Vehicle Licenses. Revenues from the operation or ownership of motor vehicles within the government's jurisdiction.

Other Licenses and Permits. Revenues from businesses and occupations or nonbusiness activities which must be licensed before doing business within the government's jurisdiction or before an activity (motor vehicle operation, hunting, marriage or pet ownership) may be conducted within the government's jurisdiction.

Fines and Forfeits. Monies derived from fines and penalties imposed for the commission of statutory offenses, violation of lawful administrative rules and regulations and for the neglect of official duty or monies derived from confiscating deposits held as performance guarantees.

Charges for Services. Charges for current services that should be segregated between public utility service provided by the government and services exclusive of public utility service that should be segregated by functions such as general government, public safety, highways and streets, sanitation, health and welfare, culture and recreation and education.

Interest. Amounts earned from investments held by the government.

Miscellaneous. Amounts earned or charged by the government for purposes other than described above.

Disbursements/Expenditures By Function

General Government. Expenditures for the legislative and judicial branches of a government. It is also charged with expenditures made by the Chief Executive Officer and other top level auxiliary and staff agencies in the administrative branch of the government. The accounts are subdivided into three groups: legislative, executive and judicial.

Public Safety. Expenditures for the protection of persons and property. The majority of subfunctions under Public Safety are police protection, fire protection, protective inspection and correction.

Corrections. Expenditures for the confinement and correction of adults and minors convicted of offenses against the law and pardon, probation and parole activities.

Judiciary. Expenditures for judicial activities of the government, including criminal courts, grand jury, public defender, civil courts and the law library.

Public Works/Transportation. Highways and Streets and Roadways—Expenditures for roadways and walkways according to the type of facility involved. However, roadways and walkways in parks are not charged to this account but to appropriate accounts under the function of Culture and Recreation. *Bridges, Viaducts and Grade Separations* is charged to expenditures for the construction, maintenance, and repair of bridges (stationary and movable), viaducts, grade separations, trestles and railroad crossings. *Sanitation* is a major function of government which includes all activities involved in the removal and disposal of sewage and other types of waste matter.

Health and Welfare. Health is a major function of government which includes all activities involved in the conservation and improvement of Public Health. *Welfare* is a major function of government which includes all activities designed to provide public assistance and institutional care for individuals who are economically unable to provide essential needs for themselves.

Culture and Recreation. Expenditures for cultural and recreational activities maintained for the benefit of residents, citizens and visitors.

Development. Urban Redevelopment and Housing is a major function of government which is concerned with the planning and provision of adequate housing and with the redevelopment of substandard and blighted physical facilities in urban areas. *Economic Development and Assistance* is a function whose activities are directed toward the economic development of the area encompassed by the government and the provision of assistance and opportunity for persons and businesses who are economically disadvantaged. *Economic Opportunity* is charged with expenditures for various programs designed to eliminate or ameliorate poverty and its causes.

Debt Service. Includes interest and principal payments on general long-term obligations and interest amounts applicable to other debt instruments.

Other. Is charged with expenditures for miscellaneous activities which cannot be properly charged elsewhere.

Other Financing Sources/Uses

Other Financing Sources. Amounts such as those derived from significant proceeds of fixed asset dispositions, interfund operating transfers, proceeds from the sale of general long-term debt or amounts financed by long-term leases.

Other Financing Uses. Includes items such as amounts utilized for interfund operating transfers and other transactions, as appropriate.

Other Changes in Fund Balance/Retained Earnings

Amounts attributable to such items as residual equity transfers, appropriate prior-period adjustments allowed for certain changes in accounting principles and changes in reserves for inventories accounted for under the purchase method.

Source: Office of the State Comptroller, State of Illinois, 1987.

Municipal Auditing Law

8-8-3. Annual audits and reports

§ 8-8-3. The corporate authorities of each municipality coming under the provisions of this Division 8 shall cause an audit of the funds and accounts of the municipality to be made by an accountant or accountants employed by such municipality or by an accountant or accountants retained by the Comptroller, as hereinafter provided.

The accounts and funds of each municipality having a population of 800 or more or having a bonded debt or owning or operating any type of public utility shall be audited annually. The audit herein required shall include all of the accounts and funds of the municipality. Such audit shall be begun as soon as possible after the close of the fiscal year, and shall be completed and the report submitted within 6 months after the close of such fiscal year, unless an extension of time shall be granted by the Comptroller in writing. The accountant or accountants making the audit shall submit not less than 2 copies of the audit report to the corporate authorities of the municipality being audited. Municipalities not operating utilities may cause audits of the accounts of municipalities to be made more often than herein provided, by an accountant or accountants. The audit report of such audit when filed with the Comptroller together with an audit report covering the remainder of the period for which an audit is required to be filed hereunder shall satisfy the requirements of this section.

Municipalities of less than 800 population which do not own or operate public utilities and do not have bonded debt, shall file annually with the Comptroller a financial report containing information required by the Comptroller. Such annual financial report shall be on forms devised by the Comptroller in such manner as to not require professional accounting services for its preparation

In addition to any audit report required, all municipalities, except municipalities of less than 800 population which do not own or operate public utilities and do not have bonded debt, shall file annually with the Comptroller a supplemental report on forms devised and approved by the Comptroller.
Amended by P.A. 78-592, § 15, eff. Oct. 1, 1973.

8-8-4. Failure to comply with audit and reports

§ 8-8-4. In the event the required audit report for a municipality is not filed with the Comptroller in accordance with Section 8-8-7 within 6 months after the close of the fiscal year of the municipality, the Comptroller shall notify the corporate authorities of that municipality in writing that the audit report is due, and may also grant an extension of time of 60 days, for the filing of the audit report. In the event the required audit report is not filed within the time specified in such written notice, the Comptroller shall cause such audit to be made by an accountant or accountants. In the event the required annual or supplemental report for a municipality is not filed within 6 months after the close of the fiscal year of the municipality, the Comptroller shall notify the corporate authorities of that municipality in writing that the annual or supplemental report is due and may grant an extension in time of 60 days for the filing of such annual or supplemental report.

In the event the annual or supplemental report is not filed within the time extended by the Comptroller, the Comptroller shall cause such annual or supplemental report to be prepared or completed and the municipality shall pay to the Comptroller reasonable compensation and expenses to reimburse him for the cost of preparing or completing such annual or supplemental report.
Amended by P.A. 78-592, § 15, eff. Oct. 1, 1973.

8-8-5. Audit report—Contents

§ 8-8-5. The audit shall be made in accordance with generally accepted auditing standards. Reporting on the financial position and results of financial operations for each fund of the municipality shall be in accordance with generally accepted accounting principles, insofar as possible. The audit report shall consist of the professional opinion of the accountant or accountants with respect to the financial statements or, if an opinion cannot be expressed, a declaration that the accountant is unable to express such opinion and an explanation of the reasons he cannot do so. Municipal authorities shall not impose limitations on the scope of the audit to the extent that the effect of such limitations will result in the qualification of the opinion of the accountant or accountants.

Audits under this Division may be made upon either an accrual or cash basis of accounting depending upon the system followed by each municipality.
Amended by Laws 1965, p. 2503, eff. Aug. 4, 1965.

County Auditing Law

2013. Annual audits and reports

§ 3. In counties having a population of over 10,000 but less than 500,000, the county board of each county shall cause an audit of all of the funds and accounts of the county to be made annually by an accountant or accountants chosen by the county board or by an accountant or accountants retained by the Comptroller, as hereinafter provided. In addition, each county having a population of less than 500,000 shall file with the Comptroller a financial report containing information required by the Comptroller. Such financial report shall be on a form so designed by the Comptroller as not to require professional accounting services for its preparation.

The audit shall commerce as soon as possible after the close of each fiscal year and shall be completed within 6 months after the close of such fiscal year, unless an extension of time is granted by the Comptroller in writing. Such extension of time shall not exceed 60 days. When the accountant or accountants have completed the audit a full report thereof shall be made and not less than 2 copies of each audit report shall be submitted to the county board. Each audit report shall be

signed by the accountant making the audit.

Within 60 days of receipt of an audit report, each county board shall file one copy of each audit report and each financial report with the Comptroller and any comment or explanation that the county board may desire to make concerning such audit report may be attached thereto. One copy of each such report shall be filed with the county clerk of the county so audited, and one copy shall be filed with the Commission created by "An Act to create a Commission to survey and study the problems pertaining to counties in the State, to define its powers and duties and to make an appropriation therefor", approved July 6, 1957.[1]
Amended by P.A. 83-536, § 1, eff. Sept. 17, 1983.

[1]Paragraph 1201 et seq. of this chapter.

2013a. Overdue reports—Notice to county board

§ 3a. In the event the required reports for a county are not filed with the Comptroller in accordance with Section 3[1] within 6 months after the close of the fiscal year of the county, the Comptroller shall notify the county board in writing that the reports are due, and may also grant an extension of time of up to 60 days for the filing of the reports. In the event the required reports are not filed within the time specified in such written notice, the Comptroller shall cause the audit to be made and the audit report prepared by an accountant or accountants.
Amended by P.A. 83-536, § 1, eff. Sept. 17, 1983.

[1]Paragraph 2013 of this chapter.

2013b. Funds managed by county officials—Filing audit—Report— Definitions

§ 3b. In addition to any other audit required by this Act, the County Board shall cause an audit to be made of all funds and accounts under the management or control of a county official as soon as possible after such official leaves office for any reason. The audit shall be filed with the county board not later than 6 months after the official leaves office. The audit shall be conducted and the audit report shall be prepared and filed with the Chairman of the County Board by a person lawfully qualified to practice public accounting as regulated by "An Act to regulate the practice of public accounting and to repeal certain acts therein named", approved July 22, 1943 as amended.[1]

As used in this Section, "county official" means any elected county officer or any officer appointed by the county board who is charged with the management or control of any county funds; and "audit" means a post facto examination of books, documents, records, and other evidence relating to the obligation, receipt, expenditure or use of public funds of the county, including governmental operations relating to such obligations, receipt, expenditure or use.

Added by P.A. 84-1017, § 2, eff. Oct. 30, 1985.

[1]Chapter 111, § 5500.01 et seq.

2014. Audit report—Contents

§ 4. The Audit report shall contain statements that are in conformity with generally accepted public accounting principles and shall set forth, insofar as possible, the financial position and the results of financial operations for each fund, account and office of the county government. The audit report shall also include the professional opinion of the accountant or accountants with respect to the financial status and operations or, if an opinion cannot be expressed, a declaration that such accountant is unable to express such opinion and an explanation of the reasons he cannot do so.

Audit of Accounts

702. Annual audits and reports

§ 2. Except as otherwise provided in Section 3,[1] the governing body of each governmental unit shall cause an audit of the accounts of the unit to be made by a licensed public accountant. Such audit shall be made annually and shall cover the immediately preceding fiscal year of the governmental unit. The audit shall include all the accounts and funds of the governmental unit, including the accounts of any officer of the governmental unit who receives fees or handles funds of the unit or who spends money of the unit. The audit shall begin as soon as possible after the

close of the last fiscal year to which it pertains, and shall be completed and the audit report filed with the Comptroller within 6 months after the close of such fiscal year unless an extension of time is granted by the Comptroller in writing. The licensed public accountant making the audit shall submit not less than 3 copies of the audit report to the governing body of the governmental unit being audited.

Amended by P.A. 78-592, § 34, Oct. 1, 1973.

[1]Paragraph 703 of this chapter.

703. Financial report

§ 3. Any governmental unit appropriating less than $200,000 for any fiscal year shall, in lieu of complying with the requirements of Section 2[1] for audits and audit reports, file with the Comptroller a financial report containing information required by the Comptroller. In addition, a governmental unit appropriating less than $200,000 may file with the Comptroller any audit reports which may have been prepared under any other law. Any governmental unit appropriating $200,000 or more for any fiscal year shall, in addition to complying with the requirements of Section 2 for audits and audit reports, file with the Comptroller the financial report required by this Section. Such financial reports shall be on forms so designed by the Comptroller as not to require professional accounting services for its preparation.

Amended by P.A. 84-744, § 1, eff. Jan. 1, 1986.

[1]Paragraph 702 of this chapter.

704. Failure to file report

§ 4. If the required report for a governmental unit is not filed with the Comptroller in accordance with Section 2 or Section 3,[1] whichever is applicable, within 6 months after the close of the fiscal year of the governmental unit, the Comptroller shall notify the governing body of that unit in writing that the report is due and may also grant a 60 day extension for the filing of the audit report. If the required report is not filed within the time specified in such written notice, the Comptroller shall cause an audit to be made by a licensed public accountant, and the governmental unit shall pay to the Comptroller actual compensation and expenses to reimburse him for the cost of preparing or completing such report.

Amended by P.A. 78-592, § 34, eff. Oct. 1, 1973.

[1]Paragraph 702 or 703 of this chapter.

705. Audit report—Contents

§ 5. The audit report shall contain statements that conform with generally accepted accounting principles and that set forth, insofar as possible, the financial position and results of financial operations for each fund of the governmental unit. The audit report shall also include the professional opinion of the licensed public accountant with respect to the financial statements or, if an opinion cannot be expressed, a declaration that he is unable to express such opinion and an explanation of the reasons he cannot do so.

706. Signing and filing report

§ 6. When the audit is completed the licensed public accountant making such audit shall make and sign at least 3 copies of the report of the audit and immediately file them with the governmental unit audited. Governmental units appropriating $200,000 or more for any fiscal year shall immediately make one copy of the audit report and one copy of the financial report required by Section 3 of this Act[1] a part of its public record. Governmental units appropriating less than $200,000 shall immediately make one copy of the audit report, or one copy of the report authorized by Section 3 of this Act to be filed instead of the audit report, a part of its public record. These copies shall be open to public inspection. In addition, the governmental unit shall file one copy of the report with the Comptroller and with the county clerk of the county in which the principal office of the governmental unit is located. A governmental unit may, in filing its audit report with the Comptroller, transmit with such report any comment or explanation that it wishes to make concerning the report.

Amended by P.A. 82-422, § 1, eff. Sept. 4, 1981.

[1]Paragraph 703 of this chapter.

1988
Annual
Financial
Report

Roland W. Burris
Comptroller
State of Illinois

State of Illinois Center
100 West Randolph Street
Suite 15-500
Chicago, IL 60601

312-917-6963

Check box opposite appropriate government	
☐ County	
☐ City	
☒ Village	
☐ Township	
☐ Road and Bridge District	
☐ Drainage District	
☐ Fire Protection District	
☐ Park and Forest Preserve District	
☐ Road District	
☐ Sanitary District	
☐ Special District	

Name of governmental unit
VILLAGE OF SMALLTOWN

County
PRAIRIE

Street address
R.R. #1

City
SMALLTOWN

ZIP Code
60000

Fiscal year	From	Through
	5/1/87	4/30/88

Written signature of government official
John Doe

Printed or typed signature
JOHN DOE

Title
TREASURER

Area code	Telephone number
217	555-1212

FOR OFFICE USE ONLY

Record	
County number	
Unit number	
Special type	
TR code	
Population	
Employees	
Assessed value	
Date	

FORM **AFR** (2-5-88)   Printed by Authority of the State of Illinois 3/88 – 20,050 – Job 17785

285

1. Latest —

	Number	As of
a. Estimated population	200	4/30/88
b. Number of employees	2-3	4/30/88
c. Equalized assessed valuation . . .	345,249	4/30/88

2. Total appropriations (for townships and special districts only) . . . .

010

3. Fiscal year *(List each year if different fiscal year used for different funds.)*

4. List each auditing firm employed for all funds, activities, boards, and commissions of the unit of government.

Firm name	State of Illinois registration number
NONE	

5. Basis of accounting used in completing this report:

☒ Cash

☐ Modified accrual/Accrual

6. Please indicate any payments your government made to other governments for services or for programs performed on a reimbursement or cost-sharing basis. Exclude payments made to the State retirement system.

Amount paid to State

020 L88
$

Amount paid to other local governments

030 D89
$

7. Report total salaries and wages paid to all full-and part-time employees of your government. Include also salaries and wages paid to employees of any utility or other enterprise owned and operated by your government. These figures may be taken from the W-3 form filed by your government for the year ended December 31, 1987.

Total salaries and wages

040 200
$ 800.50

Inquires may be forwarded to: Director, Local Government Fiscal Programs, State of Illinois Center, 100 West Randolph Street, Suite 15-500, Chicago, Illinois 60601. The telephone number is 312/917-6963.

Combined Statement of Position
All Fund Types and Account Groups

Government: VILLAGE OF SMALLTOWN

Date: 8/30/88

Assets	Code	Total memorandum only	REPORT AMOUNTS IN DOLLARS ONLY Governmental fund type	Proprietary fund type	Fiduciary fund type	General fixed assets	General long-term debt
Cash	101	$ 17,658. W81	$	$	$ W81	$	$ 17,658.
Investments	102	20,000. W70			W70		20,000.
Property tax receivables	103						
Accounts receivable from other governments	104						
Accounts receivable	105						
Special assessments receivable	106						
Interfund receivable	107						
Other receivable	108						
Inventories	109						
Prepaid items	110						
Fixed assets	111	33,800.					33,800.
Other assets	112						
Amount available in debt service fund	113						
Amount to be provided for payment of long-term debt	114						
TOTAL ASSETS	120	$ 71,458.	$	$	$	$	$ 71,458.

FORM AFR (2-5-88)

All Fund Types and Account Groups

Government
VILLAGE OF SMALLTOWN

Date 8/30/88

REPORT AMOUNTS IN DOLLARS ONLY

Liabilities and fund balance	Code	Total memorandum only	Governmental fund type	Proprietary fund type	Fiduciary fund type	General fixed assets	General long-term debt
LIABILITIES Accounts payable	125	$ -0-	$	$	$	$	$
Wages payable	126	-0-					
Accounts payable to other governments	127	-0-					
Other payables	128	-0-					
Interfund payables	129	-0-					
Other liabilities	130	-0-					
Customer deposits	131	-0-					
Deferred revenue	132	-0-					
Debt service payable	133	-0-					
TOTAL LIABILITIES	135	$ -0-	$	$	$	$	$
EQUITY Fund balance — reserved	136	-0-					
Fund balance — unreserved	137	-0-					
Retained earnings — reserved	138	-0-					
Retained earnings — unreserved	139	-0-					
Contributed capital	140	-0-					
Investments in general fixed assets	141	-0-					
TOTAL EQUITY	142	$ -0-	$		$	$	$
TOTAL LIABILITIES AND EQUITY (135 + 142)	145	$ -0-	$		$	$	$

FORM AFR (2-5-88)

Combined Statement of Receipts/Revenues, Disbursements/Expenditures, Other Financing Sources/Uses and Changes in Fund Balance

Year ended 4/30/88

REPORT AMOUNTS IN DOLLARS ONLY

Receipts/Revenues	Code	Total	General	Special revenue	Debt service	Capital projects	Special assessments	Expendable trust
							U01	
LOCAL TAXES								
Property taxes	201	T01 3,303.						3,303.
Sales tax	202	T09 90.						90.
Utility tax	203	T15 -0-						
Other taxes	204	T19 -0-						
TOTAL LOCAL TAXES (201 + 202 + 203 + 204)	210	3,393.						3,393.
INTERGOVERNMENTAL STATE SHARED								
Income tax	211	C30 4,821.						4,821.
Motor fuel tax	212	C46 3,739.						3,739.
Replacement tax	213	C28 279.						279.
Other	214	C80 -0-						
TOTAL STATE (211 + 212 + 213 + 214)	220	8,839.						8,839.

FORM AFR (2-5-88)

Combined Statement of Receipts/Revenues, Disbursements/Expenditures, Other Financing Sources/Uses and Changes in Fund Balance

Year ended 4/30/88

REPORT AMOUNTS IN DOLLARS ONLY

Receipts/Revenues	Code	Total	General	Special revenue	Debt service	Capital projects	Special assessments	Expendable trust
FEDERAL SHARED								
Revenue sharing	221	$ 297. [827]	$	$	$	$	$	$ 297.
Other	222	-0- [899]						
TOTAL FEDERAL (221 + 222)	225	$ 297. [D99]	$	$	$	$	$	$ 297.
Other intergovernmental	226	-0- [D99]						
TOTAL INTERGOVERNMENTAL (220 + 225 + 226)	230	$ 9,136. [T24]	$	$	$	$	$	$ 9,136.
Vehicle licenses	231	-0- [T99]						
Other licenses and permits	232	-0- [T99]						
Fines and forfeits	233	-0- [U99]						
Charges for services	234	-0- [A99]						
Interest	235	1,560. [U20]						1,560
Miscellaneous	236	104. [U99]						104.
TOTAL RECEIPTS/REVENUES	240	$ 14,193.	$	$	$	$	$	$ 14,193.

FORM AFR (2-5-88)

Combined Statement of Receipts/Revenues, Disbursements/Expenditures, Other Financing Sources/Uses and Changes in Fund Balance

Year ended 4/30/88

REPORT AMOUNTS IN DOLLARS ONLY

Disbursements/Expenditures	Code	Total	General	Special revenue	Debt service	Capital projects	Special assessments	Expendable trust
BY FUNCTION								
General government	251	E29 -0-	$	$	$	F29 $	F29 $	$
Public safety	252	E62 -0-				F62	F62	
Corrections	253	E05 -0-				F05		
Judiciary	254	E25 -0-				F25		
Public works/ transportation	255	E44 7,694.				F44		7,694.
Health and welfare	256	E79 -0-				F79		
Culture and recreation	257	E61 1,740.				F61		1,740.
Development	258	E89 -0-				F89		
Debt service	259	E89 -0-				F89		
Other	260	E89 8,450.				F89		8,450.
TOTAL DISBURSEMENTS/ EXPENDITURES	270	$ 17,884.	$	$	$	$	$	$ 17.884

FORM AFR (2-5-88)

Combined Statement of Receipts/Revenues, Disbursements/Expenditures, Other Financing Sources/Uses and Changes in Fund Balance

Year ended 4/30/88

	Code	Total	General	Special revenue	Debt service	Capital projects	Special assessments	Expendable trust
				REPORT AMOUNTS IN DOLLARS ONLY				
Excess of receipts/ revenue over (under) disbursements/ expenditures (240 – 270)	301	(3,691.)						(3,691.)
Other financing sources/ uses Operating transfers in	302	-0-						
Operating transfers out	303	-0-						
Bond proceeds	304	-0-						
Other (explain below)	305	-0-						
Net increase (decrease) in fund balance (301 + 302 – 303 + 304 + 305)	306	(3,691.)						(3,691.)
Beginning fund balance	307	41,609.						41,609.
Other (explain below)	308	-0-						
Ending fund balance (306 + 307 + 308)	310	37,918.						37,918.

EXPLANATIONS

FORM AFR (2-5-88)

Combined Statement of Receipts/Revenue, Disbursements/Expenses and Changes in Retained Earnings/Fund Balance All Proprietary Fund Types and Similar Trust Fund

Government VILLAGE OF SMALLTOWN

Year ended 4/30/88

REPORT AMOUNTS IN DOLLARS ONLY

Operating receipts/revenues	Code	Total memorandum only	Proprietary fund types		Fiduciary fund types	
			Enterprise	Internal services	Pension trust	Nonexpendable trust
Charges for services	325	-0-	◆ A91	◆	◆	◆ A89
Interest	326	-0-	U20			U20
Taxes	327	-0-	T01		T01	T01
Other	328	-0-	A91			U99
TOTAL OPERATING RECEIPTS/REVENUE	330	-0-	◆	◆	◆	◆
OPERATING DISBURSEMENTS/EXPENSES						
Operations, other than depreciation	331	-0-	E91			E89
Depreciation	332	-0-				
Interest	333	-0-	I91			I89
Other	334	-0-	E91			E89
Benefit payments	335	-0-				
TOTAL OPERATING DISBURSEMENTS/ EXPENSES	340	-0-	◆	◆	◆	◆
Operating income (loss) (330 – 340)	341	-0-				
OTHER FINANCING SOURCES/USES						
Operating transfers in	342	-0-				
Operating transfers out	343	-0-				
Other	344	-0-				
Increase (decrease) in retained earnings/ fund balance (341 + 342 – 343 + 344)	345	-0-				
Retained earnings/fund balance beginning of year	346	-0-				
Other changes in retained earning/fund balance	347	-0-				
Retained earnings/fund balance end of year (345 + 346 + 347)	348	-0-				

FORM AFR (2-5-88)

Indebtedness

REPORT AMOUNTS IN DOLLARS ONLY

Items	Code	Outstanding beginning of year	Code	Issued this fiscal year	Code	Retired this fiscal year	Code	Outstanding end of year
REVENUE								
Water	351	-0- [19A]	360	-0- [29A]	369	-0- [39A]	378	-0- [44A]
Sewer	352	-0- [19X]	361	-0- [29X]	370	-0- [39X]	379	-0- [44A]
All other revenue bonds	353	-0- [19X]	362	-0- [29X]	371	-0- [39X]	380	-0- [44X]
General obligation bonds	354	-0- [19X]	363	-0- [29X]	372	-0- [39X]	381	-0- [41X]
Industrial revenue bonds	355	-0- [19T]	364	-0- [24T]	373	-0- [34T]	382	-0- [44T]
Tax anticipation warrants or notes	356	-0- [61V]	365	-0- [29X]	374	-0- [39X]	383	-0- [64V]
Contractual commitments: lease purchases, installment contracts, notes, etc. with duration of one (1) year or more.	357	-0- [19X]	366	-0- [29X]	375	-0- [39X]	384	-0- [41X]
Special assessments payable	358	-0- [19X]	367	-0- [29X]	376	-0- [39X]	385	-0- [41X]
TOTAL	359	-0-	368	-0-	377	-0-	386	-0-

EXPLANATIONS

14.

Local Government Finance

DOUGLAS WHITLEY

All aspects of government ultimately rely on fiscal resources. It does not matter whether the question is one of delivering service, providing grants, employing people, investing in brick and mortar, satisfying pension obligations, promoting economic development, or providing tax relief. The question will always remain, "Can it be afforded?"

Local government finance occurs in an ever-changing environment. A great variety of questions must be considered on a regular basis. Does the economic activity in the community show adequate growth to maintain or increase existing government services without raising rates or adding new revenue sources? Will new or higher taxes have an economic impact? Who presently pays taxes? If there are tax increases, where will the burden fall? Are the proposed taxes broad-based or will there be special exceptions? Is the proposed tax general in nature or is it tailored to generate a predetermined amount of money designated for special purposes? Will the tax fall primarily upon the beneficiaries of a particular program or government service? How much revenue can be expected from intergovernmental sources? How are economic and legislative changes at the federal and state level going to affect local revenue? Even international affairs may influence the ability or willingness of local residents to finance government services or programs. For example, farmland prices have a major influence on Illinois local government finances because over 40 percent of the state's 102 counties rely upon farmland assessments for more than half of their real estate tax base. The property tax is the primary local revenue source, so speculative ownership of farmland, grain embargoes, bankruptcies, and international commodity markets have an effect on financing government in rural communities.

Whether by design or by chance, local government officials' tax choices ultimately influence Illinois state and local tax policies. Their choices, often made independently to address specific local concerns, have consequences for the state as a whole. The state's tax structure and total burden then is a reflection of the accumulated actions taken by thousands of elected officials working to serve their respective constituents' interests. The result is a complicated, multifaceted tax structure which mirrors the state's diversity, encourages self-reliance, and continues to evolve without the benefit of an overall tax plan or policy.

Structure and Finance: An Interrelationship

The most distinctive feature about Illinois local government is the multiplicity of units. This diversity has occurred over many decades because of a provision in the Illinois constitution of 1870 which limited the amount of debt a government unit could accrue. Although the 1970 constitution eliminated the debt limitation provision, the pattern for governmental structure was well established and has not changed.

The preponderance of government at the local level is responsible for an extremely diverse and complex system of taxation. The approximately 6,500 units of local government are classified into roughly thirty different types of taxing districts, most having the authority to levy real estate taxes. A list of twenty-five Illinois special-purpose districts follows:

1. airport authority
2. cemetery maintenance
3. civic centers
4. conservation
5. fire protection
6. forest preserve
7. hospital
8. library
9. mass transit
10. mosquito abatement
11. multitownship assessing
12. park
13. port
14. public health
15. public water
16. river conservancy

17. road
18. sanitary
19. soil and water conservation
20. solid waste disposal
21. street lighting
22. surface water protection
23. tuberculosis sanitarium
24. water authority
25. water service

General-purpose governments—cities and counties—have more extensive revenue-raising capabilities than do special districts, which are often limited to property taxes, fees, and intergovernmental sources. In recent years, newly established special districts have been given access to sales taxes rather than the more traditional property tax. Home-rule governments have considerably more liberty to raise revenue than do other local governments that remain dependent upon the legislature or voters to grant more tax authority.

The existence of so many units of local government with independent taxing authority exerts a major influence on the financial structure of the state. A comparison of Illinois's reliance upon local taxes with that of other major industrial and regional states reveals that only New York has a greater reliance upon locally generated revenues than Illinois. Almost half of Illinois's total state and local tax collections are attributed to local governments. This contrasts with national figures which show that local governments usually account for less than 40 percent of total state and local taxes. When taxes levied by the state but returned to local governments in the form of shared intergovernmental funds are counted, it becomes apparent that a significant percentage of the total state and local tax revenue in Illinois is spent by local governments.

The traditional reliance upon local resources and local control has much to do with the existence of many "have" and "have-not" situations among Illinois local governments. This occurs both in the case of property and sales tax collections. Communities with a heavy industrial base or the existence of an electric generating plant have the benefit of exceedingly high local property wealth compared to the state average. For example, in 1984, DeWitt County had the highest total per-capita property tax extension in the state at $881. Yet the per-capita property tax burden for residential taxpayers in the county was only $129—$28 less than the statewide average. Eighty-five percent of the tax base in DeWitt County is attributable to nonresidential property.

Likewise, because local sales tax receipts are returned to governments, which impose them on a point-of-sale basis, communities with regional shopping malls benefit. The advantage of a substantial amount of retail activity in Schaumburg has allowed that city to avoid levying real estate taxes for many years. Schaumburg, home of one of the largest shopping malls in the country, received a per-capita return of almost $242 per person from its local sales taxes in 1986. East St. Louis, a city of similar size, had a per-capita return of only $17 from its local sales taxes. The state-wide average per-capita local sales tax receipts were approximately $61 in 1986.

The state's commitment to local control and revenue self-sufficiency is illustrated by the special status afforded home-rule governments by the framers of the 1970 constitution. Constitutional limitations on the revenue-generating power of home-rule units are relatively few. Home-rule governments may not incur debt payable from property taxes that mature more than forty years from the time the debt is incurred; and they may not license for revenue or impose taxes upon income, earnings, or occupations. However, home-rule units have no property tax rate limitations and are, therefore, the only governmental units in the state with independent authority to use the property tax base to generate as many dollars as deemed necessary.

Although the general assembly retains the power to deny or limit the taxing powers of home-rule units, it has rarely done so. As a result, home-rule cities have frequently chosen to exercise their independent taxing authority. The use of this independent taxing power has added diversity to revenue structures and encouraged creativity as cities have attempted to design special taxes and fees to address what they considered to be special local problems and needs. For example, Naperville has imposed impact fees on new housing developments, while Schaumburg added taxes on restaurant meals to fund road projects considered vital to a community whose economy is dependent upon automobile commuters.

Some municipal leaders have sought voter approval to establish home rule in hopes that the independence associated with home-rule taxing powers would help resolve fiscal needs. Conversely, opponents to home rule have often focused on the unlimited property tax authority as a major objection. Home-rule authority may also be rescinded by referendum, as occurred in Rockford, the state's second largest city, in 1983. The majority of votes cast in that election favored a restraint on the city's taxing powers; the decision served fair warning to other home-rule cities. Where home-rule powers exist, local officials may use the added revenue flexibility, but must remain sensitive to the possibility of a voter-initiated campaign to rescind home rule. Municipal officials know that once home-rule authority is lost, it is not easily regained. Presiding over the repeal of home rule is not a legacy most progressive mayors would welcome.

While local control is an important concept to Illinois government officials and citizens, it also causes severe difficulty in trying to keep track of the fiscal affairs of local government in the state. In addition to the three general-purpose governments—counties, cities, and townships—more than two dozen other types of special districts are organized to tax and provide governmental services. The most prominent of these are the nearly 1,000 public school districts: 444 unit districts serve grades K–12; 431 elementary districts serve grades K–8; and 122 high-school districts serve grades 9–12.

Separate elementary and high-school districts are commonly referred to as dual districts. While not limited solely to Illinois, the dual district structure exists in just a dozen of the fifty states. Where the dual district structure exists, elementary and high-school district boundaries frequently do not coincide. Nor do school district boundaries change as municipal annexation occurs; residents in the same city may be sending their children to different school districts. These parents may also find their property tax liability for public schools to be considerably different because of the variation of tax rates and assessment bases available to the respective school districts.

Most special-purpose districts have been created by local referendum; thus the boundaries of the taxing districts are often drawn to assure success at the polls. Coterminous boundaries with other governmental units are extremely rare. It is not unusual for residents of the same community (as in the public school district example cited above) to find variable rates of taxation for similar services being delivered by separate governmental units. For example, a taxpayer may be paying for park and recreation facilities delivered by a forest preserve district, park district, township, and a municipal government. It is also possible that residents of the same community will experience variation in their tax bills because the mix of taxing districts serving the community may cover some but not all portions of the city. This multifaceted structure makes financing local governments in Illinois extremely complicated.

To understand local government finance in Illinois, citizens must not only acknowledge the existence of a multiplicity of governments that lack coterminous boundaries, but also be aware that those governments do not operate on uniform fiscal years or use uniform reporting standards (see chapter 13). The reports and records of the obligations, receipts, and use of public funds of local governments are public records available for inspection by the general public. Local units must prepare annual budgets, provide

notice in newspapers of common circulation, and hold an annual hearing on the proposed budget prior to adoption if the district asks for an increase in property taxes that exceeds the prior year's request by 5 percent. These notice and budget-hearing procedures are commonly referred to as the Truth in Taxation Act. The general assembly adopted the disclosure provisions in 1981. Concerned citizens who want to make a change in the level of spending or spending priorities must attend these meetings and be heard. Unfortunately, even though the opportunity exists, it is unlikely that the average citizen can keep well informed of the fiscal plans of all the governmental units levying taxes on his or her property.

The highly decentralized system makes it extremely difficult for an individual to affect the collective local government spending choices that ultimately result in a property tax bill. Simply attending the meetings and studying the numerous budget documents could be a full-time job. The fact is that few citizens make the effort to attend budget meetings and express opinions. Since an individual taxpayer is likely to have minimal influence on spending decisions, most choose to focus their energy toward making sure the assessment on their particular property is accurate and thus acquiesce to the spending choices being made by the elected officials. Presumably, excessive spending will result in the removal of incumbents at the next election.

Property Taxation

The primary funding source for local government is the property tax. Property taxes are levied independently by each local government and collectively generate more than $7 billion in annual revenues. This is twice as much revenue as the state receives from either the income or sales tax. (The state receives no revenue from the property tax.) Property tax originates from only two sources: from the authorization of the Illinois general assembly and from the adoption of local referenda to create taxing districts and/or approve tax rate increases. Governmental bodies, composed of locally elected or appointed members, establish their property tax reliance each year, thereby ensuring that the system is largely influenced by local officials. Property assessments are handled locally, as are the determination of budget requests and the collection and distribution of the taxes. But the general assembly retains the power to determine maximum tax rates and assessment bases. It sets the state-wide level of assessment and authorizes exemptions and special assessments as well.

The general assembly established a variety of property tax rates for non-home-rule units, limiting local government financing to specially authorized tax funds granted by the statutes. Some of the taxing funds, such as those provided for debt retirement, pensions, and insurance costs, are open-ended and allow the taxing body to levy as much as is needed to meet the obligation annually. But the majority of the funds are subject to maximum property tax rates authorized by referenda.

The existence of these maximum property tax rates is intended to protect real estate taxpayers from unlimited spending on the part of local government and to provide a cap on the maximum property tax burden imposed on property taxpayers. Because of the existence of statutory rate limitations, there are only two methods by which a local government may exceed them: by seeking and gaining the approval of voters who will be affected by the property tax rate to be levied; or by getting the approval of the legislature for an increase in the maximum rate authorized by statute. Consequently, dozens of bills are introduced each year in the Illinois General Assembly for the purpose of establishing new rates or increasing previously authorized property tax rates for the various taxing districts.

Unfortunately, rate limitations tend to focus taxing districts' and taxpayers' attention on the property tax rate authorized and imposed rather than the governments' actual spending pattern. Tax rates are only half of the equation. Equally important is the assessment base upon which the tax rates will be imposed. The assessed valuation of the districts' real estate is determined by local authority. Tax rate limitations are a serious consideration where the real estate tax base fails to grow or is significantly declining. In such situations, the local government has to gain referendum support again and again just to provide consistent services. A similar local government with the advantage of a growing tax base does not need to increase rates. For example, the equalized assessed valuation in Naperville Township in DuPage County has grown by 279 percent from 1980 to 1986 while 75 percent of the counties of the state were experiencing decreases in assessed valuations. Thus, the tremendous amount of diversity that exists perpetuates a system of "have" and "have not" districts. The contrast between the Byron Unit School District with over $350,000 of assessed valuation behind each pupil and the East St. Louis Unit School District with less than $10,000 in valuation per student helps to illustrate this point.

The existence of a multiple tax rate structure for local governments encourages the creation of new special funds and tax rates whenever there appears to be a new governmental crisis or special need, instead of increasing the general operating fund of the taxing district. Confronting such issues on a piecemeal basis may be politically appealing, but the resulting financial structure perpetuates the concept of fund accounting for local governments. Fund accounting retains a considerable amount of political appeal because of the ability to explain or gain support for special needs, but most accountants and government fiscal agents acknowledge that the system is outdated.

Property Tax Cycle

Property taxation has two major components that work independently to influence individual tax bills. The first is the assessment responsibility through which the property tax burden is apportioned to individual parcels. Usually, the first half of a calendar year is devoted to determining assessments, while the balance of the year is set aside for assessment appeals by individual taxpayers and the determination of intercounty and intracounty equalization factors.

In general terms, assessment means that valuation of real estate for purposes of determining the share of the property tax obligation that will be borne by each parcel of land. Most property is assessed by local officials, and Illinois law requires that all property be reassessed every four years.

The initial assessment of property in most counties is done by elected township or multitownship assessors. The majority of Illinois county boards appoint a supervisor of assessment, who serves as the chief assessment official for the county and oversees the work of the township or multitownship assessors. The appointed supervisor of assessments is responsible for original assessments in the seventeen commission counties which do not have townships. Seven Illinois counties (Alexander, Clark, Cook, Hamilton, Shelby, St. Clair, and Vermilion) have county-wide elected assessors. In Cook County, the assessing responsibility rests solely with the elected county assessor's office. Elected township assessors in Cook County continue to hold office without the responsibility for determining original assessments.

The Illinois real estate tax appeals system is extensive. Each taxpayer has the right to seek assessment relief from the original office of assessment or from a county board of review (in Cook County, from the Board of Tax Appeals). In all counties except Cook, taxpayers may appeal their assessments to the State Property Tax Appeal Board as well. Taxpayers also have the right to seek relief through the courts. The appeals process may be a lengthy one, but for most taxpayers the resolution of an assessment is completed within a calendar year.

State law establishes that the assessed valuation upon which a tax bill is to be calculated is to be one-third of fair market value. County assessment offices and the Illinois Department of Revenue monitor the level of assessments within jurisdictions and impose equalization factors that either raise or lower the median level of assessment within the jurisdiction to the appropriate one-third of market value. Although an assessment of one-third of the market value remains the norm, there are exceptions and exemptions that influence the effective tax rate paid. State statute establishes special assessments for certain classes of real estate such as farmland, minerals, and undeveloped lots. The legislature has also interceded to ease the property tax burden on individual taxpayers by granting exemptions for both senior citizens and homeowners, among others. (The state also operates a circuit breaker grant program which, although not a direct part of the property tax system, helps senior citizens and disabled individuals with low income meet a portion of their property tax obligation.)

The major exception to uniformity in assessment levels exists in Cook County, the only county to establish separate levels of assessment for individual classes of property. Examples of real estate classes are: unimproved lands, single-family residences, real estate owned by nonprofit corporations, residential buildings with more than six living units, and commercial and industrial property. The classification system used in Cook

County also provides for special assessments for economic development purposes. The result of a classified assessment system is that the incidence of the real estate tax burden is not borne equally by each class in proportion to the share each class represents of the total amount of taxable property. In 1984, the residential class accounted for approximately 60 percent of the parcels and 38.9 percent of the assessment base in Cook County.

The second major component of property taxation, the local government budgeting and tax levy cycle, operates independently of the assessment cycle. Each governmental body prepares a budget and annually files a levy that specifies an amount of property tax dollars the governmental unit seeks to receive from the real estate tax base. The budget and levy process occurs in the fall. Most taxing districts file with the county clerk in September; counties and school districts make their final levy in December (see table 14-1).

The county clerk calculates property tax bills by applying each taxing district's dollar request by fund against the equalized assessed valuation as determined for the year the tax levy was filed. The government's requested dollar amount is limited only by the existence of maximum property tax rates on individual funds. Not every taxing district has access to the same authorized funds, nor are the maximum tax rates uniform for all districts. For example, the maximum authorized tax rate for the county corporate fund is influenced by the county population as well as whether or not the county imposes the ¼ percent supplemental sales tax.

Non-Home-Rule Counties (Ch. 34, par. 406)

.28% (28¢ per $100 of assessed valuation) for counties of 80,000 or more, but less than 3,000,000 inhabitants; .30% (30¢ per $100 of assessed valuation) for counties of 15,000 or more, but less than 80,000 inhabitants; exceptions: 35% (35¢ per $100 of assessed valuation). If a county of less than 80,000 inhabitants has, authorized by referendum, a tax pursuant to Section 7-2 of the Juvenile Court Act prior to 1-1-86; .40% (40¢ per $100 of assessed valuation) for counties with less than 15,000 inhabitants. Any county which elects to impose collection of the ¼% sales tax shall reduce its respective rate limitations by .03% (3¢ per $100 of assessed valuation). May be increased by referendum.[1]

It is not common for each taxing district to use every authorized tax rate

1. Illinois Department of Commerce and Community Affairs, *The Illinois Tax Rate and Levy Manual,* Spring 1987.

Table 14-1

Levy Certification Dates to County Clerk

Local Government	Deadline	Legal References
Cities and Villages Under 500,000 Population	Sept. — 2nd Tuesday	Ch. 24, par. 8-3-1 Ch. 120, par. 638
Counties Under One Million Population	Sept. Board Session	Ch. 120, par. 637
Townships	Sept. — 2nd Tuesday	Ch. 120, par. 638
Road Districts	Sept. — 1st Tuesday	Ch. 121, par. 6-501
Park Districts	Sept. — 3rd Tuesday	Ch. 105, par. 5-1
Fire Protection Districts	Sept. — 2nd Tuesday	Ch. 120, par. 638
Library Districts[1]	Sept. — 4th Tuesday	Ch. 81, par. 1004-15
Hospital Districts	Oct. — 1st Tuesday	Ch. 23, par. 1270
Forest Preserve Districts	Nov. — 3rd Monday	Ch. 96½, par. 6324
School District[2] (Fewer than 500,000 Inhabitants)	Dec. — last Tuesday	Ch. 122, par. 17-11
Most Other Special Districts	Sept. — 2nd Tuesday	Ch. 120, par. 638

Source: Illinois Department of Commerce and Community Affairs, *The Illinois Tax Rate and Levy Manual,* Spring 1987.

1. Amend Tax Certificate: see Ch. 81, par. 1004-15
2. Amend Tax Certificate: see Ch. 122, par. 17-11.1

that exists in the statutes for that type of district. The statutes authorize thirty-seven separate rates for townships, but not every township has ambulance, hospital, or library services. Where these services are not delivered by the township, it is unnecessary to levy a tax for them.

The application of tax rates to a parcel of property is called the extension. The responsibility for extension rests with the county clerk, who must accurately determine the aggregate property tax rate that will be applied against the assessed valuation for each parcel of property. Because of the multiplicity of local governments and the absence of coterminous boundaries, county clerks calculate a tax code that may cause individual taxpayers

TOWNSHIP		TOWNSHIP FACTOR	ASSESSED VALUE	STATE MULTIPLIER		EQUALIZED VALUE
TAX RATE	PAYABLE 1988		TAXING BODY	TAX RATE	PAYABLE 1989	DIFFERENCE

REAL ESTATE TAX BILL REVENUE YEAR 1988 PAYABLE IN 1989

Remit To JACKSON COUNTY TREASURER
SHIRLEY DILLINGER BOOKER, COUNTY TREASURER
P. O. BOX 430, MURPHYSBORO, IL. 62966-0430
(618) 684-2159

CASH_____
CHECK_____
MAIL_____
BANK_____
WINDOW_____

1½% penalty charged per month or each part of a month after each due date, till tax sale. It is your responsibility to forward this bill to your mortgage company. Taxes can be paid by mail, in person or at most banks.
Court Ordered Judgement Signing Oct. 17, 1989
Tax Sale October 23, 1989

RETURN YELLOW BILLS WHEN PAYING 1ST INSTL.
RETURN WHITE BILLS WHEN PAYING 2ND INSTL.
INFORMATION FOR TAXPAYER
LAST DAY TO APPEAL TO THE BOARD OF REVIEW
IS AUGUST 10TH   (618) 684-2152
ANY CHANGE OF OWNERSHIP OR ADDRESS,
REFER TO SUPERVISOR OF ASSESSMENTS.
(618) 684-2152

NON-CLEARANCE OF CHECK MAKES THIS RECEIPT VOID. THE COUNTY TREASURER ONLY COLLECTS AND DISBURSES TAXES AND IS NOT RESPONSIBLE FOR FAILURE TO RECEIVE TAX BILL, FOR ANY OMISSION, OR FOR PAYMENT ON WRONG PROPERTY.

ANY DRAINAGE OR BACK TAX IS INCLUDED IN TOTAL TAXES DUE.
IF YOU HAVE SOLD THIS REAL ESTATE IN 1988 PLEASE FORWARD BILL TO NEW OWNER.   **NOTICE**

DRAINAGE	BACK TAXES	EXEMPTION	1ST INSTAL.	2ND INSTAL.	COST	INT.	TOTAL TAXES

Figure 14-1. Sample property tax bill.

to experience considerable variations in the numbers of taxing districts and aggregate tax rates applied against their property.

Once the tax bill (see fig. 14-1) has been calculated, it becomes the county treasurer's responsibility to mail, collect, and distribute property taxes owed to the county's assorted governmental units. Most property taxes in Illinois are paid in two equal installments, one being due on 1 June and the second on 1 September. Illinois statutes also allow county treasurers to send an estimated tax bill based on one-half of the prior year's total tax bill. Several counties have used this method of tax collection on occasion, but only Cook County uses this as an annual method of collection. In Cook County, the first installment of estimated property taxes is collected on 1 March with the balance due on a finalized tax bill in September. Obviously, with so many parties and offices involved in the property tax process, it is not uncommon for many of Illinois's 102 counties to experience delays during the tax extension process. Although such delays are usually measured by only a few days, any delay may cause fiscal stress and cash flow problems for governments awaiting the distribution of property tax collections. Lengthy delays may result in short-term borrowing and increase the overall cost to the taxpayer.

The budget preparation cycle occurs simultaneously but independently of the assessment cycle. Consequently, Illinois local governments are often unaware of the final real estate assessment base upon which property tax extensions will be made at the time budgets are being prepared and estimated property tax receipts calculated for the upcoming calendar year. The normal property tax cycle in Illinois takes almost two years to complete (see fig. 14-2). The date of original assessment is 1 January each year, but payment of the second installment of the taxes due on the assessment does not usually occur until September of the following calendar year. The tax extension process that occurs each year is actually a collection of taxes due on the prior year's assessment. Meanwhile, the current year's assessment is being determined and taxing districts are preparing budgets that will be reflected in a tax bill which will be mailed the following year.

Other Sources of Revenue

The sales tax is the second most important revenue source for Illinois local governments. It is, in fact, not a true sales tax, but a series of taxes on retail occupations and service occupations based on the sale of tangible personal property. These taxes are used to generate revenue for more than 1,300

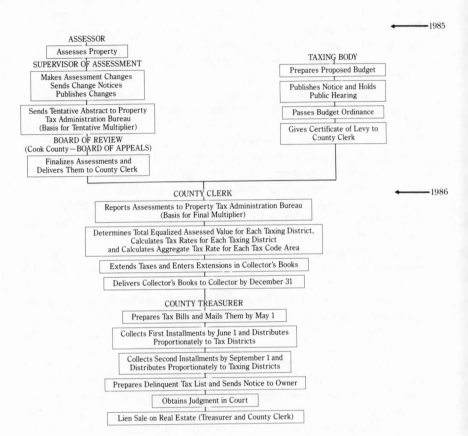

Figure 14-2. The property tax cycle: 1985.

local governments, counties, municipalities, and special districts. These local governments adopt ordinances to impose the taxes, but the collection authority rests with the Illinois Department of Revenue, which redistributes the money back to the proper government on a point-of-sale basis, that is, these local taxes are returned to the government within whose boundaries the transaction occurred. Since separate governments have the power to impose sales taxes, the rate applied to a transaction usually reflects an accumulation of rates. Sales and use tax may be imposed not only by the state, but also by counties, cities, certain transit authorities, and a multicounty water commission. Home-rule governments and all counties may impose additional sales taxes. Thus, a transaction in DuPage County may include sales taxes for the state, county, city, transit authority, water commission, and perhaps a home-rule transaction tax.

Exceptions to state collection of sales taxes began to occur during the 1980s. Several of the state's home-rule cities imposed and collected local transaction taxes while the municipal retailers' occupation tax continued to be collected by the state. Similar to the retailers' occupation and service occupation taxes used by local governments since the 1950s, the new transaction taxes have allowed home-rule cities to tailor local taxes for special purposes or to generate specified amounts of revenue. Some of the new taxes have been broad-based, whereas others have been limited to a single industry such as restaurants. The broad-based taxes even included special features such as a cap on the amount of purchase to which the tax might be imposed; in Peoria, for example, only the first $500 is taxed. At the other extreme is a tax only on purchases which exceed a certain amount, such as in Danville, where the ordinance applies to amounts that exceed 1,200. The net result is a local sales tax structure that is uncertain, changing, and inconsistent throughout the state.

Illinois is one of only seven states that allows local governments to administer independent sales taxes. Normally, states impose taxation at a common rate and on a common base, to be collected and redistributed for local government purposes. Once again, Illinois's devotion to local control, diversity, and emphasis on linking taxes to specified services or special governmental units is demonstrated, but the price is the further complication of an already difficult sales and use tax structure. These actions by home-rule cities clearly represent the most significant challenge to the future of Illinois's tax structure and intergovernmental fiscal relations. Such independent action is encouraged in the constitution, but the assault such action has on consistency, uniformity, simplicity, and compliance in Illinois is only beginning to be comprehended.

Another important source for local government finance is intergovernmental revenue, that is, state and federal funds channeled to local units. Even though Illinois has established a high reliance upon locally imposed taxes, three kinds of taxes are imposed and collected by the state and benefit local governments through state revenue-sharing formulas: the income tax, the motor fuel tax, and the corporate personal property replacement tax. First among these is the individual and corporate income tax. From the inception of the state income tax in 1970, the legislature has shared one-twelfth of the receipts with county and city governments. One-twelfth of all individual and corporate income tax receipts is placed in the local government distributive fund and disbursed each month to counties and cities on the basis of population. The state motor fuel tax is distributed to counties, cities, townships, and road districts. The formula for distributions is set by statute and has changed from time to time, usually as tax increases have occurred. Local governments that have road-related responsibilities are reliant upon the state motor fuel tax and are treated as partners in the distribution and spending of motor fuel tax revenues. The distribution of these dollars is determined by the number of vehicle registrations in the jurisdiction. The third source of intergovernmental funds is the corporate personal property replacement tax fund. With the abolition of the corporate personal property tax in 1979, the Illinois General Assembly imposed new taxes on corporations, partnerships, trusts, and public utilities for the purpose of generating revenues to be returned exclusively to local governments. The Illinois Department of Revenue collects and distributes these funds ten times a year based on a statutory formula that reflects the proportion of reliance each individual taxing district may have had on the state-wide total collections of the abolished corporate personal property tax. For additional information on state aid, motor fuel tax, the local government distributive fund, and personal property replacement tax, see chapter 2.

Another state funding source for local governments is the common school fund, but it is not linked to the receipts of a single tax. Revenues earmarked for the common school fund include all net lottery receipts, 25 percent of state sales and use tax receipts, and a portion of bingo, cigarette, and interstate message taxes. Elementary and secondary education are not exclusively dependent upon the common school fund because additional support comes from the state general revenue fund. In 1986, the common school fund sources accounted for slightly more than half of the state treasury's investment in public schools. The matter of state financial support for public education is debated annually during the general assembly's appropriations process. During the 1980s, elementary and secondary education have received slightly less than 30 percent of the total dollars

available in the state general and common school funds. These dollars are allocated through statutory formulas or categorical grant awards determined annually by the general assembly. (For a fuller description of school funding, see chapter 8.)

Although imposed only by a quarter of the municipalities, the public utility tax is nonetheless worthy of note. Major cities in Illinois make use of the municipal public utility tax. This tax may be imposed on utilities engaged in the delivery of gas, electricity, water, or telecommunications services. The municipal gross receipts taxes have rates that range up to 5 percent and may be imposed on any or all of the services delivered in the community. Because it is a gross receipts tax, municipalities have seen annualized growth in collections. Municipal utility taxes are imposed by the cities and villages and collected by the public utilities. The 1980s saw growth in the use of this tax in part as an alternative to increased reliance upon real estate taxation.

The balance of local government revenue sources is a mixture of miscellaneous taxes, fees, and special charges. Although these sources do not represent large dollar amounts when compared to the generally imposed taxes, it is likely that there will be an increased reliance upon them in the future as governments begin to calculate the true cost of services and, where possible, attempt to apportion a greater amount of the cost to the users of the services. In the past, local governments could rely on substantial direct aid from the federal government through revenue sharing and categorical grants. With the elimination of federal revenue sharing in October 1986, this aid was significantly diminished. From 1980 to 1987, Illinois local governments received nearly 20 percent less from the federal government. All signs indicate a trend toward greater self-reliance for local and state governments.

What the Future Holds: Revenue Trends

With the reduction of federal funding, the future of financing local government in Illinois will depend upon more state intergovernmental funds or the state assuming additional functions and expenses presently under the control of local government. The desire to reduce the unpopular local real estate tax has not diminished. Some counties and cities have made strides during the 1980s to reduce their reliance upon this tax source by increasing sales and utility taxes, and fee income. Yet local real estate taxes primarily benefit elementary and secondary education. As long as the state does not provide more money for schools, there will be a continued use of referenda to generate education dollars—by raising the property tax rate to offset a declining tax base, especially in rural Illinois. Significant property tax relief in Illinois is not likely to occur unless there is an increased assumption of educational cost by the state or the imposition of a statutory or constitutional limitation on property taxation. If the latter action is taken, the result will probably be an increase in state taxes. This is what occurred in California after Proposition 13 was adopted.

Another means of reducing real estate tax reliance—but less likely to bring about significant reduction—is for the state legislature to assume all or a portion of the cost related to some local government functions. During the 1980s, there was an increase in the assumption of fiscal responsibilities for what had traditionally been thought of as local government costs. This is particularly true for counties, where there has been a greater recognition that the county government is an arm of the state and must carry out its mandates. The relationship between county and state government offices is becoming increasingly blurred. For example, the state now pays all or a portion of the salaries for many local government officials, including regional superintendents of schools, judges, county supervisors of assessment, state's attorneys, assistant state's attorneys, county treasurers,

"AW, THAT'S NOT A GHOST-THAT'S SOMEONE OPENING THEIR PROPERTY TAX BILL."

county clerks, deputy assessors, township assessors, and court personnel. A reasonable argument could be made that the state should assume the full cost for financing elections, the courts, and local pensions, especially since these three areas essentially reflect the dictates of the legislature.

If the 1980s are any indication, it is likely that local governments will continue to rely upon sales taxation or other consumption-related taxes as an alternative to increased property taxation. Most of the new taxes imposed by either the state or local governments in Illinois during the last decade have been in the nature of consumption taxes, and public opinion surveys still suggest that sales taxation is preferable to the use of property or income taxes. Although it is still possible that sales tax rates might be increased in portions of the state, it is unlikely that the aggregate rate would exceed the 8 percent currently imposed on purchases of general merchandise in the city of Chicago; this is one of the highest rates in the nation. New sales tax rates may continue to appear as a means to finance special-purpose governments or projects, but there is a greater awareness of the inconsistencies that exist throughout the state. Consequently, new rate increase proposals will compete with efforts to limit and restructure the tax.

A more likely avenue for expanded sales taxation is an expansion of the state's sales tax base. By most characterizations, the Illinois sales tax base is relatively narrow. This is in part because of the legislature's tendency in the last decade to grant tax relief by exempting many transactions from the states sales tax (see table 14-2). Expansion of the base to include consumer-related services, such as cleaning, repairs, and maintenance contracts, is a possible remedy. It is the means for revenue generation which has been followed in other states, such as Texas, Minnesota, Iowa, and Florida. Such an action on the part of the general assembly has the advantage of increasing revenues for many units of local government, in addition to the treasury. Expanding a tax base is never easy, but it is one of the few available choices with the potential to generate significant amounts of revenue. If the general assembly fails to pursue sales tax revisions to stabilize and expand the local government tax base, special districts and home-rule cities will continue to seek incremental changes which will further complicate the state's sales tax structure.

Local officials are not likely to relinquish easily their claims on local control and special taxes in exchange for greater intergovernmental funding. But the demand for revenue is undoubtedly going to increase. During the last decade, there has been a steady reduction in the fiscal relationship between the federal government and its state and local counterparts. As federal revenue dollars have diminished, local governments have been faced with three choices: reduce services, increase locally imposed taxes, or turn to the state for more revenue. Increasing state aid to local governments is the only choice for equalizing the financial capabilities between the "have" and "have nots," but do to so necessitates state tax increases. The most likely candidates for enhanced state resources are the local government distributive fund, the state school aid formula, road funds, and greater state participation in capital projects such as highways, mass transportation, water and sewer projects, and the construction of public buildings.

As cost benefit analysis becomes a more important part of local government expenditures, it is inevitable that an evaluation of user fees, services charges, and the use of private contractors will have a more prominent role in local government finance than it has had traditionally. In many quarters of local government, financial planning, improved business practices, and detailed cost analysis are becoming common practice. Perhaps the most frightening conclusion local government officials might draw from their experiences in the eighties is the lack of a consistent and stable tax plan on the part of state government. The state legislature attacked the local government revenue base by authorizing exemptions in sales and property taxes. Although to a lesser degree, the general assembly also altered the

Table 14-2

A Partial List of Exemptions from the Illinois Sales and Use Taxes

Sales Exempt from the Retailers' Occupation Tax	Sales Exempt from the Use Tax
1. Sales to governmental bodies, charitable, religious and educational organizations, or nonprofit corporations organized for the recreation of persons age 1 or older.	1. Property brought into the state for temporary use by a nonresident.
2. Isolated or occasional sales by persons other than retailers; sales through a bulk vending machine.	2. Property already taxed in another state, to the extent of the tax paid.
3. Newsprint and ink.	3. Temporary storage in Illinois of property acquired and subsequently used outside the state or which is altered and, as altered, is used outside the state.
4. Occasional dinners of charitable, religious, or educational organization.	4. Building materials temporarily stored in Illinois acquired by a registered combination retailer and construction contractor either in Illinois or outside the state and used outside Illinois by incorporating the property into realty outside Illinois.
5. Proceeds from sales of property to interstate carrier for hire for use as rolling stock in interstate commerce or lessors under leases of 1 year or longer executed or in effect at the time of purchase to interstate carriers for hire for use as rolling stock moving in interstate commerce.	5. Property acquired outside this state by a nonresident and used for at least 3 months before being brought into Illinois for use here, including property purchased in Illinois and delivered outside the state.
6. Sales of fuel consumed or used in ships, barges, vessels used primarily to transport or convey persons or property on rivers bordering Illinois if the fuel delivered while such ship, barge, or vessel is afloat on such river.	
7. Motor vehicles sold in Illinois to nonresidents, not titled in Illinois, if a driveaway permit is issued for the vehicle.	
8. Proceeds of sales of farm chemicals.	
9. Sales of property as pollution control facilities.	
10. Sales of machinery and equipment for use primarily in manufacturing or assembling tangible personal property for sale or lease.	
11. Mandatory service charges (tips).	
12. New and used farm machinery used for production agriculture and valued at over $1,000 exempt for entire value.	
13. Graphic arts machinery and equipment and replacement parts.	
14. Distillation machinery and equipment used for making ethyl alcohol for personal use as a motor fuel.	
15. All machinery, equipment, structures, and associated apparatus of a coal gasification operation.	

Table 14-2 *continued*

16. Motor vehicles, designed to carry up to
    10 people, which are used for renting by
    leasing companies.
17. Proceeds from sales of petroleum prod-
    ucts where federal law prohibits seller
    from charging tax.
18. Tangible personal property sold to a rail-
    road which is transported outside Illi-
    nois for use elsewhere.
19. Personal property sold to a nonprofit
    Illinois county fair association for fair
    use.
20. Motor vehicles subject to the Replace-
    ment Vehicle Tax.
21. Personal property sold by a teacher-
    sponsored student organization affili-
    ated with elementary and secondary
    schools.
22. Food consumed off the premises (except
    alcoholic beverages, soft drinks, and food
    prepared for immediate consumption).
23. Medicines and medical appliances.
24. Legal tender, currency, medallions, or
    gold or silver coinage issued by Illinois,
    the U.S., or any foreign country except
    the Republic of South Africa, and bul-
    lion.

Source: *Illinois Tax Handbook for Legislators, 1985,* Legislative Research Unit, February 1985.

Note: Sales exempt from the retailers' occupation tax are also exempt from the use tax.

corporate and individual income tax base which contributed to the local government distributive fund. Despite adjustment to the tax system, which reduced revenue availability, the general assembly continued to pass laws which mandated local government expenditures.

Summary

The financial affairs of Illinois local governments reflect the diversity and local control characterized by the great variety and number of local governments in the state. The local government fiscal structure lacks uniformity, consistency, and simplicity. Uniform fiscal years, levy dates, tax rates, coterminous boundaries, and strong centralized general-purpose governments are nonexistent. Nearly half of all the state and local taxes in Illinois are collected by local governments. The real estate tax is the primary revenue source for local government. The property tax assessment and budget process occur independently and require almost two years to complete. In general, real estate assessments are determined by locally elected officials, as are budgets and property tax bills.

State government receives no revenue from the property tax, but influences the local tax base by setting the state-wide level of assessment, determining intercounty assessment equalization, and granting exemptions or special assessments for certain classes of property, such as farmland. In addition, the general assembly may grant new or increased property tax rate authority for local governments.

During the last decade, the dual desires to reduce property tax reliance and still develop new tax sources for cities and special-purpose governments led to increased usage of sales taxes. Sales taxes are the second most important funding mechanism available to local governments. This revenue choice has become more common among home-rule cities, but the result has been an increasingly complicated sales and use tax structure for the state. The existence of many local governments, guided by elected officials, does, however, offer Illinois citizens a unique opportunity to participate in their governments. It is unusual to go to a public meeting, attend a church gathering, or visit a civic organization without encountering people who are or have been directly involved in managing their local governments. Thus, local government finance continues to be based on citizen participation, interaction with neighbors, and an awareness of community needs.

Bibliography

Bohlen, Brent S. *Illinois Tax Climate.* Springfield: Taxpayers' Federation of Illinois.

———. *Practical Guide to Illinois Real Estate Taxation.* Springfield: Taxpayers' Federation of Illinois, 1985.

Chicoine, David L., and J. Fred Giertz. *Property Tax Assessment in Illinois: Structure and Performance.* Springfield: Illinois Tax Foundation, 1986.

Illinois Department of Commerce and Community Affairs. *The Illinois Tax Rate and Levy Manual: Spring 1987.* Springfield, 1986.

Illinois Department of Revenue. *Annual Report 1986.* Springfield, June 1987.

Illinois Department of Revenue. *Illinois Property Tax Statistics 1984.* Springfield, 1986.

Minert, Charles L. *Illinois Tax Handbook for Legislators, 1985.* Springfield: Legislative Research Unit, 1985.

Revenue Review Committee. *Proposals to Reform the Illinois Tax System: April 1987*. Springfield: State of Illinois, 1987.

15.

How to Find, Apply for, and Receive Grants

H. BRENT DE LAND

Perhaps the most difficult aspect of grantsmanship is not filing an application, waiting for a reply, or even getting rejected, but rather identifying the needs, goals, and objectives of the unit of local government submitting the grant request. Often, the individual responsible for the preparation of a grant proposal is not the individual who identified the community need to be addressed. The grant writer may find that he or she is requesting funds based on political expediency that may or may not address a real community need. Therefore it is critical that a grant writer be intimately involved in the determination of the needs, goals, and objectives of the community. As part of the needs assessment process, the grantsman should have a thorough knowledge of both the needs to be addressed and the results anticipated.

Community needs can be as simple and uncomplicated as the desire to replace traffic signals at all four-way intersections within a given town. An even less complicated need might be the establishment of a crime prevention bureau within the local police department. However, most community needs are far more complex than these two illustrations. For example, a given community might need to locate, obtain, and develop a one-acre parcel of property for the establishment of a community park. Although the need is fairly straightforward, the dynamics of obtaining the necessary funding can dazzle the imagination.

Let us first examine the problem of location. We are in a small city with a population of 4,500 residents. There is no taxing district or park authority established. Therefore, the project must be undertaken by the city itself. Although incorporated and of modest size, no full-time city manager or mayor is available to develop the project. The process of locations identification requires a complete survey of the community in terms of available land, demographic conditions, community infrastructure, and the politics of park location. Far too often, units of government jump at donated land for such a project. They fail to consider all the dynamics of the sound needs assessment required for grant funding of the entire development. The town in question may well seek a donated parcel of property fitting the general geographic needs of the project. Yet for various political and demographic reasons that particular location may doom a grant proposal.

For instance, one must consider the community infrastructure; the locationof pipelines, sewers, water distribution stations, and necessary natural resources to develop the proper environment for a city park. For a moment, consider what would occur should the city accept a donated parcel of property with no accessible water supply and all of the shrubbery, green grass, and trees were to die from a lack of water. This would create both an intolerable situation and a negative political reaction. If your community's demographics indicate that the park would principally be utilized by young people but the average age of your population by the year 1995 will be 40 years of age, most grant sources would turn down your application. How would you explain the expenditure of resources for a project that will be underutilized? It is ill-advised to proceed on any project without clear needs identification and proper advance planning. A key rule is to assume nothing. Rather, collect the necessary data to make a prudent decision on behalf of your community. Know its needs and its direction for growth and development.

The following is a needs analysis checklist for your consideration:

• Identify the need to be met or problem to be solved.
• Why does the need or problem exist?
• Whom does the need or problem affect (target population)?
• Identify existing resources to meet the identified need or problem.
• Survey the available literature dealing with the need/problem.
• Confirm that the need/problem is real.
• Locate, whenever possible, similar case examples in similar communities.
• Identify problems preventing or obstructing the need from being addressed.
• Develop a clear definition of the problem/need.
• Create an inventory of available and unavailable resources.
• Analyze the data, reevaluate the need/problem, prepare and present the needs assessment.[1]

1. One example of an excellent needs assessment approach can be found in human services used by the United Way of America, which employs UWASIS—United Way of America's Service Identification System. A copy can be obtained at the local office of most United Way chapters.

After the problem and the program requiring funding have been defined, the need arises to determine what type of funds are required to secure the desired results. The following funding sources are generally available to local governments:

1. *Grants:* This funding option is best described as a source of revenue usually provided by the state or federal government which does not have to be repaid. Grants often require some local financial match and/or in-kind requirement. In-kind sources of support include volunteer or nondirect cost to the project. An example of in-kind would be the salary and fringe package of a park district employee who will work 20 percent time on the project without the use of grant funds to support the position.

2. *Contracts:* Contracts are agreements which usually provide a fee to local government to provide a given service or product. An example of a government contract is a city providing transportation for the elderly which is paid for by a regional transportation authority.

3. *Loans:* Loans are often available to local governments from the federal or state government. Most federal loans are available to local units of government at lower than market rates of interest. Loans, although perhaps the least attractive means of financing because they have to be repaid, are often the only sources available.

4. *General Revenue:* This revenue source includes but it is not limited to taxes, fees, fines, deferred payment bonds, and notes generated by a unit of local government.

This chapter concentrates on grants: how to find them, apply for them, and secure nonrepayable sources of revenue for your unit of government.

Finding Grants

Three good sources to review in attempting to locate potential funding sources are the *Catalog of Federal Domestic Assistance,* published by the U.S. Government Printing Office; the *Handbook of Federal Assistance* published by Warren, Gorham, and Lamont; and the *Catalog of State Assistance to Local Governments,* published free of charge by the State of Illinois, Commission on Intergovernmental Cooperation. No potential grant seeker should be without a desk copy of each of these books, which will be discussed later. Highly unlikely sources of revenue to units of government are foundations, corporations, and united funds. Information on these sources of revenue can be found in the bibliography for this chapter.

A listing of ten potential funding sources is provided below to illustrate grant possibilities.

1. Rural Self-Help Housing Technical Assistance
Federal Agency: Farmers Home Administration, Department of Agriculture

Objectives: To provide financial support for the promotion of a program of technical and supervisory assistance that will aid needy, very low and low-income individuals and their families in carrying out mutual self-help housing efforts in rural areas
Eligibility: Must be a state or political subdivision
Amount available for distribution: FY 1988, $5,403.81 (in thousands)
For information contact: Local telephone FMHA district office number.

2. Justice Research and Development Project Grants
Federal Agency: National Institute of Justice, Department of Justice

Objectives: To encourage and support research and development to further understanding of the causes and control of crime and to improve the criminal justice system
Eligibility: State and local governments
Amount available for distribution: FY 1988, $21,694 (in thousands)
For information contact: National Institute of Justice
                        Department of Justice
                        Washington, DC 20531
                        (202) 724-2942

3. Coal Miners' Respiratory Impairment Treatment Clinics and Services
Federal Agency: Health Resources and Services Administration, Public Health Service, Department of Health and Human Services

Objectives: (1) To develop high quality, patient-oriented, integrated systems of care which assure access to and continuity of appropriate primary, secondary, and tertiary care with maximum use of existing resources; (2) to emphasize patient and family education to maximize the patient's ability for self-care
Eligibility: State and local government agencies
Amount available for distribution: FY 1988, $3,400 (in thousands)
For information contact: Department of Health and Human Services
                        Bureau of Health Care Delivery and Assistance
                        Health Resources and Services Administration
                        Room 7A-55, 5600 Fisher Lane
                        Rockville, MD 20857
                        (301) 443-2260

4. Wastewater Treatment Facilities Construction
Federal Agency: Environmental Protection Agency

Objectives: The state assists local governments in construction of wastewater treatment facilities. This is done to prevent pollution of state waters by local discharge. Grants are distributed by formula. Local governments must provide 45 percent of the total project cost.
    Eligibility: Municipalities, townships, sanitary districts
    Amount available for distribution: FY 1987, $27,000 (in thousands)
    For information contact: Environmental Protection Agency
                            Division of Water Pollution
                            2200 Churchill Road
                            Springfield, IL 62706
                            (217) 782-1654

5. Library Services for the Blind and Physically Handicapped
State Agency: Secretary of State

Objectives: Assistance is given to help libraries provide and coordinate specialized library services for the blind and physically handicapped. This includes special radio information services. The grant award is based on a formula using population and number of institutions served.
    Eligibility: Public library systems
    Amount available for distribution: FY 1987, $1,917.2 (estimate; in thousands)
    For information contact: Secretary of State
                            Illinois State Library
                            275 Centennial Building
                            Springfield, IL 62706
                            (217) 782-2994

6. Low-level Radioactive Waste Siting Reviews
State Agency: Department of Nuclear Safety

Objectives: The counties or municipalities in which alternative sites for a permanent disposal facility have been selected are eligible to receive state matching grants for siting reviews. Local governments can be reimbursed for up to 50 percent of costs incurred to independently review the proposed disposal site for technical suitability up to a maximum of $50,000.
    Eligibility: Counties, municipalities
    Amount available for distribution: FY 1987, $50 (appropriated; in thousands)
    For information contact: Department of Nuclear Safety
                            Office of Environmental Safety
                            1035 Outer Park Drive

Springfield, IL 62704
(217) 546-8100

7. Bridge Replacement or Rehabilitation
State Agency: Department of Transportation

Objectives: Funds are provided to replace or rehabilitate structurally deficient bridges on or off the federal aid system for the safe and expeditious transportation of the general public. The funds are allotted to districts based on a formula involving square footage of eligible bridges. Local governments are required to provide a 20 percent match.

Eligibility: Counties and municipalities
Amount available for distribution: FY 1987, $13,880.1 (estimate; in thousands)
For information contact: Department of Transportation
                        2300 South Dirksen Parkway
                        Springfield, IL 62764
                        (217) 782-7868

8. Alternative Energy
State Agency: Department of Energy and Natural Resources

Objectives: General obligation bonds are sold by the state to fund alternative energy research and development projects. These include techniques such as solar, wind, and biomass. Local governments are eligible to participate in the program by submitting proposals in response to program opportunity notices announced by the department.

Eligibility: Counties, municipalities, townships, park districts
Amount available for distribution: FY 1987, $1,253.9 (estimate; in thousands)
For information contact: Department of Energy and Natural Resources
                        Division of Energy and Environmental Affairs
                        325 West Adams Street
                        Springfield, IL 62706
                        (217) 785-5222

9. Financial Management Assistance
State Agency: Office of the Comptroller

Objectives: The program provides technical and advisory assistance to make financial management practices of local governments more effective and efficient.
Eligibility: Counties, municipalities, townships
Amount available for distribution: Not applicable
For information contact: Office of the Comptroller
                        Local Government Fiscal Programs

325 West Adams
Springfield, IL 62706
(217) 785-7414

10. Tourism Promotion
State Agency: Department of Commerce and Community Affairs

Objectives: Grants are provided to finance up to 60 percent of the cost of local tourism promotional projects, which include, but are not limited to, brochures, flyers, posters, and newspapers, radio and television advertising. A county, municipality, or a not-for-profit organization must provide a 40 percent match.
Eligibility: Counties, municipalities
Amount available for distribution: FY 1987, $1,281.0 (estimate; in thousands)
For information contact: Department of Commerce and Community Affairs
Office of Tourism
620 East Adams
Springfield, IL 62701
(217) 782-7139

Applying for Grants

Except for very few units of government blessed with an abundance of revenue, getting grants is essential to survival. The following general tips for writing grants should prove helpful as you enter the competitive world of grantsmanship. The term "grantsmanship" is used to describe the ability to apply for and receive grant money. It is often misunderstood and considered a mystery. Like most things, once you look closely, you find a rather straightforward process which requires hard work, common sense, dedication, and a few skills. Basically, grantsmanship is both a political and a technical process. Political in that you have to identify those people and organizations who can help or hinder your grant application. Technical in that you have to utilize the "tools of the trade."

Before beginning the process of writing a proposal and contacting potential funding sources, you should take a comprehensive look at your agency, its priorities, programs and potential funding sources.

Priorities

What are the major tasks to be performed?
What is your track record in these areas?
What new directions or new services are planned for the future?

Does your unit of government have an existing policy or procedure for grant application?

Can you find a grant source to pay for a service now using local tax revenues?

Programs

What particular issues tend to receive support in your community?

Should any existing program be discontinued?

What has been the response of the community to previous new programs?

What is the major focus of the program for which you are seeking financial support?

What population groups will be served by your program?

What geographic area?

Will the program require new staff?

Retraining of staff?

Reassignment of staff?

Will the program, if it is new, support, complement, or compete with existing programs?

Funding

What is your major revenue source?

How stable is it?

What other base of financial resources do you receive?

What kind of assistance will your program require?

How much money will your project cost?

Have other programs similar to yours been funded in the community?

The answers to the above questions should help you develop a strategy that will avoid many of the pitfalls generally encountered in the search for financial assistance. Any successful grantsmanship strategy takes research. It involves the identification of potential funders, the size and types of grants they award, and application requirements. The federal government is the largest of all grant-giving institutions. Even with federal budget cuts, it provides more funding than all private giving combined. However, grant applications for the government are the most time-consuming and fraught with bureaucratic red tape. A few basic tools and procedures to help you find grant sources are:

Catalog of Federal Domestic Assistance (CFDA). This is the best source. It is published by the Office of Management and Budget and contains information on program objectives, eligibility requirements, application procedures, range of grants, and so forth, for over one thousand federal grant programs. Any person interested in federal grants should become thoroughly familiar with this publication. It is indexed by agency, program, eligibility, function, popular name, and subject. It covers most forms of federal assistance. However, because of the fast-changing pace of grants, it is almost always out-of-date.

Agency contact. After checking in the CFDA, contact the local or regional office listed under "Information Contacts" for any grant you may be interested in. Inquire about the status of the program. If the program is still in operation, ask them to send you the guidelines, procedures, forms, and other materials for a federal grant application. Their job is to help you, and your job is to interest them in what you want to do. Personal contacts are important because you can receive information not otherwise available. If the agency you contact is not funding programs you need, ask them for information on who might be interested in your proposal. A follow-up thank-you letter will be helpful in the event you have to go back to them at a later date.

Federal Register. This can be used in conjunction with the CFDA and can be found in most large public university, business, and law libraries. It contains current information on pending legislation in Washington pertaining to federal grants. This source indicates possible funding, but it does not identify where to look for federal funds. When you know the grant agency and program you are interested in, look under "Notice, Rules, and Regulations" and "Proposed Rules and Regulations" pertaining to that program.

You should also become familiar with the *Catalog of State Assistance to Local Governments* and the *Illinois Register Rules of Governmental Agencies*. Once you have become acquainted with these resources, it will be time to move on to the proposal preparation.

Proposal Writing

The proposal represents a plan of action: what you plan to do; why you plan to do it; when you plan to do it; who will do it; and how you will do it. This tells the funder what to expect and how much it will cost. But before we discuss the format, here are a few tips to consider in writing a proposal.

- You should be thoroughly familiar with the project.
- Do not put it off. Start writing and worry later about grammatical errors, mistakes, and missing facts.
- Emphasize people as opposed to things.
- Use simple English. Be warm, positive, and enthusiastic. Avoid jargon

such as "utilize," "maximize," and so on. Do not use personal pronouns like "you," "we," "us." Use "it," "that," and "the."

- Be brief. Follow guidelines provided by the granting agency. In the absence of guidelines, provide two or three typewritten, single-space pages. If the proposal is longer, add a table of contents, double-space, and use headings and subheadings. You can keep a proposal short by putting a lot of material in the addendum.
- Avoid repetition, generalizations, and rhetoric. Be factual and to the point.
- When weaknesses come up, do not apologize.
- Avoid unsupported assumptions. You must be able to substantiate everything in your proposal.
- When the draft is completed, edit carefully for grammatical errors. Have a third party check it before the final draft, which should be neat, clean, and easy to read.

Most proposals should include the following nine sections:

1. *Cover Letter:* Remember to follow any and all guidelines provided by the granting agency. The cover letter should briefly describe the content of the proposal. It should not serve as a summary.

2. *Introduction:* In this section, describe your agency's ability to qualify for and carry out the grant. The introduction should be extensive, in some cases half the length of the proposal. It tells the funder whether you have experience, ability, and community support to accomplish what you want to do. Often this determines whether you will be funded. Government applications often ask for "a description of the applicant" or "background of the applicant," instead of an introduction.

3. *Problem Statement or Needs Assessment:* The problem statement or needs assessment represents the reason for your proposal. It is why your organization is planning to act. Therefore, the problem should be carefully defined before you begin planning your program. A "needs assessment" usually refers to a particular population group in need of help.

4. *Program Objectives:* Program objectives are the result of what you wish to do. They should not be confused with methods. The difference between methods and objectives is the same as the difference between means and ends. If you use statements such as, "to provide," "to establish," "to create," you are talking about methods. If your statements are "to increase," "to decrease," "to reduce," you are probably talking about objectives. Program objectives should tell you who is going to do what, when, and how much. They should be measurable, thus providing the criteria for evaluating your program.

5. *Methods:* After defining your problem and stating your program objectives, you come to the major part of your proposal. This is the explanation of the steps you will take to achieve your objectives. Here, you set forth your program design, the step-by-step plan of action.

6. *Evaluation:* A good proposal has proposed means of program evaluation included in it. This section can be simple or complex, depending on the size and purpose of the program. But a good evaluation procedure should provide feedback information so that you can change or redirect your program as you go along. Moreover, it should set forth the ground rules for determining whether the program was successful and how successful.

7. *Budget:* The proposed budget is an estimate of the total costs of the program. It should be as specific as possible. Do not underestimate or overestimate your figures. Most funders are experts at reviewing budgets and estimating costs. When figuring costs, take into account projected inflation, cost of living increases, and the anticipated time for purchase. Round off your figures to the nearest dollar and do not use categories like "miscellaneous" or "contingency." The latter should be accounted for in your planning. Most government funders have a specific budget format with very detailed instructions.

8. *Addendum:* This is the section where you attach those documents that do not properly fit in the proposal narrative. This is an important section for the short, two-page or three-page letter proposal and gives the fund provider the opportunity to examine areas of your proposal in greater detail. However, it should be used carefully and not as a dumping ground to pad your proposal.

9. *Follow-up:* Finally, after you have completed your proposal and submitted it to the funding agency, prepare yourself for the next step. If the grant is accepted, congratulations are in order. Write a thank-you letter, briefly restating what you plan to do and how you will keep the fund provider abreast of your progress. Also, explore with the provider the handling of publicity regarding the grant award. Who should do the press release and press conference? If your grant was not awarded, do not despair. You are not alone. Write a letter thanking the funding agency for considering your application. Ask them if they would be more specific about their decision and be willing to meet with you to discuss the limitations of your proposal. Information gathered by such a meeting should help you in developing and writing future proposals. Quite often your proposal may be an excellent one, but outside the current interests of the funder.

This chapter has attempted to provide the basis for understanding both the need to obtain external grants as well as some "how-to" ideas for the grant writer. Once you know what is needed, how to address the need, and from what source funding might be obtained, you will be able to try your hand as a grantsman.

Bibliography

Catalog of Federal Domestic Assistance. Washington: U.S. Government Printing Office. Published Annually.

Catalog of State Assistance to Local Governments. 2d ed. Springfield: Illinois Commission on Intergovernmental Cooperation, 1987.

Corporate Foundation Profiles. 4th ed. New York: Foundation Center, 1985.

Des Marais, Philip. *How to Get Government Grants.* New York: Public Service Materials Center, 1975.

The Foundation Directory. 10th ed. New York: Foundation Center, 1985.

The Foundation Directory Supplement. New York: Foundation Center, 1986.

Grantsmanship Made Easy. Springfield: Illinois Association of Community Action Agencies, 1985.

Handbook of Federal Assistance. Boston: Warren, Gorham, and Lamont, 1980.

Horgen, Gregory C. *Playing the Funding Game.* Sacramento: Human Services Development Center, 1981.

PART FOUR

Support Services, Media, and Community Relations

16.

Services Available
to Local Government

RICHARD BURD

Every year, perhaps hundreds of people are appointed for the first time to fill a vacancy on a city council, township board of trustees, county board, or other unit of local government. Every two years at the general elections, thousands more may be elected for the first time to a position within local government. The first question asked is, "Where can I find information about the duties of my office?" Or, "I've just been elected to the village board and I want some information about what I am supposed to do." Even the veteran local official who continues to seek information to make improvements to the operations of his government may ask, "How can I and my fellow officials get better financial information about our operations so that we can make better management decisions?" Still others may ask, "Can our township improve programs for senior citizens?" This chapter sorts out the many different sources of information available to local government officials so that the recently elected mayor, councilman, township trustee, county board member, or the veteran official can have a better idea where help can be obtained for his or her government. "Help" refers to information and technical assistance. (Financial assistance is covered in chapter 15.)

Illinois Constitution and Illinois Revised Statutes

There are two primary sources of information that every student of local government will rely on: the Illinois constitution and the Illinois Revised

Statutes. Article 7 of the Illinois constitution sets out the basic framework of local government in the state. Familiarity with article 7 is essential for an understanding of the Illinois system of local government.

Getting a basic understanding of the revised statutes, however, is an entirely different matter. A Springfield attorney recently complained to a group of township officials that when he started practicing law two decades ago, the state's law was found in a three-volume set of books, which included the index. Today, Illinois laws are contained in five volumes. The annotated set of statutes takes up six shelves of a four-foot bookcase. Although local government law covers only a fraction of the five-volume set, it does present a formidable challenge to anyone desperately attempting to "brush up" on a point of law minutes before a city council meeting is scheduled to start. What makes it an even greater task is that every law regarding cities and villages, for example, should be found in the municipal code, shouldn't it? Unfortunately, that is not true. Information will be found in chapter 24, the Cities and Villages Act, but important references will also be found scattered throughout the more than nine thousand pages of the statutes. Again, one would expect to find local government law pertaining to administrative procedures to be essentially the same for all units of government and found together in a "local government section." Again, this is not the case. Law pertaining to cities and villages is found in chapter 24; county government law in chapter 34; township law in chapter 139; park district law in chapter 105; election law in chapter 46. Another problem with the statutes is that duties of local officials are only very generally described and the reader comes away with only a vague idea of what an official's legal responsibilities are. Nevertheless, the statutes are the prime source of information about Illinois local governments (see table 16-1). Illinois law is a must for information on specific duties and responsibilities of local officials.

Local Government Interest Groups as a Source of Information

The difficulty in interpreting laws to gain an understanding of an official's responsibilities is not a new problem. Neither is the desire to make local government administration more efficient and responsive. For decades, local officials have wrestled with these problems. It is for these reasons and the desire to influence legislation favorable to local governments that the Illinois Municipal League, the Township Officials of Illinois, the Illinois

Table 16-1

Chapters of the Illinois Revised Statutes Pertaining to Local Governments

Chapter Number	Subject	Chapter Number	Subject
1	General Provisions	100	Notices
8	Animals	100½	Nuisances
14	Attorney General and State's Attorneys	101	Oaths and Affirmations
15	Auditor General and State Comptroller	102	Officers
		103	Official Bonds
		105	Parks
19	Canals and Waterway Improvements	107	Paupers
21	Cemeteries	108½	Pensions
23	Charities and Public Welfare	109	Plats
24	Cities and Villages	111½	Public Health & Safety
24½	Civil Service	111⅔	Public Utilities
30	Conveyances	115	Recorders
31	Coroners	116	Records
34	Counties	120	Revenue
35	County Clerks	121	Roads and Bridges
36	County Treasurer	121½	Sales
37	Courts	122	Schools
42	Drainage	125	Sheriffs
43	Dram Shop	127	State Government
46	Elections	127½	State Fire Marshall
53	Fees and Salaries	139	Townships
54	Fences	146½	Warrants
55½	Fire Escapes		
60	Fugitives from Justice		
67½	Housing and Redevelopment		
75	Jails and Jailers		
81	Libraries		
82	Liens		
85	Local Government		
91½	Mental Health		
95½	Motor Vehicles		

Association of Park Districts, and many other local government interest groups evolved during the early part of the twentieth century.

Probably the largest and oldest of all Illinois interest groups is the Illinois Municipal League (IML), which was established in 1904. Its major function is to influence the general assembly to pass legislation favorable to the state's approximately 1,280 municipalities. The Municipal League is regarded as one of the most influential interest groups in Springfield. Years ago, the general assembly even passed legislation authorizing cities and villages to pay annual membership dues to the IML. The Illinois Municipal League and similar organizations are effective because they provide a great deal of factual information to the members of the general assembly during legislative committee hearings. Working with local governments and the general assembly over the years, the staffs of the IML and similar organizations have gained an extraordinary amount of knowledge about the day-to-day operations of the local governments they represent. It is only natural that the expertise of the staffs is also used to provide technical assistance and information to their local official constituents.

The assistance provided by the local government interest groups takes several forms. It may range from a brief response to a mayor calling to find out the number of councilmen needed for a quorum to explain how a township can obtain liability insurance. Local government interest groups receive hundreds of telephone calls and letters each week from local officials, the news media, and state and federal agency personnel, all seeking information about duties, proposed legislation, financial data, or interpretations of the law. Ordinary citizens contact these organizations attempting to find out how they can throw their mayor out of office, what they can do about the potholes in the streets or their neighbor's barking dog. Some of the organizations with larger staffs find the telephone calls and letters a welcome break from the tedium of analyzing proposed legislation, preparing the monthly newsletters, or updating mailing lists. For the smaller organization with a limited staff, it may mean almost continual telephone conversations with officials. However time-consuming, answering local officials' questions is a vital function of all local government interest groups.

In addition to the full-time staff which the interest groups may employ, these organizations typically contract with attorneys for a variety of services including authorship of documents. These materials may range anywhere from general reference books covering all aspects of local government to short essays on specific topics such as how to finance capital projects with special assessments. Among the most authoritative and comprehensive publications is a reference book for city and village officials published by the Illinois Municipal League entitled, simply, the *Illinois Municipal Handbook*. This reference book is written to answer the most commonly asked questions about municipal operations. Local officials find it easy to use because it is well organized, has a detailed table of contents, and a comprehensive crossreferenced index that enables the reader to quickly find the section of the book which addresses his or her question. In addition, the handbook provides an interpretation of the law along with references to appropriate state statutes and applicable court decisions. It provides a municipal attorney or official with a starting point for further research on the topic. The handbook is periodically revised and provided to municipal officials as part of their membership fee.

The Township Officials of Illinois also has a handbook for its membership entitled *Township Duties and Responsibilities.* Although different from the *Illinois Municipal Handbook,* it does provide statutory references of important laws relevant to township and road districts. In addition to the general handbooks available, there are a number of publications available from the various interest groups which address specific topics. Most of the various interest groups also publish monthly magazines which feature timely topics on matters of interest to local officials. Typical information provided in such magazines includes: information on proposed legislation which affects their constituency; coverage of recent conference/workshops of the organization and registration information about future conferences; regular columns by various state officials; articles written by local officials about practical concerns; announcements of equipment to be sold by local governments; and position recruiting announcements for engineers, police/ fire chiefs, and so forth.

As a third important service, interest groups provide workshops and conferences for their members. The Illinois Municipal League conducts the largest conference of any of the interest groups. Its annual conference (almost always held in Chicago in late September or early October) regularly hosts an audience of over three thousand elected and appointed city and village officials. The Township Officials of Illinois usually conducts its annual conference in the fall in Springfield or Peoria. The Park District Association rotates it location. The County Officials Association meets in the fall in Chicago.

A common theme for all the local government interest groups' annual conferences is to provide timely information on the important issues facing the officials. The liability insurance crisis brought about numerous conference sessions in recent years, as did the congressional debate over the extension or termination of the Federal Revenue Sharing program. In addition to the regular annual conferences held by the interest groups, conferences are conducted for special purposes and issues. For example, the Municipal League conducts "Newly Elected Officials Conferences" in

Arlington Heights and Springfield every two years to provide basic information for those just elected.

The Township Officials of Illinois (TOI) holds the most workshops and conferences each year. TOI is devoted to providing a high standard of training for its members. In addition to its annual conference, TOI conducts a series of five to seven early-spring workshops jointly sponsored by Governors State University and the Illinois Department of Commerce and Community Affairs. It also conducts two spring conferences held each year, in Olney and Nashville, a series of supervisors' and clerks' workshops held during the summer, and numerous jointly sponsored county-wide workshops throughout the state. All of these sessions are extremely well attended.

The value of the conference and workshops sponsored by the various interest groups is twofold: First, the material presented at the sessions is of obvious value, for its serves to keep the local official informed of his or her duties and responsibilities and the constantly changing set of issues that confronts local officials. Second, the meetings establish an informational network for the local officials. The conferences bring together people with similar positions from different parts of the state facing the same kind of problems. They provide opportunities to learn from each other's successes and mistakes. They also enable participants to become acquainted with others so that informal communication networks can be developed.

Many interest groups have standing subcommittees to review proposed legislation or to prepare printed materials. For example, the TOI has a general assistance subcommittee composed of a number of township supervisors. This group has prepared a manual to instruct township supervisors on the procedures which should be followed in handling general assistance cases. This group also works with representatives of the Illinois Department of Public Aid to ensure that the state is aware of the impact that a proposed law or regulation will have on the general assistance programs operated by all of the state's townships.

Regional Organizations

There are essentially three kinds of regional organizations in the state although there are some organizations that defy any classification. The first is a survivor of the old regional planning organizations that received funding from the U.S. Department of Housing and Urban Development to undertake regional planning activities. In the early 1980s, this funding source was cut off. Many of these organizations still exist by charging service fees for

preparing grant applications or administering grant or economic development programs for the local governments. Also, some of the regional
planning commissions charge local governments membership fees. The
basic membership fee entitles the government to receive certain basic
services and information. Additional work done for the local government is
on a fee-for-service basis. Generally, the organizations are staffed by
people with planning or public administration backgrounds and offer technical assistance to local governments.

A second type of organization has developed out of growth and development pressures. There are a number of these organizations in the Chicago
metropolitan area that serve their member communities extremely well.
These include the Northwest Council of Public Officials, the DuPage
Mayors and Managers Association, and the South Suburban Mayors and
Managers Association. These organizations provide high-quality professional services on special research projects of regional importance, such as
solid waste management planning, testing of police personnel, land use/
zoning matters, and so on. Some of these organizations directly lobby the
general assembly on issues they feel are important.

A third type of regional organization exists scattered throughout the
state. These tend to be organizations of elected or appointed local officials — usually mayors, township supervisors, or highway commissioners.
The level of activity of these organizations depends on the personalities of
the people in the region. After lying dormant for many years, a mayor's
organization may have new life breathed into it by an aggressive mayor who
takes the initiative to call the mayors in nearby communities and encourage
them to attend meetings. Some of these organizations may provide little
more to their members than a once-a-month or quarterly dinner meeting.
The dinner meetings often feature a speaker to address a particular topic of
interest to the audience. The speaker may be an area legislator or other
political figure, a representative of the county clerk's office to explain some
aspect of the property tax system, or a speaker representing a state agency
to explain a grant or loan program. The value of such organizations is that
they provide their members the opportunity to meet other officials like
themselves and discuss common problems and issues that affect their local
governments.

Specific Officer Organizations

In addition to the various interest groups which represent local governments, there are a number of other state-wide organizations that serve

specific local officials. These include the Municipal Treasurers' Association, Municipal Clerks' Association, County Highway Superintendents, and so forth. These organizations reflect the need of their members to have an organization that represents just their group without attempting to address the competing interests of other local officials. Because the membership to these organizations is limited, the members of the organization tend to share common interests and problems. Often, these organizations, because they are able to focus their interests, prove to be the most valuable to their members. These organizations usually conduct a state-wide annual conference and several regional conferences during the year. The conferences are particularly valuable to the members since the workshops focus on common problems. They also provide an exchange of ideas, an opportunity to take positions on proposed legislation, and a friendly atmosphere conducive to learning.

Universities and Community Colleges

The state's universities and community colleges also provide assistance to local governments on a variety of issues. Assistance may be provided by faculty, graduate class projects, or sponsorship of special classes or conferences. The faculty of universities or community colleges may see the opportunity of helping a local government in meeting their own needs, such as preparing research materials for a publication. There are instances when the needs of a faculty member have dovetailed into the needs of a community—the community needing help on a particular matter and the faculty member needing a research subject. Such mutually beneficial arrangements may lead a professor to assign his or her class to research a particular problem faced by the community. Examples of such projects include land use planning and zoning questions, financial management matters, and community surveys.

Universities and community colleges may also at times sponsor workshops or offer special local government classes for local government officials. Some of these classes have met with considerable success. If a local official desires a degree or is looking for an "enrichment" course that provides a background on local government, then these classes tend to be quite worthwhile. If the local official is looking for information which will directly help him with his government problems, he or she may be disappointed in the course offering. For example, a course in accounting or municipal finance may not be of great benefit to the local official wishing to make changes since most accounting courses are designed for businesses and not governmental accounting. Even public finance courses may not meet the needs of a local official who has specific questions and applications in mind. Of course, the instructor is the one who can make the difference. By working with the official, he or she can design the course content and reading for the direct benefit of the official.

An example of this is the Illinois Municipal Clerks' Association, which has pooled resources with the University of Illinois (and, most recently, Northern Illinois University) and the National Clerks' Association to establish the Municipal Clerks' Institute. The Institute features a week-long training program conducted each fall. It brings together a blend of academics and practitioners to provide a well-balanced program. The Illinois Municipal Treasurers' Association has established a similar relationship with Eastern Illinois University. Governors State University teams up each spring with the Township Officials of Illinois and the Illinois Department of Commerce and Community Affairs to cosponsor a series of five to seven, day-long workshops held on Saturdays at different locations throughout the state.

National Professional Organizations

There are a number of national professional organizations which may be of benefit to local officials. The International City Management Association (ICMA) and the Government Finance Officers Association (GFOA) are among the nation's most respected organizations and provide a full range of educational and career development courses and publications. These organizations tend to appeal mostly to the "professional," appointed local government official rather than to the elected mayor or board member. They were established to provide government managers and finance directors with career development opportunities. Over the years, both ICMA and GFOA have developed a library of professional publications. ICMA's "Green Book" series is a classic in the field and is considered a basic reference tool to public administration students and practitioners who want to further their knowledge. Most of the publications have been written by professional city managers from the perspective of their own experience. As a result, the information is of a high quality, coming from people who have actually been responsible for running local government. This contrasts to material written at the university level by public administration and political science professors with little or no local government experience, who stress "what ought to be" rather than "what really is" and what is practical.

These organizations have Illinois chapters which encourage membership of managers, assistant managers, finance directors, treasurers, and local government personnel. Again, the network of people in similar positions provides members great opportunities to learn from each other. The state chapters also offer a number of conference and seminar opportunities.

Assistance from the State of Illinois

A great deal of information and technical assistance is available from various agencies of the State of Illinois. The Illinois Department of Commerce and Community Affairs (DCCA) offers a number of programs which are geared to meet the needs of local officials. DCCA is the state's economic development agency charged with the overall responsibility of creating and retaining jobs in the state. Although the agency's emphasis is on economic development issues, DCCA also provides services and information to local government officials. Part of DCCA was created from the former Department of Local Government Affairs, so it has a long history of assisting local governments. Over 90 percent of the state's 1280 municipalities have less than twenty thousand population. Many of these municipalities and other local governments do not have any full-time staff. As a result, many of DCCA's informational and technical assistance programs are directed at providing information and technical assistance to these small units of local government. Hundreds of phone calls and letters are received each month from local officials. DCCA also has a field staff to provide direct technical assistance to local governments. Moreover, DCCA conducts a number of workshops designed specifically to meet the needs of local officials.

The assistance available from DCCA is of particular value to local officials because DCCA provides information designed to fit the specific needs of local officials under Illinois laws and operating procedures. Much of the International City Management Association's material on budgeting is excellent for the full-time professional, but it does not provide information on what the part-time official must do to meet the specific public hearing and publishing requirements under Illinois law. Because DCCA is not a regulatory agency such as the Illinois Environmental Protection Agency, all of its assistance is purely advisory and is not binding upon the local governments. DCCA's technical and information programs can be classified into three major categories: (1) general management; (2) financial management; (3) economic development. (Loan and grant programs are discussed in chapter 15.)

General Management

DCCA offers a great deal of general government information to local officials. This information ranges from how to comply with the legislative requirements of the Truth In Taxation Act to a checklist of the requirements of the Open Meetings Act. Recently, the agency implemented a telephone tape information system which features a toll-free number whereby the caller is able to hear over one hundred prerecorded messages dealing with local government administration.

Financial Management

DCCA offers information and technical assistance to local officials on all aspects of financial management. Such assistance includes: identifying local revenue sources; helping local officials adopt sound accounting procedures; listing revenue sources available to governments, including the different property taxes which the government may choose; recommending the proper ordinances to be adopted in order to implement new taxes; pointing out a variety of other nonproperty taxes which the governments may choose to implement; and recommending sound budgeting procedures which will provide an effective means to allocate funds.

DCCA staff also assists in explaining the various publishing and hearing requirements which must be met to satisfy state requirements. Revenue raising and spending is only a part of the local government's financial operations. A government must be able to record revenues and expenditures properly. Revenue and expenditure reports are compiled from the accounting system to provide the governing board with the information needed to manage effectively. The agency can provide technical assistance to help local governments set up an accounting system to record all transactions of the community properly and generate needed financial reports. More importantly, DCCA can train local government staff. Little lasting benefit will result if a budgeting or accounting system is established without training the employees of the local government in how to use it properly. Therefore, DCCA staff works directly with local government personnel to establish step-by-step procedures.

Another important area of assistance available from DCCA is capital improvement planning and capital budgeting. DCCA staff leads the community through the process of surveying the condition of its public works system, determining what projects are needed for the future, setting priorities, identifying project financing techniques available, and scheduling projects for implementation. During the process of putting together a capital improvement plan and budget, questions often arise as to how the community will finance the project. DCCA staff is able to help the community review its financing options and help it project the annual revenue requirements needed to construct the project. For example, DCCA can analyze a community's water user charges to see if they are sufficient to support improvements to the system. If current user charges are not sufficient to produce adequate revenues for improvements to the system, the staff can provide the community with a series of user charge schedules which would provide sufficient revenue to undertake the capital improvements.

Economic Development

As the state's economic development agency, DCCA has a separate field staff that specializes in economic development matters. This staff assists local governments in such matters as industrial and commercial expansion, tax increment financing, and industrial development bonds.

Illinois State Treasurer

The office of the Illinois state treasurer offers a program which is of particular interest to officials of small local governments. The program allows local governments to invest their money along with state money. The advantage of such an investment pool is that it is managed full-time by investment professionals, resulting in high rates of interest which a part-time official would have a difficult time matching. Of even greater importance, it is fully collateralized, which makes the investment completely safe. The investment pool also offers a degree of liquidity difficult to find elsewhere, for money can be invested on one day and be withdrawn on the following day. The treasurer's office charges a slight administrative fee to participate in the pool; however, the part-time local government treasurer would have a difficult time finding investment opportunities which offer the earnings, safety, and liquidity provided by the program.

Office of the State Comptroller

The office of the state comptroller also has a field staff to assist local officials. The field staff is available to provide information about the filing requirements of the various financial statements that must be compiled and filed with the comptroller's office. The comptroller's office also prepares various publications of interest to local officials (such as a recent guide on investing local funds) and conducts training workshops around the state.

In addition, the state comptroller has three local government advisory boards that provide assistance: the Municipal and County Advisory Boards and the Local Government Advisory Board. The Municipal and County Advisory Boards were established years ago to advise the comptroller on local government finance issues and to aid in developing an overview of local government spending practices. Each board consists of three local officials, three certified public accountants, and three public members. The Local Government Advisory Board was created in 1984 to give local officials a greater voice in regulations affecting them and to improve the quality of financial information used by local officials, the public, and the media. This board consists of eighteen members: six local officials, six certified public accountants, and six public members, including representatives from the Department of Commerce and Community Affairs, the Township Officials Association, the Illinois Press Association, the C.P.A. Society, the State Board of Education, the Taxpayers' Federation of Illinois, and others.

Other state agencies also provide technical assistance to local governments. For example, the Bureau of Local Roads and Streets within the Illinois Department of Transportation (IDOT) provides assistance concerning street maintenance and repair. IDOT has a number of district offices, each with a district engineering staff providing assistance to municipalities and township road districts. These district offices provide technical information and conduct workshops on the permissible uses of motor fuel tax monies, new materials and maintenance techniques, and information about other programs of interest to local officials.

Finally, the State Board of Elections has a staff of experts which can answer questions concerning the timing of elections, technical questions on petitions and referendums, and the filing of local official vacancies.

Almost all of the state's various agencies can provide at least some assistance to local governments. Even though most state agencies have regulatory authority over some aspect of local governments, invariably, they will be willing to provide at least some assistance to local governments. Obviously, there is a limit to some of the assistance which regulatory agencies can provide. For example, the Illinois Environmental Protection Agency regulates local public water supplies and sewage discharge into the state's waterways. Although agency staff is more than willing to discuss local water and sewer problems, obviously staff cannot perform engineering services for local governments or waive legal requirements.

17.

Interest Groups

JAMES F. KEANE

It is difficult to determine whether political parties predated interest groups or if the interest groups by natural association joined together to form political parties. Historically it may not make much difference, but it is obvious that both political parties and interest groups have become crucial extraconstitutional bodies that function between the people of the United States and various levels of government.

People naturally gather in alliances to oppose government actions which they individually find abhorrent or to call on government to provide them with protection or benefits based on some similar background. This becomes especially evident to appointed or elected officials in the lawmaking process, when allies come together either to oppose or support an ordinance or a local government ruling. One astute observer noted that political parties are the basis of interest groups. The most obvious examples are the historical relationships between the Republican party and the business community as well as the relationship between the Democratic party and organized labor.

David Truman, in his book *The Governmental Process,* provides a good definition of an interest group. He describes it as any group that "on the basis of one or more shared attitudes, makes certain claims upon other groups in the society for the establishment, maintenance and enhancement of forms of behavior that are implied by the shared attitudes."[1] Quite obviously, interest groups are nothing more than natural outgrowths of the representative form of government. When one person who is interested in a particular governmental action meets another who feels the same, a basic

1. David Truman, *The Governmental Process* (New York: Alfred A. Knopf, 1971), 33.

interest group has been established. Because of the natural tendency for people to associate with those that have the same interest, special interest groups have existed and have been easily formed. As noted, individual pressure groups provided the core for political parties, and while much of this is not as clear-cut as it has been in the past, in general it still holds true.

A few more characteristics of interest groups should be recognized. Organized interest groups, also called pressure groups, play a role in American politics and generally possess an upper-class bias. They also represent a very small percentage of the population. According to E. F. Schattschneider, probably 90 percent of the population within the United States are not in the formalized interest group system. He notes that pressure politics is essentially the politics of small groups.[2] For those interested in the organizational structure and operation of pressure groups, the books by Schattschneider and Truman are worthy sources.

Growth

Interest groups have multiplied rapidly in the last forty years. The growth of revenues by a unit of government—be it federal, state, or local—attracts people to government to ensure that they receive their fair share of the goodies and that their position within the society is not in anyway diminished. The most recent example of this phenomenon has been the great increase in Illinois state government in the number of lobbyists who have become registered since the advent of Reagan federalism. Because of the lack of fiscal revenue growth on the federal level in relation to past growth, many interest groups, as represented by their lobbyists, are finding that state and local government is where the action is.

There is also a natural multiplication of interest groups built into the process, because any time one organization or unit within an organization receives some legislative or executive benefit, similar organizations appear to claim the same rights for their membership. Examples of this in Illinois in the past five years have been the demands by public pension bodies to receive equal treatment. This occurred when firefighters in Illinois were successful in expanding their pension benefits. During a recent session, police representatives came to Springfield to urge the passage of similar pension benefits for their membership. The police were successful in piggybacking upon the gains made by the firefighters. At the present time,

2. E. F. Schattschneider, *The Semi-Sovereign People* (Hinsdale, IL: Dryden Press, 1960), 35.

all other groups representing state and public employees are attempting to have their pension benefits brought up to par with that of firefighters and police officers.

New interest groups are also formed when new problems arise. Sometimes the new interest group is made up of the same people who had previously united over a given issue, but quite often the new interest group consists of members of different interest groups, and once in a while a brand-new organization is formed on a permanent basis. Some interest groups go out of existence simply because they have either reached their goals or their specific interest is no longer relevant. An example of this was the free-silver special interest group, which disbanded after it lost its cause.

Types

It is impossible to provide, at any given time, a comprehensive list of all the special interest groups that exist and influence particular units of government. Special interest groups are constantly coming into and going out of existence. Historically, interest groups can be categorized in broad terms, such as those connected with labor. Over the years, different trade unions were formed, quite often based upon apprentice training and defined skills. In later years, general membership unions were formed, encompassing all those who labored within a given industry. There have also been unions that have differed on philosophical aspects of the rights of the working man versus the employer.

A large segment of interest groups is formed on the basis of business. These originally started as trade or product associations, such as the tobacco groups and the sugar interest groups. Another category of interest groups would be classified as a professional interest group. This group would include doctors, lawyers, dentists, nurses, psychologists, and any other group that considers itself a profession. Over the last few decades there has also been tremendous growth in the citizens' rights and social rights area. Probably the most prominent has been the civil rights movement interest group, closely followed by the emergence of the senior citizen community as an interest group.

A short listing of the more obvious interest groups follows:

manufacturers
distributors
transportation

finance
insurance
national association of businessmen
professional and semi-professional labor unions
women
veterans
stock and commodity exchanges
farmers
blacks, hispanics
fraternal
public officials

Dealing with Interest Groups

Over the years, our attitudes determine whether interest groups represent
a good or bad force in government. Generally, those who have positions
similar to our individual positions are considered to be good, while those
who disagree with us are bad. A local public official may or may not have an
opinion as to whether a given interest group or the influence of interest

groups as a whole is good or bad. However, we must recognize their existence and their rightful participation in the governmental process.

A study of United States history indicates that interest groups will be involved in government issues as long as our existing constitution is in place. The right of the people to petition and the right of the people to organize for furtherance of their political objectives are well established under the U.S. Constitution. Therefore, it is incumbent upon all public officials to accept the existence of interest groups. Once this acceptance is established, it is important for the appointed or elected official to develop a working philosophy that he or she will use in dealing with these groups.

When an official takes office, he or she will usually find that a number of interest groups monitor and participate in his or her unit of local government. Some groups will have a constant presence; others will come and go and limit themselves to a few issues. It is essential for the newly elected official to determine the scope and impact that various interest groups have on the decision-making process so that he or she can become a more effective public official. Not only is it important to know the identity of the special interest groups but also their major goals and objectives.

Although many interest groups concentrate heavily on the national and state scene, there is a trend for interest groups to focus increasingly on local governments. This is especially true as the federal government is cutting back on many domestic programs. More and more, interest groups are looking to state and local governments to take over abandoned federal programs. The willingness of national interest groups to become involved on the local level is exemplified by the involvement of the National Rifle Association when there is an attempt to pass an ordinance that would outlaw the use or ownership of handguns within local boundaries. Such legislation assures heavy lobbying activity by the National Rifle Association on the local level.

Once a local official has determined who the special interest players are, he or she may then wish to review their past activities in terms of his or her unit of local government. Quite often, once a special interest group has achieved its purpose and been successful in implementing its legislative goals, it may withdraw from the local government arena. However, it is important for the local official to take the time to understand how the group has affected his or her unit of local government. In this way, the official can not only judge the effectiveness of a group but also better understand the process by which interest groups function.

Probably the best method for determining the impact of a special interest group on a unit of local government is to discuss the matter with old-timers who are familiar with the governmental history. They can provide a background on the development of the issue and the fights that have occurred in the past over different issues. A good political history of the local government, especially over the past twenty-five years, will usually give the newly elected local official an indication as to who the special groups are and which interest groups have been successful and which have not.

Perhaps the best indication of the relative strength of an interest group is the budgetary process of the unit of local government. If a newly elected public official looks at his or her government's budget over the past twenty years, certain spending swings may become obvious. Perhaps the easiest way to review this budget history is to develop a series of pie charts in which each expenditure of the local government unit is divided into its proportionate slice. If a series of pie charts is compiled for the past twenty or twenty-five years and a comparison is made, one can easily spot where there has been a general change of direction in spending. The official can also see changes in the funding for existing programs as well as new programs coming into existence and older programs being phased out. Quite often the older programs have realized their objective (for example, street resurfacing). New programs, however, usually represent the impact of the wishes and desires of the community as represented by interest groups.

While one may argue that the decision to implement a program is not a decision brought about by interest groups but rather by the housekeeping and infrastructure needs of the unit of local government, one need only point out that there is a group of individuals as well as interest groups within the community that demand housekeeping services. Once one realizes that the unit of local government does not have sufficient funds to provide all the services requested of it, one becomes more aware that the budget changes reflect the success of one group over another. The increased influence over government exercised by senior citizen associations on all levels of governmental decision making is an obvious example. If one reviews the growth and development of new programs that serve senior citizens on a national, state, and local level, the political impact of senior citizens as an interest group becomes obvious. In the federal deficit reduction discussions, among the few items that cannot be considered for reduction are the social security and medicare programs. On the state level, there has been an increase of services for senior citizens. Similarly, on the state level, the last programs to be cut, should fiscal hard times occur, would be those that serve the senior citizen. The same is true on the local level. While some may consider this the result of the large percentages of senior citizens that vote, senior citizen programs represent an influence by an interest group.

In summary, while the influence of interest groups is not as extensive in state and local matters as it is in national politics at the present time, there may be a change forthcoming. It is important for local officials to recognize the existence of interest groups and their rightful role in the governing process. To many people the term "interest group" may have a negative meaning. The local official must remember the right of interest groups to participate in the democratic process. This is a right that is not only well established in reality but has been protected under the terms of the U.S. Constitution.

The Future of Interest Groups

Local government will continue to be influenced by interest groups as it has over the years. Each school board referendum to increase real property taxes for educational improvements is in fact the effort of one interest group to provide its constituency with a larger share of real estate revenues. Senior citizens lobbying a unit of local government to provide free or reduced-fare bus services is an attempt by a special interest group to have a bigger piece of the action. Legislation to provide special handicapped transportation services is an expansion of rights that are being demanded by the handicapped.

Every local official is constantly exposed to demands by different groups for expanded services. This process has become more sophisticated over the years and especially in regard to larger units of local government will become only more so in the future. Local governments will be exposed to more professional lobbyists than they have seen in the past as special interest groups look to state and local governments to replace domestic programs terminated by the federal government.

Bibliography

Morrow, William L. *Public Administration, Politics, and the Political System.* New York: Random House, 1975.

Schattschneider, E. F. *The Semi-Sovereign People.* Hinsdale, IL: Dryden Press, 1960.

Truman, David B. *The Governmental Process.* New York: Alfred A. Knopf, 1971.

Waldo, Dwight, ed. *Public Administration in a Time of Turbulence.* Scranton, PA: Chandler, 1971.

18.

Media Relations

GARY KOCH AND JAMES F. KEANE

For many elected and appointed government officials, one of the most difficult aspects of their job is dealing effectively with the media. A phone call from a reporter for a newspaper or radio or television station can strike fear into even the most experienced or knowledgeable official.

This need not be. Reporters and editors in the media are simply doing their job by reporting on government activities. Sometimes their role is adversarial. As the "public watchdog," the media review government activities with a skeptical eye, and rightly so. The U.S. Constitution declares that the public has a right to know. Sometimes the role is simply information-seeking—the routine gathering of information for a story. The smart official soon realizes that the easier he or she makes a reporter's job, the better the relationship between the government and the media. This chapter focuses on the development of the relationship between an appointed or elected official and the media. This relationship is complex and ever-changing, but it does not have to be difficult.

Media relations are generally two-way. Sometimes the local newspaper, radio or television station is the aggressor in tracking down the facts of a story. Other times the local government itself may be pressuring the media to present a specific issue or to focus on a particular side to a story. Reporters and government officials have particular biases against each other which have developed over the years through poor communication or a lack of communication altogether. Reporters complain about the following: government uses too much "red tape" and jargon to make some issues more difficult than they need to be; government officials send out too many self-serving news releases; officials are notorious for not returning telephone calls; there is too much ignorance of reporter's needs and deadlines; and reporters often feel used by government officials.

Officials counter with their own set of gripes about reporters. They claim that reporters do not tell the "whole story" or reporters do not always take the time to understand a story or get the proper background information. They also maintain that reporters are distrustful of anything coming from government officials; that too many reporters have an arrogant attitude toward government and government officials; and that officials resent wasting their time reeducating new reporters because of the high turnover in the journalism field. This chapter is an effort to make dealing with the media an easier task. The relationship with the media may be adversarial but it does not have to be acidic. It is possible to develop a good working relationship with reporters based on mutual respect and trust.

According to the Illinois Press Association, Illinois has roughly 700 newspapers publishing within its boundaries. Seventy-six of these are dailies and the remainder are published weekly. There are 350 publishing companies which publish one or more newspapers. Added to that, there are 60 television stations and 207 radio stations in Illinois. This means that there are a lot of reporters looking for news. Besides covering the usual sources—disasters, accidents, deaths, the weather—they will direct some of their coverage toward local government and you, as its representative. The question thus becomes: "How can I effectively deal with the news media?" And taking that a step further, "How can I successfully get my message across?" Or, "How can I get fair coverage from the local press?"

In their book *Effective Public Relations,* Cutlip and Center[1] list six basic rules:

1. *Shoot squarely.* Be fair, be honest, and be accurate. It will increase your credibility and the local media will trust and respect you for it.

2. *Give service.* Helping a reporter to make his or her job easier will make yours easier as well. This can range from providing information in a timely manner to offering easy access to it.

3. *Don't beg or carp.* News stories are printed on their own merits, not because an official requests it. Also, don't complain about how you're treated in a story unless the facts are completely false. Remember that the media has the last word.

4. *Don't ask for kills.* The best way to prevent a negative story is to do your homework so the unfavorable situation does not exist in the first place.

5. *Don't flood the media.* Don't waste a reporter or editor's time with

1. Scott M. Cutlip, Allen H. Center, and Glen M. Broom, *Effective Public Relations,* 6th ed. (Englewood Cliffs, NJ: Prentice Hall, 1985), 431.

unnecessary stories or information. It will ruin your credibility to the extent that when you do have something newsworthy, reporters will assume you're "crying wolf."

6. *Keep updated lists.* Get to know your local reporters, their "beats" and deadlines. Your media coverage will reflect how well you maintain this aspect of media relations.

Taking these rules a step further, Chester Burger[2] outlined the "10 commandments" of getting along with the media:

1. Talk from the viewpoint of the public's interest, not your own.
2. Speak in personal terms whenever possible.
3. If you do not want a statement quoted, do not make it.
4. State the most important fact at the beginning.
5. Do not argue with the reporter or lose your cool.
6. If a question contains offensive language or simply words you do not like, do not repeat them even to deny them.
7. If the reporter asks a direct question, give an equally direct answer.
8. If you do not know the answer to a question, simply say, "I don't know but I'll find out for you."
9. Tell the truth even if it hurts.
10. Do not exaggerate the facts.

Reporters will periodically contact you for information, quotes, or reaction to the news, but there will be times when you are the aggressor, when you want to influence the news. There generally are three ways to do this: the interview, the news release, and the news conference.

Interview

In an interview, it is important that you provide the direction or focus of the interview so you can cover the material you wish discussed. It is also important that ground rules are established at the beginning so that both you and the reporter know what is and is not "on the record" (everything said is directly attributable to the official). You should do your homework so that you are ready to talk with some authority about the subject matter.

2. Chester Burger, "How to Meet the Press," *Harvard Business Review,* (July–Aug. 1975).

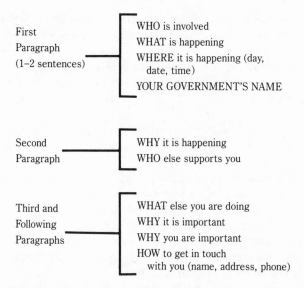

First
Paragraph
(1–2 sentences)

WHO is involved
WHAT is happening
WHERE it is happening (day,
    date, time)
YOUR GOVERNMENT'S NAME

Second
Paragraph

WHY it is happening
WHO else supports you

Third and
Following
Paragraphs

WHAT else you are doing
WHY it is important
WHY you are important
HOW to get in touch
    with you (name, address, phone)

Figure 18-1. A style of writing for public relations.

Any handout materials necessary should be readily available. If the interview includes the taking of a photo, arrangements should be made beforehand.

News Release

The news release is the easiest and most common means of providing information on your government's activities. It makes a reporter's job easier as it provides background information and can save you time because the release, if done well, will cut down on the number of phone calls from reporters. A news release is very simply the who, what, where, when, and why of a story. It should be written in an inverted pyramid style so that the most important information is listed first (see fig. 18-1). Then, if the newspaper prints only the first paragraph of your story because of space limitations, it will have the most important part. Similarly, if the reader only reads the first paragraph, he or she will also have the most important information of the story.

A good news release follows certain rules.

1. A news release should be on your government letterhead, preferably with your logo or symbol, so it is easily recognizable.

2. The date of the release should be listed.

3. The release date should be listed. In most cases, it would be "For Immediate Release."

4. The name and phone number of a contact person should be listed.

5. Do not use headlines. Editors will give the story a title if they choose to use it.

6. The lead paragraph should contain many of the "5Ws" (who, what, where, when, and why) of your story.

7. The second paragraph should contain answers to any of the "5Ws" not listed in the first paragraph.

8. Double-space the release and use wide margins.

9. End the press release with the traditional "30" or "end" or "# # # # #".

10. Most releases should be one page in length. If yours goes on to a second page, end page one with the word "more."

11. Use short, active sentences as much as possible.

12. Always proofread releases before they are distributed. It will save you the possible embarrassment of having to correct information later.

News Conference

News conferences are a good means of getting several reporters together at one time to cover an important issue, such as the need for a new school, higher taxes, or a new executive appointment. For the most part, news conferences are overused and, in local government, should be seldom considered. How do you determine if a news conference is justified? If the information you want to disseminate is complex or controversial, the need may exist. If an issue is of a broad public nature, a news conference may be necessary. If a visiting celebrity passed through your community, a news conference may be in order.

If you decide that a full-blown news conference is required, make sure you contact all the area media. You do not want to exclude anyone for any reason. Try to make the location and time of the news conference convenient for reporters. The site should be large enough for the media people and any visitors, and it also should be conducive to the taking of photos. Any news releases, handout materials, press kits, and so forth should be available for reporters who want background information. Be prepared to go into detail regarding the subject matter of the news conference. Reporters will assume you have something important to say so expect some thorough and perhaps lengthy questioning. You should do your homework beforehand and try to anticipate the difficult questions. This will allow you to be more poised and relaxed at the news conference.

Newspapers

It is important for local officials to realize that there are two roles in dealing with newspapers, and to a lesser extent, with television and radio. As an elected or appointed official, you are a provider of information concerning the government's activities. From this standpoint, you will deal with a reporter or possibly the editor. On another level, you may purchase advertising space in the newspaper for an employment ad or possibly a legal notice or copy of the treasurer's report. In this role, you would work with the advertising or business office. A newspaper office generally has six departments: news, editorial, advertising, business, circulation, and production. A small paper may combine some of these functions, but most officials can expect to deal with the editorial, news, advertising, and business departments during their term of office.

When tailoring your message specifically to newspapers, keep in mind their deadlines. All media like timely information—if it is not timely, it is not news. Learn what the deadlines are for your area newspapers. If the paper is a daily, the deadline may be early morning or early afternoon depending on when it is printed. If it is a weekly paper, the deadline for news (and advertising) may be on Monday or Tuesday. Newspapers, because of their type of coverage, can provide more depth to a story, so it is important to provide them with enough material. In a similar vein, because of the format and type of deadlines, feature stories are more acceptable than in radio or TV. Officials should always be looking for an interesting slant to get their government activities in the news.

Opportunities for photos should always be explored. Newspapers love visual aids to tell a story. An important reminder: when sending out news releases that include a photo, remember to omit the photo in your release to a radio station. You would be embarrassed.

An important resource for working with newspapers is an annual publication entitled the *Editor & Publisher Yearbook*. This volume, available in most libraries, lists all newspapers in the country with respective addresses, phone numbers, departments and personnel, deadlines, and advertising rates. Any official wanting to establish a good relationship with area newspapers is encouraged to review this book.

Radio

Radio is a very diverse medium. Listening audiences are segmented into rock, pop, classical, country, all talk, all news, Spanish, and others. Because of this diversity of stations, local officials can target their news to a particular segment of the population if desired. Local officials should make use of all aspects of radio. Many radio stations have a daily or weekly talk or interview show. Stations managers are always looking for interesting guests, so the aggressive official will want to participate in any talk show format available. Similarly, most radio air public service announcements that are of interest or benefit to the community. Local governments can use this to their advantage to advertise a particular service, announce an important meeting, provide health information, or any similar type of message.

As the International City Management Association notes in its publication *Effective Communication: Getting the Message Across,* radio is an immediate medium.[3] Radio deadlines can be hourly so it is important that radio news people have access to news and information as soon as it is humanly possible. A local official should expect to deal with reporters or the news director at a radio station. Radio stations are structured similarly to newspapers, yet usually have less staff, so a reporter may double as a news editor or station manager. Large stations can have similar bureaucracies and levels of administration as large newspapers.

News releases prepared for radio news should be written for the ear, not the eye. They should be written more informally. They should be short, usually no more than five hundred words, and should avoid abbreviations or acronyms. Figures should be rounded off whenever possible. Names that are are difficult to pronounce should include some phonetic help to aid the reader.

Television

TV stations generally receive their news from the print media and are more interested in providing news and stories which are visual and have a visual impact. Quite often they will do a short segment or a story that was covered in much depth in a newspaper. The visual aspect of television can not be emphasized too much. Camera crews are always looking for stories that will

3. "Working with the Media," in *Effective Communication: Getting the Message Across.* (Washington: International City Management Association, 1983), 114.

look good on the "tube." Your story will have a much better chance to be aired if you think in advance of what visual aids or setting will improve your story.

Television has special deadlines as do newspapers and radio. When catering to television reporters, keep in mind that their stories run on the 5 and 10 P.M. news. But first they have to file and edit their reports, so if you want your story on the evening news, schedule your interview or news conference by midmorning. In case your local TV station is some distance away, take the reporter's drive time into consideration. If the reporter may not have had time to eat breakfast, you may want to provide coffee and donuts. You also may want to notify the station a few days in advance so it can adjust its schedule.

As in radio, talk shows and interview-type programs are common and should be used to the fullest extent possible. Television also airs many public service announcements (PSAs). These need to be well done to be carried, but most television personnel are happy to assist organizations to make PSAs as good as possible. When you are on the air, remember to dress conservatively, preferably in a dark suit, so you will look better on camera. Try to avoid wearing a lot of jewelry or anything else that distracts from you and your message. Obviously, there is great competition for space and air time. The better your message or story, the more thought-out it is and the better prepared, the more likely it is that you will receive the type and amount of publicity you desire.

Rules for Newly Elected Public Officials

Probably the best course of action for you as a newly elected or appointed public official would be to identify the media outlets that exist in your area and to visit each media editor and reporter. Often you may have already met the reporters and editors (print, radio, TV) during the campaign. Even so, it is wise for newly elected as well as veteran public officials to meet with the reporters and the editors of the district. In the course of the visit, you should provide the media representatives with an agenda of what you hope to achieve in the coming term of office. This can often result in a positive feature story and, at the very least, will have a positive impression on the editor or reporter.

If you do a good job of briefing the media upon election, then follow-up stories based on the original briefing are inevitable. This process involves the media in your political and public program. They have a better understanding of what you are attempting to do. Often they become involved in the development of the program they have discussed with you.

A reporter's phone calls should be returned as soon as possible even if you know what the reporter is calling about and you are not prepared to answer the anticipated inquiries. If it is impossible for you to return the phone call, have your secretary or someone else call and indicate that you are unable to talk to the reporter at the present time but that you will get back to him or her as soon as possible.

If you are involved in a difficult situation or you are aware of a major problem that has developed in which you are involved, it is quite often the best course of action to initiate the contact with the media to describe the situation in your terms rather than have the press report the story a few days later using someone else's background and terms. This is nothing more than one of the basic rules of public relations: get your side of the story out first, so your interpretation of events becomes the accepted one. It is best to "share" the problems of your office or unit of government with the general public and with the media rather than to have them discover the problem. As a general rule, it might be said that conducting the public business in the open is the best way to maintain a good reputation and to stop any charges of "cover-up."

In line with the above-noted openness, it is better not to have any public secrets. When an audit is received, it is good practice for you, as the local official, to brief the press on the findings of the audit, be they good or bad, prior to its final publication. The briefing allows you to put the audit interpretations into your own terms and to explain any peculiarities rather than to have a possible misinterpretation of audit findings or even a negative interpretation of part of the findings which is not justified.

As much as possible, try to prevent reporters from developing a bad attitude about you or your government. Quite often if there is an ongoing adversarial or combative relationship between a reporter and a local public official, an attitude of cynicism may develop on the part of the reporter to the point that he or she is unwilling to believe that a public official is capable of doing any good deeds. It is not necessary for you to prostrate yourself before the media, but the old saying of "don't get into an argument with people who buy ink by the barrel" has to be kept in mind. If you have a problem with a reporter, one of the best things to do is to sit down and discuss the problem with the reporter. Before you go to the editor or publisher, try to resolve your problem with the reporter. Just as you would not want somebody going over your head, you should give the same consideration to the reporter. Quite often an open and honest approach such as this can resolve the problem and improve relationships.

In a social or working relationship with members of the media, there is no overall accepted protocol as to who buys lunch, who might buy tickets for a ball game, or any number of other social situations. In some cases, the newspaper has a code of conduct that it expects its reporters to follow and in other instances the reporters are free to accept lunches and other favors on their own. It is important for you to understand what the custom is so that embarrassments can be avoided.

One of the major complaints made by public officials and candidates is the turnover of reporters, especially in small newspapers. You must keep in mind that this is a fact of life. It is in the nature of small local newspapers that they often are the first job or training ground for reporters and the turnover is high. In spite of the turnover, it is well worth the effort and time to cultivate relationships with new reporters. You have a new opportunity to explain your goals and objectives as well as the operation of your office. Quite often, a new reporter will make a feature story out of the operation of a local office, whereas an experienced reporter would not even consider such a story.

Working with reporters from newspapers, radio, and television can be a rewarding experience. It should be your goal to develop a two-way relationship in which you initiate news as well as provide it upon request. By doing your homework, being honest and fair with reporters, tailoring your message to the appropriate forum, and making it as easy as possible for the reporter to do his or her job, you and your government can generate favorable publicity to the taxpayer, who is the ultimate critic of your work.

19.

Community Relations

GARY KOCH

Equal in importance to media relations are community relations. What exactly are "community relations?" Very simply, they are public relations aimed at a particular geographic area, in this case, the area administered by your particular government. Community relations revolve around your government's participation with and within the community. A reasonable question to ask at this point is "Why are community relations needed?" Or, "Aren't community relations accomplished through effective media relations?"

Not exactly. Media relations are only a part of it. In a community, a local government has three publics—voters, taxpayers, and other citizens or residents. These publics want and expect certain things from their community[1]:

1. commercial prosperity
2. support of religion
3. work for everyone
4. adequate educational facilities
5. law, order, and safety
6. population growth
7. proper housing and utilities
8. varied recreational pursuits
9. attention to public welfare
10. progressive measures for good health
11. competent government
12. good reputation

1. Scott M. Cutlip, Allen H. Center, and Glen M. Broom, *Effective Public Relations,* 6th ed. (Englewood Cliffs, NJ: Prentice-Hall, 1985), 399.

For most of these needs, the community looks to its government. Unfortunately, many residents are fearful and cynical about their local government and its ability to meet those needs. Why is this? Six reasons come to mind:

1. People, for the most part, do not understand how large and complex government is today.
2. They do not comprehend the amount of dollars involved in administering government.
3. They do not understand how government works.
4. They do not understand how laws, resolutions, and other government activities are approved.
5. People have a difficult time separating government from politics.
6. Governmental power has shifted from local to state and now to the federal level, thus increasingly removing government from the average citizen.

Community relations are more of a local government concern today than in any previous time because citizens have become more active. They want and expect more from government and are more vocal in their efforts to get it. Providing what citizens want and keeping what they want within the ability of government to provide is what community relations are all about.

To establish successful community relations between a government and the community, it is first important to determine and analyze the local power structure. Who actually runs the community? Obviously, local officials play a key role, but so do many other people. Some of the important persons in a community are: major employers; wealthy families; large landowners; business executives; prominent attorneys and doctors; civic leaders; publishers and editors; owners of businesses; and teachers. Major groups and associations also are vital to the future of the community. Some examples are the local Kiwanis, Rotary, American Legion, Lions, Knights of Columbus, PTA, Masons, League of Women Voters, Chamber of Commerce, political organizations, and so on. These groups work hand in hand with the "movers and shakers" of a community to get important tasks completed.

Community relations have two primary objectives: first, to make the community associated with the local government a better place to work and live; and second, to allow the government to carry out its appointed tasks more easily. These objectives can be realized if they are tied to the needs of the community and involve the key people and groups within the community.

A local government can provide many valuable services to a community beyond the traditional or legally required (police protection, for example).

These include: creating something needed that did not exist before; eliminating something that causes a problem; developing means for self-determination; broadening the use of something that exists to include have-nots; sharing equipment, facilities, or professional expertise; tutoring, counseling, and training; reconstituting, repairing, or dressing up; promoting the community outside its confines; and activating others.[2] When these services are applied, it is important to "act in regard to the community, think of terms of groups, and address yourself to the individual."[3] However, what a government can do for an area it represents is not limited to the above items. Far from it, the possibilities are almost endless. Let us examine a few of them in more detail.

Open House

An open house is a simple way to make government accessible to a large number of people. If city hall, the county courthouse, or other government offices are opened up, citizens are made to feel more a part of their government and are inclined to take more of an interest. Open houses also generate pride among government staff and improve morale.

Special Events

The types of special events possible are only limited by the scope of your imagination. Special events can range from the commonplace such as a ground-breaking or ribbon-cutting ceremony or the placement of a time capsule in a building to working with businesses to place employment offices in poor areas, offering scholarships, providing free blood pressure tests, and other nontraditional events. Police departments often conduct meetings to offer tips to cut down on home burglaries. Some governments offer courses on safe driving and conserving energy in the home. In one central Illinois city, the municipal government and a local hospital worked together to provide free medical assistance (excluding major surgery) to anyone who stopped in during regular business hours on Valentine's Day.

2. Philip Lesly, ed., *Lesly's Public Relations Handbook,* 3rd ed. (Englewood Cliffs, NJ: Prentice-Hall, 1983), 79.

3. Philip Lesly, ed., *Lesly's Public Relations Handbook,* 3rd ed. (Englewood Cliffs, NJ: Prentice-Hall, 1983), 85.

Newsletters

Some local governments publish a regular newsletter for their citizens, carrying news of local interest. Sometimes the newsletter is distributed with a utility or phone bill or with other government mail. Included in the newsletter may be a community calendar of events, home improvement and safety tips, health tips, comments from local officials on important public issues, and articles on local history or culture.

Advisory Groups

People like to feel involved in government decisions. An easy way to accomplish this is to appoint different citizens representing all areas of interest of the community to specially assigned advisory boards. An advisory board which "helps out" on particular issues can lay the groundwork for the government when it is ready to act upon the matter. The more people you have participating in the government process, the broader your base and the more acceptance you will have for future projects and activities.

Public Hearings

Public hearings are an effective means of bringing a broad public issue to the attention of citizens. They generate active citizen participation. They can also provide direction for the local government for the future. Unfortunately, most citizens do not take the time to attend public hearings. It is therefore important specifically to invite people to attend and participate and make them feel that their thoughts, recommendations, and ideas are appreciated and encouraged.

Welcome Packets

New citizens to a community should not be excluded from community relations activities. A "welcome packet" is very welcome indeed to a new resident. Such a packet can be mailed, hand-delivered, or made available for pick-up at city hall, the courthouse, public library, or other convenient location. Although often prepared by municipalities or chambers of commerce, an effective welcome packet can also be developed and distributed by a local government. Packets can include: a welcome letter from the mayor (if a municipality is responsible for the packet) or head of the respective government; a local map; information on schools, churches, parks, and other recreational activities; information on shopping areas; utility and telephone service; history of the community; special events; and emergency telephone numbers for police, fire protection, and health care.

Community relations are an effective tool in winning the support of local residents, keeping the public informed generally, and breaking down barriers between the government and its citizens. They can make the task easier when it becomes necessary to raise taxes, make zoning or annexation changes, or make other important and difficult decisions. Community relations are a very basic aspect of a local official's job today.

PART FIVE

The Future of Local Government

20.

What Does the Future Hold?

JAMES F. KEANE AND GARY KOCH

What does the future hold for local government? This chapter reflects a lack of common sense on the part of the editors because it is terribly risky to try to predict where local government will be in five, ten, or twenty years. But a number of things do seem obvious to us. President Reagan's years in the White House have tremendously affected the role of state and local government. Prior to 1932 and the onset of the New Deal, approximately one-third of public funds were collected by the federal government with two-thirds of the funding of state governments being raised and spent at the state and local level. The New Deal, World War II, and the Great Society of President Johnson reversed these proportions, with approximately two-thirds of public funds going to the federal coffers and one-third to state and local sources.

The Reagan administration has initiated another reversal of this trend, but whether or not the trend will continue depends on a number of uncontrollable factors. The first and foremost is political. If our nation continues to support the conservative policies of President Reagan to return to the states those functions which originally belonged to the state and local government and rigorously enforces limitations of federal involvement in local affairs, then local government will experience a growing responsibility. If an administration is elected which returns us to the Great Society days, then the opposite would be true. In our estimation, reality will fall somewhere in between. This means that local government would have a growing share of responsibility and duties via the public. Specifically, we envision six emerging trends for local governments.

1. *The request for services will increase, as will the need for more revenue.* The public has evidenced an insatiable desire for ever-expanding services,

especially those that historically have been provided at the local level. Unfortunately, the willingness of the public to tax itself to pay for those services has been historically absent. Local government will have to become very selective in paying for the provision of those services. The introduction of user fees and similar charges to those who utilize public facilities and enjoy public services will become more widespread. The search for revenue to fund new and existing services must and will continue. As Doug Whitley states in his chapter, local governments have basically three choices: They can reduce services, increase local taxes, or ask state government for more money. While none of these options is particularly appealing, there are few alternatives.

It can be expected that various local government associations will apply pressure to the general assembly to assume full costs of expenditures that the state is already partially paying. Again, to use Whitley's example, it is possible that in the future, we will see the state assuming the responsibility of paying for elections, administration of the courts, and local pensions. Local officials themselves will be expected to cut waste where possible, stretch existing tax dollars, and look for innovative ways to reduce costs. Intergovernmental cooperation between units of government will also be more fully explored.

2. *There will be a strong movement to consolidate local government.* The excessive number of units of local government in Illinois reflects unnecessary public administrative costs, and it is the editors' opinion that the future will see a reduction in the number of local government units in Illinois. School consolidations are a prime target because of their sheer number and the economics involved. Obviously the demand for consolidation will grow in relationship to the growth in taxes. Once the public becomes aware of the fact that Illinois has 700 percent more units of local government than comparable states, there will be a push to consolidate.

Recent series of articles in the *Chicago Tribune* and the *St. Louis Post-Dispatch* suggest that township government has outlived its usefulness and should be consolidated or absorbed into some other type of government. However, because of its strong grassroots support among its twelve thousand officials and the unwillingness of other governments to take on new responsibilities, a reduction in the number of Illinois townships in the near future is unlikely. Any consolidation that does occur will probably affect school districts, as mentioned above, and special districts. Many special or single-purpose districts, particularly the smaller ones, could easily be absorbed into an adjacent city or county. Legislation approved in 1987 (PA85-0672) would permit certain special districts to become part of an adjoining township.

3. *Greater professionalism will be stressed.* As Comptroller Burris correctly points out in the second chapter, many local officials throughout the state are only part-time officials—they earn their living from another job. Often, they have little or no government experience prior to taking office. As government continues to grow more complex and the duties of local officials become more difficult, greater emphasis will be placed on professional standards. Mandatory requirements for certain offices will be established. Persons holding certain positions or titles will be expected to be certified as experts in their particular field.

Taxpayers will demand more efficient operations within the courthouse, city hall, or other local government office. Computerization of routine functions, such as record keeping, issuing of tax bills, and so forth, will increase, not just in larger or more sophisticated communities, but also in small rural governments. As technology continues to make computers more and more affordable, many officials will see the need to upgrade their operations. They will be able to "sell" the idea to the public as a cost-effective measure. The Illinois Municipal League has already developed computer systems that are applicable to almost any type or size of local government for a moderate cost. In the future, we will see widespread marketing of computer applications for local government.

4. *Public accountability will increase.* As the public becomes more sophisticated in its understanding of local government and more vocal in its opinions, it will continue to expect more and better information from the government. It will want to know, in detail, where the money comes from and where it goes, and why particular decisions for spending it were made. Richard Haas, in his preface to *Governmental Accounting, Auditing and Financial Reporting,* sums up future accountability as follows:

> In the public sector, accountability must be achieved by harnessing a variety of complicated economic, legal, political, and social forces into a delicate matrix of equilibrium checks and balances.

> Governmental accounting and financial reporting standards have recently improved and may be expected to further improve. . . . We must each improve upon our own past performance . . . if we are to collectively assure ourselves of acceptable governmental organizational performance and effective public sector management stewardship.

> Government finance officers must more actively encourage reporting in conformity with generally accepted accounting principles and independent annual audits. Government budget officers need to better understand the importance of budgeting. . . . Government chief executive officers need to

better appreciate the importance of sophisticated integrated financial management to effective public administration. Elected officials must more carefully consider the financial consequences of public policy decisions. Voters must become more informed and less apathetic about the financial management activities of their governments.[1]

5. *Greater emphasis will be placed on public image.* We agree with Jim Nowlan's statement in his foreword that the public image of local officials is low—very low. This is usually due to poor communications or lack of communication entirely. The modern local official knows that it is not sufficient to just do a good job; he or she must act as a salesman and "sell" his or her performance and that of the government to the community and the media. State Comptroller Roland Burris has often said in speeches that the biggest problem facing local officials is not a lack of revenue or new state mandates—it is the lack of communication; communication between officials and staff, other officials, the community, and the media. Simply put— you may be doing a good job, but if for whatever reason the community or the local newspaper does not think so, you are headed for trouble. Local officials in the future will increasingly reach out to members of the community, reporters, and others to form a partnership to broaden the understanding and acceptance of government.

6. *Uniformity among local governments will increase.* Because local officials in Illinois have traditionally been an independent group and because there is very little training available, most officials and many governments have developed their own way of performing various tasks. There often are no right or wrong ways to accomplish these tasks, but some are more efficient than others, and some allow for better record keeping. As chapter 13 points out, there is relatively little uniformity in Illinois local government finance. With the advent of greater professionalism and accountability, we foresee greater emphasis on uniformity between types of government. Better record keeping and better information will allow for more knowledgeable decisions to be made.

Local government plays a vital role in the American way of life. There is no better training ground for anyone who wants to improve his or her understanding of how the American system of government works. We, in Illinois, are fortunate that our system of local government is so accessible. Virtually anyone can serve on a city council or county or park board, or even run for mayor or county sheriff. Even though local officials, like all

1. *Governmental Accounting, Auditing, and Financial Reporting* (Chicago: Municipal Finance Officers Association, 1980), v.

public servants at any level, occasionally are chided for their actions, we do not see this as discouraging people from wanting to participate. Rather, countless thousands of Illinois citizens will heed the call and run for local office. That is one prediction you can count on.

Notes on Contributors
Index

Notes on Contributors

Richard Burd is chief of Local Government Management Services in the Department of Commerce and Community Affairs. He serves on the state comptroller's Local Government Advisory Board. He received bachelor's and master's degrees in Public Administration from Southern Illinois University.

Roland W. Burris is serving his third term as state comptroller of Illinois. A former vice-president of Continental Illinois Bank, he also served as director of general services under Governor Dan Walker. A past president of the National State Comptrollers Association, he has also served as president of the National Association of State Auditors, Comptrollers, and Treasurers. He is listed in *Who's Who in America, Who's Who in Law, Who's Who in Government,* and has been named by *Ebony Magazine* as one of the "100 Most Influential Black Americans."

H. Brent De Land is executive director of the Illinois Community Action Association and adjunct associate professor of organization management at Sangamon State University. He holds B.A. and M.A. degrees in social planning from Sangamon State University and a Ph.D. from the Union Graduate School.

Ted Flickinger is the executive director of the Illinois Association of Park Districts. He is a former park and recreation director, college professor, and regional director of the National Recreation and Park Association. He received B.S. and M.S. degrees in park and recreation management from Southern Illinois University, and a Ph.D. in natural resources management from Ohio State University. He is president of the American Park and Recreation Society. In 1988 he received the Certified Association Executive (CAE) credentials from the American Society of Association Executives.

Kurt P. Froehlich is a partner in the law firm of Evans and Froehlich in Champaign, Illinois. A former technical advisor with the Illinois Department of Local Government Affairs, he has also served as Champaign's city attorney. He is a graduate of the University of Illinois (B.S. chemistry, M.Ed. secondary education, and J.D. law). He also serves as visiting professor of architecture at the University of Illinois. Many of his articles concerning municipal law, intergovernmental relations, and public and municipal finance have been published at the state and national level.

Michael Igoe is secretary to the Board of Cook County Commissioners. As secretary, he is responsible for all matters relating to the finance, public service, and roads and bridges committees. He is an attorney and member of the Chicago Bar Association. Igoe attended Canterbury Preparatory School, Georgetown University, and the University of Chicago Law School. He saw military service as a lieutenant in the army.

James F. Keane has served as state representative from the 28th District (Chicago) for the past decade and is Deputy Majority Leader in the Illinois House. He has chaired the House Revenue Committee and the Legislative Audit Commission. He is also a member of the state-federal assembly of the National Conference of State Legislatures. Prior to that, Keane served as assistant to the senate president and was assistant professor of political science at Chicago State University. He is founder and former president of the American Federation of Teachers, Local 1700. Keane received a B.S. degree in psychology from Loyola, an M.A. in history from Chicago State University, an M.Ph. P.A. in public administration from Roosevelt University, and a Doctorate in Public Administration from Nova University, Florida.

Gary Koch is special assistant to the state comptroller. He is also adjunct assistant professor of communications at Millikin University and is former national chairman of the Public Relations Society of America's government section. He formerly served as executive director of the Legislative Local Accounting Task Force and as public information officer in the Department of Commerce and Community Affairs and the Department of Local Government Affairs. A graduate of Illinois College, Koch has M.A. degrees in journalism (public affairs reporting) and communications from Sangamon State University. He has served on various state-wide commissions and guest-lectured at Richland Community college, Lincoln Land Community College, and Sangamon State University. He is listed in *Who's Who in the Midwest, Who's Who in the World, Who's Who in Emerging Leaders, Personalities of America,* and was an Outstanding Young Man of America in 1980.

John Lattimer is executive director of the Illinois Commission on Intergovernmental Cooperation. Prior to this, he was chief of intergovernmental relations for the Ohio Legislative Service Commission and a research associate for the Kansas Legislative Coordinating Council. He is a past staff chairman of the National Conference of State Legislatures and past president of the Central Illinois Chapter of the American Society for Public Administration. Lattimer has served on a variety of advisory committees and boards and as guest lecturer at Sangamon State University and Lincoln Land Community College. He is a graduate of Southern Illinois University, received an M.A. degree in political science from the University of Kansas, and has done postgraduate work at the University of Kansas and St. Louis University.

William McGuffage is legislative liaison for the attorney general's office. He also directs the attorney general's Election Watch Program, in which lawyers are assigned to monitor voting in state and local elections and investigate complaints of election law violations. He has served as legislative liaison for the State Board of Elections and was author of the Consolidated Election Law. He is a graduate of Southern Illinois University and is working toward an M.A. in Public Administration from Governors State University.

George Miller is executive director of the Township Officials of Illinois. He has served as president of the Township Officials of Cook County and was twice elected president of the Township Officials of Illinois. In 1976, he was one of the founders of the National Association of Towns and Townships (NATAT) and was elected president in 1982. Also that year, he was appointed to a five-member White House advisory council on "new federalism."

William B. Morris was one of the youngest persons ever elected to the Illinois Senate at age 29. He was elected mayor of Waukegan, Illinois, at 31. Following nearly a dozen years of elected public service, Morris entered the private sector as a vice-president of Continental Illinois National Bank, handling investment banking for local governmental units. He serves on advisory committees to Illinois Comptroller Roland Burris and Illinois House Speaker Michael Madigan. He also teaches public administration and state and local politics courses at Loyola University, Lake Forest College, and the College of Lake County. A former journalist, Morris holds a Bachelor of Science degree in journalism from Northern Illinois University and a Master of Arts degree in Public Administration from Webster University.

Peter M. Murphy is the legal/legislative counsel for the Illinois Association of Park Districts. He received a B.S. degree from the University of Michigan and a J.D. from the New England School of Law in Boston. He has served as staff attorney for the Illinois General Assembly's Reference Bureau. He recently received the designation of Certified Association Executive (CAE) from the American Society of Association Executives and is active in the legislative affairs of the National Park and Recreation Association. He has authored numerous publications, including one on lobbying, and regularly writes a column for the Illinois Parks and Recreation magazine.

James D. Nowlan is a professor of public policy at Knox College in Galesburg. He was elected to the Illinois House at age 26 and ran for lieutenant governor in 1972. He has served as director of two state agencies, as executive director of Governor James Thompson's transition team, and organized John Anderson's presidential campaign. During the 1970s, he owned newspapers in Peoria and Stark counties. From 1981 to 1985, he directed graduate programs in public management and taught political science at the University of Illinois. He has written two books, *The Politics of Higher Education* and *Inside State Government*. Nowlan received a Ph.D. in political science from the University of Illinois. He has been a member of the Roosevelt Center for American Policy Studies and the White House Intergovernmental Council on Education.

Michael E. Pollak is a principal with Pollak and Hoffman Ltd., Chicago Attorneys at Law. He is also parliamentarian for the Illinois House of Representatives. A graduate of Miami University, he earned a J.D. degree from Loyola University. He is author of the *The Legislative Game: You Can Win if You Know the Rules*. He is chairman of the board of directors of the Illinois Tax Foundation and is vice-chairman of the Franchise Committee for the American Bar Association.

Laurel Lunt Prussing is three-term county auditor of Champaign County and was one of the first women ever elected to the Champaign county board. A graduate of Wellesley College, she has an M.A. degree in economics from Boston University and has done postgraduate work in economics at the University of Illinois. Prussing served as president of the Illinois Association of County Auditors in 1984 and 1985. She serves on advisory committees for the state comptroller and the Government Finance Officers Association of the United States and Canada. She was the first county auditor in Illinois to receive the Award for Excellence in Financial Reporting and also the first to receive the Award for Distinguished Budget Presentation, both from the Government Finance Officers Association.

Ted Sanders is U.S. Undersecretary of Education and formerly the Illinois state superintendent of education. Previously, he served as Nevada's superintendent of public instruction and as the second-ranking official in the New Mexico Department of Education. He was president of the Council of Chief State Schools Officers and has chaired the Council's Committee on Teacher Education, Preparation and Accreditation, which in 1984 authored the report "Staffing the Nation's Schools: A National Emergency." Sanders also chairs the American Association of Colleges of Teacher Education. He is a member of the National Council for Accreditation of Teacher Education and the National Council on Science and Technology Education.

Steve Sargent is executive director of the Illinois Municipal League. He has been associated with the league for the past three decades. A graduate of Millikin University, he earned an M.P.A. degree from the University of Illinois. He has served as staff coordinator for the Illinois Municipal Problems Commission and has served on the board of directors of the National League of Cities, the Illinois Law Enforcement Commission, and the Illinois Commission on Criminal Justice.

Douglas Whitley is president of the Taxpayers' Federation of Illinois, a position he has held for the past ten years. He recently served as chairman of Governor Thompson's Revenue Review Committee. He currently serves on a committee of fifty Illinois citizens studying the call for a revision of the 1970 Illinois constitution. A graduate of Southern Illinois University, Whitley serves on advisory panels to the National Institute on State and Local Taxation and to State Comptroller Roland Burris. He previously served on the Local Government Finance Study Commission and the State Board of Education's School Finance Panel.

Index